Strategic IS/IT Planning
Edwin E. Tozer

BUTTERWORTH
HEINEMANN

Boston • Oxford • Melbourne • Singapore • Toronto • Munich • New Delhi • Tokyo

Copyright © 1996 by Butterworth–Heinemann

ℛ A member of the Reed Elsevier group

Library of Congress Cataloging-in-Publication Data

T
58
.6
.T669
1996

Tozer, E. E.
    Strategic IS/IT Planning / by Ed Tozer.
        p.   cm. – (Datamation book series)
    Includes bibliographical references and index.
    ISBN 0-7506-9666-4 (pbk.)
    1. Management information systems. 2. System design. I. Title.
II. Series.
T58.6.T669   1995
658.4'038–dc20

95-21570
CIP

British Library Cataloguing-in-Publication Data

A catalogue record for this book is available from the British Library.

The publisher offers discounts on bulk orders of this book. For information, please write:

Manager of Special Sales
Butterworth-Heinemann
313 Washington Street
Newton, MA 02158-1626

10 9 8 7 6 5 4 3 2 1

Composition by Graham Douglas, Bath, UK
Printed in the United States of America

PREFACE

The philosophy of this book

The best laid schemes o' mice an' men Gang aft a-gley.

Robert Burns, 'To a Mouse' (1786)

All too often, even today, we prove Burns right. But he doesn't actually suggest that we shouldn't plan, just that we may fail to bring in the planned results unless we are both careful and lucky.

This book suggests that we can eliminate much of the luck from the process. Planning for information systems and technology can be worthwhile, but only if we approach the task with appropriate humility, and make sure that we build a realistic plan which is in tune with the mood, intentions and plans of the business, and remains so. We must also make sure that we track regularly how we are doing against the plan, and whether the plan is still relevant. Every so often, we will have to change the plan, even quite radically; in extremis, circumstances may dictate that we abandon it for a while and improvise, but in a controlled manner. Then maybe we can shade the odds in our favor and defy Burns' warning.

A note on references

References to source materials in this book follow the Author-Date system. All references are placed together in Appendix I, References and Bibliography, in Author's surname order. References in the body of the text generally give the Author's surname and publication date of the work referenced, enclosed in parentheses, e.g. (McFarlan 1984), or, according to context, the date only parenthesized immediately following a reference to the Author, e.g. '...this was extended by Ward, Griffiths and Whitemore (1990)'.

This book embodies a formal but practical approach for the development of the information systems strategy necessary to support the management of medium and large organizations. But it is not just a conventional book. It is also a complete 'how-to' manual which will enable you to establish an effective process for developing, implementing and maintaining an effective, business-led strategy for successful exploitation of information systems and technology in your organization, however large or small it may be, and regardless of whether your business is commercial, industrial, financial or public service.

This manual originated from training and project team support materials developed and used by the author in his consulting practice. Its primary structure follows the sequence of an in depth course in the techniques for practitioners developing or maintaining IS and/or IT strategy for an organization. This structure is augmented by:

- reference materials
- worked examples of key deliverables
- discussion papers and sections on particular topics
- the availability on request of templates in PC processable form (usually in Microsoft Word for Windows or Excel format) for most of the working papers.

The book's origin in training materials has carried over into its format, much of which has retained the character of the original presentation materials. For this reason, and also because of the use to which the material is put in the Author's consulting practice, key sections of many of the chapters remain in note form. The result of this is that the text is considerably more concise than would have otherwise been the case. I hope that the reader (or 'user' as I prefer to regard you) will adapt easily to this style, and will appreciate the advantages of the brevity thus achieved.

To those readers who would prefer all of the ideas to be expressed in flowing, elegant prose, I can only say that the resultant expansion factor would have caused this book, already too long, to run to several thousand pages. I didn't have time to write that book, and you wouldn't have time to read it.

This manual is aimed at:

- organizations wishing to establish, perhaps for the first time, an effective and continuing linkage between their business planning cycle and the information systems planning function;
- organizations already having a mature planning approach, who wish to make their planning cycles leaner and more responsive, and to incorporate recent developments;
- project managers and potential team members about to undertake work in this area;

- individuals who wish to develop their career towards business and information systems planning; ·
- business schools planning to offer a course in this field.

The method presented - which goes under the brand name of SP4IS (Strategic Planning for Information Systems) - is designed to help to ensure accurate and continuing alignment of an organization's IS/IT strategy with business goals and intentions. It embodies a clear framework, which is populated with up to date, proven techniques. It is has its roots in the body of experience and best practice which has evolved over the past fifteen years, and is compatible with UK Government CCTA Guidelines on Strategic Planning, development methods (SSADM) and project management (PRINCE). The approach embodies especially rigorous processes for analysis of business plans and intentions, establishing requirements and identifying potential business benefits. This ensures delivery of maximum business value where it is most needed. It supports a range of business planning techniques such as Portfolio Management and Value Chain Analysis, and is compatible with Business Process Reengineering techniques. The process does not stop at vague vision, or a set of outline architectures: it proceeds to delivery of a phased, costed set of plans, along with the means for maintaining them. The techniques presented include measures for coping with highly volatile environments, and for retaining some degree of control when improvisation becomes necessary. The approaches cater for package implementation as well as custom; and for overhaul of existing investment as well as 'green field' implementation. The methods are compatible with the latest advances in information technology, including Open Systems and Client/Server, and support a variety of CASE techniques and software.

I would like to hear from persons who put these ideas into practice, both of the frustrations and the successes, but especially any lessons learned or improvements achieved - we are all still learning how better to do this type of work. I am also willing, within reason, to respond to queries about the approaches - or even, for a fee, to come along and undertake a consulting assignment. Please contact me at the address below:

Edwin E Tozer Ltd
Dolphin House
St Peter Street
Winchester
Hampshire
S023 8BW, UK

Tel: 44-1962-869465
Fax: 44-1962-866116
E-mail: edtozer@winchester.win-uk.net

CHAPTER 1

Introduction

Objectives of this chapter

- Highlight the changing pressures on businesses today.
- Outline the ways in which information systems contribute to business success; both at present and potentially in the future.
- Show what needs to be done to exploit IS and IT more effectively for business success.

The strategic role of information systems

Introduction

Mankind has traded since the dawn of history. Wherever there were surpluses or shortages between communities, there has been some form of exchange - by means of barter if there was no currency. Once the notion of currency as an abstraction of value became common, then wherever there was advantage to be gained by holding a commodity for a time whilst its price varied, or by transporting it so another place where its price differed, then enterprising traders would do so - and still do. Likewise, once there was scope to specialize, those with skills to offer have traded those skills for reward. In these ways arose our commercial organizations. It quickly proved necessary to keep some form of written record of these transactions. In this way arose the needs of commerce for some form of bookkeeping.

Once society came to mean more than a single extended family living in close proximity, then there arose a need for some form of community infrastructure and social administration. These quickly grew in complexity as societies became more complex. Thus there came into being our public sector organizations, with their need also for some form of record keeping. This all happened long before information technology (IT) came on the scene. Bureaucracies grew, and have not so far been eliminated by automated information systems (IS) based on IT. Consideration of human nature suggests that both the trading activity and the tendency to bureaucracy will continue long after information technology as we know it today has left the scene.

With the advent of IS and IT, people began to expect that much of the 'pen-pushing' and basic bookkeeping in organizations could be done more cheaply using more automation and fewer people – or so it seemed. We could free up many of the clerks to do something much more useful. But how often did we measure the resulting efficiency improvement – how much money we *really* saved? And did we really help those remaining to do the job better – did we even define criteria for 'better'? And what useful things do all those displaced clerks do today?

Using 'batch processing' systems in the 1960s, we dismantled the clerical worker's job structure; we took away their pen (metaphorically still a quill, if not literally), the ledger, in which he or she often took such pride, and the high stool. Instead we provided a pad of data preparation forms, which had to be filled in. A few days later, we would send back a (usually badly printed) computer listing which told the clerk that he or she had filled in some of the data entry forms wrongly (or that good entries had been wrongly keyed). They dug out the source forms and tried again. After another few days, there would be a further report of residual errors, and so on. Some errors would never be fixed. The clerk's sense of contact with the computer master files became very remote compared to the old hand written ledgers. They probably often forgot that there were any customers involved at all!

But it was cheaper – sometimes. More effective? Occasionally.

Now, as computing power has become cheaper, we have re-discovered 'real time' transaction processing systems. It is very modern for today's clerk to have a well structured job, with more responsibility for processing the whole transaction – to be 'empowered'. He or she is 'Customer focused'. With modern desktop 'GUI' interfaces, I fully expect to see soon a business accounting package which uses icons of quill pens, ledgers, etc. In case you, the reader, are using such an animal, I hasten to add that it wasn't released, even as vapourware when I wrote this. This is all very pessimistic. Hindsight makes it easy to poke fun at our previous follies, but this is all intended to make a number of serious points:

1.   Not all application of IS/IT in the past has been either well considered or effective.

2.   Advances in what is possible do not necessarily guarantee advances in delivery of business benefits. Some apparent advances are actually regressive.

3.   Some change is cyclic – we are only now beginning to undo the damage

to job and responsibility structures which early data processing did caused many cases.

4.   Unquestioning automation of a poor clerical system can only yield marginal improvement at best, and may often accentuate its worst features. Fundamental re-thinking of the process, or even its purpose, is essential before automation.

5.   The technology needed to do a much better job is now freely available. IT is the only known commodity in the world which is growing cheaper at around 50% p.a. compound, and is showing every sign of continuing to do so.

6.   The expertise to make effective use of IT is much scarcer, but a little should go a long way, and we should be prepared to learn from our and other's mistakes as we go.

7.   There are tremendous benefits still to be gained in most organizations from enlightened exploitation of IS/IT, but we need to think much harder about the impact of systems on the organization, and to be very clear on:

   ■ business goals;
   ■ benefits sought;
   ■ the manner in which the benefits are expected to materialize;
   ■ how we will determine whether we have done good or harm to the organization as a whole, both locally, and in its broader social context.

8.   The IS/IT mistakes of the past remain endemic in many organizations. There is a tremendous source of competitive advantage in being just a little smarter in use of IT, in gaining some of the benefits without all of the pitfalls.

9.   These mistakes have yet to be made in many of the businesses and public sector organizations in the developing or re-emerging nations. We should be able to help them to avoid some of the grosser follies.

10. IS/IT exists to serve the needs of the business, and not the other way round.

11. An effective IS/IT strategy, linked with, and compatible with, the business strategy is critical to business success.

12. Success in developing and implementing such a strategy can be difficult, unless you make use of existing experience – i.e. follow a method.

Developments in business pressures and climate

The pace of change in many aspects of business, both private and public sector, is increasing, apparently without slackening. Much of this change comes in sudden steps, or discontinuities, which are especially hard to cope with. This appears to be accompanied by a growing realization that accurate forecasting is impossible in very many cases. Many despair of planning in consequence, but this is a false deduction. We need to change and lighten the style of planning adopted. The name of the game becomes to attempt to position our business strategy and the accompanying organization and systems so as to cope with a wide range of possible scenarios.

This means that we have to choose between gambling, by optimizing for some of the most likely medium term outcomes, versus covering a more conservative spread of scenarios. If we adopt the latter approach, and find ourselves out of gear with the actual outcome in consequence, we may have to cope with the consequences of some of our competitors getting lucky in their guesses, and cleaning up in some of our markets.

All of this suggests a shift in planning and control style towards a strategic vision which is robust to a range of likely scenarios, and is supported by:

- closely integrated short and medium term implementation plans, covering business and systems
- close and frequent monitoring of outcomes
- frequent review of the relevance of the plans to business circumstances and need;

We should avoid wherever possible 'lock in' to long term strategic programs which will not deliver benefits until they come to fruition, and which are predicated on business circumstances behaving as we have forecast in the mean time.

IS/IT as the key to survival in Drucker's vision of Post Capitalist Society

The rise of knowledge-based organizations

In his book *Post Capitalist Society* (1993), Drucker builds a convincing case that Capitalism, as traditionally understood, in fact preceded Marxism to its doom, and that knowledge, and its exploitation is supplanting as a key organizational resource the traditional assets of Labor and capital. He sees knowledge-based organizations as being a driving force in the 21st century. He points out that during the later part of the 19th century and most of the 20th, dependence on capital and labor limited the flexibility of organizations – they are both difficult to accumulate, and have a damping effect once accumulated.

Organizations needed to become large and relatively rigid to be efficient. Knowledge-based organizations can be much smaller and more flexible. Such an organization can react much more quickly and flexibly in future to changes in their environment – and can thus be much more competitive.

Drucker suggests that knowledge and its supporting processing systems can be exploited as the basis for a much more systematic and focused approach to innovation, enabling organizations to initiate change, rather than merely react to it.

IS/IT as knowledge enablers

Knowledge requires communication. Information is the embodiment of knowledge. Drucker uses this line of argument to show that information communication and processing systems, along with the technology to support them have become the key enablers of knowledge exploitation and processing, and thus of adaptability and survival.

In the past, productivity – the watchword of the Industrial Revolution – consisted largely in the worker performing the same process ever-faster, so as to produce more and yield more profit. This obviously hit the point of diminishing return, limited by human and mechanical capability. With the advent of the knowledge-based view, it has become clear that there is more often than not a better or more intelligent way of achieving the same or an equivalent outcome, at far less effort on the worker's part – if he or she only knows how. This usually involves radical alteration to the processes, achieved by ruthless re-examination of all of the assumptions involved. 'Work smarter' has replaced 'work harder' as the key to productivity.

Drucker suggests that this view is the key to the West's regaining competitive predominance over the East, exploiting creativity and innovation, despite the huge differential in labor costs. He points out that the value of knowledge was recognized for centuries, but its systematic analysis and transmission was limited by human capabilities and cultural attitudes. Guilds and apprenticeships were devoted – largely successfully – to its protection and jealous transfer only to the chosen few.

Communist countries foresaw the danger of uninhibited information transfer. They tried, eventually without success to limit use of telephones, and to ban faxes and computer modems. They were right, as it turned out, as the freer flow of information which these devices enabled when unleashed quickly exposed the gigantic frauds which the Communist ruling elite usually practised.

In a similar way, in the West, once restrictions on the flow of capital and on financial and trading information – common in the '60s and '70s – were largely removed, IS and IT became the key enablers of truly global trading systems. Drucker argues that it is now unlikely that any national Government will ever again be able to exert absolute political power or truly control its own economy – the genie is well and truly out of the bottle.

This is not all for the good. Free transfer of information does not guarantee that greed and unscrupulous behavior are no longer possible. IS and IT are ethically neutral – literally amoral; they enable global fraud as easily as fair trading. However, they do make it much harder to cover up fraud and sharp practice. Effective audit trails and controls are ever more essential, and we must learn how to apply them to better effect in the knowledge based world.

The need for a theory of 'Knowledge Economics'

Drucker argues that much of conventional economic theory is overturned by knowledge based thinking. He suggests that a new economic theory is needed, which takes account of the real value of knowledge and information. Such a knowledge-based economics will have a number of key characteristics:

1. effective means for assessment of knowledge quality, potential and value as an asset;

2. better means for assessing the non-intuitive ways in which economies of scale operating;

3. much greater tolerance of an imperfect marketplace;

4. recognition of qualitatively different types of knowledge, such as:

    - incremental improvement;
    - exploitation of developments;
    - step changes.

Levels of investment in information systems

Senior managers want to be sure that they are investing wisely in information systems. They often ask *"are we are spending the right amount"*, e.g. compared to the competition. But of course, it is still possible to spend the 'right' amount on IS/IT, but still not to spend it wisely. A more important question is *"are we spending what we spend right?"* – i.e. in the right way. The second question is harder to answer, but that's what this whole book is about – it shows how to make sure you are.

In the mean time, the table below casts some light on the first question. It embodies old survey data, but reliable later versions are hard to come by. Based on spot checks with co-operative clients during 1993, the 1987 survey data appear mainly still to lie within the ranges now indicated. Between 1984 and 1993, spend on IT in the UK, adjusted for inflation, appears to have stayed roughly flat (Price Waterhouse 1991/2/3). It is of interest that, assuming a conservative rate of improvement of technology cost/performance of 45% to

50% compound p.a. (some authorities claim 60%), spending the same ratio now as in 1987 will buy you around 15 times as much technology.

Table 1-1:   *IT investment as a percent of revenue by industry*

Primary source: Datamation Sept. 1987 survey of 120 major US corporations

		1987 data	Likely present range
Banking & finance		4.5	3–5
Electronics		3.7	3–4
Industrial & automotive	2.7		
Insurance		1.7	1.5–3
Food & beverage	1.6		
Process industries		1.6	
Petroleum & petrochemicals		1.3	
Transport		1.3	
Metal & metal products	1.1		
Utilities	1.0		
Health care & pharmaceuticals	0.6		
Retail		0.2	0.3–0.6
Sample average	1.8		

Planning terminology

Before we go further, it is best if we define some basic terms. The term 'IT Strategy' is widely and loosely used to imply some or all of the elements of and effective systems strategy. Its use in this sense is dangerous and misleading, as it implies that you can think first about technology solutions, before business needs or systems solutions. This places the cart firmly before the horse. The terms used in this book, and which are recommended are:

Business Strategy

Must come first and drive everything else. It doesn't have to be terribly formal – direction or vision are often all that you have – but someone, somewhere needs to be clear *what the business is trying to do and how to set about it.*

Information Systems (IS) Strategy

This concerns the information systems of the business in the widest sense, manual as well as automated, informal as well as formal. The formal, automated systems are often termed 'applications'. The IS Strategy also embraces stored data, the user interfaces, and the manner in which they serve the needs of the business. It should be derived from the business strategy by a process which is covered in this manual.

Information Technology (IT) Strategy

IT Strategy is about technology solutions to support systems – and sometimes business needs directly. It concerns all aspects of the boxes, wires and systems software which forms the environment on which information systems run. It must be driven both by business strategy and systems strategy. Due to the rapid rate of change, both of business pressures and needs, and of the capability and cost/performance of the underlying components, IT solutions are the most volatile. They must be highly adaptive; often the IT strategy turns out to be in large part to not become strategically committed to directions which can become a straitjacket.

Reacting to competitive pressures

The organization's chosen stance influences the nature of the contribution expected from IS/IT.

1   Are you 'least cost' oriented – i.e. aiming at the high volume utility end of your market, or 'differentiated', e.g. on premium quality – i.e. offering a quality difference which the customers will pay for?

A focus on high quality of service and excellence in product support will have very different implications for the application portfolio than will a primary thrust towards cost reduction.

2.   Are your business strategies mainly reactive and defensive, or are they more proactive trying to lead the competition?

Adventurous business strategies are likely to lead to greater volatility, and to require flexible and innovative systems to support them, whereas a risk averse business management style will need to be supported by a relatively sober and conservative approach to information systems. Surprisingly, the more reactive and volatile the business style, the greater the stress placed on effective IS/IT planning. Not only will the IS/IT strategies need to be more flexible and adaptive, but the planning process itself needs to be leaner and more focused to be tolerated at all by entrepreneurial management.

Some IS/IT related constraints to business competitiveness

Ways in which IS/IT shortcomings can translate directly into competitive disadvantage include:

- Inability to support new/changed products or services quickly enough.
- Lack of up to date information as to real business performance versus plan.
- Failure to recognize opportunities or competitive threats quickly enough to respond effectively.
- Failure to identify clearly and agree across the business the critical IS/IT priorities for attention.
- Inappropriate, inflexible or misleading reporting of performance indicators.
- Inadequate base of current systems and data:
  - poor/missing information from operational systems into MIS/EIS
  - lack of cross-functional view, e.g. of customer or product stream
- Application famine and development backlog.
- Shortage of appropriate IT skills/resources.
- Uncertainty over why/how to automate business processes – lack of effective criteria and/or failure to keep up with technology developments.

Principal management concerns over IS/IT

This amalgam of surveys gives some indication, despite the mismatch of scales, of how perceived concerns have evolved over time.

Table 1-2:   *Sources: AA & Co Surveys '86, '89, Price Waterhouse IT Reviews 1991/92/93*

Area of Concern	Percent of responders concerned				
	Andersen Consulting		Price Waterhouse		
	1986	1989	1990	1992	1993
Communication between IT staff and senior management	–	92			
Better systems development productivity	66	76	10	35	
Translating IT into competitive advantage	72	74			
Capability to handle rapid business change or uncertainty	–	73	–	15	18
Managing information resources	63	69			
Training of users to use systems effectively		–			
Facilitating/managing end-user computing		76			
Meeting project deadlines	–		27	22	24
Integration of IT	62	53	40	30	26
Cost containment	low	low	10	35	37
Staff recruitment/retention	–		20	negligible	

The most recent survey data, from Price Waterhouse, clearly shows the UK recession affecting attitudes, in that cost containment comes to dominate the issues, and staff retention becomes of negligible significance. Those surveys also show the rapid rise in concern over coping with change and uncertainty.

Success factors and 'barrier' factors in exploiting IT

In 1985 and 1990 AT Kearney undertook DTI sponsored research into what they called the success factors and 'barrier' factors in exploiting IT. Their findings are summarized below:

TOP SIX SUCCESS FACTORS:

- Top management support
- Quality of DP staff
- Quality of user staff
- Co-operation between IT and users
- Training
- Software package fit for purpose

TOP FIVE BARRIER FACTORS:

- Quality of user staff
- Availability of skills
- Clear requirements definition
- Software package fit for purpose
- Managerial awareness

Source: AT Kearney: 'Barriers 2' survey - UK 1990

Business planning horizons

Definitions of these terms vary widely, and no real consensus is possible - or even strictly necessary. However, working definitions are needed for our purposes.

- *Tactical:* Survival - now to one year
- *Operational:* 1–2 years horizon
- *Strategic:* 3–5 years. In some cases, 10 years plus

Also any issue critical to survival, however short term

NB: The definitions of Tactical and Operational are sometimes reversed. Figure 1-1 illustrates the way in which even short term issues can assume strategic significance if they are sufficiently critical.

Figure 1-1:   *How timescale and criticality are related in the definition of 'strategic'*

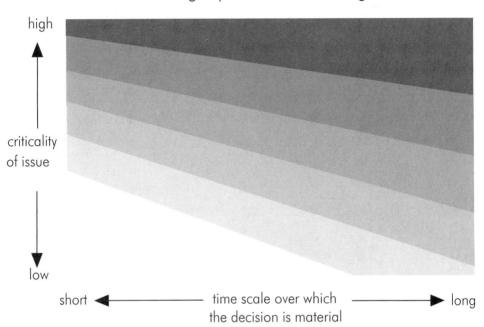

Darker gray = more strategic

high

criticality
of issue

low

short ◄────────── time scale over which ──────────► long
the decision is material

Planning approaches – coping with uncertainty

'My business/market is un-forecastable' is one of the most frequently used, but least valid excuses for not planning. In a relatively stable business climate (increasingly less common), it is possible to rely on forecasting – extrapolating from current status – to predict key trends. This is termed *extrapolative planning*.

In the increasingly common case where a number of key business factors are likely to vary in unpredictable ways, possibly rapidly, extrapolation or forecasting cease to be valid or useful. Volatility of markets or business climate bring the need to react fast to unexpected opportunities or threats. Under these circumstances, another approach, termed scenario planning, becomes useful in its place. Scenario planning is based on the thesis that, rather than optimizing for a single, forecast outcome, it is better to identify the range of possible outcomes, and to devise a strategy which is resilient to any of them. It leads to robust but possibly sub-optimal strategies being favored over optimal but fragile – i.e. it improves the chances of business survival in volatile conditions. These issues are covered in more detail in Chapter 6.

Interrelation of planning cycles

IS and IT planning do not take place in isolation. As illustrated in Figure 1-2, there is in any organization an interlocking set of planning cycles. Some may be informal, or their existence even denied, but they, and their interactions, must not be ignored. Everything must be directed from the top – the Corporate Business Plan – however informal this may be. That being said, the Corporate planners must be alert to feedback from the lower cycles as to the outcome and feasibility of their directives.

Figure 1-2:   *Interdependent planning cycles*

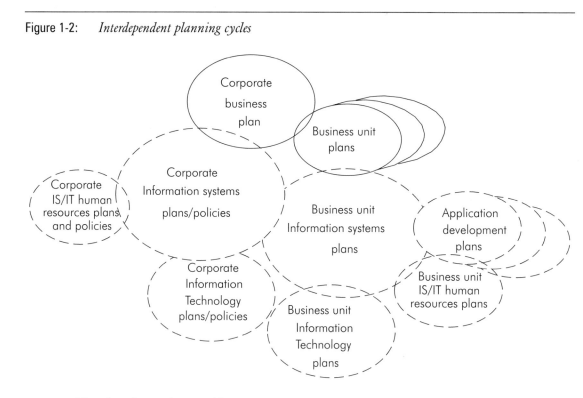

The planning and control loop

It is a military adage that no plan survives first contact with the enemy. It is not sufficient to make a plan, then to sit back complacently and watch it fail. Effective tracking of performance against plan, the willingness to assess the effect of departures from it, and in all humility to admit error and to modify the plan are all critical attributes for success. This is often forgotten. Figure 1-3 illustrates this.

Figure 1-4 suggests that there can be as much risk in over controlling as in under controlling. At the right hand end of the curve, the 'Geoffrey Boycott' approach, to use a cricketing analogy, carries risk of stifling innovation and creativity. This can lead to effects as serious as, but different to, those resulting from too little control. The 'David Gower' approach on the left may be long on flair, but is short on safety measures. In the middle is the place to be, unless you can guarantee that all your projects will be staffed by geniuses (and are willing to try to manage them).

Figure 1-3:   *The closed-loop planning and control cycle*

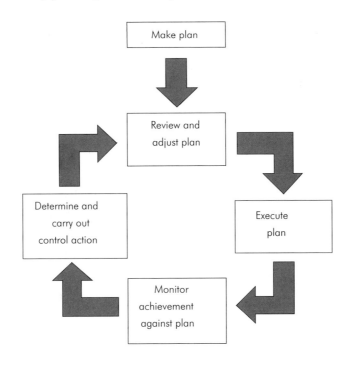

Figure 1-4:   *Risks involved in managing risk*

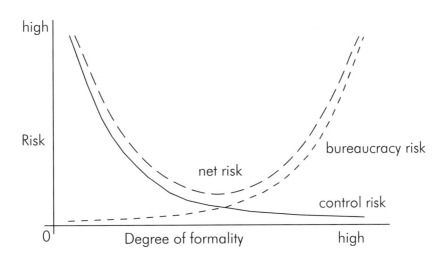

Categorization of the ways in which information systems can contribute to business success

Types of benefit delivered

The categories set out below represent a progression from the relatively mundane automation of existing manual processes through complete integration of IS/IT into the fabric of the organization and its products.

EFFICIENCY E.G. COST CONTAINMENT

This was first type of application of IT in many organizations. Cost saving gains are easy to identify (although less easy to demonstrate afterwards in many cases). Benefits tend to be in terms of marginal percentage savings, often with un-quantified – and sometimes undesired – side-effects.

Core databases built as a result of the automation of the basic processes of the organization can provide an essential platform for the other types of contribution listed below. Beware, however, that such databases, if developed from too narrow a perspective, may not offer the range of data, nor the effective integration necessary. Rectifying such fundamental problems often involves re-building core systems.

EFFECTIVENESS E.G. BETTER SERVICE

Benefits from carrying out our business processes not just more cheaply, but to better effect can be far more wide-ranging than mere cost saving. This is especially so if the opportunity is taken to re-think – 'Re-Engineer' to use the current jargon (Hammer, 1990) – the business processes themselves. Benefits gained in this way, such as more contented and loyal Customers, may be harder to express in purely financial terms. Business sponsors facing this challenge should be encouraged to think in terms of more fundamental sources of benefit, such as increased revenue from satisfied Customers or reduced costs incurred in handling complaints and problems.

'PROACTIVE' SYSTEMS

Once the foundation of core data and transaction systems is sound, there are many ways in which systems can contribute in a more creative or constructive manner. Which of these is most important will vary by organization and culture, but some examples are:

- ability to change products or marketing approach faster
- better, faster management decisions
- improved competitive awareness
- IS opportunities enabling radical business process redesign
- advanced product delivery systems

Business cases for this type of system become a different proposition. Quantified cost savings are almost entirely irrelevant. Increased market share or product penetration are more likely sources of benefit. Their quantification is very much a matter of business judgement (or 'subjectivity' if you disagree with the judgement!) However, such subjective business judgements are valid, just harder to get right. The higher up the management tree you look in an organization, the more decisions are based on judgement. Although quantified analysis to back up 'hunches' at this level is very comforting, it often turns out itself to be based on judgemental assumptions.

IS/IT BECOMES THE PRODUCT DELIVERY VEHICLE

The mature stage is where IS/IT are so closely embedded in the fabric of the organization and its products that they are almost inseparable. In some parts of the Finance sector this trend has gone so far that key payment systems such as SWIFT and CHAPS serve the joint needs of an entire community of organizations who, whilst they co-operate closely to trade, also compete fiercely among themselves. Pursuit of competitive advantage in such communities no longer depends even on systems excellence, where these are common; but is becoming ever more demanding in terms of business creativity and subtlety.

Classification of business information

The Anthony triangle (Anthony 1965), is shown in an adapted form in Figure 1-5 below.

Figure 1-5:   *Information systems classes current and potential coverage (adaptation of the Anthony Triangle)*

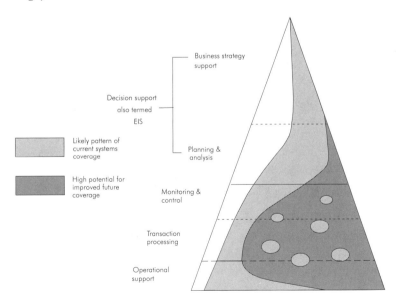

It leads to another useful categorization of business information – the layers are discussed below. The lightly shaded area illustrates the degree of coverage of business needs which is likely to be offered by an organization's current application systems portfolio. The areas of darker shading indicate the increase in coverage which is likely to result from an IS/IT strategy study. The 'Swiss cheese' effect is intended to represent weaknesses which may be detected in the older generation of current systems present systems – it is also discussed further below.

The modified Anthony triangle categories are, starting from the bottom of the triangle:

OPERATIONAL SUPPORT

Routine administration functions – e.g. Office Automation, e-mail, etc. These have recently become increasingly fashionable, as the competitive advantages of high quality customer service have become more widely appreciated. Changing technology costs have radically altered the criteria for deciding what should be automated in this area.

TRANSACTION PROCESSING

These systems process the relatively high volume routine business events of the organization. This is where most DP shops started 20 or more years ago, and where some of them have stayed! Often regarded as a 'solved problem', and superficially offering little potential for increasing competitive advantage, this class of system can prove to be in desperate need of re-build when assessed against current needs.

The continuing improvement in technology cost/performance means that it is now usually cheaper and simpler to implement such systems in fully interactive form, with shared, integrated databases. This can offer important business benefits also, as long as jobs and work flow are re-structured to take advantage. Superficially, you are often perceived as merely replicating existing functionality. This can make business cases based on narrow cost saving criteria difficult to substantiate.

To counter this, heavy weighting should be placed on:

- improved quality and service levels
- cheaper and faster adaptation in future to business change
- improved quality and integration of core databases.

MONITORING AND CONTROL

Often built early, on the basis of the detailed data available from the initial generation of transaction systems, these systems were intended to monitor the routine operation of the business and to produce routine MIS (Management Information) reports. Often this has meant little more than production of large quantities of waste paper. Like transaction systems, this area also may prove to be in poor shape when investigated. A better term in some cases might be management dis-information systems. A re-build, with a switch to interactive access by managers and supervisors to computer-held exception reports and MIS databases may prove appropriate.

PLANNING AND ANALYSIS

Needs in this area tend to be less predictable and more volatile than the above, with a strong focus on interactive use. Neglected in the past, due to their heavy computational needs, especially for on-line interactive use, these days they are a 'natural' for local PC based processing, albeit against shared MIS databases.

BUSINESS STRATEGY SUPPORT

This category is like planning and analysis but more-so. It is increasingly concerned with external information, and a wider range of data types, e.g. text and intelligence based. Needs are highly volatile. The potential is little tapped as yet, except in a few cases.

Decision support systems – categories

The Decision Support categories of the adapted Anthony triangle can be split vertically, as opposed to the above horizontal banding, into the following:

MANAGEMENT INFORMATION SYSTEMS (MIS)

A combination of the more valid aspects of the old monitoring and control reporting systems, and the relatively mundane elements of the planning and analysis systems. This category splits into:

- routine limited exception reporting, supported by interactive enquiry and diagnostic support, with access to relatively low levels of detail including extracts and aggregates from operational databases, where needed.
- more forward looking planning and analysis support, based on the results of routine analysis. This tends be heavily based on quantitatively based modelling, with interactive access and with graphics output. Increasingly, desktop PCs are proving the most suitable vehicle for these applications.

INTELLIGENCE GATHERING AND ANALYSIS

This term refers to systems able to cope with 'fuzzy' information, general rules and exceptions, where much of the source information may deal in probabilities rather than certainties, and/or may be in unstructured text form.

A third aspect of Decision Support applies mostly at the Operational Support level. This is termed:

OPERATIONAL DECISION SUPPORT

Here, it is becoming increasingly clear that interactive decision support processing has an important role to play. The combination of cheap computing power and rapid interactive access to up to date databases can enable the person at the 'sharp end' to benefit from a growing range of types of support. That being said, many of these applications can have contentious aspects, where we may be allowing systems to take decisions in preference to humans. When the computer fails in such a situation, the implications can be far reaching; fallback to manual operation may be virtually impossible. This should lead an alert system designer to undertake serious risk analysis, and to consider the broader issues, business and ethical, as is illustrated in the examples below:

- *Process control* – where a chemical plant or a nuclear power station can be run at a higher level of efficiency if first line operational decisions take place in real time under computer control.
- *Aircraft loading* – where last minute changes in weather or routing may influence the selected balance between fuel reserve and freight loaded, and hence the operating economics and safety margin of the aircraft.
- *Credit scoring* – where consumers expect an 'instant' decision on a credit application, and business may be lost (or unsuitable business taken on), unless a rapid decision can be taken on sound and consistent criteria.
- *'Fly-by-wire' controls* – in which high performance aircraft are configured to be flyable only if the human pilot's reactions are augmented by computerised decision-making.
- *Service despatching* – where vehicles in a service or emergency fleet are despatched to events according to criteria which are based on the objectives of meeting defined service levels with limited resources. The complexity of this situation may overwhelm the human operator, who may also miss opportunities for the optimal disposition of resources where they are non-intuitive.

Some chronic IS problems

The prospects are vast; opportunities almost limitless. But today, we often find our IS/IT performance in a sorry state. Problems which simply will not go away, and which an effective IS/IT strategy must address, include:

- Development still takes too long
- Changing existing systems takes even longer
- Forbidding replacement costs for inflexible, out of date systems
- There is excessive spend on 'maintenance'
- Systems functions as delivered are out of date
- Inadequate IS support impedes rapid response to market needs
- Users lose patience, but their d.i.y. solutions soon get out of control
- Critical MIS data may be locked away in inaccessible mainframe systems
- IS/IT investment is out of phase/focus with business priorities
- DP staff don't understand business needs

- Senior management don't understand DP constraints
- IS/IT operation appears misdirected, unplanned

To be effective, any IS/IT strategy must help to overcome these problems, as well as addressing the high profile competitive advantage requirements.

What do we need to do to get it right?

This chapter has shown that:

1. Business survival increasingly depends on attainment of excellence in IS/IT.

2. Information systems in most organizations fall far short, even of the traditional criteria for effectiveness.

3. Those criteria are changing rapidly, as a result of:

    - increasing competitive pressures
    - shortening time scales for delivery of new functionality
    - changing perceptions of the benefits of radical overhaul of business processes
    - the increasing integration of IS and IT into our products and delivery channels
    - rapidly changing IT cost/performance.

4. More creative or pro-active systems can only be delivered on the basis of a solid foundation of complete, up to date, accessible data, which itself is often lacking.

What must we do about this?

My suggestions are as follows:

1. Shift your planning style so that:

    - Business, IS and IT plans, both long and shorter term, are more closely integrated;
    - there is regular review to ensure that plans remain relevant, and are being followed.

2. As a basis for IS/IT planning, ensure that business plans, intentions and priorities are clear, and that areas of high uncertainty are properly explored.

3. Establish an effective IS/IT plan, which is clearly based on and linked to the agreed business needs and priorities, which is robust to identified uncertainties.

4. Make sure the plan covers 'proactive' exploitation of IT opportunities

for business and product/service support as well as the more mundane needs.

5. Ensure that the plan is clearly understood and committed to by senior management, and that it can be followed and maintained.

6. Establish effective board level structures such that responsibility for business results carries with it responsibility for the IS/IT facilities required to achieve them.

7. Provide a sound basis for implementation, including:

- verifiable business cases
- resources/skills in place
- effective IS organization and management controls
- sound systems development method
- realistic & practical migration plans

The remainder of this manual sets out a proven approach to achieving the above.

Table 1-3 sets out a summary of the way in which one organization has found it useful to link its IS/IT objectives to its business objectives.

Table 1-3:   *IS/IT objectives in support of business objectives*

Typical IS/IT Objective	Type of business objective					
	Improve customer satisfaction	Gain market share	Reduce costs	Improve profitability	Develop new/ improved products	Develop new markets
Support new insights into business processes and priorities	✔	✔	✓	✓	✔	✔
Detect changes in business need and respond quickly	✓	✓	✓	✓	✔	✔
Develop and enhance applications faster and cheaper	✓	✓	✔	✔	✔	✔
Systems to be adaptive and flexible to changes in business need or volumes	✔	✓			✔	✔
Meet service level targets at minimum costs	✓		✔	✔		
Provide effective business performance measurement and analysis	✓	✓	✓	✓	✓	✓
Gain maximum return on investment in IT R&D	✓		✓	✓	✔	
Provide and operate cost effective, flexible technology infrastructure	✓		✔	✔	✓	✓

CHAPTER 2

A survey of current approaches to IS/IT planning

Introduction

A formal method for planning for IS and IT is not really necessary for success, but in practice, people from junior analyst to Managing Director have more confidence if you are using one. However, even the most complete and elegant method, however well tried and proven, will fail for certain if it is followed slavishly and without insight. Conversely, with sufficient experience and judgement, you can 'wing it' without using a formal method at all.

From an almost complete vacuum in the early '80s, there have evolved a good many approaches to IS/IT planning. A fair subset of them will actually prove successful if used with insight, and by experienced staff.

The state of the art is changing rapidly, and it is only possible here to discuss a sample of approaches. Most of these will be slightly out of date.

You will often have to improvise in this field. Another good reason to use a formal method is that it provides a better place from which to launch your improvisation than mere guesswork.

I hope that this brief review of approaches may offer some insights into the whys and wherefores of success in this field.

Categories of IS/IT planning approach

You can't really categorize methods for IS/IT planning, but it helps to try. The main 'quasi-categories' are:

- Pre-1980s
- Information Engineering based: *closely, loosely*

- Cranfield influenced: *closely, loosely*
- Other current approaches

Pre-1980s approaches

These are now of historical interest only, but acted in many ways as the test beds for many of the techniques which are now routine.

- *IBM* – with BSP, later known as EIP, and its successors.
- *Arthur Andersen*, with Information Planning which preceded Method/1.

Information Engineering based approaches

James Martin, who had been involved in developing many of the techniques of IBM's BSP (Martin 1982), launched James Martin Associates (JMA, now James Martin Consulting) in 1983. Soon afterwards, he commenced collaboration with Knowledgeware and Texas Instruments in parallel on CASE Tool development. His family of methods emerged under the general banner of Information Engineering, accompanied by such acronyms as IEF, IEW, although their manifestations through the different collaborations varied significantly.

The Knowledgeware developments were taken up by Arthur Young (now Ernst and Young), and marketed as part of their 'Navigator' methodology series, (Ernst and Young 1990), supported by a CASE tool entitled Information Engineering Workbench (IEW, now ADW). Both Ernst and Young and JMA market embody a phase for IS/IT planning in their method frameworks, although they differ markedly.

The SP4IS method presented in this manual has origins in common with Information Engineering, but does not now follow it particularly closely.

Performance Development Corporation, of Princeton, NJ market and teach a method for IS/IT Planning, which is entitled Information Strategy Planning. This is substantially based on Information Engineering, and is in wider use in the USA than in Europe.

Approaches especially influenced by Cranfield

The most important of these are:

- *Cranfield* – Strategic Planning for Information Systems (Ward, Griffiths and Whitemore 1990).
- *UK Government CCTA* – Guidelines for Strategic Planning for Information Systems (Bunn, Bartlett and McLean 1989).
- *PA Consulting* – Tetrarch

Other current approaches

- DCE – Strategic Planning for Information Systems – merged in late 1992 with James Martin Consulting (who no longer have any formal connection with the provision of IEF).
- This approach is a hybrid of an early form of SP4IS and many of the Cranfield ideas. Pat Griffiths, then of DCE co-authored a book with John Ward of Cranfield (ibid. 1990). The ideas were especially influential in the formulation of HM Government CCTA Guidelines for Strategic Planning for Information Systems (ibid.). The merger with JMA implies that there will in due course be a merging of the JMA IE and Cranfield influences.

- CSC – SPIRIT
- Coopers Deloittes – Summit
- Soft Systems Methodology (SSM)
- Arthur Andersen – *Information Planning (part of Method/1 and Foundation)*

- Nolan & Norton – Stage by Stage
- LBMS – LEAP

SSM appears to be a collection of techniques for analysis and requirements definition which are more relevant to stages later in the life cycle, but it is being used with increasing frequency in analysis to support IS planning work (CCTA 1993). Its proponents differentiate it clearly from what they regard as 'hard' methods – i.e. everyone else's – but when used rigorously, it appears to have elements in common with functional decomposition. P B Checkland (Checkland 1981) is acknowledged as the leading UK proponent of this approach.

UK Government CCTA guidelines on strategic planning for information systems

These guide lines are discussed in rather more detail, as they offer a valuable template for a staged approach to IS/IT strategy development and maintenance, and are documented in the public domain – formally by Bunn, Bartlett and McLean (1989), and in substantial parts of Ward, Griffiths and Whitemore (1990). They constitute a framework and set of guidelines, rather than a prescriptive methodology. Users may select particular techniques and incorporate them. Within reason, other 'respectable' IS/IT planning methods, such as that described in this manual, should be capable of use in a manner which conforms to these guidelines.

The thinking which underlies the CCTA view of strategic planning can be described as a series of questions:

1.   What is the scope?

2.   Where are we now?

3.   Where do we want to be?

4.   How do we get there?

I recommend strongly that you regard there as being an additional question 3a: *"How good a basis is what we have now for supporting where we want to be?"*. This is the most effective means for forcing consideration of current systems and assets at the correct stage of the process.

CCTA guidelines – the five stages

1.   **Scoping study** (Addresses question 1). This covers positioning, prerequisites and relative scope(s) of related business and IS strategy projects. This is an especially valuable stage in complex or volatile environments:

- to position any business or systems strategic work properly before it is undertaken;
- to ensure that key prerequisites and dependencies are controlled;
- to ensure that the interactions of parallel activities are managed effectively.

2.   **Strategy study** (Addresses questions 2 fully, 3 and 3a in principle). The main phase – assembles all evidence required for selection of IS and IT strategy. The title is misleading, as it implies that the result is a completed strategy, which is not the case – it yields a series of options and the basis for distinguishing between them. You have to do all of the stages to gain a usable IS/IT strategic plan.

3.   **Strategy definition** (Finalizes questions 3, 3a, and addresses question 4 in directional terms). Generation and agreement of a vision of the future IS and IT strategy. Broad solutions are selected, but are not taken to final plan form.

4.   **Implementation planning** (Finalizes question 4). Transformation of the strategy into a viable, resource loaded, phased projects plan. This may involve iteration with earlier stages, e.g. if solutions prove uneconomic or not technically viable.

5.   **Monitoring, tuning and review** Continuing cycle of review and maintenance – the plan should never be allowed to become out of date or irrelevant.

There are further CCTA guide lines available from HMSO, which cover IS/IT strategy management, review and maintenance.

Common weaknesses of current approaches – pointers for improvement

From extensive use of a variety of methods and techniques for IS/IT strategic planning, I have assessed the most important problems and weaknesses in the current state of the art in IS/IT planning. The results of this are presented below under two categories:

(a) *recognized flaws and pitfalls*, to which good solutions are now known (but which are not always practised);

(b) *less tractable difficulties*, to which energy and attention must continue to be devoted.

All of the methods referenced above suffer in varying degrees from some of these flaws, but both because my information must always be out of date, and also for legal reasons, a detailed mapping cannot be provided. The method which is put forward in the later chapters of this manual, SP4IS, is, as should be expected, reasonably free from the majority of the type (a), but remains open to improvement, especially regarding the type (b) difficulties.

The type (a) problems, 'solved in principle', are:

- *Poor links with business planning and policy development.* This usually results from a failure to gain management commitment and trust at the outset, or to retain confidence once it has been gained. Failure is almost certain in this case.
- *No provision for continuing maintenance of the plans*

Early workers often thought, wrongly, that completing the first planning cycle was the end of the process. Usually, such plans were locked in a glass fronted bookcase and ignored. The plans must embody the means for:

- monitoring and control - continuing maintenance

- *Oriented towards exercise of structured techniques rather than to really meeting business needs.* There was a vogue in the early to mid '80 for over-use of structured analysis techniques. Some people still haven't got over it. Whilst most acute at system design level, the malaise influenced some IS/IT planning approaches. Workers using approaches biased towards structured analysis rarely completed stage 2, in CCTA terms, and delivered little of strategic relevance.
- *Can't handle uncertainty or change - becomes a straitjacket.* This is a traditional heresy of second rate systems analysts. It is addressed by the techniques for management of uncertainty, such as scenario planning (Chapter 6).
- *Stops too soon - e.g. at visions or architectures.* A weakness of many of the early efforts, especially those influenced by IBM.

- *Fails to integrate smoothly with subsequent stages of the application development life cycle.* There is a need to identify target deliverables and agree formats; so that everyone knows what to expects and what to do with it. There is sometimes need to educate the putative recipients also; they may never have seen a plan before, let alone be expected to follow one.

- *Obscure or complex process.* Some approaches to IS planning or design are extremely thorough, elegant and sophisticated. However, they are operable only by geniuses, and are incomprehensible to management. They are useless. Typically, the basis for conclusions reached under these processes is neither verifiable nor re-workable by ordinary mortals.

  This is somewhat of a grey area; a degree of formalism is unavoidable, and in some parts of the process we have to get into some detail. Clarity of flow, and traceability should be the watchwords. Automation will help here - helping to carry brunt of detail, and making the detail manageable.

- *Failure to deal with application package assessment and integration.* Critical - this is a common error.

- *No effective assessment of levels of accuracy and risk.* Risk assessment at this level is very judgemental - but it is a well trodden track nowadays, and omission is inexcusable.

- *Failure to make effective use of work already done, or 'best practice'.* Though it hurts a consultant to admit it, this is most commonly a result of the arrogance of external consultants.

Some of the type (b) difficulties, where there remains room for improvement are:

- *The process takes too long, costs too much to do - loss of management patience.* This is a perpetual problem - 2 days is too long for some senior managers! They'll get you either way - senior management have a sometimes mischievous tendency to 'wrong foot' you on detail or lack of it.

  There is nowadays a heavy focus on speeding the IS/IT planning process up, but this needs great care, and carries risk of getting it seriously wrong if overdone. There is inevitably a trade-off between accuracy/risk control and flair/vision, and you are generally on a loser. The process is gradually getting faster, but is still too slow.

- *Limited applicability - cannot cope with varied environments.* This is still a 'work in progress' area. It is still hard to do the process really fast for small operations (but see the addendum to Chapter 3).

  More and more non-commercial organizations, who were at one time most difficult because of the 'You can't measure what I do' syndrome, are coming over to a quantified, objectives based management approach. Personally, I have found such a syndrome quite amenable to the *reductio ad absurdum* argument which can be summarized as: '*If that means that we cannot detect the effects of what you do, then neither would the business notice your absence.*' This usually leads to the person in question quickly discovering that they do have a measurable output after all!

- *Failure to embrace human factors.* In attempting to change any organization, we are up against human nature. The 'hearts and minds' approach is always best. A good start can be made on the basis of the sponsorship and consensus processes set out in this manual.

- *Poor or non-existent automated support.* There is no complete solution available yet, but I exhort you strongly to place whatever documentation is generated on your favorite automated media, and to make heavy use of it. See chapter 9.

Conclusion

There is no perfect method for IS/IT planning. The method which is documented in this manual will do the job well if used with insight – and so will others based on similar principles. But whichever approach you use, leaven it generously with common sense and business judgement (which those who disagree with you may term 'subjectivity'). And above all continue to question and improve both the process and the results which you achieve from it.

CHAPTER 3

Overview of strategic planning for information systems

Introduction

This chapter provides an overview of the SP4IS (*Strategic Planning for Information Systems*) method for IS/IT Planning. It is intended both for use 'stand alone' as a high level reference, and also as a guide to the remainder of the manual. For this reason, it inevitably embodies a degree of redundancy with material which is covered in greater detail later. It is important to realize that, unlike procedures for design and implementation of information systems, methods for the preparation of IS/IT plans cannot be fully prescriptive. Variations encountered in business style, complexity and environment, coupled with the variety of management styles encountered, mean that a significant degree of customization of the process may often be needed. The systematic framework presented here is therefore intended as a basis from which to customize, rather than as a straitjacket.

Objectives of the SP4IS method

- Align and focus information systems and IT strategies of the organization so as to best support and reinforce the business mission and goals
- Link the business, systems and IT planning cycles so as to ensure continuing focus on strategic priorities
- Secure and retain senior management commitment to the planning process, and to sponsoring the implementation
- Identify and exploit opportunities offered by information technology (IT) to help the organization gain and hold a competitive edge

STRATEGIC PLANNING FOR INFORMATION SYSTEMS IS AIMED AT DELIVERING A SET OF PLANS WHICH ARE:

- Manifestly necessary to the business
- Affordable
- Understandable
- Achievable
- Manageable
- Maintainable

Do you need a plan for IS/IT?

Maybe your organization doesn't need a plan for IS/IT. You can certainly save a great deal of time and trouble if this is so. As a simple check, try the questions below. If you can answer them all with a fair degree of certainty, you already have an IS/IT plan sufficient for your needs.

- What are the most important information and support needs?
- What are the overriding business concerns and priorities?
- How are both likely to change over time
- How well does the current IS portfolio meet the needs?
- How can I best rectify the gaps?
- Are we missing out on key IT opportunities for product delivery?
- How can I build systems and databases which will support my organization's future needs?
- At what rate, and in what sequence should I deliver systems?
- Is the IS/IT budget too high/too low? How can I tell?

Information systems – overall objective

We assume that today's IS Department has some form of overall mission statement, such as: '*To meet the information and support needs of the business in the optimum manner*'.

In practice, this is usually translated into goals such as the following:

- Avoid late, inaccurate or missing information being a constraint on business performance
- Improve efficiency and effectiveness of business operation:

  - *closer control*   ▪ *lower stocks*   ▪ *better customer service*

- Improve quality of management decisions by providing better information support
- Support development of new business areas, e.g. through timely and effective IS/IT support of products and/or delivery channels.

It follows directly that answers are needed to the questions set out in the preceding section, and that an effective IS/IT plan is needed to provide these answers. My thesis is therefore that an IS department, to fulfil its mission and objectives, needs an IS/IT plan. In fact, without such a plan, it cannot even formulate its objectives in anything except vague and directional terms.

Why have a method?

- A sound IS/IT plan is critical to business performance
- You only get one chance – don't risk fluffing it
- Difficult to do quickly and effectively without experience
- Exploit the proven experience gained elsewhere
- Leverage on scarce resources – a modest team can follow a method which was devised by people of greater experience
- 'Bedside manner' – good for management confidence

Inputs – the link from business planning to information systems planning

- Starting point information – the ideal – is as follows:
- Corporate mission and objectives
- Customer and competitive positioning
- Sector plans:
  - *objectives, goals, priorities*
  - *strategies followed*
- Likely factors influencing business and market change
- Business structure/organization
- Management style – level and means for control
- Functional organization
- Planning and control style
- Results from previous planning cycles
- What is needed – information and support needs plus priorities

Products from the process

The strategic IS/IT planning process has a number of different products. It is useful to divide these into:

- end products;
- business-oriented intermediate products;
- IS and IT oriented products.

This division is important, because we need to target our products at the appropriate audience. To offer all of the products to all interested parties is one of the faster ways in which to lose their interest. For example, senior management will have little interest in, or patience with the details of the architectures and interfaces of the information systems, important as they are for getting the strategy right.

End products

- Statements of strategic solutions for information systems and technology
- Phased development plans for:
    - application systems and databases
    - IT development projects
    - staff skills upgrade
- Basis for implementation and migration
- Business case with financial plan
- Criteria and process for plan review, tuning and maintenance

Business-Oriented Intermediate Products

- Consolidated and agreed statement of business information and support needs and priorities.
    - the 'charter'
    - basis for managing change
    - may be used to generate scenarios
- Indication of key areas of risk and uncertainty on which the viability of the recommended solutions depends
- Assessment of current information systems in terms of the extent and quality of coverage achieved of business needs
- Urgent actions plan for interim 'quick fixes'
- Complete audit trail and basis for traceability from requirement to solutions

IS and IT oriented products

- Assessment of current IS and IT status:
    - objective – what there is
    - judgemental – its quality and current and future relevance
- Log of options and solutions which were considered and rejected, with reasons
- Target applications and database architecture
- Target IT architecture
- Target organization and skills/resource strategy

Key features of the process

- Business/priority driven – 'tuned in'
- Top/down, focused – 'rifle bullet' approach
- Open architecture – flexible, continuing to evolve; the framework is distinct from the techniques
- Estimatable, controllable
- Complete – delivers implementable plans
- May be used in a manner which is compatible with HM Government CCTA guidelines for Strategic Planning for Information Systems
- Process and results are understandable, verifiable
- Process is proven
- Efficient in elapsed and management time
- Iterative
- Key analytic tasks amenable to automation
- The quality process is integral and explicit
- The plans as delivered are designed for maintenance and enhancement

Approach to quality

- Quality is embedded in the method in a pervasive manner
- Preventive measures seek to avoid need to rectify problems
- Diagnostic measures ensure that problems are detected and rectified
- Scope covers:
  - sponsors' involvement and commitment
  - interim and final deliverables
  - phase end checkpoints

The quality approach and process are set out in detail in Appendix III. In summary, there are two classes of quality process provided:

- preventive, or intrinsic measures, which are aimed at ensuring that quality is built in from the start;
- diagnostic, or inspection based measures, aimed at identifying and rectifying any flaws which escape the preventive processes.

Preventive quality measures

- Business systems sponsors know who they are and what they need to do
- They take responsibility (with specialist support) for the end-to-end process of identifying and meeting *their* needs
- Sponsors review and approve all key deliverables

- The approach recognizes and embraces change and uncertainty; does not try to ban or ignore them

Diagnostic Quality Measures

DELIVERABLES

- Format and assessment criteria for all deliverables are pre-defined
- Delivery stage and time are identified
- Review responsibilities and process are clear

PHASE END CHECKPOINTS

- Has the planned work been completed?
- Are the deliverables present and approved?
- Are the conclusions justified by the evidence and the analysis?
- Are the plans for the next phase still appropriate?
- Is there a sufficient basis to start work on the next stage?

The place of SP4IS in the development life cycle

- Business planning – corporate and sector
- Information systems planning – corporate and sector
- Information technology planning – corporate and sector
- Functional requirements definition – priority business area
- External design – application/user i/face
- Internal design – system/subsystem
- Construction – subsystem
- Implementation – subsystem/phase
- Maintenance
  - rectification of faults
  - extension/amendment of function

Figure 3-1 illustrates the overall flow of business, IS and IT planning, and the iterative manner of the plan maintenance process.

Figures 3-2, 3-3 and Table 3-1 give progressively more detailed and formal views of the process. Detailed work programs are provided in Appendix II.

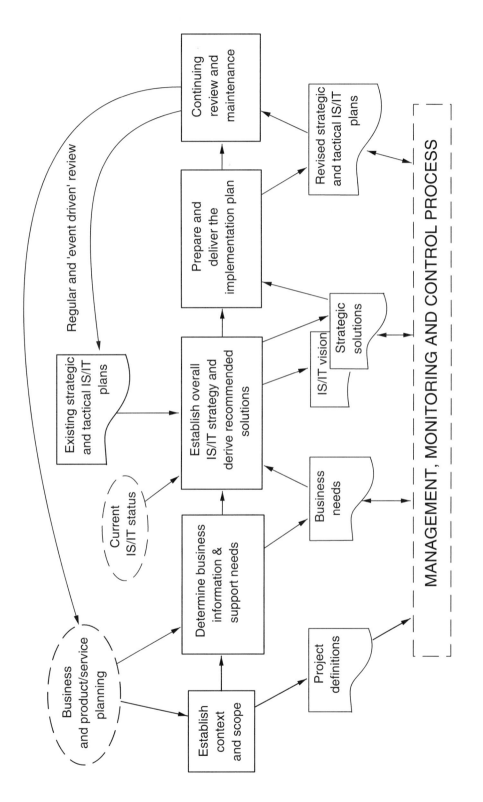

Figure 3-1: *The IS/IT strategic planning cycle*

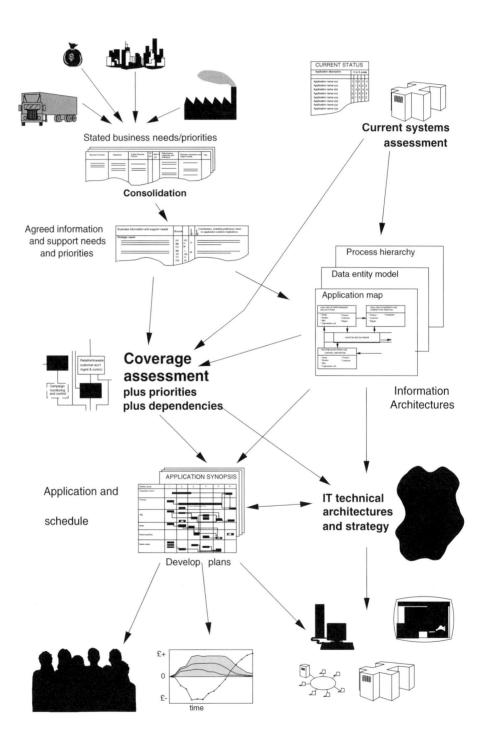

Figure 3-2: *Strategic planning for information systems overall logical flow*

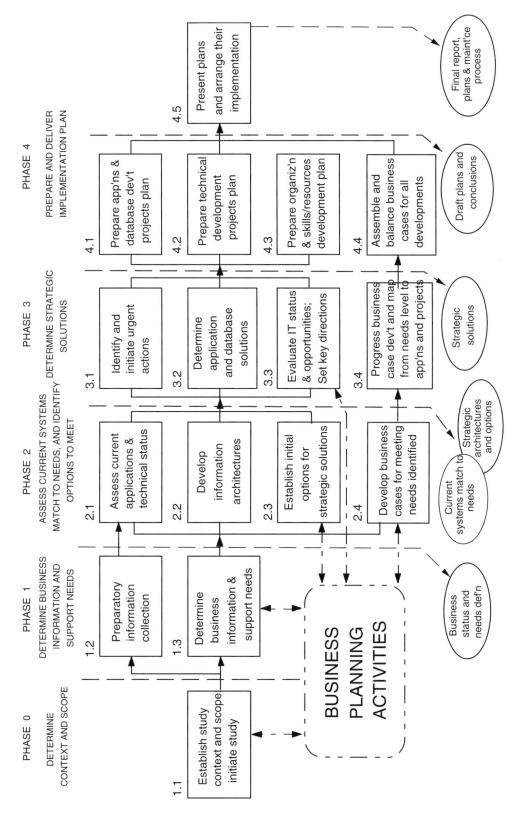

Figure 3-3: *Framework for strategic planning for information systems*

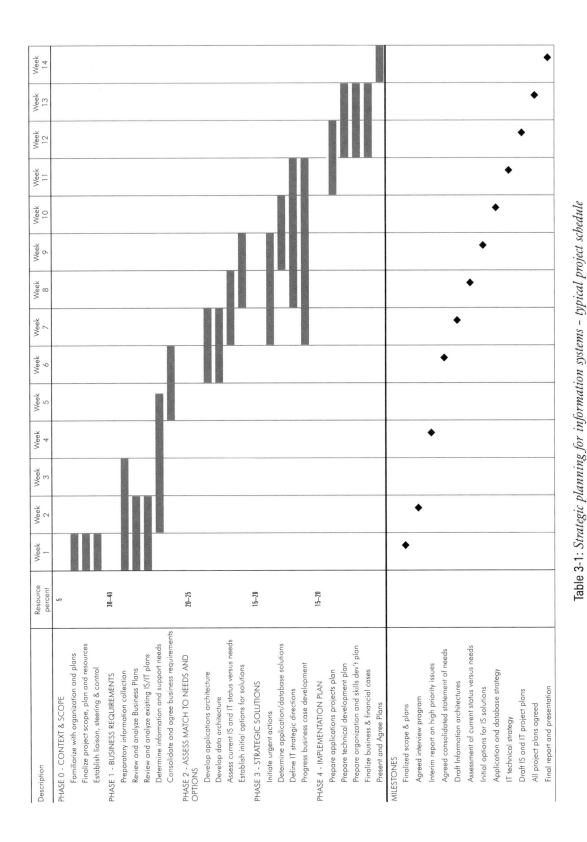

Description	Resource percent	Week 1	Week 2	Week 3	Week 4	Week 5	Week 6	Week 7	Week 8	Week 9	Week 10	Week 11	Week 12	Week 13	Week 14
PHASE 0 - CONTEXT & SCOPE	5														
Familiarize with organization and plans		▮													
Finalize project scope, plan and resources		▮													
Establish liaison, steering & control		▮													
PHASE 1 - BUSINESS REQUIREMENTS	30–40														
Preparatory information collection				▮											
Review and analyze Business Plans			▮	▮											
Review and analyze existing IS/IT plans			▮												
Determine information and support needs						▮									
Consolidate and agree business requirements							▮								
PHASE 2 - ASSESS MATCH TO NEEDS AND OPTIONS	20–25														
Develop applications architecture								▮							
Develop data architecture								▮							
Assess current IS and IT status versus needs									▮						
Establish initial options for solutions										▮					
PHASE 3 - STRATEGIC SOLUTIONS	15–20														
Initiate urgent actions							▮								
Determine application/database solutions											▮				
Define IT strategic directions												▮			
Progress business case development												▮			
PHASE 4 - IMPLEMENTATION PLAN	15–20														
Prepare applications projects plan													▮		
Prepare technical development plan														▮	
Prepare organization and skills dev't plan														▮	
Finalize business & financial cases														▮	
Present and Agree Plans															▮
MILESTONES															
Finalized scope & plans		◆													
Agreed interview program			◆												
Interim report on high priority issues					◆										
Agreed consolidated statement of needs							◆								
Draft Information architectures								◆							
Assessment of current status versus needs									◆						
Initial options for IS solutions										◆					
Application and database strategy											◆				
IT technical strategy												◆			
Draft IS and IT project plans													◆		
All project plans agreed														◆	
Final report and presentation															◆

Table 3-1: *Strategic planning for information systems – typical project schedule*

Compatibility

Strategic Planning For Information Systems May be used in a manner which is compatible with the UK Government CCTA guidelines for Strategic Planning for Information Systems. The correspondence is roughly as follows:

CCTA stage	SP4IS phase
1. *Scoping study* What is the scope?	0. Determine context and scope
2. *Strategy study* Where are we now?	1. Determine business information and support needs
Basis and options for strategy selection	2. Establish information architectures and options
3. *Strategy definition* Where do we want to be?	3. Determine strategic solutions
4. *Implementation planning* How do we get there?	4. Prepare and deliver plans
5. *Monitoring, tuning and review*	Post phase 4. Provided for in the plan as delivered

The link from business planning

What is needed from the business planners as a basis for IS/IT planning? Ideally, a very great deal – see the list below. But we must recognize that:

- not all of these items will be readily forthcoming;
- it may not be feasible to wait until they are available – they may never arrive;
- items which are provided may be rather high level or even vague.

We may need to work with the business planners, or the senior management who own the plans, in order to sharpen their definition, or clarify their interpretation to a degree sufficient to form as basis for IS/IT planning. An approach of last resort, for use in cases where business planning is especially poor is set out in the addendum to this chapter.

The ideal shopping list is as follows:

- Business mission, goals, priorities
- Specific corporate, product and sector plans
- Functional organization
- Relevant business scenarios and contingencies

- Competitive positioning and intelligence
- Key business priorities and concerns
- Leader/laggard attitude
- Results from previous planning cycles

The typical view of business plans which we expect to find is illustrated in Figure 3-4.

Figure 3-4: *Business plan typical structure – key elements and derived requirements*

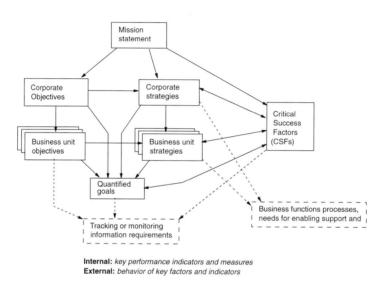

The relation between business, IS and IT plans, short and long term, and corporate versus sector, is illustrated in Figure 3-5.

Figure 3-5: *The integration of business unit plans with corporate*

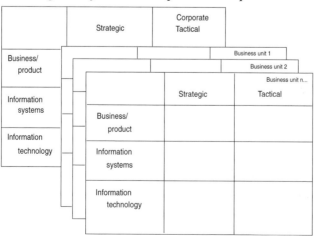

Phase and stage framework

The remainder of this chapter steps through the phase and stage structure of the SP4IS framework. For each stage the objectives and key products are presented, with examples of certain of the deliverables. More detailed task level breakdowns for the stages are presented in the illustrative work programs in Appendix II. These should not be regarded as definitive, as, due to the variety of organizational complexity and culture encountered, no recipe book approach is feasible. A degree of improvisation will always be required; it will usually be necessary to write a custom work programs, based on the phase/stage structure presented below.

Phase 0 – establishing context and scope for an information systems strategic plan

This phase addresses the positioning, prerequisites and relative scope(s) of related business and IS strategy projects. It is optional, but usually recommended. Issues addressed include:

- What are the business units?
- Are existing strategies – appropriate, relevant?
- Are they being followed?
- What needs to be covered by the new strategy(ies)?
- How many studies are needed, of what nature and depth? (The answer may be 'none')
- How should they integrate with one another:
  - business unit plans, IS and IT strategies?
  - interfaces, co-ordination, timing and time scales?
- Management, control and resourcing
- Pre-study issues to resolve

Stage 0.1 – Establish context and scope; initiate the study

OBJECTIVE

Start the most appropriate study(ies) at the right time, under control, with the right terms of reference, management commitment and expectation

PRODUCTS

1. Study context, scope and terms of reference
2. Prerequisites identified and under control
3. Essential parallel activities scoped and initiated

4.   Team in place, trained, supported

5.   Steering Group set up and aware

Other key management involved and briefed

Completed work program

Initial interview schedule

Phase 1 – determine business information and support needs

Establish the basis of fact on which to build a strategy

- Where do we want to be – in terms of business plans, information and support needs and priorities
- IS and IT achievements and assets
- Other 'givens' and constraints
- Range of uncertainty

Stage 1.2 – Preparatory information collection

OBJECTIVE

1.   Ensure a basis of fact for later analysis/assessment

2.   Be as prepared as possible for management interviews

PRODUCTS

Inventory and assessment of all available information about:

1.   business status goals, directions, environment and plans

2.   current and planned applications and data (see Table 3-2)

3.   IT assets and inventory, current and on order

4.   human skills/resources

Stage 1.3 Determine business information and support needs and priorities

OBJECTIVE

1.   Develop full and clear understanding of business status goals, directions, environment, plans, information and support needs.

2.   Agree priorities for these

3.   Gain commitment from senior management and sharpen their expectation of outcomes

APPLICATION	Status P – plan D – dev't L –live	DATE FIRST LIVE	HARDWARE & SOFTWARE ENVIRONMENT	USER INTERFACE MODE	COMMENTS	Summary ratings - 0 (poor) to 5 (good)				
						User Satisf'n	Oper'l stability	Response and thruput	Security availability integrity	Pot base for future dev't
General Accounting	L	1984	IBM 43xx Package	Interactive	Reputable package, but it is failing to meet user needs at present, mostly due to inadequate coding structures and poor discipline and controls in the manual systems.	2	4	3	2	4
Purchase Ledger	L	1972	ICL (Plan & COBOL)	Batch	Completely out of date; should have been entirely superseded by now, but is still in use in a few sites.	1	2	2	3	0
	L	1984	Converted to IBM COBOL	Batch	The conversion was at the code level, the revised system remains poor.					
Sales Ledger	L	1985	IBM 43xx Package	Interactive	Implemented to replace poor mostly manual transfer from Sales Order Processing, & to provide automated invoicing. User problems mostly due to inadequacies of the SOP system.	3	5	4	4	4
Payroll	L	1974	ICL (Plan & COBOL)	Batch	Does the job at present, but accounting interface is weak, and design limitations make further development difficult	4	3	3	3	2
	L	1985	Converted to IBM COBOL	Batch						
Personnel	L	1976	ICL (Plan & COBOL)	Batch	A batch-based extension to Payroll. Offers little flexibility for analysis or enquiry, due to constraints of parent system.	2	3	3	3	0
	L	1985	Converted to IBM COBOL	Batch						
Sales Order Processing	L	1975	ICL COBOL	Interactive	Limited system, lacking up to date facilities.	2	2	3	2	0
	L	1985	Converted to IBM COBOL	otherwise batch	Due to poor quality of design, potential for enhancement is now exhausted. Many requests for modifications outstanding.					

Table 3-2: *Trendy Products PLC – current systems and development plans inventory and assessment*

APPLICATION	Status P – plan D – dev't L –live	DATE FIRST LIVE	HARDWARE & SOFTWARE ENVIRONMENT	USER INTERFACE MODE	COMMENTS	Summary ratings - 0 (poor) to 5 (good)				
						User Satisf'n	Oper'l stability	Response and thruput	Security availability integrity	Pot base for future dev't
Finished Goods Inventory Control	L	1977	ICL COBOL	Interactive data entry otherwise batch	Well integrated with SOP, but lacking facilities to cope with Trendy's current multiple sites and more complex distribution arrangements.	3	4	3	3	2
	L	1985	Converted to IBM COBOL							
Sales & Marketing Analysis	L	1986	IBM 43xx COBOL, with some ad hoc enquiry	Batch limited reporting flexibility	System value is limited by quality and scope of source data. Users are disappointed by lack of online enquiry & lack of flexible formatting and analysis facilities.	2	3	4	4	3
Manufacturing Control - Luton	L	1973	ICL COBOL	Mostly Batch	Trendy's original system - now obsolescent.	2	3	1	3	0
	L	1984	Converted to IBM COBOL							
Manufacturing Control - Birmingham	L	1979	ICL ME29 - RPG, some COBOL	Mixed batch/ interactive	Custom system, moderately successful at Birmingham location. Doubts exist over its applicability to other sites due to technical env't and limited facilities.	4	4	3	3	1
Manufacturing Control - Bristol	L	1985	Hewlett Packard 3000 Package	Mixed batch/interactive	An up to date mfg. control package, with reputable vendor and broad user base. More advanced modules (MRP & shop floor ctl.) not yet implemented in Bristol, but early plans exist to do so.	4	4	4	4	5

NB: This version does not include W.I.P projects

Table 3-2: *(continued) Trendy Products PLC - current systems and development plans inventory and assessment*

PRODUCTS

1. Agreed consolidated statement of business information and support needs and priorities

2. Backing detail of the stated need and negotiations (see Figure 3-6 and Table 3-3)

3. Identified and committed business sponsors for each key requirement (see Table 3-4)

Figure 3-6:   *Business interview analysis format*

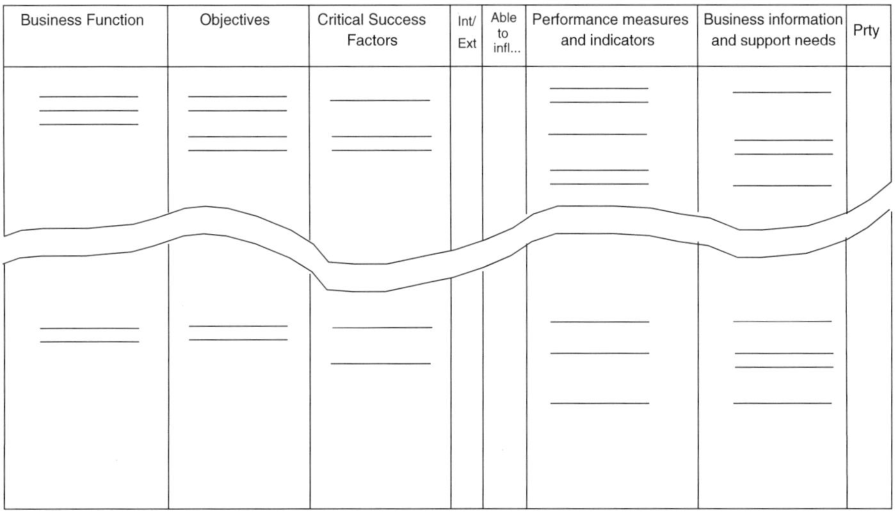

Phase 2 – establish information architectures and options for solutions

Phase objective: *Determine the strategic IS and IT goals, and establish a range of options for achieving them*

- Determine where we want to be:
  - IS/IT strategic vision to support the business needs
  - appropriate information architectures and infrastructure
- Assess the value and relevance of current IS and IT status and achievement to date:
  - coverage offered for identified business needs
  - basis for evolution towards the strategic vision
- Establish a preliminary view of implementation options:
  - implications of business information and support priorities
  - application options for meeting these needs
- Develop business cases for implementation

FUNCTION	OBJECTIVE/GOAL	CRITICAL SUCCESS FACTORS	Ext/ Int	Can infl	PERFORMANCE MEASURES	BUSINESS INFORMATION & SUPPORT NEEDS	PRTY
Set up and run Trendy's retail operation.	Get retail acquisition back to break even by 1Q '93	Ability to identify and cut key costs fast	I	Y	Store performance reported accurately and promptly	Revenue and profit volumes overall and by: ■ item ■ square foot for each: ■ store ■ region actual versus plan, this year versus last.	VH
		Ability to prune store portfolio	I	Y			
	Make 30% gross margin on turnover in 1993 i.e. 15% net profit	Have the right goods in stock at the right price and margin, in the right stores at the right time.	I	Y	Sales item performance overall and by store reported accurately /promptly		
	Grow square footage by 25% p.a. compound from 1993 onwards	Ability to find the right sites for new stroe and to exploit them.	E	Y	Site evaluation support.		
		Ability to staff new stores	I	Y	New store performance highlighted.		
		Size of new stores (need to be larger on average).	I	Y	Staffing achieved vs targets		
Stabilise current operation – 'stop the haemmorrage'	Turn around or close non-performing stores	Ability to spot poor performers	I	Y			
		Accurate identification of causes	I	Y			
		Ability to shed poor sites; close stores & sell	I	Y			
	Cut 'shrinkage' from 2.5% at least to the industry average – 1.5%	Improved controls at all points in the chain.	I	Y	Average shrinkage by location, goods type by time.		
	Make store managers more responsible as managers – mini-business concept, with each store in effect a profit centre, by mid 1993	Effective in-store systems to support the store manager	I	Y		In-store systems to enable the store to run as a business unit	H
		Effective training programmes	I	Y	Store manager preformance		
	Highlight non-performing store managers and release them.	Ability to recruit enough store managers of the necessary calibre	I	Y			

Table 3-3: *Trendy Product PLC – information systems strategy – analysis of Gerry Floggitt interview*

FUNCTION	OBJECTIVE/GOAL	CRITICAL SUCCESS FACTORS	Ext/ Int	Can infl	PERFORMANCE MEASURES	BUSINESS INFORMATION & SUPPORT NEEDS	PRTY
Plan and open new stores	Find the right new sites to meet growth objectives. 10 new stores in 1993; 15 p.a. during '94 to '96.	Capital availability to invest in new stores	I	Y		Effective cash management systems, so as to free up the working capital needed.	M
		Accurate evaluation of potential sites	I				
		Accurate tracking of new stores in the critical early stages	I	Y			
Stock the right items	Know accurately what we're really selling soon after we sold it.	Goods identified at point of sale	I	Y	Sales volume by stock item		
		Easy to operate fail safe recording of goods sold linked to cash records.	I	Y	Level of stock outs or over-stocking by store & item	EPOS at all points in all stores.	H
	Translate sales data into shipment orders.	Sales data automatically fed back into ordering cycle.	I	Y		Good information systems running all the way through: ■ the point of sale ■ in-store inventory and ordering ■ distribution chain ■ buying and warehousing	VH
	Ability to buy at the right price & lead time.						
Get the goods into the stores on time	Cut distribution costs as a percentage of revenue from 12% to 7%.	Ability to identify and ctl store costs.	I	Y	Distribution costs by: ■ region; ■ carrier type.		
	Cut late deliveries from 30% to under 5%	Enforcement of scheduling disciplines in distribution operation	I	Y	Delivery performance versus schedule by region & carrier		
Monitor sales and other store performance measures effectively.	Know accurately what we're really selling soon after we sold it, and be in position to act on the information.	Good information systems running all the way through: ■ the point of sale ■ in-store inventory and ordering ■ distribution chain ■ buying and warehousing	I	Y		Revenue and profit volumes overall and by: ■ item ■ square foot for each: ■ store ■ region actual versus plan, this year versus last.	VH
		Good information on and control over store performance and costs.	I	Y		Costs overall and by type for each: ■ store ■ region	H
						Staff turnover by store and grade.	M

Table 3-3: (continued): *Trendy Product PLC – information systems strategy – analysis of Gerry Floggitt interview*

Ref.	INFORMATION/SUPPORT NEED		Source		Joint prty (H/M/L)	POTENTIAL BUSINESS BENEFITS SOURCES AND BASIS	EXTENT TO WHICH NEEDS ARE ADDRESSED BY CURRENT SYSTEMS
	Short title	Description	Initials	prty (H/M/L)			
SM10	Market analysis - general	Capability for extensive analysis of, and modelling based on marketing database e.g.	WJ JW	M H	M	Needs new marketing database development (below), and enhanced end-user facilities & support	
SM20	Mkt analysis - new products	■ To explore potential impact of new products under range of circumstances.	B CG	M L	H		
SM30	New ventures - risk analysis	■ Risk evaluation of new ventures: eg modelling of potential market share & profitability of alternative product & promotion strategies.	FR JW	H M	M	High potential for use of interactive modelling tools.	
SM40	Marketing database	Marketing database covering all sectors, products, plus competitors activity and fiscal /economic factors. To include data from a wide range of external sources and from TC field staff.	FR WJ F	H MH M	M	Needed for above, therefore at least priority 4	
SM80	Cashflow planning	Corporate cashflow planning & modelling facilities.	EB	H	H		
PLANNING & ANALYSIS							
SM110	Cashflow forecasting	Cashflow & revenue forecasts	EB	VH	H		
SM160	Manuf'g costs analysis	Fuller & more accurate analysis of all elements of manufacturing & distribution costs.	CG JK	VH H	H	Needs integrated, uniform treatment of all costs, coding categories.	
SM170	Supplier perf analysis	Analysis of supplier performance, relating quality, returns and timeliness of delivery.	CG	H	H		
SM200	Product peformance analysis	Product and sales line performance analysis	JW	VH	H		
SM220	Treasury support	Up to date FX and money market information and Trendy's cash position and needs to support short term funds management.	EB	M	M		

Table 3-4: *Consolidated summary of business information and support needs*

| | INFORMATION/SUPPORT NEED | | Source | | Joint | POTENTIAL BUSINESS BENEFITS | EXTENT TO WHICH NEEDS ARE |
Ref.	Short title	Description	Initials	prty (H/M/L)	prty (H/M/L)	SOURCES AND BASIS	ADDRESSED BY CURRENT SYSTEMS
MONITORING & CONTROL NEEDS							
SM230	Business performance reporting	Effective overall business performance measures: ■ volume, profit, cashflow, ■ actuals versus targets, ■ analysed by: product, product group, outlet type, business unit, responsibility unit	FR EB	H H	H	Significant upgrades to base systems.	
SM240	Profitability reporting	Profitability by product, region, outlet, major customer by time, volume & margin, actual versus plan, this year versus last.	JW CG	VH VH	H	Dependent on improved sales and costs information.	
SM270	Service level reporting	Accurate, up to date reporting of service levels covering all aspects of distribution logistics, actual versus plan.	JK	VH	H	Needed for independent validation distribution contractor's invoices as well as normal perf'ce tracking.	
SM280	Costs monitoring	Costs and revenues by cost centre, product and activity type; actuals versus plan	EB	H	H		
SM300	Manufacturing performance	More accurate and complete costs and performance information for manufacturing processes, provided in a consistent format for all plants and work centres.	CG EB	VH H	H	Need compatible coding structures and information flows from all sites.	
TRANSACTION AND SUPPORT NEEDS							
SM360	External information links	Effective and timely information links with our: ■ Wholesale Customers; ■ Suppliers; ■ Bankers and financial advisors; ■ Distribution contractor(s).	FR BJ	M H	M	Communication solution should embrace EDI also.	
SM365	Better sales & acc'tg tx'n data	Cleaner, single point of entry transaction data collection and validation for all sales and accounting transaction data.	EB JW	H M	MH	Savings on repeated data entry. Removal of sales and acc'tg reports inconsistency. Improved basis for MIS	
SM370	Standard chart of accounts	Standardised high level chart of accounts and coding structures covering all Business units.	EB	VH	H	A management issue, but selected systems should support the solution.	

Table 3-4: *(continued): Consolidated summary of business information and support needs*

The manner in which business needs are matched with the cover offered by current systems and projects to give an initial view of gaps and weaknesses is illustrated in the top half of Figure 3-7.

Figure 3-7:   *Matching plans to business needs*

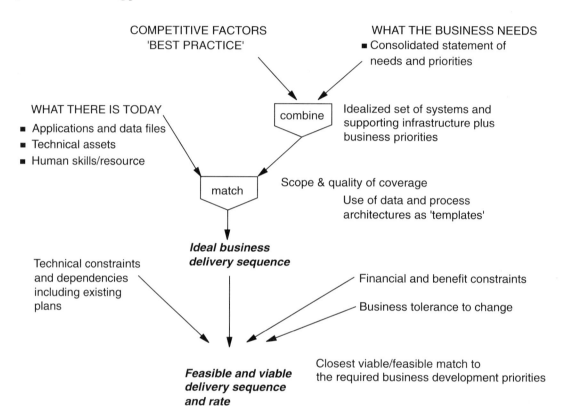

Stage 2.1 Assess current applications and IT technical status, and match to needs

OBJECTIVE

1.   Assess current IS and IT status, and the degree of match to identified and probable business needs

2.   Determine key strengths and weaknesses

PRODUCTS

1.   Full inventory of current application portfolio and IT assets

2.   Assessment of strengths and weaknesses

3.   Action plan in outline for each high priority weak area

4.   Preliminary view of rapid development opportunities where appropriate

Stage 2.2 Developing information architectures

OBJECTIVE

Establish information architectures as a basis for long term development

PRODUCTS

1.   Draft architectures for business and industry structure

2.   Draft information architectures – application systems, databases and technology requirements

3.   Identification of key gaps/weaknesses in current status which will prejudice attainment of the architectures

The key intermediate product, the Application Systems Map, which is annotated to show both business priorities and the extent of cover offered by current systems and plans, is illustrated in Figure 3-8.

Stage 2.3 Establish initial options for strategic solutions

OBJECTIVE

For high priority needs, establish a preliminary set of options for application solutions

PRODUCTS

1.   Identification of key gaps/weaknesses in current coverage which require applications solutions

2.   An overall IS strategic vision of the preferred means for meeting the business needs

3.   For high priority needs, a preliminary set of options for application solutions

4.   Feed-back to rapid development opportunities (stage 2.1)

5.   Modifications to emerging information architectures

Elements of an IS vision

1.   An overall application portfolio framework – probably framed in terms on an overall Application Systems Map, with color coded coverage assessment, and supported by brief explanatory notes. (see Figure 3-8).

2.   Proposed means for support of business product and service development.

Figure 3-8:   *Trendy products PLC – applications systems map with coverage annotation*

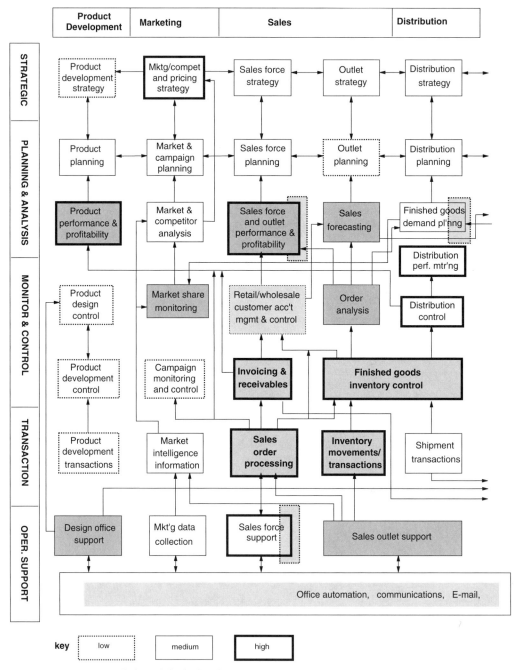

Figure 3-8: *(continued) Trendy products PLC – applications systems map with coverage annotation*

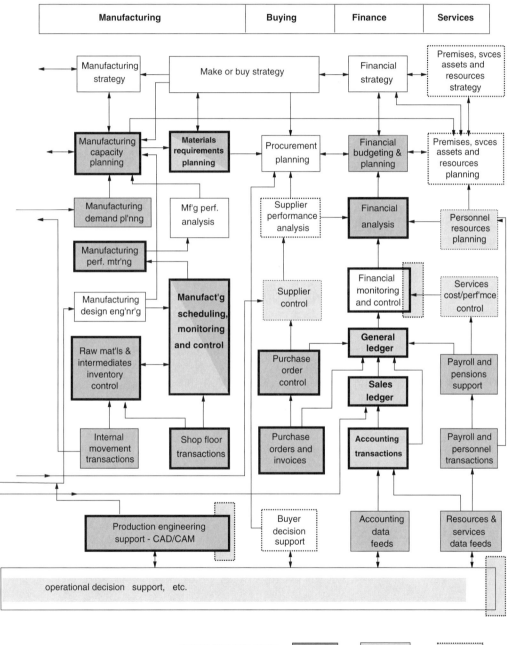

3. Capability to cope with business change:

   - Product or geographic scope   ■ volume   ■ competitive stance

4. Integration with the business planning process.

5. Style of data collection:

   - once only close to source
   - validation at the point of collection
   - direct update of core databases

6. Style of operation of core transaction systems and databases:

   - common customer view;
   - on-line processing of all core business transactions;
   - re-usable infrastructure, e.g. to support common products and functions across the organization;
   - effective reporting and analysis of key business measures such as customer and product profitability.

7. Approach to provision of timely, relevant and accessible MIS and EIS in a manner which will adapt to evolving management style.

8. Business basis for the vision.

9. Risk assessment.

10. Assumptions on which the vision is based.

11. Implications for IT strategy.

Stage 2.4 Develop business cases for meeting needs

OBJECTIVE

Have the sponsors develop the business case for each key development to meet their identified business needs

PRODUCTS

1. List of committed sponsors

2. Business case development format

3. Business cases for meeting all key needs

4. Action plan to carry business cases forward through selection of solutions and implementation planning

Phase 3 – Determine strategic solutions

Phase objective: assess and select strategic solutions

We have by now identified the revised business needs and priorities, assessed the extent to which current systems and projects cover these needs, and established the strategic IS vision and overall solution to meet the needs.

We now need to transform that vision into a specific set of IS and IT solutions. This means that we will need to investigate:

1.   Means for support of business processes

2.   Specific application solutions

3.   Technology strategy and solutions

4.   Basis for successful implementation and migration

Stage 3.1 Identify and initiate urgent actions

OBJECTIVE

Ensure that obvious and suitable needs are met rapidly, preferably during the time span of the study. This may be via rapid development projects, enhancements to existing systems, or even by management actions unrelated to IS or IT.

PRODUCTS

1.   Rapid development proposal and scope definition for a project to meet each appropriate need

2.   Completed developments

3.   Required business outcome achieved

Stage 3.2 Determine application and database solutions

OBJECTIVES

1.   Review and assess proposed application solutions from stage 2.3; select the preferred options

2.   Assess priorities, dependencies and groupings; develop the most appropriate application and database structures to support the solutions

3.   Refine the information architectures as appropriate

4.   Develop technology requirements to support the solutions

PRODUCTS

1. Selection of the most appropriate application solutions

2. Definition of the most appropriate application and database structures to support the solutions

3. Log of options considered and reasons for selection or rejection

4. Updates to the emerging information architectures as appropriate

5. Specification of workload volumes and other technology requirements to support the solutions

6. Basis for development of migration strategy to the proposed solutions

Figure 3-9 illustrates the initial, purely business based view of application priorities; Figure 3-10 illustrates the manner in which it is transformed into a realistic set of phased projects.

Figure 3-9: *Business priorities for application delivery*

Priority band	1	2	3	4	5	6
Corporate Control						
■ Profitability by product, outlet and region	▨					
Finance						
■ Cashflow planning/ management		▨				
Manufacturing						
■ Materials requirements planning				▨		
■ Shop floor control		▨				
Sales						
■ Order processing			▨			
Warehouse/Dist						
■ Finished goods inventory control						▨
■ Distribution scheduling					▨	
Retail Outlets						
■ In-store data capture		▨				
■ Store-level control					▨	

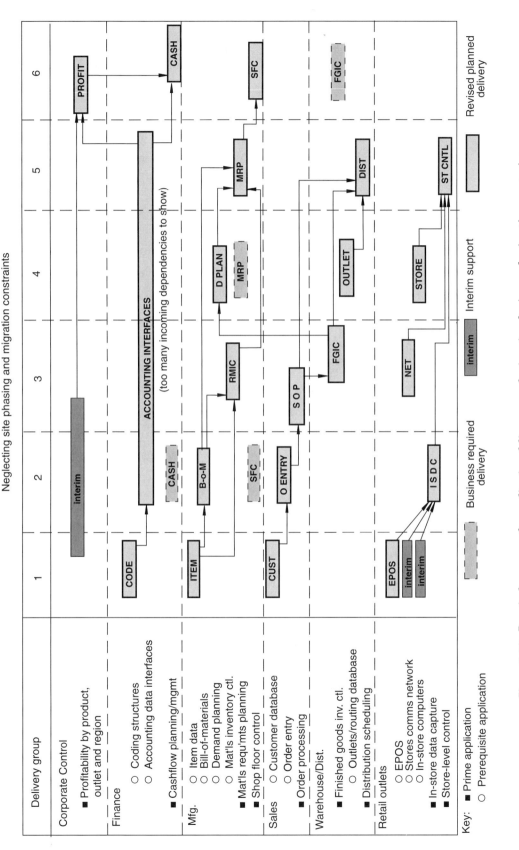

Figure 3-10: *Practical sequences for application delivery – neglecting site phasing and migration constraints*

Stage 3.3 Evaluate IT status and opportunities; set key IT directions

OBJECTIVES

1.   Assess current IT status in relation to requirements

2.   Establish and evaluate opportunities offered by IT industry and developments

3.   Set key future IT directions and options

PRODUCTS

1.   Assessment of current IT status – gaps and soft spots, blind alleys

2.   Assessment of key developments and vendors in so far as they are relevant to business needs

3.   Assessment of key industry directions – e.g. competitor activities, competitive opportunities

4.   Identification of options and opportunities for meeting business and application needs

5.   Preliminary identification of technology support options

Stage 3.4 Progress business case development

OBJECTIVES

1.   Help keep sponsors committed and involved

2.   Keep the emerging IS and IT plans closely in tune with the mood of the business

3.   Guide and negotiate the re-mapping of business case benefits and arguments from business needs through application solutions to specific implementation projects

4.   Facilitate the assessment of alternative delivery sequences and benefits profiles

PRODUCTS

1.   Sponsors still committed and involved

2.   Two way information flow concerning developments in business needs and priorities, and the effectiveness of alternative solution scenarios in meeting them

3.   Business cases for each key development, aligned to the emerging draft implementation schedule, but traceable back to the business needs statements

Template for development of business cases

- **What?** Title and one paragraph description of what is proposed.

Cross-references to acknowledged business needs, e.g. CBINs or other specific user sponsored initiatives.

Why? Business rationale for the development – qualitative.

Business benefits – costs/headcount saved:

- risks controlled or losses avoided
- revenue or profit improvement

Impact/risk of not doing it

How Much? Total costs, split by:

- internal staff
- software licenses or services
- external contractors
- equipment

When? By date: – deliverable

- £ spend, by:
- £ amount of benefit delivered

How? Who will do it

- With what training or other purchased assistance
- With what technology
- Key risks and control measures
- What are the dependencies, impacts and side effects, and how are they to be controlled.

Have available backing detail on alternatives considered/rejected if this is a contentious area.

Phase 4 – Prepare and deliver the implementation plan

Phase objective: Finalize and deliver all elements of the strategic IS and IT plans

- Information architecture development
- Applications and projects – scoping and phasing
- Technology vision, strategy and environments
- Organization, skills and resources
- Financial and business case
- Implementation plan

Migration planning

A strategic vision is useless if it is unattainable. The steps towards it must not only be feasible; they must individually be low in risk and attractive in business terms, i.e. there must be an effective and robust migration plan. Producing this plan is one of the most important stages in the entire IS/IT planning process; in it we must:

1.   Validate the strategic targets by establishing viable evolutionary routes to them.

2.   Establish an effective basis for implementation by ensuring that the IS/IT plans are integrated with relevant organizational and process changes

KEY CONSIDERATIONS

- The recommended target has to be a good place to be, and to move on from

- It has to be possible to get there from here

- There have to be sound and compelling business reasons for heading there, and for taking each step en route

In a complex environment, e.g. where a set of ageing vertically oriented product support systems are being replaced by a new unified 'horizontal' system, migration planning can become very complicated. Figures 3-11 and 3-12 below illustrate how 'T' diagrams may be used to help manage this complexity. In each case, the components of the old systems are on the left, and the new on the right. The architecture components are used as the 'pivot' in the mapping.

Figure 3-11: *Migration mapping -applications*

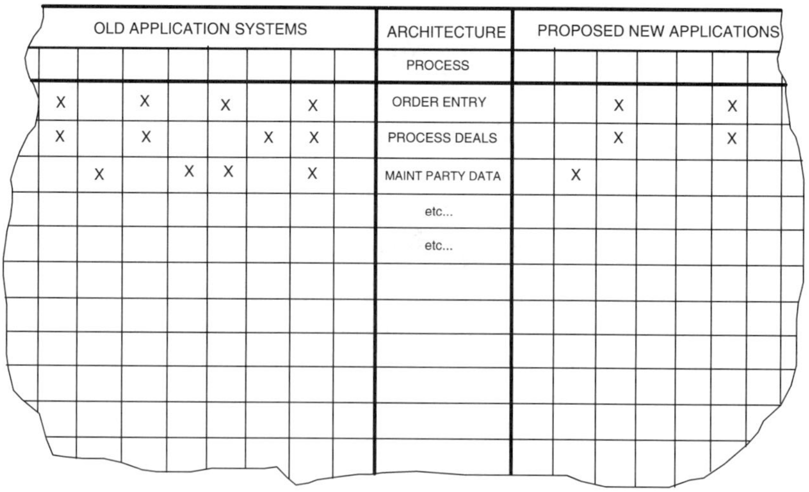

Figure 3-12:   *Migration mapping – data*

OLD FILES/DATABASES							ARCHITECTURE	NEW DATABASES				
							DATA ENTITIES					
		X		X		X	PRODUCT	X				
							LOCATION					
X			X		X		TRANSACTION				X	
X			X				LEGAL ENTITY		X	X		
	X		X				Customer		X			
					X		Agent		X			
	X						Counterparty		X			
					X		Competitor			X		
	X						Advisor		X			

Whatever else we do, eventually, we have to produce a set of project definitions; these form the basic raw material of the plan. Figure 3-13 indicates the nature of the information and style involved. However, note that, except for very small projects, this information rarely gets onto a single page.

Stage 4.1 Prepare applications and database projects plan

OBJECTIVES

1.   Finalize the preferred strategic application solutions.

2.   Assemble a development program for applications and databases which comes closest to the ideal business delivery sequence and rate

PRODUCTS

1.   Firm statement of preferred strategic application solutions.

2.   Complete development and implementation plan for applications and databases, linked to the IT and human resource plans, and balancing with the business cases.

A sample application projects plan is shown in Table 3-5.

Stage 4.2 Prepare IT technical projects plan

OBJECTIVES

1.   Assess alternative options for technology support, and select the preferred strategic solution(s)

RECOMMENDED IS/IT PROJECT SYNOPSIS ref.:

Author: _____   date: _____   reviewed: _____   date: _____

Title: _____

Type: review ☐   feasibility study ☐   requm'ts def'n ☐   design ☐   new dev't enhancement ☐   custom dev't package implem'n ☐   technical ☐   other (specify) ☐

Short description:

Cross-references to business needs:

CBINS ref.	Short name		Sponsor	Priority

Data Usage:

Business volumes and workload profile

Application and data dependencies/cross references:

Performance, security and control requirements:

Implementation options:

Technical requirements/ options:

Project/phase cross references and dependencies

Resource estimates:

Analysis:	Build:
Design:	Test:
User:	Implement:

Implementation schedule:

Summary of cost/benefit case

Costs by time phase:

Benefits by time phase: (consider cost reduction, loss/risk avoidance and revenue/profit increases)

Risk/impact of not proceeding:

Figure 3-13: *Recommended IS/IT project synopsis*

2.   Assemble a development and implementation program for computer hardware, software, communications, workstations and development environments which supports the applications and databases development plan

PRODUCTS

1.   Statement of preferred strategic technology solution(s)

2.   Complete development plan for computer hardware, software, communications, workstations and development environments which supports the applications and databases development plan

---

Table 3-5:   *Trendy products PLC - information systems strategy application development projects overall schedule*

BUSINESS AREA / PROJECT NAME	Development man yrs	style	1995/6 Q1	Q2	Q3	Q4	1996/7 Q1	Q2	Q3	Q4	1997/8 Q1	Q2	Q3	Q4	98 on man yrs
SALES															
Sales order processing and finished goods inventory	8.75 0	Pack	3	4	8	8	6	4	2						
Sales analysis phase I	1.5	Rapid			2	2	2								
Sales analysis phase II	1	Rapid						2	2						
Customer perf./profitability	1	Rapid					2	2							
Wholesale outlet support	2.25	Trad									1	3	3	2	
Retail outlet support	2	Trad											2	2	1
Sub-total	16.5		3	4	10	10	10	8	4	0	1	3	5	4	1
FINANCE															
Revised coding structures	1.25	Manual	2	3											
G/L interfaces	1.75	Mods	3	2	1	1									
Improved financial ctl reports	2.25	Rapid			1	2	2				2	2			
Budget planning support	1.13	EUC		1.5	1.5	1.5									
Cashflow planning model	1.63	EUC		1.5	1.5	1.5			1	1					
Cash management	2.5	EUC							2	2	2	2	2		
Sub-total	10.5		5	8	5	6	2	0	3	3	4	4	2	0	0
MANUFACTURING															
Bristol	0														
Mat Req. Planning	3.75	Pack	2	3	2										2
Shop floor control	2.5	Pack						2	2	2					1
	0														
Luton	0														
Basic HP systems	2.25	Pack				1	3	3	2						
Mat Req. Planning	3.25	Pack							2	2	1				2
Shop floor control	3	Pack									2	2			2
	0														
Birmingham	0														
Basic HP systems	2.25	Pack							1	3	3	2			
Mat Req. Planning	3.25	Pack										2	2	1	2
Shop floor control	4	Pack											2	2	3
Sub-total	24.3		2	3	2	1	3	5	7	7	6	6	4	3	12

(Shows no. of development staff by quarter)

Table 3-5:   *(continued) Trendy products PLC - information systems strategy application development projects overall schedule*

BUSINESS AREA / PROJECT NAME	Development man yrs	style	1995/6 Q1	Q2	Q3	Q4	1996/7 Q1	Q2	Q3	Q4	1997/8 Q1	Q2	Q3	Q4	98 on man yrs
(Shows no. of development staff by quarter)															
MARKETING															
Marketing analysis phase I	1.5	Trad		2	2	1	1								
Marketing analysis phase II	3.25	EUC				1	2	2	2						1.5
Campaign analysis	1.25	EUC										1	1	1	0.5
Sub-total	6		0	2	2	2	3	2	2	0	0	1	1	1	2
DISTRIBUTION															
Distribution control pilot	1.75	Pack						2	2	2	1				
Distribution – all sites	7.5	Pack										2	4	4	5
Sub-total	9.25		0	0	0	0	0	2	2	2	1	2	4	4	5
PRODUCT DEVELOPMENT															
Product dev't support	1	EUC			2	2									
CAD/CAM facilities	2.5	Pack					1	2	2	3	2				
Sub-total	3.5		0	0	2	2	1	2	2	3	2	0	0	0	0
PURCHASING															
Purchasing system replacement	1	Pack	1	1	1	1									
Sub-total	1		1	1	1	1	0	0	0	0	0	0	0	0	0
PERSONNEL & SERVICES															
Payroll/personnel system replacement	4.5	Pack							2	4	2	2			2
Office automation pilot	1.5	Pack					1	2	2	1					
Office automation (fuller)	3.25	Pack										1	2	2	2
Sub-total	4.5		0	0	0	0	0	0	2	4	2	2	0	0	2
GRAND TOTALS - MAN YEARS	75.5														22
GRAND TOTALS - MANPOWER			11	18	22	22	19	19	22	19	16	18	16	12	

Stage 4.3 Prepare organization and skills/resources development plan

OBJECTIVE

1.   Finalize organization and skills/resources plan.

2.   Assemble a development program for IS organization and human skills and resource which supports the applications and IT development plans

PRODUCTS

1.   Statement of organization and skills/resources solutions.

2.   Complete development plan for IS organization and human skills and resource which supports the applications and IT development plans

Stage 4.4 Integrate costs and business cases

OBJECTIVE

Support the development and fine tuning of application, IT and human resource plans by ensuring that business cases are delivered and integrated with those plans

PRODUCTS

1.   Business case statements which are structured so as to provide justification for the application, IT and human resource plans

2.   Results of negotiations with sponsors to ensure that the final recommended delivery rate and sequence are acceptable

3.   Integrated and balanced financial and business case to support the recommended strategic solutions.

Figure 3-14 illustrates a form of graphical presentation which highlights how costs and benefits of infrastructure and of application development are phased, and the overall benefits profile. Table 3-6 represents the detailed spreadsheet from which the graphs in Figure 3-14 were prepared.

Financial summary

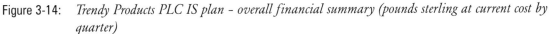

Figure 3-14:   *Trendy Products PLC IS plan – overall financial summary (pounds sterling at current cost by quarter)*

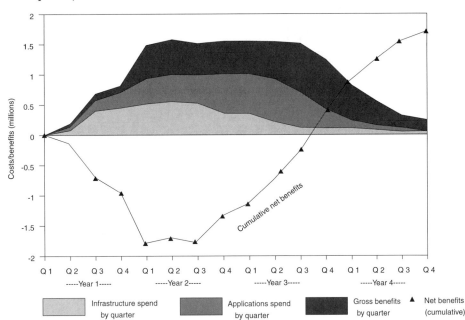

Table 3-6: *Trendy Products PLC – Information systems plan (summary and costs of benefits)*

PROJECT AREA	Total man Years	Total Costs	Total Benefits	Y1 Q1	Y1 Q2	Y1 Q3	Y1 Q4	Y2 Q1	Y2 Q2	Y2 Q3	Y2 Q4	Y3 Q1	Y3 Q2	Y3 Q3	Y3 Q4	Y4 Q1	Y4 Q2	Y4 Q3	Y4 Q4
BUSINESS APP'N AREAS																			
■ Sales	17	850	1,800		120	185	160	160	146	65	14	24							
■ Finance	11	480	1,200			60	80	75	80	86	75					75	75	65	
■ Manufacturing	25	1,500	3,500			75	65	135	150	135	145	215	160	120	85				
■ Marketing	5	160	700			20	30	25	25	40	20								
■ Distribution	9	300	550								50	40	60	65	85	55			
■ Product Development	4	170	375				15						35	45	35				
■ Purchasing	1	55	178					30	10										
■ Personnel & Services	5	185	325								25	55	75	30					
APPLICATIONS TOTAL	75	3,700	8,628	0	120	340	350	425	411	326	329	334	330	260	205	130	75	65	0
TECHNICAL INFRASTRUCTURE																			
■ Mainframe Computers	7	1,700			300			650			350	45			400				
■ Networking	3	350				200				85			20			65			
■ Workstations	1	1,010					150		220		225		50	300					
■ Systems Software	3	148					45		65		38								
■ Data Management	3	375				25		45		85		135			55		30		
■ Application Dev't Env't	1	135						25		45		20	20	20	5				
■ Standards & Methods	2	85						5	25	5	5	5	35	10					
■ ISD Development	1	75						10	5	5	10	10							
■ Architectures	2	110			15	25	15						5						
■ Specials	3	275				15	10		10	10	10	25		25	50	45	50	50	55
INFRASTRUCTURE TOTAL	26	4,263	0	0	315	265	220	735	325	235	638	240	130	355	510	110	80	50	55
OVERALL TOTAL	100	7,963	8,628	0	435	605	570	1,160	736	561	967	574	460	615	715	240	155	115	55
COSTS BREAKDOWN																			
■ Hardware		1,265																	
■ Building		480																	
■ Software		708																	
■ Manpower - tech support	10	240																	
■ - analysts	35	540																	
■ - programming	45	780																	
■ - users	50	1,450																	
■ External services	50	725																	
Distribution of Benefits			9,592		220	200	550	550	700	950	600	978	1,300	900	954	680	350	460	200
Cumulative Costs				0	435	1,040	1,610	2,770	3,506	4,067	5,034	5,608	6,068	6,683	7,398	7,638	7,793	7,908	7,963
Cumulative Benefits				0	220	420	970	1,520	2,220	3,170	3,770	4,748	6,048	6,948	7,902	8,582	8,932	9,392	9,592
Running DR/CR Balance				0	(215)	(620)	(640)	(1,250)	(1,286)	(897)	(1,264)	(860)	(20)	265	504	944	1,139	1,484	1,629

Stage 4.5 Present plan and negotiate implementation

OBJECTIVES

1. Ensure that senior management receive and understand the recommendations of the study

2. Make arrangements for successful implementation

3. Make provision for review, tuning and maintenance of the plans during continuing planning cycles

PRODUCTS

1. Agreed plans:

    ■ *application*   ■ *technology*   ■ *skills/resources*

2. Budgetary commitments

3. Implementation program

4. Agreed basis for maintaining and re-assessing the plans when business circumstances or economics alter

Addendum: An alternative 'crash' process for IS/IT planning

For use when there is neither time nor management tolerance for doing it properly

Improvisation and approximation are sometimes necessary. However, they always carry risk. The process below preserves the spirit of SP4IS, but sacrifices much of the hard work, rigor and traceability. The approach is relatively safe where several of the following circumstances apply:

■ a small, coherent organization;

■ strong management team who communicate well;

■ proven history of effective business operation in a lightly planned mode, e.g. in a very volatile environment;

■ relatively sound pre-existing business and IS/IT plans, which now need only a moderate level of tuning.

It is very tempting to take these short cuts when these circumstances do not prevail. The types of short cut indicated below are recommended only as a last resort, and should really only be used as a stepping stone to a more reasoned, planned process. It is easy to get stuck in a reactive loop – remember panic is infectious.

OBJECTIVE

For a relatively lightly planned, small to medium company or business unit, to initiate an integrated cycle of business and IS/IT tactical and strategic planning.

CRITERIA FOR USE

1. Senior management appreciate that there is a problem with IS/IT strategy, and are motivated to fix it.

2. The environment is straightforward enough that the risks of short-cutting the full process can be controlled.

PRODUCTS

Usual SP4IS deliverables, with shortcuts.

Prerequisites

1. Participants have prepared. (See below)

2. The most current set of business plans must be available, warts and all, health warnings and all. See the following section for a 'crash' approach to setting business directions.

3. A reasonably clear (or at least candid) definition of the company's product set and customer sectors must be available.

4. The most current set of IS/IT plans must be available, 'warts and all', health warnings and all.

5. There must be willingness to be candid and open about business, products and IS/IT plans and status.

6. There must be commitment of key personnel to work full time for 2 weeks on developing the solutions.

7. There must be commitment of key board-members and senior managers to attend the session, to contribute, and to own and implement the results.

Criteria for success

At the end of the process, there should be a clear, implementable IS/IT strategy. Senior management, IS/IT personnel and users should be committed to the solutions agreed, and to the means for their implementation.

Duration and Resources – 3 to 4 weeks end-to-end

PROCESS

1. Preparatory: 1–2 weeks elapsed

    - *establish all prerequisites*
    - *develop template-based starter products:*
        - function/organization/product mapping
        - candidate requirements
    - *information collection/analysis:*
        - business/product plans;
        - current IS/IT status.

2. 2–3 day intensive management workshop – see below

3. 2 week solutions development – following the action plan determined by the first workshop.

4. Presentation and approval of plan – 1/2 day workshop.

5. Implementation and follow-up – following the process and steering arrangements determined by the 1/2 day workshop..

Format for a management IS/IT planning workshop

Attendees:

-   Representative set of Board members and GMs
-   Representative sample of operational managers
-   Senior IS/IT team ▪ The 'solutions' team

Day 1

PLENARY–1

1. Agree goals and process

2. Walk through business areas and functional responsibilities, identifying an overall framework of functions, objectives, goals ands CSFs (template prepared in advance).

Split to 3 groups defined below. Each to draw up 'hit lists' as follows:

-   *Senior Management group:* Key functional priorities for information needs and support.
-   *Line managers/Users:* Forgetting IS/IT constraints and preconception:

- What do you *really* want from IS/IT: *routine* or *'sci-fi'*?
- what frustrates you most about IS/IT?

- *IS/IT Group:* What stops you giving the service which you'd like to deliver: *business factors* or *IT constraints*?

Each group to use a consensus process to condense to a top 6 list under each category.

PLENARY–2

Each group presents their list. Free discussion under a strong chairman.

Split to groups; each group to develop solutions to the lists from the other two.

- *Overnight working:* goal is for each group to come up with solutions to the lists of the other two, not excuses for the problems. Requests for information/clarification to go via the moderator.

Day 2

PLENARY-3

Each group presents their solutions. Free discussion under a strong chairman.

Chairman sums up outline solutions, and leads a categorization of the subjects and issues which have emerged.

SPLIT TO GROUPS

Re-structured into two groups now, selected so as to balance management viewpoints and skills across the groups.

One group develops the business action plan for the 2 weeks solutions development stage, and the other develops the IS/IT action plan for same.

CLOSING PLENARY SESSION

In which the deliverables, resources and action plan for the next 2 week stage are agreed.

Further addendum: An approach of last resort to business planning

For use if there are little or no tangible business plans available

This highly abbreviated and pragmatic process is intended to be catalytic in helping to stimulate formulation of business intentions and directional plans. It is not expected or required to yield definitive business plans first time through, but it may prove better than nothing as an enabler for initial IS/IT planning.

Objectives

1. Identify and agree across the senior management team the present and likely future business vision and directions of the business and its products to a level of detail sufficient to direct the formulation of the IS/IT strategy.

2. Identify and scope those areas, issues and factors which are most critical to the business, and/or which may have the greatest effect in determining future needs for management information or IS/IT support.

3. Help to establish a basis for evolution towards an integrated set of business, IS and IT planning cycles.

In certain cases the present business input may be in terms of present intentions and likely directions, rather than as firm committed plans. We also expect that there will be particular focus on areas of high uncertainty and/or great volatility, where future systems will need to be particularly flexible and responsive.

End products

Overall, and for each product stream and functional area:

1. A statement of short term business goals and strategy.

2. An indication of longer term business directions and intentions.

3. Identification of those factors which will influence future business directions most strongly.

4. Identification of the Board Member or General Manager who will be responsible for co-ordinating future planning in this area, including the co-ordination of product development with IS/IT support needs.

Process

SESSION 1

1. Agree on a working basis overall mission and goals.

2. Identify and scope business functional/product related areas.

3. For each area:

   - Identify current status of business plans and intentions;
   - Identify and agree the most important problems, critical factors and 'drivers';
   - Agree the minimum set of 'givens' and assumptions which should act as ground rules;

- Allocate lead responsibility for the between sessions planning and futures work in this area.

4. Agree products to be delivered at session 2. These are to include:

- review and confirmation of current plans, status, problems, critical factors and drivers;
- prioritization of the above, and assessment/resolution of cross-area interactions;
- recommended approaches and strategies to address the key needs;
- identification of key risks and issues requiring group level resolution – this is to include cases where givens and ground rules are questioned.

5. Agree process and co-ordination approach for between sessions task group working.

BETWEEN SESSIONS

Each functional area task group will work to deliver their agreed products on time for session 2. The details of the process to be followed are to be determined by the area co-ordinator. There should be a small number of review points at which cross-group issues are cleared and progress reviewed.

SESSION 2 (IDEALLY 10 TO 12 WORKING DAYS AFTER SESSION 1)

1. Review and approval of the reports and recommendations from each task group.

2. Agreement of:

- the nature and format of the 'first cut' planning document to be issued as a result of these sessions;
- the work remaining to be done to resolve open issues and complete that document;
- specific high priority directions for the IS/IT strategy study;
- responsibilities and mechanisms for maintenance and future evolution of the business plans for Trendy Products PLC.

Participants

Board members and GMs.

Responsibilities

This process should be facilitated by an experienced process leader who has no axe to grind, but should be Chaired by a senior Board Member.

CHAPTER 4

Project scoping and initiation

Introduction

There is no point in doing the wrong project. There is no point in carrying out any form of strategy study if one is not needed at all. Likewise, if strategy is needed, then it is vital that the right climate and prerequisites be established so that the strategies delivered can be pursued in an organized manner.

Figure 4-1:   *Phase 0 - establish scope and context*

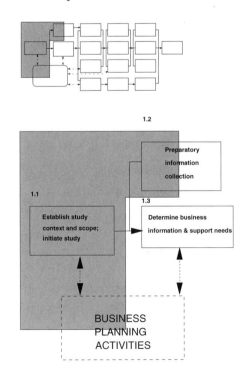

For all of these reasons, it is important that, except in the simplest of circumstances, serious – but not protracted – attention be given to getting the scope of a strategy study right, and ensuring that an effective management environment is established. Figure 4-1 illustrates which of the stages are affected by this process. The extent of involvement with Business Planning is extremely variable, but the right spirit of co-operation needs to be established from the outset. Preparatory information collection is affected, as the lead time on this can be embarrassingly long, and the sooner it is started the better.

Chapter objective

Examine the practical aspects of launching a study of this kind:

- Scope, prerequisites, synchronization aspects
- Management commitment and awareness
- Overcoming excuses for not starting
- Steering and control arrangements
- Resources/skills mix
- Managing expectations
- Starting fact collection
- Sensitivity to organizational style
- Six ways to shoot yourself in the foot at the start

Phase 0 – Establishing context and scope for an information systems strategic plan

This phase addresses the positioning, prerequisites and relative scope(s) of related business and IS strategy projects. It is optional, but usually recommended. Issues addressed include:

- What are the business units?
- Are existing strategies – appropriate, relevant?
- Are they being followed?
- What needs to be covered by the new strategy(ies)?
- How many studies are needed, of what nature and depth? (The answer may be 'none')
- How should they integrate with one another:
  - business unit plans, IS and IT strategies?
  - interfaces, co-ordination, timing and time scales?
- Management, control and resourcing
- Other pre-study issues to resolve

Stage 0.1 – Establish context and scope; initiate the study

OBJECTIVE

1. Ensure as briefly and as succinctly as possible that the positioning, prerequisites and relative scope(s) of related business and IS strategy projects are defined appropriately, and that management expectations are realistic and under control

2. Launch the project(s):

    - at the right time
    - with the right scope definition
    - with the right skills/resources mix
    - in the right management and expectations framework

PRODUCTS

1. Context, scope and terms of reference defined for IS/IT planning studies

2. Prerequisites identified and under control

3. Essential parallel activities scoped and initiated

4. Appropriate Steering Group, able to co-ordinate relevant key activities set up and aware

5. Other key management involved and briefed

6. Deliverables from the IS/IT planning work identified and outlined

7. Completed plan and work program

8. Team in place, trained, supported

9. Initial interview schedule agreed

Scoping issues

These is no point in carrying out any form of IS/IT planning exercise if it is not needed. Correspondingly, there is no value in carrying out the wrong work, or the right work at the wrong time. The scoping study should therefore examine and take account of at least the following:

1. The present and likely future scope and structure of the organization.

2. Level of management/planning maturity and culture.

3. The status and scope of existing business, IS and IT strategic and tactical plans (if any).

4. The timing of any relevant planning or procurement cycles (although it should bear in mind that if these are treated as hard dependencies, there

may *never* be a suitable planning window for IS/IT).

5. Management expectations, and any recent history which may have colored those expectations.

6. The scope of cover now required, in terms of:

   ■ *organization*　　■ *business units*　　■ *functional areas*

7. Formulation and phasing of the planning work needed – should there be one study or several.

8. Boundaries and cross-functional issues – control and integration needs.

9. What will need to be done to establish an continuing cyclic process to keep IS and IT plans relevant and in touch with business developments and plans.

10. The skills and resources needed.

11. Timing, and the approach needed to coordination of cross-study and responsibility area issues.

The context is illustrated in Figure 4-2.

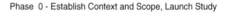

Figure 4-2:   *Strategic planning for information systems*

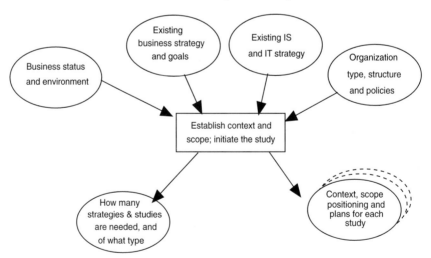

Steering and control

Like so many aspects of this work, there are few hard and fast rules for effective steering and control. Key factors are:

- there should be an effective steering group;
- it should include committed representatives of key business users;
- the members should have authority to make steering decisions;
- it should meet sufficiently frequently as to be able to make effective decisions within a useful time scale – this may be fortnightly in the middle stages of a short, sharp study.

Figure 4-3 suggests an approach which is appropriate for an IS/IT strategy study being conducted for a major business unit of a group of companies, where there is relatively strong interest in business and IS/IT policy from Group level. The shaded boxes represent the primary interests. The dotted lines represent liaison activities.

Figure 4-3:   *A typical IS/IT planning project environment*

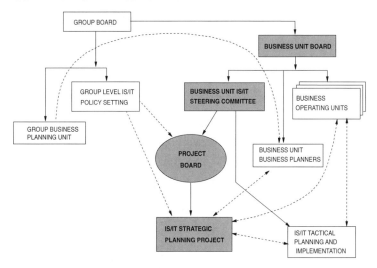

Project start-up – quality assurance

Quality assurance is covered in more detail in Appendix III, but the following checklist is valuable at this time:

- Does the business really need this study?
- Is the timing right (or near enough)?
- Are there committed sponsors with the right clout?
- Is senior management commitment firm?
- Are project plans, estimates and schedule done and approved?
- Do you have a team? Are there sufficient qualified members available?
- Do you know the status of business plans, and have you access to the necessary business expertise?

- Is information collection under way?
- Are the first cycle of interviews scheduled?
- Are key road-blocks identified – do you have a plan for each?

Planning and estimating

Estimating this type of work is notoriously difficult. The best, most reasoned schedule can be destroyed by another event capturing senior management's attention at a crucial stage. However, we must still try; the guide-lines below have proved surprisingly resilient. Rule of thumb (purely pragmatic) for the overall manpower cost: *10 man-days per management interviewee (excluding interviewee and senior management effort), weighted by factors below:*

	Effort split	*Duration*
Phase 0	5%	unpredictable
Phase 1	30–40%	35–40%
Phase 2	20–25%	15–20%
Phase 3	15–20%	15–20%
Phase 4	15–20%	25–35%

But beware that the interview schedule has a strong tendency to grow, especially after you have committed to project plans and estimates. And interviewing three managers together in a group does not save all of the resources of two one person interviews (see chapter 7).

Factors which may influence effort estimates:

Increasing factors:	*Max. impact*
Business functional complexity	+20%
High rate of business or environmental change	+15%
Team inexperienced	+30%
First time for this organisation	+20%
Decreasing factors:	*Max. impact*
Especially experienced team	–20%
Strongly committed senior management support	–15%
Pre-existing 'planned' culture	–15%
Repetition of a previous plan cycle:	
■ sound, recent plan, modest changes	–50% or more
■ out of date plan, major changes	–10%

Appendix II contains two sample work plans, which may be used as a starting point.

The launch process

- There must be sound and compelling business reasons for the study
- Timing must mesh in with the business planning climate
- There are 10 reasons why now is never a good time to do the study
- It is critical to identify and recruit senior management sponsors who will stay with it
- Develop the work program – with resource estimates, allocation of responsibilities.
- Make steering and control arrangements.
- Ensure that checkpoints are frequent, and management can 'feel good' about what's being delivered.
- Don't forget motherhood – accommodation, secure filing, support, secretarial, PCs, automated aids.

Team composition

Core Team

- Project manager
- Specialist/'coach' in methods/techniques
- Business analyst(s)
- Systems analyst(s) with sound knowledge of existing applications and databases

Liaison/Part Time

- In-depth knowledge of business areas – possibly via a series of willing co-optees
- Liaison with data administration or systems architecture group
- Operations and IT specialists for assessment and sizing
- Financial planner for business case analysis

Information collection

- Kick off information assembly as early as possible – the lead times can be startlingly long.
- Sub-contract it as much as possible, e.g. to knowledgeable analysts
- The very act of asking for it may have profound impact
- Identify sources and allocate responsibilities

- Use questionnaires, forms and procedures (see Appendix III)

Information categories

It is easy to forget whole categories of information. People also have a way of being coy about things which they are not proud of – so a degree of persistence is necessary.

BUSINESS

- Plans, organization, marketplace, products/services, competition
- Supplementary information – find what's missing on the first pass

APPLICATIONS AND DATA

- Current systems and databases
- Current projects and plans
- External services
- PC and LAN-based systems
- Development environments

IT ASSETS AND INVENTORY

- All kinds/sizes of computer including PCs and workstations
- Local and wide area Networks
- External services
- Plans and contracts
- Systems software
- Standards and policies

HUMAN SKILLS/RESOURCES

- Business organization
- DP organization
- Identify all application developers/operators, even end-users
- Permanent staff/contract
- Skills and experience
- Training done, plans, perceived needs

Supporting documentation

Appendix III includes sample documentation and checklists for use in this phase, including:

1. A typical statement of project scope and terms of reference

2. A pre-study questionnaire for use in highlighting scope issues

3.   A set of questionnaires for use in information collection

4.   A questionnaire for use in scoping management interviews

5.   A sample format for analysis and presentation of current systems assessments

6.   A sample of a management information pack, defining and launching an IS/IT planning project

CHAPTER 5

Case study profile: the Trendy Products Group

Introduction

This chapter provides background to case study examples which appear later in the book. It firstly describes a hypothetical business organization, Trendy Products Group Plc, firstly *as it was in 1990*, and summarizes the results of an information systems strategy study assumed to have been carried out around that time. The latter section of the chapter outlines events involving the Trendy Group between 1990 and the present day. It presents the results of preparatory work for a new planning study, around which case study examples in the book are centered. The material is intended for use as background to case study/ syndicate work in a classroom environment. Some of the more pathological features of Trendy Products Group Plc may appear to readers who work in well-behaved organizations to have been somewhat exaggerated, but I can assure you that all of the types of problem indicated have been encountered in real life, although not all at the same time.

The Trendy Products Group Plc

The Trendy Products Group have been in existence since 1934. Traditionally they have dealt in toys and games, mostly manufacturing their own products, with a fairly slow steady growth until the late 1950s. During the late 1960s, they expanded rapidly and opened several overseas operating companies, primarily in Australia, South Africa and Hong Kong. During the late 1970s and early '80s, Trendy gradually started to move into electronic toys and games, and the growth and profitability of traditional lines began to falter. At the same time, Trendy started to distribute their products more seriously in Western Europe, opening subsidiaries in France, Germany, Italy and Holland. The electronic toys and games business has developed well, but, partly because many of these lines are still bought out, the profit margins are less than satisfactory.

In 1985, as part of a deliberate diversification program, Trendy took over a small car hire firm and a small hotel chain. In 1990, at the time of the first IS/ IT Strategy study, it is still not yet clear whether this action will bear fruit. Revenues and profitability are flat, due, it is believed at Group level, to weak management. Group structure, as at 1st January 1990, is shown in Figure 5-1.

Figure 5-1:   *Trendy group structure in 1990*

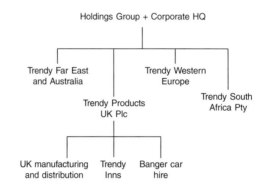

As a result of disappointing recent performance, a review of Group organization has recently taken place, which has resulted in Trendy Products (UK) Plc (as an operating unit, with significant new blood in its management team) being made responsible for all UK business. This includes:

- Car hire
- Manufacturing and distribution
- Hotels and leisure
- Product research and development

As the UK market (and the UK company) is the largest in the Group, it remains the strongest influence on Group strategies and policy. The organization structure of Trendy Products (UK) is shown in Figure 5-2.

Figure 5-2:   *Trendy Products (UK) Plc Organization in 1990*

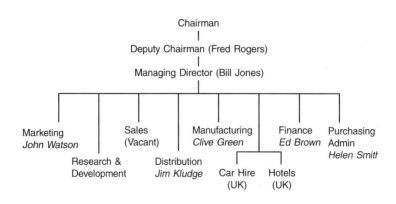

Scope of the 1990 IS/IT planning study

A major strategy and policy review of the UK company has already been undertaken, headed by Fred Rogers, the Deputy Chairman. This includes overall business goals and strategies and has now been extended specifically to include information systems strategy. The information systems strategy study objectives were set by Fred Rogers as follows:

1. Establish a basis for providing the most effective level of information systems support for Trendy Products (UK) Plc for the next five years.

2. Ensure that likely changes in business direction and strategy can be accommodated.

3. Identify the most important business needs, and the most effective systems strategy to meet them.

4. Produce a specific plan in terms of:

    - Applications enhancement and new developments needed – what and when;
    - Financial basis;
    - Resources and personnel skills;
    - Time scales.

The car hire and hotel subsidiaries were excluded from the study, although if it goes well, then they would be encompassed in a second phase.

Revenues and profitability of the Trendy Group 1986 – 1990

The revenues and profits for the Group and UK companies for the period are shown in Figure 5-3 below:

Figure 5-3: *Revenues and profitability of the Trendy Group (£ millions)*

	1986		1987		1988		1989		1990	
	Gp	UK	Gp	UK	Gp	UK	Gp	UK	Gp	UK
Revenue	460	395	530	420	650	440	730	475	415	265
Gross profit (before tax)	18.6	24.7	21.8	15.4	26.2	8.34	31.3	(3.6)	11.8	3.2

Business operations of Trendy Products (UK)

Trendy Products (UK) operate manufacturing plants in Birmingham, Luton and Bristol and import bought-out goods from other Trendy Products companies and other suppliers. They also export direct to external companies and to other Trendy Products companies overseas. Approximately 70% of goods sold in the UK are manufactured within the UK by Trendy. The remainder are bought out, about equally split between overseas Trendy plants and third party suppliers.

At present, Trendy Products do not own any retail outlets and prefer to deal direct with some of the high street retailers. One option under consideration is the acquisition of one of these chains as an outlet.

In the last five years, Trendy Products have bought out two of their suppliers in Birmingham and Bristol and have, unsuccessfully, attempted to run their own distribution operation. Recently, they sold this distribution operation and now subcontract all transportation and depot stocking throughout the UK. Their own warehouses are located at Luton, Birmingham and Bristol. Orders are taken from UK and overseas customers and distribution is then scheduled through the distribution operation outlined above.

Manufacturing plants are located in:

- *Luton* (general, traditional toys and games, mostly board games);
- *Bristol* (specialized plastic-forming operations);
- *Birmingham* (specialized assembly of electromechanical units).

The Birmingham and Bristol factories are those acquired when the suppliers were bought. They still operate in the main as they did before purchase.

Management structure and personalities

The key persons in the Trendy Products (UK) management team as at June 1990 are described below.

Deputy Group Chairman: Fred Rogers, age 50, has been with Trendy a very long time and is widely expected to become the new Group Chairman on the retirement of the current Chairman in two years' time. He is energetic and clear thinking and has been the chief architect of the recent restructure of the Group.

Managing Director: Bill Jones was brought back from Trendy Australia last year to take on the Managing Directorship of Trendy Products UK when the previous incumbent was retired early. Relatively young and energetic.

Marketing Director: John Watson has been Sales and subsequently Marketing Director for Trendy for a considerable time. He is nearing retirement and tends to take a short-term view of marketing strategy. In particular, he has been highly sceptical of the Group's recent ventures into electronics and other diversification.

Sales Director: Currently vacant – John Watson is looking after this role as well at present.

Manufacturing Director: Clive Green is the other member of the management team, apart from John Watson, who has been with Trendy for some time. He has been prominently involved in many of the recent rationalization and cost-cutting operations and has a reputation for running plants at high efficiency.

Purchasing and Administration Director: Helen Smith has recently been promoted from a personnel management role within the company. She has recently been spending a great deal of time in the Far East negotiating supply contracts for some of the new product lines.

Distribution Director: Jim Kludge has run distribution for Trendy since his transport company was bought out by them in 1981. Now that the transport fleet has been sold off, he deals with a variety of outside truckers and distributors. He is 54, made his money when he sold out to Trendy and is looking forward to retirement.

Finance Director: Ed Brown is 36 and an unknown quantity within Trendy UK. He became Finance Director at the end of 1988; before that, for three years he was General Manager, Corporate Financial Planning in Trendy's Group HQ. Before that he ran a small Trendy company in Singapore.

Information Systems Division Manager: John Dore reports to the Finance Director. He was hired in mid '89 from one of Trendy's competitors where he was the Systems Development Manager.

1990 Information systems status

By 1987, many of the traditional data processing functions had been automated within Trendy on ICL equipment. During 1987–88 Trendy converted to IBM mainframe equipment and there has been a hiatus following this conversion, whilst current applications and basic needs were cut-over. During this time little or no new systems development has occurred, apart from Phase 1 of Sales and Marketing (below). There are significant shortfalls in the existing systems, because of their age and because of the backlog of needs which has built up since that time.

The major systems with their ages and styles are set out in Table 5-1.

In 1988/1989, a two stage sales and marketing planning and analysis project was undertaken. Phase I was to take information from sales orders input and:

- Highlight market trends and demand patterns
- Provide a basis for improved manufacturing, purchasing and distribution schedules
- From analysis of orders and usage, help management to determine future product directions and needs.

The system was implemented a year late, de-scoped and over budget by a factor of two, and is regarded by many users as totally unsatisfactory because of a lack of the reporting and analysis flexibility which is needed.

Phase II was intended to build on this by collating the information gained from Trendy's own sales with market and competitive intelligence acquired from industry sources, providing a strategic market analysis and planning capability. Authorization has not yet been given for this to proceed, because it is not believed by the board that Phase I provides an adequate basis for it to succeed.

There is now a widespread view that far more truly interactive systems are required generally, with a significant reduction in printed chapter output. Several user departments have implemented local systems on PCs themselves, and like the interactive style involved. They are asking why the mainframe systems cannot operate in the same interactive manner.

One of the complaints at Group level is that some of Trendy's financial control reporting streams cannot be reconciled with other outputs; this is due to the use by separate user departments of separate PC systems to produce their own parts of the operating statements. The Finance Director is proposing the implementation of a major new accounting system on the mainframe which will resolve this problem. He believes that the finance department should have absolute control over all data which relates to financial control reporting of any sort.

1990 IT Technical status

On conversion to IBM equipment a 4341 configuration was installed in 1987, which was soon upgraded to dual 4381s which are now getting near capacity limits.

CICS/DL/1 software was used from the outset. Computer resource consumption was considerably greater than expected. IBM are now pressing strongly to upgrade to 3090 series, and DB2.

Between 1982 and 1984, a great deal of money was spent on a data analysis project conducted by outside consultants, which resulted in a 'corporate data

APPLICATION	Status P – plan D – dev't L –live	DATE FIRST LIVE	HARDWARE & SOFTWARE ENVIRONMENT	USER INTERFACE MODE	COMMENTS	Summary ratings - 0 (poor) to 5 (good)				
						User Satisf'n	Oper'l stability	Response and thruput	Security availability integrity	Pot base for future dev't
General Accounting	L	1984	IBM 43xx Package	Interactive	Reputable package, but it is failing to meet user needs at present, mostly due to inadequate coding structures and poor discipline and controls in the manual systems.	2	4	3	2	4
Purchase Ledger	L	1972	ICL (Plan & COBOL)	Batch	Completely out of date; should have been entirely superseded by now, but is still in use in a few sites.	1	2	2	3	0
	L	1984	Converted to IBM COBOL	Batch	The conversion was at the code level, the revised system remains poor.					
Sales Ledger	L	1985	IBM 43xx Package	Interactive	Implemented to replace poor mostly manual transfer from Sales Order Processing, & to provide automated invoicing. User problems mostly due to inadequacies of the SOP system.	3	5	4	4	4
Payroll	L	1974	ICL (Plan & COBOL)	Batch	Does the job at present, but accounting interface is weak, and design limitations make further development difficult	4	3	3	3	2
	L	1985	Converted to IBM COBOL	Batch						
Personnel	L	1976	ICL (Plan & COBOL)	Batch	A batch-based extension to Payroll. Offers little flexibility for analysis or enquiry, due to constraints of parent system.	2	3	3	3	0
	L	1985	Converted to IBM COBOL	Batch						
Sales Order Processing	L	1975	ICL COBOL	Interactive	Limited system, lacking up to date facilities.	2	2	3	2	0
	L	1985	Converted to IBM COBOL	otherwise batch	Due to poor quality of design, potential for enhancement is now exhausted. Many requests for modifications outstanding.					

Table 5-1: *Trendy Products PLC – current systems and development plans inventory and assessment*

APPLICATION	Status P – plan D – dev't L –live	DATE FIRST LIVE	HARDWARE & SOFTWARE ENVIRONMENT	USER INTERFACE MODE	COMMENTS	Summary ratings - 0 (poor) to 5 (good)				
						User Satisf'n	Oper'l stability	Response and thruput	Security availability integrity	Pot base for future dev't
Finished Goods Inventory Control	L	1977	ICL COBOL	Interactive data entry otherwise batch	Well integrated with SOP, but lacking facilities to cope with Trendy's current multiple sites and more complex distribution arrangements.	3	4	3	3	2
	L	1985	Converted to IBM COBOL							
Sales & Marketing Analysis	L	1986	IBM 43xx COBOL, with some ad hoc enquiry	Batch limited reporting flexibility	System value is limited by quality and scope of source data. Users are disappointed by lack of online enquiry & lack of flexible formatting and analysis facilities.	2	3	4	4	3
Manufacturing Control - Luton	L	1973	ICL COBOL	Mostly Batch	Trendy's original system - now obsolescent.	2	3	1	3	0
	L	1984	Converted to IBM COBOL							
Manufacturing Control - Birmingham	L	1979	ICL ME29 - RPG, some COBOL	Mixed batch/ interactive	Custom system, moderately successful at Birmingham location. Doubts exist over its applicability to other sites due to technical env't and limited facilities.	4	4	3	3	1
Manufacturing Control - Bristol	L	1985	Hewlett Packard 3000 Package	Mixed batch/interactive	An up to date mfg. control package, with reputable vendor and broad user base. More advanced modules (MRP & shop floor ctl.) not yet implemented in Bristol, but early plans exist to do so.	4	4	4	4	5

NB: This version does not include W.I.P projects

Table 5.1: (continued) Trendy Products PLC - current systems and development plans: inventory and assessment

model', but it bore little relation to any implemented systems. Most of the operational systems currently on the IBM equipment consist of the original ICL applications converted to IBM COBOL and with the ICL file structures converted to the DL/1 databases. Most of the CICS application consists of on-line data entry, with overnight batch update.

There are considerable difficulties with report printing and distribution, due to the volume of paper produced.

Recent takeovers have resulted in the acquisition of small computer centres in Birmingham, where there is an ICL 2950 running simple manufacturing control applications, and in Bristol, where there is a large HP 3000 configuration running manufacturing and order entry applications. Neither of these computer installations is compatible with the Head Office IBM installation, and neither is regarded as satisfactory.

There are about 35 (at the last count in March 1990) personal computers installed in various offices, from a variety of manufacturers, including IBM, Compaq, Apple, Epson and Apricot. They mostly run a mixture of Wordstar, Multimate, Supercalc and Lotus 123. Some of these run communications software, and can access the IBM mainframe on a dial-up basis using 3270 emulation, but it is not clear what systematic use is made of this.

Extracts from the Trendy Products (UK) business plan for 1990

This plan was a product of the 1989 Planning review; it has not yet been fully communicated, nor have all of the organizational implications been followed through. It has been provided on a confidential basis by Bill Jones.

Corporate Objectives of Trendy Products Plc

The corporate objectives are as follows:

1.   Regain acceptable profitability by remaining in consumer products and services, manufacturing and distribution. Select product lines and markets to regain the market share and profitability of the late 1970s.

2.   Retain the 'British and responsible' image for customer service gained by Trendy in the past (subject to the necessary price differential not being a constraint on market penetration).

3.   Assist the Group to diversify geographically in Europe and the Far East as insurance against fluctuations in the UK business climate.

4.   Update the product line, especially in the areas of electronic toys and microcomputers.

5.   Diversify selectively into new market areas, especially consumer services

rather than products, where market opportunities of adequate profitability can be identified.

Group goals of Trendy Products Plc

The group goals are as follows:

1. Achieve revenue growth of inflation plus 10% in the UK, South Africa and Australia and revenue growth of 25% in Western Europe and the Far East.

2. Achieve profitability of 15% on gross revenue. (This is a significant increase over the poor profitability displayed recently.)

3. Identify and exploit new products and service areas to replace the declining lines which were the mainstay of the early '80s.

4. Seek, in particular, to improve manufacturing efficiency and quality, specifically, in the UK and European manufacturing plants, to achieve productivity and quality within 30% of those being exhibited by our Far East suppliers.

5. Maintain customer service performance at a level in excess of the competition.

Operating strategies of Trendy Products

The operating strategies are as follows:

1. Reduce head count in the sales force by 25% over the next two years. Improve sales force productivity by improved information, improved route planning and improved information support.

2. Negotiate advantageous outlet deals with key high street retail outlets. Establish an entrepreneurial attitude in the sales force, by granting them a degree of flexibility on bulk discounting and other pricing and bonus deals.

3. Increase the level of closely targeted marketing via such channels as TV promotion and telephone selling. This needs to be based on well-researched market profile analysis.

4. Reduce the level of manufacturing and finished goods stocks, through improved tighter development of demand and manufacturing schedules based on customer orders. In particular, achieve an overall reduction in working capital employed of 20% in real terms over two years.

5. Improve quality, service and profitability rapidly in car hire and hotels. If this cannot be achieved, consider other options.

6.   Investigate carefully:

- Moving into high street retailing
- The remaining opportunities and possibilities in home and small business microcomputers.

1990 Study – interview notes

Interview with Fred Rogers

At the inception of the study, we conducted an interview with Fred Rogers, partly to let him see the style, and partly because it was best to interview him first anyway. The notes from this follow.

Trendy have been in business since the 1930s. There was rapid growth in the 1950s and 1960s and Trendy were ahead of many of their competitors in moving into Europe. During the 1970s, certain specific business lines remained highly profitable, especially board games and a variety of mechanical and construction toys.

Recently, the long-term viability of these profitable business lines has clearly declined and Rogers is most anxious to pick the high yield 'winners' which will be Trendy's main business lines in the years to come. Rogers sees his main functions as follows:

1.   To identify areas where change is needed and encourage the other Board members to face this need.

2.   Keep the Boards' collective eyes on a three-to-five year event horizon (rather than their natural six months).

3.   Help Bill Jones to complete the 'rationalization' of Board composition and responsibilities.

4.   Negotiate Group-level funding and support for Trendy Products (UK)'s key projects.

5.   As a member of the Holdings Board:

- Balance the product and geographic mix of the group to insure against excessive exposure to any one economy (he feels Trendy is too dependent on the UK and is interested in more Far East manufacturing and in the EEC and US as markets)
- Ensure that investment and rationalization of operations and skills is adequate to get Group performance back on target over three to five years.

The recent reorganization was prompted mainly by the sharp decline in profitability in the UK over the past five years and the need to get the Group in shape to fight off any repeat of some recent take-over attempts. Rogers clearly believes that change is the most important factor in his role at present and that, if Trendy does not manage to change with the times, it will disintegrate and get taken over or go out of business. Rogers also complains that many of his co-directors are concerned mainly with the current month or the current year; he sees one of his major roles as encouraging them to look three to five years ahead, rather than just at the current year. Rogers indicated that the corporate review identified some of the main sources of current problems as:

EXTERNAL FACTORS

1.   Increasing price competition.

2.   Competitors becoming very innovative.

3.   Rapid market shifts.

INTERNAL FACTORS

1.   Loss of Marketing insight and flair by Trendy.

2.   No clear sales direction.

3.   Inability to control manufacturing and distribution costs closely enough, despite changes of strategy.

4.   The recent diversions into car hire and hotels have yet to start pulling their weight.

5.   Information systems seem to have got badly out of date.

Therefore, the IS/IT study is seen as being very much in the mainstream of implementation of the conclusions of the corporate review, and has extremely high visibility. The key issues arising from the interview with Fred Rogers can be summarized as follows:

1.   Rapid decline in profitability of traditional lines.

2.   Failure of recent attempts to diversify.

3.   Failure to control costs in recent times of flat performance.

4.   View of costs in Trendy Products (UK) is piecemeal – operating units 'rob Peter to pay Paul' and look good at others' expense.

5.   Some 'dead wood' at Board level, but also risk of 'young tigers' trying to move too quickly and make an immediate impact.

6.   Marketing innovation is needed – can we try some 'technology push'?

7.   Information systems are a shambles and at least five years out of date.

8.   This study must 'grasp the nettle', and make sure that the information systems are modernized rapidly, and aligned properly with business strategies.

See also the full interview analysis (Table 5-2).

Interview with John Watson – Key issues summary

1. Eroding margins of the mid '80s and have just got worse – radical action is needed.

2. Admits to being the wrong man for the job – too immersed in day-to-day sales thinking. Performing a 'holding action' – applying textbook marketing, but without flair. Need for Trendy to become 'proactive' in the market.

3. Trendy is now targeted on productivity and profit goals, but there is a lack of ability to measure the degree of achievement – information flows are either totally lacking, or late and unreliable.

4. The Sales and Marketing analysis system came in too late, and isn't meeting needs. Phase II should have started to offer better control information – what happened to it?

5. Acute need for external information – market share, competitor pricing, customer attitudes. Legal constraints concerning level of information we're allowed to seek of competitor's market shares, but with good analyses, we could make 'educated guess'.

6. Need for integrated and up to date information on key distributors and retail outlets – credit problems, and making fools of ourselves through my not knowing what sales had said to them.

7. Competition is cut-throat, and margins are low – no room for errors, but no time for risk analysis before key decisions. Doubtful if information systems can help here.

8. Feels let down by poor manufacturing quality, and weak cost control – creates embarrassment over complaints, and leaves little room for keen pricing.

9. Sad to see sales force cuts – feels we're risking throwing out the baby with the bath water, as much depends on sales rep/agent goodwill.

10. Doesn't think Trendy has any marketeers – only converted salesmen like himself.

See also the full interview analysis (Table 5-3).

FUNCTION	OBJECTIVE/GOAL	CRITICAL SUCCESS FACTORS	Ext or Int	Able to infl	PERFORMANCE MEASURES	BUSINESS INFORMATION & SUPPORT NEEDS	prty
Identify and cause to happen the changes needed to avoid problems	Identify the most important areas of risk or opportunity and respond in time	Ability to identify key trends	E	Y	Business outcome achieved	Early warning of all classes of problem	M
	–	Ability to react quickly enough	I	Y	Business outcome achieved	Effective overall business performance measures: ■ volume ■ profit and cashflow versus targets	H
Help Board members to keep to a long enough event horizon	–	–			–	–	
Rationalise & improve the Board's performance	Set and monitor key performance indices by division	Ability to establish effective control measures	I	Y	–	–	H
		Ability to monitor same on a timely cycle	I	Y	Degree of control achieved & predictability of business performance	Effective overall business performance measures: ■ volume ■ profit and cashflow versus targets	H
	Take appropriate control action in response to exceptions	Awareness of options & likely outcomes of actions	E/I	P	Extent to which effective action is able to be taken	An effective MIS system for presentation and delivery of key control information (WE ARE FAILING ON THIS)	VH
Implement business strategies	Oversee the shift into retailing – have the retail division into profit by mid 1993.				Volume and profitability by store and region	Sales volume & profit by: ■ product ■ sector ■ customer type ■ outlet type ■ sales force organizational unit	H
		Availability of high caliber retail expertise at Board level	I	Y			
		Sufficient capital available to fund the growth of retail out of its Midlands base.	E/I	P		Good cash management systems	M
					Sales force head-count by time vs target	Sales force head-count by time vs target	M
	Grow UK revenue by inflation +10%	Ability to grow market share in existing lines	E	P	Market share by product & sector by time	Market share by product & sector by time	H
					Absolute sales volume by product & sector	Sales volume by: ■ product ■ sector ■ customer type ■ outlet type	
		Achievement of success in the venture into retail	I/E	P	Growth rates in new market sectors	Market share by product & sector by time	H

Table 5-2: *Trendy Products PLC – information systems strategy – analysis of Fred Rogers interview*

FUNCTION	OBJECTIVE/GOAL	CRITICAL SUCCESS FACTORS	Ext or Int	Able to infl	PERFORMANCE MEASURES	BUSINESS INFORMATION & SUPPORT NEEDS	prty
	Achieve 15% profit on gross revenue	Ability to control manufacturing and distribution costs	I	Y	Profitability achieved	Sales volume & profit versus target by: ■ product ■ sector ■ customer ■ outlet type	H
					Ability to set & hold prices	Competitors' prices	M
	Replace old products & services	–			Volume & profit achieved by product & sector	Sales volume & profit by: ■ product ■ sector vs target	H
	Improve mfg efficiency to within 30% of Far East standards	Ability to achieve manpower productivity	I	Y	Productivity by work center	Productivity by work center	M
		Ability to control fixed costs	I	Y	Costs vs budget by cost center	Costs vs budget by cost center	H
Negotiate Group-level funding for strategic projects	Identify prime candidates for funding	Availability of suitable candidates	I	N	Satisfactory flow of investment into chosen areas	–	
		Suitable criteria for selection	I	Y	–	–	
	Get funding for prime candidates	Knowledge of external factors influencing funds available	I	Y	Satisfactory flow of investment into chosen areas	External financial market status	M
						Activities of competition	H
						Investment against plan	H

Table 5-2: *(continued) Trendy Products PLC – information systems strategy – analysis of Fred Rogers interview*

FUNCTION	OBJECTIVE/GOAL	CRITICAL SUCCESS	Ext or I	Able to Y	PERFORMANCE MEASURES	BUSINESS INFORMATION & SUPPORT NEEDS	prty
Plan and manage Trendy's existing markets	Develop markets and channels to support the revenue growth objective of 15% pa	Accurate identification of markets and needs			Rate of growth in market share	Market analysis by: ■ product ■ customer type ■ geog. region current & forward projection	H
						Overall shipment volumes by product and customer class	H
					Market share	Total market size & potential	M
						Accurate information on outlets & channels	M
						Total market analysis by: ■ product ■ customer type ■ geog. region current & forward projection	H
		Appropriate products	I	Y	Shipment volumes by product	Shipment volumes by product	H
		Activities of competitors	E	N		Competitor market shares and pricing strategies	M
	Retain current market share in books & games	–			Market share by product	Market share by product	H
		Accurate and competitive pricing	I	Y	Total profit volume	Profit, shipment volumes and market share, by: ■ product ■ region ■ customer class ■ outlet type with trends related to pricing showing demand/profit elasticity	VH
					Customer satisfaction and 'image'	Complaint levels	M
		Product Quality	I	Y		Results of product comparisons with competition, and opinion surveys	M
	Avoid excessive price competition	Ability to spot areas where competition will be keenest	I	Y	Profit margins achieved in relation to the competition	Profit, shipment volumes and market share, for current and year-on-year, seasonally adjusted, by: ■ product ■ region ■ customer class ■ outlet type ■ individual key outlet	VH
	Achieve target profit levels in current markets	Accurate and competitive pricing	I	N	Profitability/market share index	As above; also, the nearest we can get to the same for the competition	H

Table 5-3: *Trendy Products Plc – information systems strategy – analysis of John Watson interview*

FUNCTION	OBJECTIVE/GOAL	CRITICAL SUCCESS	Ext or I	Able to Y	PERFORMANCE MEASURES	BUSINESS INFORMATION & SUPPORT NEEDS	prty
Plan and carry out specific marketing promotions	Gain higher returns from marketing promotions	Knowing where to aim	E	Y	Profit and volume changes resulting from campaigns	Accurate, up to date costings for all stagesin the chain, by outlet type	M
						Analysis of impact of specific campaigns, by region, consumer class, product group and time	M
		Ability to separate out the impact of specific factors				Support for the process of analyzing the effect of multiple conflicting factors on sales	M
	Ensure all marketing activity is according to a co-ordinated plan	Speed of feedback concerning execution of plans	I	Y	Actual versus plan for campaigns: ■ spend ■ achievement ■ outcome	Accurate and up to date reports of marketing costs and activity by campaign, cost center and project	H
Identify and address new marketing opportunities	Become able to identify and react faster to threats, opportunities, and to changes in image	Getting to know about new trends and developments in time, and in a way he can react to	E	N	Rate of development of new marketing and product areas	Profit, shipment volumes and market share, for new products, by: ■ product ■ region ■ demographic category ■ outlet type and key outlet.	VH
					Profitability/market trends in new markets	Market research to identify favorable profitability/market trends in new areas	M
	Be sufficiently in touch with technical and product developments that they can become pro-active, and make consumer taste trends happen rather than just react				Rate of development of new marketing and product areas	Accurate knowledge of consumer and trade reaction to specific products and campaigns	M
Formulate and aim appropriate products at the selected new markets	Gain rapid growth in market share, while avoiding excess risk	—			Rate of development of new marketing and product areas	Profit, shipment volumes and market share, for new products, by product	VH
		Flexibility in the organization so as to be able to react fast	I	Y			

Table 5-3: *(continued) Trendy Products Plc – information systems strategy – analysis of John Watson interview*

Ref.	Short title	Description	Source Initials	Source prty (H/M/L)	Joint prty (H/M/L)	POTENTIAL BUSINESS BENEFITS SOURCES AND BASIS	EXTENT TO WHICH NEEDS ARE ADDRESSED BY CURRENT SYSTEMS
INFORMATION/SUPPORT NEED			**Source**				
SM10	Market analysis - general	Capability for extensive analysis of, and modelling based on marketing database e.g.	WJ JW	M H	M	Needs new marketing database development (below), and enhanced end-user facilities & support	
SM20	Mkt analysis - new products	■ To explore potential impact of new products under range of circumstances.	B CG	M L	H		
SM30	New ventures - risk analysis	■ Risk evaluation of new ventures: eg modelling of potential market share & profitability of alternative product & promotion strategies.	FR JW	H M	M	High potential for use of interactive modelling tools.	
SM40	Marketing database	Marketing database covering all sectors, products, plus competitors activity and fiscal /economic factors. To include data from a wide range of external sources and from TC field staff.	FR WJ F	H MH M	M	Needed for above, therefore at least priority 4	
SM80	Cashflow planning	Corporate cashflow planning & modelling facilities.	EB	H	H		
PLANNING & ANALYSIS							
SM110	Cashflow forecasting	Cashflow & revenue forecasts	EB	VH	H		
SM160	Manuf'g costs analysis	Fuller & more accurate analysis of all elements of manufacturing & distribution costs.	CG JK	VH H	H	Needs integrated, uniform treatment of all costs, coding categories.	
SM170	Supplier perf analysis	Analysis of supplier performance, relating quality, returns and timeliness of delivery.	CG	H	H		
SM200	Product performance analysis	Product and sales line performance analysis	JW	VH	H		
SM220	Treasury support	Up to date FX and money market information and Trendy's cash position and needs to support short term funds management.	EB	M	M		

Table 5-4: *Consolidated summary of business information and support needs*

Ref.	Short title	Description	Initials	prty (H/M/L)	Joint prty (H/M/L)	POTENTIAL BUSINESS BENEFITS SOURCES AND BASIS	EXTENT TO WHICH NEEDS ARE ADDRESSED BY CURRENT SYSTEMS
MONITORING & CONTROL NEEDS							
SM230	Business perform-ance reporting	Effective overall business performance measures: ■ volume, profit, cashflow, ■ actuals versus targets, ■ analysed by: product, product group, outlet type, business unit, responsibility unit	FR EB	H H	H	Significant upgrades to base systems.	
SM240	Profitability reporting	Profitability by product, region, outlet, major customer by time, volume & margin, actual versus plan, this year versus last.	JW CG	VH VH	H	Dependent on improved sales and costs information.	
SM270	Service level reporting	Accurate, up to date reporting of service levels covering all aspects of distribution logistics, actual versus plan.	JK	VH	H	Needed for independent validation distribution contractor's invoices as well as normal perf'ce tracking.	
SM280	Costs monitoring	Costs and revenues by cost centre, product and activity type; actuals versus plan	EB	H	H		
SM300	Manufacturing performance	More accurate and complete costs and performance information for manufacturing processes, provided in a consistent format for all plants and work centres.	CG EB	VH H	H	Need compatible coding structures and information flows from all sites.	
TRANSACTION AND SUPPORT NEEDS							
SM360	External information links	Effective and timely information links with our: ■ Wholesale Customers; ■ Suppliers; ■ Bankers and financial advisors; ■ Distribution contractor(s).	FR BJ	M H	M	Communication solution should embrace EDI also.	
SM365	Better sales & acc'tg tx'n data	Cleaner, single point of entry transaction data collection and validation for all sales and accounting transaction data.	EB JW	H M	MH	Savings on repeated data entry. Removal of sales and acc'tg reports inconsistency. Improved basis for MIS.	
SM370	Standard chart of accounts	Standardised high level chart of accounts and coding structures covering all Business units.	EB	VH	H	A management issue, but selected systems should support the solution.	

Table 5-4: *(continued) Consolidated summary of business information and support needs*

TPG 1990 IS and IT Strategic Plan

Management Summary

1. BUSINESS REQUIREMENTS

1.1   *Introduction*

By and large, the conclusions drawn from the management interviews reflect the factors which had already been identified, and which had led to the restructuring of Trendy Products Plc. The observations summarized below are a commentary on the specific information needs which are summarized in the Consolidated Statement of Business Information Needs above. They embody those aspects of the conclusions which are most relevant to information systems needs; they omit consideration of wider aspects of business strategy, and general organizational issues.

1.2   *Business Planning and Control*

At present in Trendy Products, basic information concerning actual costs incurred and business unit performance is not complete or accurate enough to provide necessary levels of business control. Meaningful and consistent analysis of such information as is available is difficult, because coding structures are neither uniform nor sufficiently comprehensive. Most aspects of cost reporting and control disciplines need to be tightened up, as do the channels for reporting of actual results achieved. Until this is achieved, there is not sufficient reliable, up to date information on costs and achievement to provide the basis for profitability reporting, which must form the core of a new set of performance monitoring systems.

With such poor performance monitoring and control facilities, management have been disinclined to plan seriously, and have resorted to fire-fighting instead. This must change, and in to support this thrust, in parallel with the urgent overhaul of accounting and control systems, revised procedures and support for proper business analysis and planning are needed.

1.3   *Marketing*

Strategic marketing has been neglected, and the management team needs to be strengthened in this area. Far more hard information on the markets, their potential, the competition and Trendy's position in relation to these needs to be assembled, and analyzed in a systematic manner.

1.4   *Finance*

The need for improved financial control has been covered above, under business control. Once this basis of 'actuals' is available, and there are firmer plans against which to compare performance, then more realistic and responsive management of cash flow and funding will be possible. Until this stage is achieved, the strategic management of finance in Trendy is hampered, and a more tactical, reactive approach is needed in the short term.

1.5   *Manufacturing*

The recent acquisitions in Bristol and Birmingham have different approaches and problems. There is still much to learn from and about them, but in the short term, the priorities must be to get manufacturing planning and control on a uniform basis. Despite the different types of manufacturing process involved, there is strong commonality of need. There are particularly serious gaps in the means used to control operations in the Luton factory, where the systems are most out of date.

1.6   *Sales*

Reporting and measurement of sales is neither accurate nor prompt enough. We are unable to identify trends in potential demand, or even actual sales, in sufficient time, nor with precision to react effectively. Pricing strategy is also hampered by being somewhat in the dark concerning the gross margins available, and hence the scope for aggressive pricing. Also information concerning marketing strategies is insufficient to help to decide when and when not we should attempt to buy market share.

1.7   *Distribution*

Costs are the big problem in distribution. They are undoubtedly excessive, but there is not sufficiently precise information to tell us exactly where. Also, better information is needed to help to determine whether the chosen distribution strategies are the most cost effective, and whether distribution costs are being properly reflected in our prices to outlets.

1.8   *'Brand' Performance*

Trendy needs to become more 'brand oriented' – the competitive climate is quite between different markets and between different ranges of products. The only way to formulate effective strategies is to discriminate more clearly between the various market targets, and to aim individual products and ranges at these targets. To do this, far more extensive information is needed about the market areas, and greater precision is needed in good time concerning the performance actually achieved.

2. APPLICATIONS SYSTEMS NEEDS

2.1   *Introduction*

Overall, Trendy Products' information systems have got seriously out of date, and the lack of investment during the latter part of the '70s shows clearly. The attempt to catch up in the early 1980s misfired because a code level conversion was undertaken of applications which were already obsolescent. This was partly due to an attempt to cut costs by removing the ICL equipment as soon as possible. The conversion program took far longer then planned, and this had the result of stifling virtually all new application development for several years. Notable exceptions were the general accounting and sales ledger packages, which were reasonably effective, except for the shortcomings due to inadequate flow of data from underlying systems.

The current portfolio of applications, which was summarized in Table 5-1, is a long way from meeting the current and likely future business information systems needs of Trendy Products Plc. The coverage offered by these systems of the business needs identified in the 1990 study is summarized in Figure 5-4 below.

A radical overhaul of information systems cannot be postponed, and a balance must now be struck between getting a sound long term foundation for the first time, against meeting the most pressing of needs. The recommended program of application development is summarized in Table 5-5. The financial summary, Figure 5-10 includes an indication of the quantified business benefits associated with the recommended projects.

2.2   Business Planning and Control

The current general ledger is ineffective as a control tool. The underlying package is potentially good enough, despite known shortfalls, but the problem lies in the information which is input to it (or rather not input). Three key needs apply:

- overhaul the basic accounting and coding disciplines and structures, so that uniform, comparable information is collected at source.

- tighten manual procedures and disciplines, so that this information is not lost or corrupted.

- make the interfaces from underlying systems into the general ledger more consistent, complete and automatic, so that the information actually gets into the G/L.

Table 5-5:   *Trendy Products PLC - Information systems strategy application development projects overall schedule*

BUSINESS AREA / PROJECT NAME	Development man yrs	style	1995/6 Q1	Q2	Q3	Q4	1996/7 Q1	Q2	Q3	Q4	1997/8 Q1	Q2	Q3	Q4	98 on man yr
SALES															
Sales order processing and finished goods inventory	8.75 0	Pack	3	4	8	8	6	4	2						
Sales analysis phase I	1.5	Rapid			2	2	2								
Sales analysis phase II	1	Rapid						2	2						
Customer perf./profitability	1	Rapid					2	2							
Wholesale outlet support	2.25	Trad									1	3	3	2	
Retail outlet support	2	Trad											2	2	1
Sub-total	16.5		3	4	10	10	10	8	4	0	1	3	5	4	1
FINANCE															
Revised coding structures	1.25	Manual	2	3											

BUSINESS AREA / PROJECT NAME	Development man yrs	style	1995/6				1996/7				1997/8				98 on man yrs
			Q1	Q2	Q3	Q4	Q1	Q2	Q3	Q4	Q1	Q2	Q3	Q4	
G/L interfaces	1.75	Mods	3	2	1	1									
Improved financial ctl reports	2.25	Rapid			1	2	2				2	2			
Budget planning support	1.13	EUC		1.5	1.5	1.5									
Cashflow planning model	1.63	EUC		1.5	1.5	1.5			1	1					
Cash management	2.5	EUC							2	2	2	2	2		
Sub-total	10.5		5	8	5	6	2	0	3	3	4	4	2	0	0
MANUFACTURING															
Bristol	0														
Mat Req. Planning	3.75	Pack	2	3	2										2
Shop floor control	2.5	Pack						2	2	2					1
	0														
Luton	0														
Basic HP systems	2.25	Pack				1	3	3	2						
Mat Req. Planning	3.25	Pack							2	2	1				2
Shop floor control	3	Pack									2	2			2
	0														
Birmingham	0														
Basic HP systems	2.25	Pack							1	3	3	2			
Mat Req. Planning	3.25	Pack										2	2	1	2
Shop floor control	4	Pack											2	2	3
Sub-total	24.3		2	3	2	1	3	5	7	7	6	6	4	3	12
MARKETING															
Marketing analysis phase I	1.5	Trad		2	2	1	1								
Marketing analysis phase II	3.25	EUC				1	2	2	2						1.5
Campaign analysis	1.25	EUC										1	1	1	0.5
Sub-total	6		0	2	2	2	3	2	2	0	0	1	1	1	2
DISTRIBUTION															
Distribution control pilot	1.75	Pack						2	2	2	1				
Distribution – all sites	7.5	Pack										2	4	4	5
Sub-total	9.25		0	0	0	0	0	2	2	2	1	2	4	4	5
PRODUCT DEVELOPMENT															
Product dev't support	1	EUC			2	2									
CAD/CAM facilities	2.5	Pack					1	2	2	3	2				
Sub-total	3.5		0	0	2	2	1	2	2	3	2	0	0	0	0
PURCHASING															
Purchasing system replacement	1	Pack	1	1	1	1									
Sub-total	1		1	1	1	1	0	0	0	0	0	0	0	0	0
PERSONNEL & SERVICES															
Payroll/personnel system replacement	4.5	Pack							2	4	2	2			2
Office automation pilot	1.5	Pack					1	2	2	1					
Office automation (fuller)	3.25	Pack										1	2	2	2
Sub-total	4.5		0	0	0	0	0	0	2	4	2	2	0	0	2
GRAND TOTALS - MAN YEARS	75.5														22
GRAND TOTALS - MANPOWER			11	18	22	22	19	19	22	19	16	18	16	12	

(Shows no. of development staff by quarter)

Figure 5-4:   *Trendy Products PLC - Application systems map with coverage annotation*

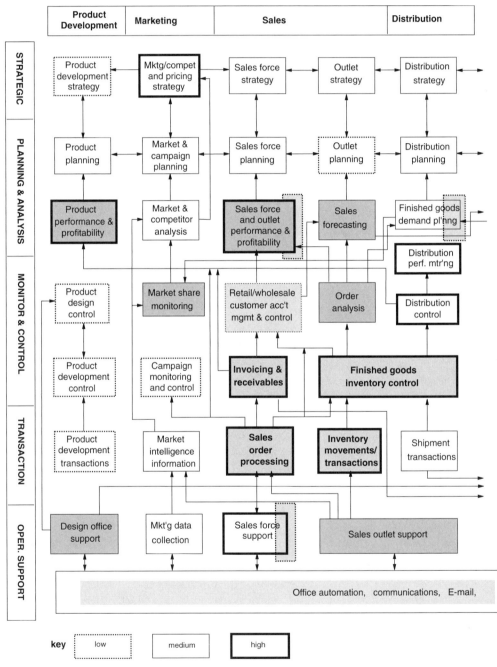

Figure 5-4:   (*continued*) *Trendy Products PLC – Application systems map with coverage annotation*

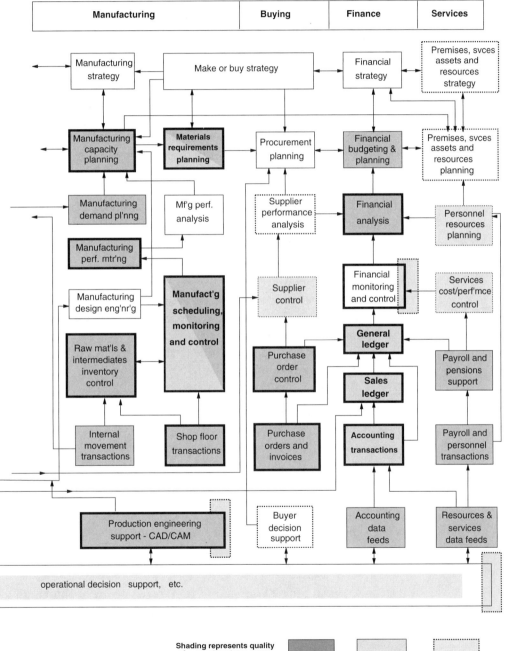

2.3   *Marketing*

Phase I of a marketing analysis system can be implemented, based on the analysis of Trendy's orders and goods shipments, once good information from sales analysis is available.

Phase II market analysis, concerned more with external factors, will be suitable for rapid development techniques, and can follow along shortly after.

2.4   *Finance*

General accounting, covered above should also be made the pivot of better financial control reporting, and of improved performance and profitability analysis. There are also several urgent developments, including budgeting support and cash management, which are suitable for rapid development/end-user computing techniques, and which may therefore be commenced early.

2.5   *Manufacturing*

The manufacturing control systems at Luton are obsolescent, and need complete replacement urgently. Those at Birmingham are adequate for the time being, although will they not be suitable for much expansion, nor for use at the other sites.

Fortunately, the manufacturing systems at Bristol are a success story, and it is believed that the Bristol approach offers the best practical way to upgrade the manufacturing systems at the other sites. It is recommended that, in parallel, the implementation of the remaining modules, of materials requirements planning (MRP), and shop floor control be pushed ahead in Bristol, and that the basic manufacturing systems modules be installed in Luton on a new HP 3000 configuration as soon as possible, to replace the old systems.

Extension of this environment to Birmingham, and the installation of the later phases at all three sites can follow later.

2.6   *Sales*

As a matter of urgency, an effective integrated set of packages should be selected and implemented to cover sales order processing and finished goods control. Once these are operation efficiently, the next most urgent needs are to implement flexible reporting and enquiry for sales analysis, and to ensure the flow of sound, up to date information through to the performance reporting systems.

Later, there is potential benefit to be gained from investigating the provision of on-site systems to the primary retail and wholesale outlets of Trendy Products.

2.7   *Distribution*

The most pressing distribution problems are more of management than information systems, but by mid 1990 there may be a good case for investigating the use of an automated distribution control package by implementation at a pilot site. If this proves successful, then fuller implementation during 1991/92 can be considered.

2.8   'Brand' Performance

The provision of effective performance information for Customer, Outlet and Product is a matter of extreme urgency. However, it cannot be achieved until a number of key prerequisites, addressed by the application program set out above, have been met. The most vital of these are:

- effective analysis of complete, up to date and accurate sales data
- prompt and accurate information on all aspects of costs, stemming from improved manual disciplines, and from the overhaul of the sales, manufacturing and distribution systems.

2.9   Other application needs

There is considerable benefit to be gained from early replacement of the purchasing/supplier control system, because of the need to control suppliers and deliveries far more closely. It is believed that a package solution could be implemented reasonably quickly and cheaply. There are several other areas where there are significant needs, but mostly these will have to give precedence to the top priority items identified above. Those items which will be kept under review, and which have been booked provisional places in the latter part of the priority queue include:

- CAD/CAM design support
- Overhaul of the payroll and personnel information areas
- Make or buy out modelling support

2.10   Databases

The most important of the databases to be created or to be consolidated from existing information are:

- Customer profiles – distinguishing between wholesale outlets, retail outlets and direct customers
- Marketing information
- Orders
- Finished goods inventory
- Suppliers/procurement Product design/definition
- Manufacturing control
- Business performance and control, including general accounting
- MIS/information database

The sequence of establishment and form of technical realization of these databases will depend on the application delivery sequence, and on the nature of the packages selected for sales order processing and finished goods control. The manufacturing databases will reside on the individual HP 3000 factory computers, and the MIS and marketing databases will reside on the central IBM mainframes.

2.11   *Development plans*

Recommended application development plans were summarized in Table 5-5. Overall resources, budgets and expected benefits are summarized in Table 5-6.

Overall financial summary

3. IT TECHNICAL ENVIRONMENTS

The primary information systems technical environments needed to support the applications defined above are:

Central operational batch and on-line processing. This environment will be based on IBM 30xx mainframes running a current generation transaction monitor and DBMS, and will support a shared integrated database of customers, orders, finished goods inventory, and distribution and accounting data. This environment will support:

- pre-defined transaction processing
- ad-hoc enquiry, reporting and analysis
- routine reporting
- summarization and extract to the MIS/information database.

Manufacturing environment. Based on dedicated general purpose HP 3000 computers at each factory. These will run proprietary manufacturing control packages, and will pass inventory, demand and delivery schedule, accounting and consolidated performance information to the central mainframe on a daily basis.

Central MIS and end user computing environment. This will also run on the IBM mainframes, but the information database will be separate from the operational environment, linked by an overnight 'refresh' cycle. The DBMS and language facilities offered will be chosen for their ability to support MIS and decision support processing, as well as capability to maintain and synchronize the information database with the operational database.

There will be extensive facilities to support the generation of data extracts and aggregations for downloading to local departmental/PC environments for end-user analysis. However, this freedom of access implies the need for rigorous control over rights to re-input modified data to the centrally controlled 'official' environment.

This environment is intended to support most forms of planning and analysis applications where access to centrally controlled 'official' data is needed. It must cover the three classes of MIS, numerical and text-based needs.

General purpose local DP support for single users and small groups. This will support a range of facilities, including records entry and management, planning and modelling, and will interface to the centralized operational and

Table 5-6 presents the figures as below. Note: empty cells indicate no value in that quarter.

PROJECT AREA	Total man Years	Total Costs	Total Benefits	YEAR 1				YEAR 2				YEAR 3				YEAR 4			
				Q1	Q2	Q3	Q4	Q1	Q2	Q3	Q4	Q1	Q2	Q3	Q4	Q1	Q2	Q3	Q4
BUSINESS APPLICATIONS AREAS																			
■ Sales	17	850	1,800		120	185	160	160	146	65	14								
■ Finance	11	480	1,200			60	80	75	80	86	75	24							
■ Manufacturing	25	1,500	3,500			75	65	135	150	135	145	215	160	120	85	75	75	65	
■ Marketing	5	160	700			20	30	25	25	40	20								
■ Distribution	9	300	550								50	40	60	65	85				
■ Product Development	4	170	375										35	45	35	55			
■ Purchasing	1	55	178				15	30	10										
■ Personnel & Services	5	185	325								25	55	75	30					
APPLICATIONS TOTAL	75	3,700	8,628	0	120	340	350	425	411	326	329	334	330	260	205	130	75	65	0
TECHNICAL INFRASTRUCTURE																			
■ Mainframe Computers	7	1,700			300			650			350				400				
■ Networking	3	350				200				85		45	20						
■ Workstations	1	1,010					150		220		225		50	300		65			
■ Systems Software	3	148					45		65		38								
■ Data Management	3	375				25		45		85		135			55		30		
■ Application Dev't Env't	1	135						25		45		20	20	20	5				
■ Standards & Methods	2	85							25	5	5	5	35	10					
■ ISD Development	1	75				25	10					35	5						
■ Architectures	2	110			15	15	15	15	15	15	20								
■ Specials	3	275												25	50	45	50	50	55
INFRASTRUCTURE TOTAL	26	4,263	0	0	315	265	220	735	325	235	638	240	130	355	510	110	80	50	55
OVERALL TOTAL	100	7,963	8,628	0	435	605	570	1,160	736	561	967	574	460	615	715	240	155	115	55
COSTS BREAKDOWN																			
■ Hardware		1,265				450	160	200				550			65				
■ Building		480			120	30		30	35	20	20	20	65	28					
■ Software		708			150	25	45	45	130	15	150	15	85	15	15	15	15	15	15
■ Manpower - tech support		240			15	20	15	15	15	15	15	30	15	15	15	15	15	15	15
- analysts		540		10	15	20	25	25	15	15	35	30	15	28	15	35	30	30	30
- programming		780		35	45	40	45	35	35	40	35	50	30	35	40	55	50	50	50
- users		1,450		45	110	120	110	130	55	60	55	50	50	45	60	60	60	50	50
■ External services		725		50	25	150	150	75	75	30	25	55	75	30	35				
Distribution of Benefits			9,592	0	220	200	550	550	700	950	600	978	1,300	900	954	680	350	460	200
Cumulative Costs				0	435	1,040	1,610	2,770	3,506	4,067	5,034	5,608	6,068	6,683	7,398	7,638	7,793	7,908	7,963
Cumulative Benefits				0	220	420	970	1,520	2,220	3,170	3,770	4,748	6,048	6,948	7,902	8,582	8,932	9,392	9,592
Running DR/CR Balance				0	(215)	(620)	(640)	(1,250)	(1,286)	(897)	(1,264)	(860)	(20)	265	504	944	1,139	1,484	1,629

Table 5-6: Trendy Product PLC I S plan – overall financial summary (pounds [thousands] sterling at current costs by quarter)

MIS facilities. This environment will be based on current generation personal computers, running terminal emulation software as well as general purpose modelling and text management facilities. They will be linked into local networks (LANs), which will have departmental minicomputers acting as co-ordinators and managers of shared data, and controlling gateways into the main network.

Office administration support and automation. This will include what has come to be called office automation, but also a wider range of administration support facilities. The facilities will be delivered through the network of general purpose workstations defined under 4.

Any other special-purpose or customized systems, e.g. laboratory analysis, CAD/CAM, etc., will be entirely dependent on the specialized needs of individual departments and centres of expertise. These environments will be described more fully the technical Appendices to the full report.

4. HUMAN RESOURCE AND ORGANIZATION

The resource and skills profile of the Information Systems Division of Trendy Products needs radical overhaul. The most important new functions to be established include:

- effective support for end-user computing
- integration and control over information architecture
- improved planning and management of mainframe computer and network capacity

The Appendices to the full report describe in more detail the most important of the revised functions and will contain a proposed revised organization chart as well as a manpower capacity plan.

5. FINANCIAL SUMMARY

The application systems proposals, along with costs and benefits were summarized by time in Table 5-6.

TPG 1990 IS/IT Vision Statement

1. INTRODUCTION

This section sets out an idealized medium term future IS strategic vision for Trendy Products Plc, under which information systems and technology would provide all of the important support required by the business, and would impose only minimal constraints on business or product development. Whilst this scenario is unlikely to be worth pursuing to completion, it is seen as an important guideline, and as a starting point for future systems architecture for several reasons:

1. it is based closely on high priority business needs articulated by senior management during the course of the study;

2. 'fit' with the vision will be a useful criterion for distinguishing between options for interim solutions (along with cost effectiveness of course);

3. examination of means of attaining key features of the vision can lead to consideration of relatively radical options which may not otherwise be considered;

4. the interfaces which need to be considered when adding or modifying products, support infrastructure or systems are well isolated and limited in nature;

5. it provides a good model for accommodating current product support systems 'warts and all', and in planning migrating from the weaker of the current systems;

6. future tactical decisions, e.g. those involving use of non-strategic packages can be recognized more readily as temporary exceptions, and treated as such, thereby limiting their impact.

2. OVERALL SYSTEMS FRAMEWORK

The overall framework on which this vision is based is illustrated in outline in Figure 5-5.

2.1 In this view, relatively separate product or service related support systems can be viewed as 'columns' as long as:

- they are well supported by common lower layers of:
  - integrated support for a common Customer view;
  - common administrative and operational support.
- they 'plug into' a co-ordinated upper layer of integrated common management reporting, MIS and EIS.

2.2 The main goals and objectives of a full implementation of this scenario are:

1. New or changed directions in products, market sectors or business ventures should not be seriously constrained by IS/IT development lead times or costs.

2. The IS and IT infrastructure should be sufficiently flexible and general that they are not serious constraints on the development of products and services, and the business organization and processes to support them. This includes the ability:

    - to cope with significant growth in business volumes at short notice;
    - to vary product and service formulation as required;
    - to set up and monitor (e.g. on a P&L basis) profit centres, business

units and strategic partnerships, based on a standard 'template' of systems and procedures.

Figure 5-5:   *TPG medium term integrated systems vision*

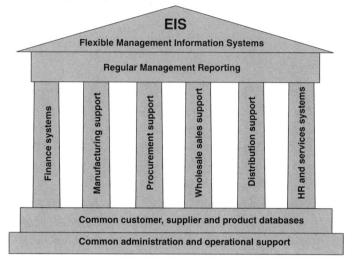

3.   The short and longer term planning cycles covering:

- business development;
- product/service development;
- information systems;
- information technology;

should be sufficiently well synchronized to avoid major mismatches. Reviews of all types of plans, both regular and event-driven, should take place efficiently and under control.

4.   There should be a common, complete, consistent, integrated, up to date view available of core business data, for all products, services, agreements and clients. There should be the *appearance* of a single, integrated logical database in each category, regardless of the actual underlying mechanism, covering:

- customer/contract;
- supplier/supply contract;
- product/service;
- operating company and business unit;
- MIS and management reporting.

5.   There should be sufficient concise and timely information on key management parameters and performance indicators, such as product and customer profitability.

6. Management reporting and MIS should be based on a common, consistent set of data, and a common, responsive architecture, having the following features:

    - common data feeds from operational systems, with minimal need for re-keying and manual adjustment;
    - access to a reporting database covering both reconcilable financial data and appropriately controlled non-financial operational performance data whose content is complete and consistent with financial performance reporting data and cycles;
    - up to date MIS information should be accessible on-screen, with no need for high volume printed reports, and no need for any re-keying;
    - subject to authorization controls, ready user access where needed to underlying customer, account and product level data, including full history of orders and contract performance, along with the ability to extract and analysis this information as required.

7. Users should be able to select appropriate reporting cycles, such as daily, weekly, monthly etc., and should be able to rely on data being complete and up to date within the tolerance for that cycle, as well as being reconcilable with other reporting cycles;

8. Delivery and formatting/presentation should be controllable by, and customizable by users, subject to appropriate controls over source data and authentication;

9. It should be relatively easy to add or modify key performance indicators (KPIs), subject to appropriate controls.

10. Means should exist for effective exploitation of the base of Customer/ Contract data across all products, for example for marketing purposes, or for aggregation of cover. There should be effective cross-functional co-ordination over the use of this data, e.g. between Marketing, Wholesale Sales, Retail, Purchasing, Manufacturing and Accounts.

11. Re-invention of the wheel should be avoided wherever possible. There should be a high level of re-use of business and systems infrastructure support. Similar problems and requirements should be met where possible by use of common processes and mechanisms.

Figure 5-6:   *Trendy Products PLC - application portfolio showing new and regraded applications*

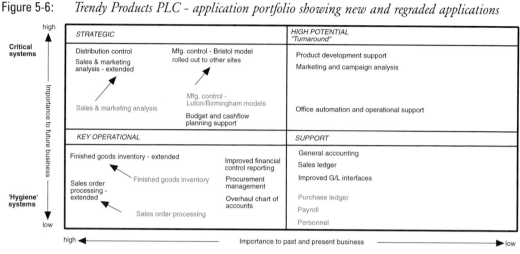

3. THE APPLICATION PORTFOLIO

Figure 5-6 sets out both the present set of applications (shaded in grey), and the recommended changes (in black), by categories of:

1. *support* – i.e. utility systems whose value is limited and/or declining, and in which further investment is not recommended;

2. *key operational* – systems upon which Trendy depends heavily, but whose value is unlikely to be increased by significant further investment, but where it is important that they be maintained to the requisite standard;

3. *strategic* – systems which are, or should become the mainstay of Trendy's competitive edge, and where investment should be focused;

4. *high potential* – where the next generation of strategic systems may arise, and where high risk/reward investment should be considered, but carefully monitored.

4. APPLICATION DEVELOPMENT AND ENHANCEMENT

Core systems and databases and their interactions and integration should be controlled by a set of centrally administered information architectures which should be enforced. Application development and enhancement needs must be met reasonably rapidly in relation to their business urgency, in a cost effective manner.

All developments/enhancements must be performed using the approved guide lines. Full control and progress monitoring must occur across all projects, under the ultimate control of a project steering group. Whatever the time constraints, quality must always be a major consideration.

The backlog of application development and enhancement requests should be within acceptable tolerances. Response to change requests, in terms of cost and lead times quoted should be prompt, accurate, and satisfactory. Backlog priorities should be:

- well under control;
- managed in a manner which reflects the business urgency;
- reviewed regularly in the light of significant change in business needs or priority.

There should be proven criteria for implementing systems solutions in a manner which preserves an appropriate balance between:

- simple well defined product-oriented systems, which are relatively independent from one another, yet are easy to deliver early and to modify;
- cross-functional 'infrastructure' based systems, which provide greater economies of scale and lower marginal cost of extension within predefined parameters.

There should be clear criteria, for deciding between rapid 'quick fix' approaches which are needed to meet business expediency, and more considered approaches to system enhancements which may preserve greater flexibility in the long term.

Control over the formatting and presentation of MIS and operational information should be devolved to the end-user to the maximum extent possible, consistent with:

- effective control over data values presented and verifiability of conclusions drawn;
- effective authentication of report contents;
- the user's need and willingness to customize or move away from default formats.

There should be maximum effective exploitation of application packages, subject to:

- preservation of the option to custom build 'competitive edge' systems;
- control over the conflict between package architecture and the preferred information and technical architectures;
- retention of the ability to develop enhancements rapidly and in a sound manner.

5. USE OF INFORMATION TECHNOLOGY

There should be, to UK HQ based users, key Customers and Suppliers, UK sites and regional offices and overseas HQ locations, the *appearance* of a single, integrated logical network and set of services offered on it – a 'single system image' – regardless of the physical topology, transmission media or protocols.

Whilst preserving the 'single system image' there should be flexibility to vary the types and deployment of application solutions, databases and technology platforms including appropriate distribution and/or replication. This will be subject to meeting business systems service, performance and value for money requirements. There should be no impact on the users' perception of the service, save for the addition of functionality from time to time.

Specific technical options should be able to be selected or changed, e.g. on cost/performance grounds, without undue disruption of the application code or the database views. There should be the minimum level of diversity in the range of technical solutions offered at any one time consistent with meeting the goals of flexibility, scaleability and cost/performance. I.e. there will be a standard recommended technical solution for each type of environmental need; exceptions should be by negotiation only, and justifiable only in case of overriding business need.

The technical platforms recommended should be open-ended in terms of capacity. Their cost/performance should be in line with industry norms, and should be scaleable in a linear manner over the expected range.

The communications network and systems should be as open as possible, subject to considerations of commercial security and confidentiality. The increasing requirements for interaction with Customers' and Suppliers' systems, as well as other remote systems such as third party databases and services should be supported by the technical architectures implemented.

6. RECOMMENDATIONS FOR IMPLEMENTING THE VISION

1.   Planning cycles covering:

- business planning
- product development
- IS/IT strategy
- IS/IT tactical planning

need to become better integrated.

2.   Reviews, both regular and event-driven, should take place efficiently and under control.

3.   The business planning process for product amendment or innovation needs to encompass organization, business process and IS/IT planning from the earliest possible stages.

4.   Where, inevitably, short term expediency pressures force departure from the plans, then subsequently the plans should be 'mended' around the change, and then followed, rather than abandoned.

5.   Future product support systems should be based as far as possible on a set of general product parameters, thereby enabling significantly quicker and cheaper response to business changes.

6.   There should be a common architecture for MIS, management account-
     ing and operational performance reporting. This should cover:

     ■ a uniform 'single source' data collection, with minimal bypasses or
       manual adjustment;

     ■ a common MIS database, covering a wide range of financial; and
       other performance data and reporting cycles;

     ■ a common delivery and presentation architecture which places the
       maximum possible proportion of analysis and formatting as close as
       possible to the user.

7.   There should be a common approach to developing business processes,
     organization and systems for product support. This should be based on
     re-use where possible of common elements of infrastructure support.
     Similar problems and requirements should be met where possible by use
     of common mechanisms, which should be built once, and then
     maintained in a manner to meet the common range of needs.

8.   Future databases for core common data, covering:

     ■ customer/contract   ■ supplier/supply contract
     ■ product/service   ■ operating company/business unit
     ■ MIS and management reporting

     should be designed with a view to providing a common logical view,
     whilst permitting flexibility in the physical implementation, migration
     and placement of data. Suitable database access interface software or
     protocols should be adopted to support the common logical views
     across varying physical implementations.

9.   As a basis for orderly and efficient exploitation of information technol-
     ogy developments with minimum diversity of solutions, there should be
     defined:

     ■ a range of IT technical environments, each suited to the needs of par-
       ticular classes of application;

     ■ clear criteria for assigning applications and databases to these envi-
       ronments;

     ■ a development plan for each type of environment, which specifies:

       ■ how it should be supported at present;

       ■ how its support will evolve so as to offer good cost/perfor-
         mance with linear scaleability in the future;

10. A standard set of programming interfaces which will help isolate
     applications from evolution of the underlying technology.

11. There should be increasing exploitation of client/server architecture to
     meet the goals of:

- placing core databases on secure, cost effective computing platforms;
- placing application logic on low cost PC based workstations, and developing client applications in maximum productivity graphical user interface (GUI) based environments;
- enable access from PC based client workstations to the databases of existing systems which can then remain based on existing platforms for as long as it is economic to keep them there.

12.   The application development life cycle, methods techniques and environments in use should be re-oriented so as to support:

- design of long-life systems and databases, and the architectures to support them;
- incremental delivery of business subsystems;
- relatively high maintenance workloads economically;
- effective exploitation of client/server technology;
- maximum use of low cost workstations to run client processes;
- the ability to re-locate MIS and, in the longer term, product and agreement databases to different server platforms as and when the economics of mid-range computer hardware change.

Summary of key events at TPG since 1990

Soon after the previous study in 1990, Trendy divested themselves of their Car Hire and Hotels operations. Late in 1990 they bought Grommetts, a family owned chain of high street retail outlets, originally based mainly in the Midlands, but which had started to expand into out of town hyperstore sites. This was very much Bill Jones' initiative – his vision of how Trendy could gain direct access to the high street market, with accompanying improved margins. When bought from the Grommetts family, the chain of retail stores consisted of 62 stores, with a combined turnover of £450M p.a. Profitability had collapsed, and growth had ceased, due to lack of capital.

Since January 1991, 7 new stores have been opened in the South East, and 6 in the North West. Growth plans have been stalled due to lack of investment capital. Some systems improvements have been undertaken (see later).

The retail chain is now being run as a separate subsidiary, with Gerry Floggitt as Chief Executive, alongside Trendy UK, but it is felt that it should be incorporated in this planning cycle because:

- it is not proving to be the long term cash generator which was hoped, due to the UK recession, and to the run-down and under-automated state of the business when it was acquired;
- its role is seen as critical to Trendy's wish to control the UK market;

- its operations will be closely integrated with those of Trendy UK.

In fact, despite its problems, Trendy Retail was still a bargain, as it was ailing, in good part because of the almost complete lack of effective management and control systems. It had outgrown the entrepreneurial flair of those who started it up. Trendy have recently (mid '91) hired Gerry Floggitt as Director of Retail Operations from one of its competitors; he has a brief to revitalize it.

The revenues and profits for the Group and UK companies for most recent periods are shown in Figure 5-7.

Figure 5-7:   *Revenues and profitability of the Trendy Group (£ millions)*

	1990		1991		1992		1993		1994	
	Gp	UK	Gp	UK	Gp	UK	Gp	UK	Gp	UK
Revenue	823	502	1460	1080	1686	980	2325	855	2768	1055
Gross profit (before tax)	24.5	5.6	25.8	(5.2)	15.5	(13.6)	32.6	(8.3)	48.7	(0.54)

It is clear from the results for 1990 through 1994 that the newly acquired UK retail operation (Jan. 1991) is still not pulling its weight. The extent to which this is due to the inherent problems of the business, as opposed to the UK recession is less clear.

Key directions, business and policy issues

The business focus and balance of the Trendy Group has changed radically since the previous study. Many of the plans and recommendations from the previous cycle have been overtaken by events, or have become irrelevant for other reasons. The relative priorities of those which remain relevant need to be completely reviewed.

Much of 1991 was lost time; Trendy waited for retail to deliver, and gradually went into a state of shock when they realized just why it was such a bargain. The Board eventually realized that retail needed special attention; they took the decision to run it as a separate business unit, and to hire a retail specialist. Gerry Floggitt joined in mid-1991 to fill this role.

During 4Q '91 and 1Q '92 an IS review was carried out, with the aim of identifying what was needed to integrate retail systems with those of the rest of Trendy UK. Some of the relevant interview notes from this review are available (FR, GF). This review served to highlight the following:

- the systems of the retail unit were very weak indeed – non-existent in many cases;
- the results of the previous IS/IT plan conducted in 1990 were not being

followed with any precision, and in any case had become seriously mis-matched to the business.

As a result of the 91/92 IS review, Bill Jones took responsibility for IS/IT away from Ed Brown, and set about hiring a GM for IS/IT of a calibre to make him a candidate for a full Board position, i.e. to sit above John Dore. Andy Barnes has recently joined in this role (mid '92). He is anxious to make his mark, and is keen to launch a full IS/IT strategy study. This is supported by Rogers and Jones, but there are concerns over the timing on the part of other Board members.

The Trendy Group is still wrestling with the issues of how to tackle the EC in the post 1992 climate, and how to address the opportunities of Eastern Europe. Revised business scope and responsibility definitions were developed late in 1992 covering these needs. Detailed business plan reviews will follow in mid 1993.

The UK company has currently short term focus on the following:

1.   Completing the overhaul of financial control systems, which has rather lost momentum.

2.   Getting the retail operation into shape to exploit the end of the UK recession.

3.   Overhaul manufacturing and distribution operations so as to be able to act as the 'supplier hub' of Trendy's thrust into Europe.

The Distribution Director, Jim Kludge has retired. The operation is still sub-contracted; the contractor's performance has slipped badly with the advent of the demands of the retail operation – he is too small and is over-stretched. This contract needs to be reviewed. Organizationally, Distribution is currently part of Floggitt's empire, but this is temporary.

It is now felt that two levels of IS and IT strategic review are needed, and should take place in close conjunction with the development of relevant business plans:

1.   Group level scoping, to determine which business areas should seek to co-ordinate IS and IT policies, and if so, what the criteria should be. This process is expected to lead to the launch of a number of separate IS/IT strategy studies in parts of the group;

2.   A rapid but thorough overhaul of the UK's IS and IT strategies, which are seen as having got seriously out of date.

Key organizational and personnel changes

Fred Rogers now Group Chairman.

Bill Jones still MD.

Ed Brown still Finance Director – but for how long?

Andy Barnes, the new IS/IT GM, Director designate, keen to make his mark.

Gerry Floggitt Joined mid '91 as Retail Operations Director responsible for Trendy Retail and the sub-contracted distribution operation, plus special responsibility at Group level for planning the moves into Europe. He used to work for a well known British maker of consumer electronics and PC clones.

John Watson is about to retire as Marketing Director. Trendy are recruiting a replacement, there being no good candidate in house.

A new Sales Director is in the process of being recruited. Floggitt has been caretaking this for a while.

Outcomes from the 1990 IS/IT plan

On average, the previous IS and IT plan has been implemented slightly slower than recommended – about 2 years of it have been implemented. In systems terms, significant achievements have been:

- The general ledger package has been implemented, and all base level accounting is now running fairly smoothly. However, problems remain with financial data reconciliation, due to the lack of discipline in the retail organization.
- Sales order processing and finished goods inventory has been implemented centrally, but not yet adapted to service Trendy's retail operation.
- Full MRP and shop floor control are now working well in Bristol and Luton. In Birmingham, the first phase of new basic systems were scheduled for mid '91, with MRP 12 months after.
- The distribution control pilot was successful – but the advent of Trendy Retail has changed the nature of the problem and requirements, and development has stalled.

Other IS and IT developments

1. The IBM 4381s at Head Office were replaced in 1989 by a 3090-400 running MVS, CICS and DL/1. This is now nearing its capacity limits, for reasons which are not fully understood. DB2 is installed on a pilot basis, but for its use to extend much, it appears that another major upgrade of mainframe capacity will be needed.

2. The Hewlett Packard equipment and manufacturing application packages in the manufacturing plants has proved successful. It is now being progressively upgraded to the current range of HP equipment. There is pressure from this vendor to adopt Open Systems, UNIX based policies.

3. A 'backbone' SNA network has been installed linking HQ, Bristol, Luton, Birmingham and the regional Sales Offices. Some of the bigger stores are now linked in. Many other sites, including the remainder of the retail stores need better communications; there has been an outbreak of un-planned and poorly controlled renting of leased lines and purchasing of modems.

4. The in-store PCs have proved a great success, but ran out of capacity quickly. Stores are working their way through generations of successively larger PCs. In some of the flagship stores, there are pilot implementations of 486 server class machines running SCO UNIX supporting multiple EPOS terminals as well as payroll and inventory management. These are working well individually most of the time, but there are incompatibilities between the software packages, and these machines themselves are running out of capacity. Larger UNIX boxes are under consideration. There are also serious support problems because the local users do not have the expertise to handle problems with UNIX.

5. The regional Sales and Distribution Offices have observed the apparent success and cost effectiveness of the in-store computers. They have acquired a proliferation of PC-based systems, and are now very keen to move into larger systems. Some are being heavily sold IBM AS/400 based solutions, others are being pressed to adopt UNIX based solutions. They are all chafing at not having the authority to procure what they see as the tools of the trade. Trendy's centralized IS function is hurriedly reorganizing to provide better support.

6. There are several Office Automation trials in progress, mostly not properly authorized, using three different software solutions and two different hardware/networking environments.

7. There is a desperate scarcity of communications expertise in Trendy. No-one seems to know how to select the type of local area networks needed for a particular site, nor when to move from leased lines to a link to the SNA network.

8. The design offices and manufacturing plants have standardized on AutoCAD on Silicon Graphics workstations. These will network, but not over SNA, and are presently running standalone, with dial-up for file transfer. Data corruption during the transmission of very large files is a problem, as are line costs.

Key current IS and IT issues

Remaining application problems include:

- There is still no sound and accurate sales analysis, let alone accurate and flexible MIS or truly integrated financial control.

- Development of financial control systems progressed to implementation of the general ledger and a core business basic financial reporting system.

- Further progress is stalled on a variety of issues, including:
  - the advent of Trendy Retail, with different coding structures, lacking in automation disciplines;
  - failure so far to achieve a uniform level of automation and timeliness of information flows;
  - residual incompatibility of cut-off periods and coding structures

On the technology front:

- PCs, LANs and small to mid-range systems are running out of control, in terms of standards, spend and compatibility.

- The prospect of further major upgrades to the IBM mainframe is not relished. There is an impression among informed users that smaller systems could do the job at far lower cost. Many of the 'old guard' in Trendy's IS department have serious reservations about decentralization, but are hard pressed to justify another major upgrade of the centralized mainframe installation.

- Communications is fast becoming the biggest headache, in terms of capacity, cost, compatibility and control. For example, there are three different LAN approaches in use in different parts of Trendy.

Undercurrents and hidden agendas

Rogers is probably contemplating retirement; his main ambition is most likely to leave things in sound shape rather than to rock the boat with risky ventures.

Floggitt hasn't yet had the expected impact on the UK retail operation yet, for a complex range of reasons. He is now perceived as having his eye more on the European Operations.

Bill Jones was the driving force behind the acquisition of Trendy Retail, and is very disappointed that it has taken so long to turn around. Has high hopes that Floggitt can achieve this, and is now very bound up with what he sees as the next innovative venture – the Group's move into a higher profile in Europe. Some other Board members feel strongly that if Trendy UK do not get their manufacturing and distribution operation running really smoothly and fast, then the European moves will probably bypass the UK company entirely.

The new IS/IT GM, Andy Barnes, is an unknown quantity. The Board of Trendy (UK) appreciate that they should have an IT Director, but they want to see how he does first. In the meantime, although he reports direct to the MD, he has to carry the senior Board members with him on all of his proposals.

Scope and terms of reference for the new study

The objectives for the UK based study have been set by Fred Rogers as follows:

1.   Establish a basis for providing the most effective level of information systems support for Trendy Products (UK) Plc for the next five years.

2.   Ensure that likely changes in business direction and strategy can be accommodated, whatever they turn out to be! Ensure that IS/IT are not on the critical path.

3.   Identify the most important current and likely future business needs, and the most effective systems strategy to meet them.

4.   Produce a specific plan in terms of:

- Applications enhancement and new developments needed – what and when;
- IT support
- Resources and personnel skills
- Financial basis
- Time scales

5.   Ensure that the plan will be:

- implemented;
- maintained in step with business developments;
- followed in the future.

You, the reader, should regard yourself as having the dual role of head of Application Systems Development for Trendy Products (UK) and currently being the Project Manager for this study. Your line report is to John Dore, the IS Manager, but for the purposes of this study, you report direct to Andy Barnes.

CHAPTER 6

Review of business planning techniques

Sagen Sie mir nicht, dass Friede ausgebrocchen ist, wo ich eben neue Vorräte eigenkrauft hab.

"Don't tell me peace has broken out, when I've just bought some new supplies"

Bertold Brecht, *Mutter Courage (1939) sc. 8*

Chapter objectives

This chapter is not a comprehensive tutorial on business planning. It aims rather to introduce some of the approaches which are commonly followed in developing business plans, and to highlight certain more recent developments which are especially valuable or relevant to exploitation of IS and IT. The main objectives are:

1. Introduce a range of planning approaches commonly encountered

2. Identify common elements of effective approaches

3. Provide insight to support interpretation and refinement of business plans to the point where they can form a basis for IS/IT planning.

4. Indicate ways in which planning style may vary by industry and organisation type

Business planning – categories of approach

Since the 1950s, there has been a discernible evolution in business planning approaches. Whilst this process has not really been very linear, and not all 'advances' have necessarily proven beneficial, it is still useful to set out some of the landmarks in the sequence in which they have arisen. These may be viewed as:

1.   Pragmatic or intuitive approaches–where we all started.

2.   Traditional mainstream – including Management by objectives (MBO), of which Peter F Drucker and John Humble were the key proponents.

3.   A variety of formal analytic techniques which originated in the leading USA business schools in the '60s and '70s, and which came into widespread use by the leading USA based management consulting firms.

4.   Critical success factors (CSF) techniques (e.g. Bullen and Rockart, 1981).

5.   Techniques for management of uncertainty – scenario planning

6.   Competitive advantage based approaches, typified by the work of Michael Porter (e.g. Porter, 1985).

7.   More formal approaches to business process analysis and reengineering (e.g. Hammer, 1990).

Selected techniques from the above list are discussed later in this chapter.

There appears to be a widespread consensus that in many normal cases, business plans are formulated on the basis of an amalgam of common sense and MBO, leavened by CSF based thinking. A generic model for assessment of business plans constructed on this basis is presented in Figure 6-1. Use will be made of this in later chapters 7 and 8.

Figure 6-1:   *Business plan - typical structure*

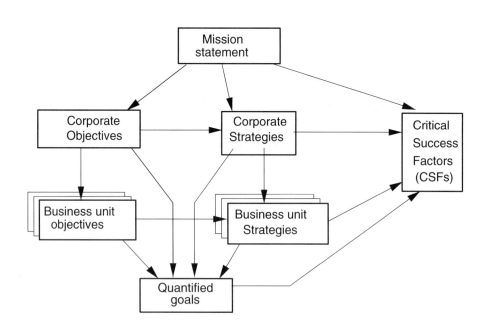

Business planning concepts and definitions

Introduction

This section sets out pragmatic definitions of a number of terms commonly used (and misused) in business planning. They have particular significance in the analysis of business plans for the purposes of identification of information and support requirements. They are put forward here solely for the purpose of establishing a working vocabulary, and not in any attempt to provoke academic dispute. The diagram above illustrates how these concepts interrelate.

Several of the concepts would be expected to be quantified in a mature and stable planning environment. However, it is recognized that planning is an imperfect and iterative process, and that early, tentative versions of some of the plan elements may be high level, directional, or even downright woolly. This is acceptable during the process of evolution of a sound business plan, but greater precision and more rigorous quantification will lead to a better business plan, and hence to a sounder basis for formulation of IS and IT strategy.

Mission Statement

A succinct statement of an organization's reason for existence – *what* it is intended to achieve overall, but not how it will achieve it. Clarity is paramount at this level.

Objective

Any clearly defined target set and agreed at any business level, including:

- corporate
- business unit
- functional or organizational responsibility area

Objectives should preferably be quantified, or should offer a suitable basis for the derivation of quantified measures of their attainment. Higher level objectives may be directional, and are expected to be directly relevant to the achievement of the overall mission.

Strategy

A broad plan to be followed in the pursuit of the business mission itself, or of specific contributing objectives.

Goal

A specific quantified aim of any strategy or action plan. May be directly derived 1:1 from an objective, or there may be many goals stemming from an overall objective and the strategies adopted in its pursuit.

Tactical Action Plan

Any series of plans or actions which are more detailed or shorter in term than a strategy. Strategies are normally pursued through such action plans.

Critical Success Factor (CSF)

Any factor, event or circumstance which is regarded as critical to the success or failure of a business mission, objective or strategy. May either be directly quantifiable, e.g. 'Ability to reduce the defect rate below 0.3%', or may be 'binary' in nature, but amenable to some form of tracking or measurement criterion, e.g. 'A significant upturn in the UK economy by the middle of 1992'.

Support Service

Any function or service which is required to support the pursuit or discharge of a business goal, objective or function. Typically such services are already automated to some degree, or may be regarded as candidates for automation.

Performance Measure

Any quantified variable which it is desired to monitor as a means for tracking:

- the degree to which a strategy or action plan is actually being followed in practice;
- the degree of success resulting from the pursuit of any objective, strategy or action plan;
- the behavior of a CSF.

NB: Performance measure and CSFs are sometimes used interchangeably. This can be very confusing.

Key Performance Indicator (KPI)

KPIs are a special case of performance measure, designed to enable the effective monitoring of:

- the degree of adherence to a business plan or strategy;
- the degree of success attained in meeting an objective or goal as a result of the pursuit of a particular course of action.

Key performance indicators may be derived as a composite of performance measures. Their selection is governed by such factors as the nature and quality of tracking data available and the human user's need for a coherent feedback and control mechanism which is operable in practice. The very act of tracking KPIs can lead to change in the organization being monitored, the managers tending to operate in a manner which leads to optimal performance as measured by the KPIs. The overall effect is thus not always that which was intended; for this reason, the effects of KPIs must be monitored closely, and they may need to be varied regularly.

Figure 6-2 illustrates typical business plan elements from Figure 6-1, extended to show the derivation of tracking/monitoring information, and the relation to business processes.

Figure 6-2:   *Business plan typical structure - key elements and derived requirements*

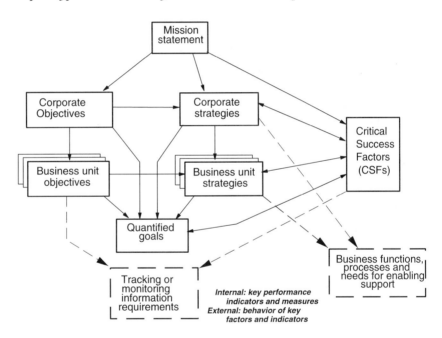

Basic planning/control process

For the purposes of deriving business information needs and KPIs, we will assume that the principles for business planning and control are along the following lines:

1.   Identify and agree Corporate mission and goals

2.   Establish an overall strategy to achieve them

3.   Identify business functional areas and associated responsibilities

4.   'Cascade' the strategies down the resulting hierarchy

5. Establish functional:

- objectives
- tracking criteria
- quantified goals and performance measures

at each level

6. Develop procedures for:

- monitoring of achievement versus objectives/measures
- selecting and implementing control/rectification actions

At each level, the strategies of the higher tend to influence the objectives pursued at the lower.

Organizations are staffed by people. We are all aware that this process is not always followed rigorously or systematically, even where it is documented policy to do so. Further, the existence of such a process does not guarantee that objectives and strategies will be interpreted in a sensible and realistic manner, nor that other hidden agendas will not be pursued. That's one of the things which make corporate life so interesting.

Corporate and business unit planning levels

In a typical corporation, the business may be divided into a number of business streams or units, which, according to current fashion, may be run very closely coupled, a loose federation of operating companies, or anything between.

In whichever case, it is important to take account of the differing level of detail and purpose of plans at corporate and business unit level. Also, if the business unit plans conform to a common template, then it becomes much easier to identify opportunities for 'roll-up' across the business, and thereby for identification of opportunities for provision of common resource, service and infrastructure requirements.

Note that the same considerations apply to plans across short and long term time scales, and across different types of plan.

Figure 6-3 illustrates some of the interrelated planning cycles which may exist in a moderately complex organization.

Figure 6-4 shows how it is important for the planning and control templates to be so aligned as to permit lower level plans and reports to be 'rolled up' to higher levels for reporting and control purposes.

Figure 6-3:   *Interdependent planning cycles*

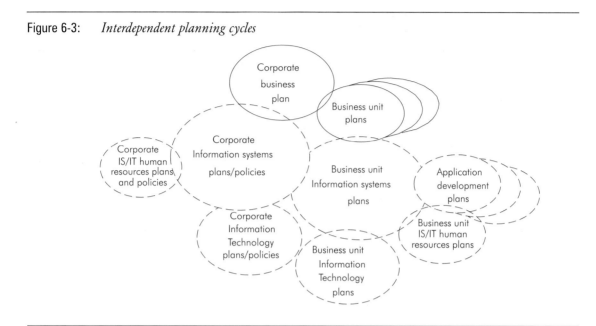

Figure 6-4:   *The integration of business unit plans with corporate*

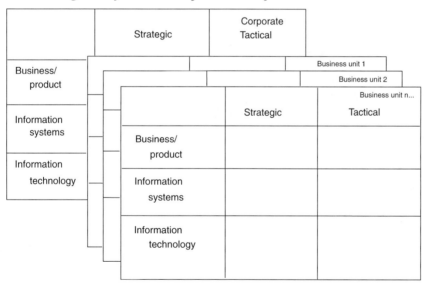

Review of the range of relevant techniques

Many techniques for analysis of business or systems processes have proved of use in contexts far broader that for which they were initially conceived. Process analysis, also termed functional decomposition, is a prime example. Initially arising from the areas of formal programming, under the guidance of Dijkstra and Knuth, this family of techniques has proved remarkably powerful in the analysis of systems and business processes. It is now at the core of business process re-engineering. The same is true of a number of other techniques, and may well yet prove so for others, as yet un-explored. The matrix which follows, Table 6-1, is an attempt to express this multi-disciplinary view of utilization of techniques. It encompasses techniques which are commonly used in later stages as well as in early business modelling, and is intended as a link between the work which is done at many different stages of the IS/IT planning process.

I will also mention here a warning, repeated at key stages in later chapters, against over-use of analytic techniques. Because I advocate their use, it does not means that I advocate exclusive reliance on them, or their use to the extent that they place the process before the outcome. If you ever experience a doubt that in a particular piece of planning work that you may be in danger of over-using a technique, or that in focusing on its practice you are losing sight of the intended business outcome, then you are almost certainly right.

That being said, on with the techniques!

USA Business Schools business analysis and planning style

This school of business management is typified by especial stress on:

- Quantification
- Proper alignment of responsibility/authority/resources
- A thoughtful approach to segmentation – Michael Porter's contribution to the process
- A general tendency to use scattergrams and indices, even where the axes are not necessarily fully orthogonal

For example, analysis of competitive position versus sector potential – see below

Examples:

MCKENNY SQUARE

In this technique, the past importance of IS is assessed against its likely future importance – McFarlan portfolio analysis (Figure 6-5) is a special case of this.

PLANNING WORK AREA IN WHICH THE TECHNIQUE IS MOST RELEVANT

Technique	origin	2D matrix?	Business planning	Investment appraisal	Business information requirements definition	Information architectures	Current status assessment	Application strategy selection	Application portfolio assessment	Migration planning	Technical strategy & architecture
Critical success factors	R		XXX		central role						
Scenario planning	*		Coping with uncertainty		XXX			XXX	XXX	XXX	XXX
Stakeholder analysis	C		Motivational								
Arkush square	C	Y		Especially relevant for IT							
PEST analysis	C		Environmental assessment								
McKenny square	C	Y	Evaluation of ventures	Identifying areas for IT potential				XXX			
Boston square	*	Y		XXX							
Multi-dimensional decision drivers	T		Subsumes 2D matrix techniques					XXX		XXX	XXX
Value chain analysis	P		Structural and environment					(XX)	(XX)		
Business process (re) engineering	HDS		Process/organization redesign			Process scoping		Enabling new processes	Enabling new processes		
Functional decomposition	*		Structural assessment		Responsibility structure	Process scoping		System scoping & interfaces		Scoping of phases	
Information needs analysis	T				Identification of needs	Basis for components					
User needs survey	C	Y			XXX	XXX					
Coverage assessment	T						Core technique for GAP analysis	XXX			
Group consensus	*		XXX		XXX			XXX	XXX		
Business impact analysis	C	Y					XXX	XXX			
Entity modelling	*				Often mis-applied here!	Core tool	XX	Core database strategy	XXX	XXX	
Information/data flow modelling	*				XX	Core tool	XXX	XXX	XXX	XXX	
Portfolio analysis (McKenny squ)	M	Y	Products and business units	For ventures			XXX	XXX	XXX		
Soft systems analysis	CH		Experimental stages		Getting at diffuse requirements		XXX	XXX			
SWOT analysis	*		Strategy selection	XXX	XXX		XXX	XXX	XXX	XXX	XXX

Source ref: *=many   C=CCTA A2 Guide   CH=Checkland   HDS=Hammer/Davenport/Short   M=McFarlan   P=Porter   R=Rockart   T=Tozer

Table 6-1: *Relevance of selected techniques to planning work stages*

Figure 6-5:   *Application portfolio approach - McFarlan*

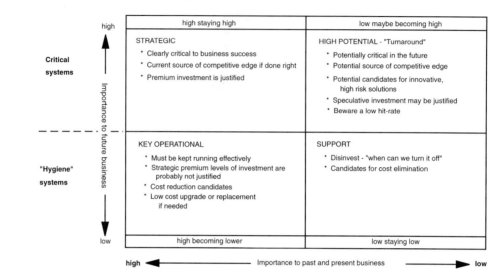

BOSTON SQUARE

In this technique (Figure 6-6) growth in an area of need or opportunity is assessed against organization's ability to meet that need.

Figure 6-6:   *Current position versus market potential*

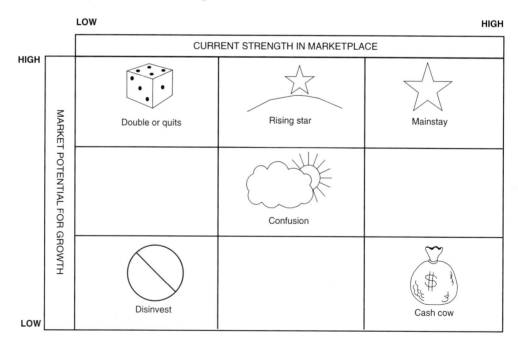

This view is often used to track product or business ventures in the manner illustrated in Figure 6-7.

Figure 6-7:   *Current position versus market potential*

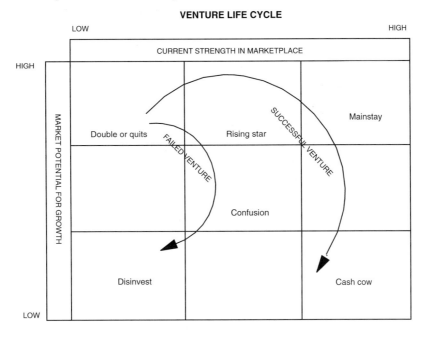

STAKEHOLDER ANALYSIS

Thesis: the net pressures on the organization are the vector sum of the individual forces.

Approach:

- Identify magnitude and direction of all of the:
    - major external influences on the organization
    - likely perceptions
    - potential interactions
- Determine the net sum of these forces
- Identify means to alter or exploit the forces

Value – helps to:

- understand pressures
- highlight potential conflict
- identify key factors needed to facilitate change
- assess future change in pressures
- identify what may or may not be possible

P.E.S.T ANALYSIS

- Analysis of the organization's environment under four headings:

    - Political   - Economic   - Social   - Technical

- Tends to be used in conjunction with Strengths Weaknesses Opportunities Threats (SWOT) analysis (see later) and Stakeholder analysis (above). These are also useful categories of Critical Success Factors (CSFs) see later.

BUSINESS DIMENSIONAL ANALYSIS

Analysis of business dimensions, as illustrated in Figure 6-8, is a powerful tool for identifying areas of commonality, or potential for introducing common processes, and hence for identifying opportunities for economies of scale. Selection of the dimensions if a matter of judgement, as is the decision as to whether the benefits of enforcing commonality outweigh the potential dilution of business focus.

Figure 6-8:   *Business dimensions*

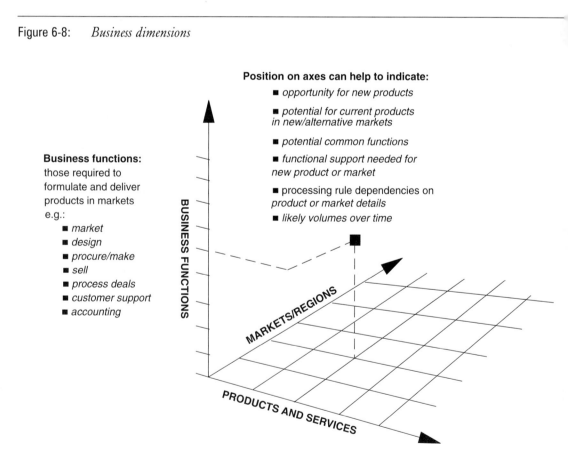

A generalization of the matrix based approaches to business planning

Reflection on the range and variety of the business planning and analysis techniques, such as Boston Square, which are based on two dimensional grids, has led me to wonder whether it is possible to get away from the over-simplified view imposed by only two dimensions without making the process too obscure to be useful. I now believe that this can be achieved. The discussion which follows reflects some partly formed ideas, but it is hoped that the reader will find them sufficiently useful to pursue in his or her own business area.

I have come to the following conclusions:

1. There are only a relatively small number of candidate matrix dimensions – about 13 in the case of business strategy selection. They can be treated as criteria, or 'drivers' to use the jargon. (But note that picking any two dimensions from 13 to form a matrix can be done in factorial 12 (12!) ways. This means that this approach can encompass all of the current generation of two-dimensional approaches documented, plus something over 6 billion more not yet invented).

2. Often, for a given matrix axis, only a small number of usefully different states are relevant, e.g. low/medium/high, absent/present or good/moderate/poor. I have borrowed the term Domain from the mathematicians for this concept.

3. Within the very large multi-dimensional space represented by all possible combinations of all domains of all drivers, we are only interested in a relatively few combinations which correspond to 'real' business options or scenarios. These rare relevant combinations would be hard to find in a 'sparse' matrix which embodied all the combinations. Therefore an approach is required which focuses on the 'real world' combinations only.

4. Each of the useful combinations must be associated with a business decision or outcome. It follows that an outcome-based approach, in which we start by considering only valid outcomes, or decision options, is likely to be most useful in practice.

5. There is one particularly simple diagramming technique – Decision Tables – whose age (it dates from the '60s at least) belies its value. This approach permits only the useful intersections of the dimensions to be documented in a simple table, along with the decisions or outcomes associated with each.

In outline, the approach which I believe will prove useful is as follows:

1. Identify:

    - the times at which decisions need to be made – e.g. business strategy selection, selection of IS support options;
    - the types of decisions to be made at each time;
    - the decision options – possible outcomes – e.g. get in, stay in, pull out, re-focus, reinvest;
    - the most likely drivers and other criteria which may govern the selection of the most effective solutions.

2. For each *decision time*: for each *type of decision* to be made and for each *decision option*:

    - specify the rules by which the drivers and criteria
    - determine the outcome.

3. Re-integrate the resulting solutions, conducting analysis of:

    - interactions and apparent contradictions
    - risk/reward • cost • cost/benefit sensitivity

The approach as applied to business strategy selection is illustrated in Table 6-2, where:

- the bottom left quadrant (which we would normally complete first) lists the business decisions which we want to take, along with the available options;
- the top left quadrant lists the decision drivers, and their associated domains;
- the right hand section of the chart sets out the decision rules which link the drivers and domains with the decisions.

The hard part, of course, is in completing the decision rule columns – I have provided some samples, which I am sure can be improved upon. This process is equivalent to capturing business expertise in a rule base.

A particular advantage of the decision table format is that there is no precedence implied between the rules, or between the criteria. Criteria sequence is immaterial; each rule (each column in Table 6-2) is wholly self-contained, and we can add, remove or change them on a trial and error basis. Any rule may select several options, and there is no constraint on specification of mutually inconsistent rules. Whereas this may correspond with real business strategy, it is unsatisfactory, and simple checks will be needed to eliminate such logical errors. These could be done by software.

It appears that the technique may be relevant in at least four areas:

- business strategy selection – see Table 6-2;
- selection of IS support style for business strategy implementation – see Chapter 10;
- selection of IS implementation options to meet business needs – see Chapter 11;
- selection of IT technical options – see Chapter 12.

The reader is invited to extend the scope of this applicability as and when they see fit.

The Critical Success Factors (CSF) approach

This approach originated from the work of John F Rockart and his co-workers (Bullen and Rockart 1981). A Critical Success Factor (CSF) is defined as: *A feature of an organization or its environment which, by its nature, has such an impact on success that its tracking, measurement, achievement, or avoidance, becomes critical to success.*

CSFs are often confused with KPIs; they are very different. CSFs are things which might stop you achieving your objective; KPIs are things which you may choose to measure to tell how you are doing, either in achieving the goal, or in managing the CSFs.

Critical Success Factors Approach – characteristics

- Proven in many industries over 20+ years
- Focused – 'rifle bullet' approach
- Fast to learn and apply for all levels of management
- Sound basis for identification of performance measures/indicators.

Methods of identification of CSFs

- Interviews/analysis
- Sieving out top 6 to 8 CSFs
- Group consensus/prioritization

CSF types and sources

- **Active**, where the manager may be able to directly influence the factor; he needs information is to help to identify control action, and outcome, versus
- **Passive**, where the manager cannot influence the factor directly, but needs to track it

Description	Domain/option	Decision matrix - rule definitions																								
Business criteria – 'drivers'																										
Present position in the market	Dominant/So-so/Weak/Not In	NI	NI	NI	NI	NI	NI	NI	NI	NI	NI	NI	S	W	S	W	S	W	S	W	D	S	D	W	S	W
Market future potential	High / Med / Low / Uncertain	L	U	H	H	H	H	M	H	H	H	H	L	L	L	L	H	H	H	H	H	H	L	H	U	U
Present relevant capability - expertise	High / Med / Low			H	M	H	H	H	H	L	L	L					H	M	H	H	H	M	H	H	H	H
Present relevant investment	High / Med / Low				L					L							H	M	H	H	H	M	H		H	H
Achievable return on investment	Good / Tolerable / Poor / Uncert			P	T	G	G	G	G	G	G	G	U	U	P	P	G	G	G	G	T	G	T	G	U	U
Present market share	High / Med / Low																M	M	M	M	H	M	H	L		
Future rate of innovation in market	High / Med / Low / Uncertain									H												H				
Furute volatility of the market	High / Med / Low / Uncertain					L		H	H	H	H	H														
Synergy with other ventures	High / Med / Low						H			H	H	L					H	H	H	H	H		L	H	H	H
Level of competitive activity	High / Med / Low				M		H					H														
Entry costs	High / Med / Low				L	H		L	L	H	L	L												L		
Availability of investment capital	Yes / No / Uncertain				Y	Y	H			N		Y					H	Y	N	N		Y				
Legislative climate	Lax / Tolerable / Restrictive																									
Decisions / options																										
GET IN – toe in water					Y																					
■ invest for strategic venture						Y				Y																
■ buy market share							Y																			
■ early entry for high margins								Y																		
■ focused attack on market leaders						Y	Y		Y	Y																
■ substitution / innovation										Y																
■ strategic partnership											Y															
■ takeover												Y														
STAY OUT		Y	Y	Y																						
STAY IN – hang in at least cost – 'Cash Cow'																							Y			
■ re-inforce early success																	Y									
■ buy market share																								Y		
■ invest for long haul																					Y					
■ back burner - wait and see																									Y	Y
■ focused attack on competition																	Y	Y	Y	Y	Y	Y				
■ shift ground - innovate or substitute																						Y				
■ strategic partnership																			Y	Y						
■ re-engineer for turnaround																	Y	Y								
GET OUT													Y	Y	Y	Y										

Table 6-2: *Selecting business strategies – a multidimensional approach (a simplified example)*

- **Internal** to the organization, versus external

Other categories valuable in helping to generate candidate CSFs include:

- Political or environmental
- Customer or supply chain
- People related factors

- Industry/competitive
- Cost drivers
- Product differentiation/development

Critical Success Factors – an example

- **Business aim**: Control physical inventory
- **Specific goal**: Achieve 95% ex-stock service to customer site within 4 hours at minimum overall inventory holding cost

Sample CSFs		*Implications/needs*
1.	*Measuring true demand*	improve tracking information
2.	*Channelling investment in inventory*	influence policy; potential for decision support system
3.	*Managing inventory levels*	support system needed
4.	*Managing distribution*	support system needed
5.	*Measurement of service levels*	track and influence
6.	*Measurement of inventory holding value*	track and influence
7.	*System controllability*	human interface
8.	*Customer acceptability*	industry/competitive

Management of uncertainty

The limitations of extrapolative planning

Under certain circumstances, increasingly common in the business world, extrapolative planning approaches, based on the assumption that we can forecast the future on the basis of the past, break down. Even in simple cases where cause and effect appear related in a smooth, predictable manner, this relationship may apply only over a limited (and undefined) range. If an accountant were to fly an aircraft purely on the basis of the proportion of fuel expended in overcoming air resistance, he would likely fly slower and slower, performing ever better against this particular performance indicator (KPI) until he reached stalling speed, whereupon he would most likely crash the aircraft. This also tells us something about the need to select appropriate KPIs – of which more anon. And something about the risks of putting accountants in charge of things they don't understand!

Most of the simple cause and effect relationships upon which we rely in business also apply over a limited range – but we often have no idea what are the 'boundary conditions' where things break down. As business pressures grow, we are at ever greater risk of straying into our local equivalent of a stall. Other approaches are needed, if we are not to flounder.

It is not all bad news. I believe that, where conventional approaches to planning and control break down, e.g. in cases of great volatility or uncertainty, there is potential to make use of some of Michael Porter's thinking (1985) on cost (and other) drivers. We should seek those areas where things start to behave unexpectedly – points of discontinuity, or 'chaotic attractors' in Chaos theory terms (Coveney and Highfield, 1991), of which our aircraft approaching stalling speed is an example. In Porter's terms (1985). the cost drivers tend to become non-linear in these areas. Wherever it appears that there may be a sudden, large change in business outcome (beneficial or otherwise) in response to a small change in an input or driver, if we know how to operate in that area, there may lie a fruitful source of competitive advantage or risk avoidance.

Beware, however, that mathematical theory suggests that this may be quite difficult in some cases. Penrose (1989, pages 218–221) shows clearly that, even to a mathematician, many simple, natural systems, such as a billiard table, can be beyond forecastability. Whilst they may be fully deterministic (i.e. the future is fully determined by the past, as long as you know enough about it), they can be non-computable – i.e. in principle non-calculable. He goes further, and shows that many simple systems are not even deterministic. On a more optimistic note, later in the book he indicates a potential basis for the phenomenon which we observe frequently in business, that sheer persistence, will power or business vision can win out, even in these situations.

There is more work to be done in this area, especially in terms of highlighting better ways of tracking the 'boundary conditions' where our business assumptions become invalid; the payoff in improved understanding and exploitation of such phenomena is potentially immense.

Improvisation

When we find that our current plans, and the assumptions on which they are based have become invalid, then we have little choice but to make things up as we go along for a while. The respectable term for this is improvisation. The risk is that we become convinced that the situation is inherently un-plannable, or even un-controllable, and we continue to 'wing it' for too long. What is needed is a systematic basis for improvisation. The goals should be to:

- identify quickly that we have exceeded the limits of our existing planning and control framework;
- move as quickly as possible from the resulting lack of control to some

more systematic basis for improvisation;

- determine what revised assumptions and planning and control process may serve us better in the new situation;
- implement it.

Almost inevitably, good information on current status will prove vital. If you know where you are, and have a clear sight of your intended outcome, then improvisation can be effective, even inspired. Otherwise, it is merely a symptom of panic. We may not know initially what information we need; there is a risk that if we stick to our previous KPIs we may be blinding ourselves to key features of the new situation. Therefore a rapid and fundamental questioning of KPIs must be a critical element of any period of improvisation.

Scenario Planning

Scenario based planning is an especially valuable approach in environments which are highly volatile, or which embody elements of significant uncertainty. It is at identifying the likely range of circumstances under which we may need to operate.

The basic assumptions are that:

- We cannot predict tomorrow on the basis of historical data.
- The future environment may assume any one of several inherently different states.

OBJECTIVES OF SCENARIO PLANNING

- Ensure that the planners consider a broad enough realistic set of possibilities.
- Identify strategies which are sufficiently resilient, through assessing the likely behavior of the organization, and the probability of attainment of its objectives under the scenarios considered.
- Achieve a compromise between over-optimization towards the 'most likely' scenario, and a general approach which will survive but not necessarily be competitive under all scenarios.

USEFULNESS OF SCENARIOS

- Reveal strategically significant uncertainties.
- Flush out CSFs or potential causes of failure.
- Identify IT opportunities.
- Help to align IS plans with business missions and goals.

PROCESS FOR DEVELOPMENT OF SCENARIOS

1. Brain-storm to identify possible scenarios. Initially include a deliberately wide range, including some really 'way out' cases. The scenarios should not just be a set of alternative values within a single model.

2. Develop each possible scenario so as to establish its usefulness and relevance.

3. Analyze and identify:

   - threats/opportunities.
   - strategies for succeeding under, or avoiding the adverse consequences of each scenario.

4. Ensure that a range of contingencies are considered:

   - environmental   ■ industry   ■ economic

USING THE SELECTED SCENARIOS

1. Select a small number (between three and six) materially different scenarios on the basis of the above analysis.

2. Explore ranges and combinations of variables where instability arises; identify key 'drivers' in each case.

3. Evaluate the organization's ability under each set to thrive or at least survive – identify critical survival factors.

4. Iterate with alternative assumptions concerning and external factors.

5. Select for further evaluation those business options and strategies which prove relatively stable across the range of scenarios.

6. Continue to review and question the relevance of the scenarios considered, and the basis on which others were excluded from consideration.

Competitive advantage approaches

The work of Michael E Porter epitomizes in many ways the competitive advantage approaches of the 1980s. His book *Competitive Advantage* (1985) contains valuable descriptions of his key techniques.

Some of Porter's approaches are summarized below, including:

- The five competitive forces.
- Value chain analysis.
- Cost analysis, leading to the identification and analysis of 'cost drivers'.

The five competitive forces

Figure 6-9 illustrates Porter's approach of breaking an industry down into components, and then analyzing the forces and the interactions involved. It shows a typical mature industry (a), in which there is an established market structure and a set of existing participants, who engage in competitive activity (b). There may be a number of potential entrants (c), who, due perhaps to a lack of imagination on their part, would be expected to compete broadly within the present ground rules of the industry. There may be serious 'entry barriers', such as start up cost, for potential participants.

Other potential competitors may take a more creative approach, either because the barriers to traditional entry are prohibitive, or because they have a genuine innovation to offer. They offer substitute products or services (d), which offer the same outcome for the customer, but by a different means. An example is Midland Bank's First Direct service, where retail banking is offered as a wholly telephone and mail based service, without the need for high street premises.

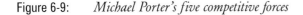

Figure 6-9:   *Michael Porter's five competitive forces*

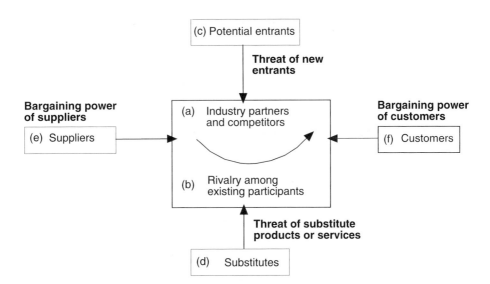

The horizontal dimension illustrates what Porter calls the customer chain and the supply chain (which is the customer chain viewed from the other end!). Larger players, in either customer or supplier roles, can often exert pressure on their smaller trading partners. There is therefore great potential for competitive activity in the horizontal dimension, as well as the vertical. There is also potential for co-operative activity; a present trend is for ever growing integration of this horizontal chain between companies through increasing linkages between information systems.

Value chain analysis

Value chain analysis is based on the notion of breaking down a business or business area into natural functions or processes, and then investigating the means by which the processes interact, especially in terms of their customer/supplier relationships as defined above, and the means whereby value is added (or subtracted!). The customer/supplier chain concept is extended for this purpose to embrace internal inter-process interfaces also. Porter uses the term 'cost driver' for any factor which bears an identifiable and significant relation to costs, and much is made in his methodology of the means to identify and analyze the behavior of them (see below).

Figure 6-10:   *Generic value chain*

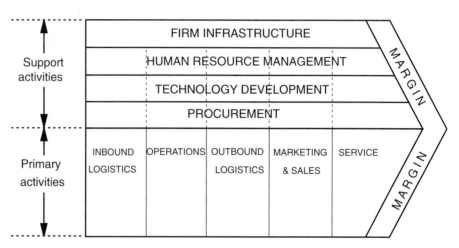

Michael E Porter - Competitive Advantage

The value chain approach, as illustrated in Figure 6-10, is very close in style to the Business Process Schematic described in chapter 8, which is used as a formalized 'map' of the organization on which to place candidate application systems. There is considerable synergy between the two concepts. As with so many analytic techniques, it is very easy to 'overwork' the process, leading to too much detail and loss of sight of the intended end. Business planners suffer from the same temptations in this regard as do systems analysts. The art of effective use of value chain analysis lies in picking a fairly small but useful set of business functions, and concentrating on those customer/supplier links and cost drivers which have a material impact, and which can be influenced in accessible ways. In rigorous application of the approach, even internal customer/supplier interfaces become subject to a tightly specified service level agreement (SLA) or contract.

Porter contends that the improved disciplines and the cost advantage gained in this way is a powerful source of competitive advantage. It can open the options for clearer differentiation between low cost and premium quality differentiated products (another of Porter's trade marks). It can also indicate where potential gains can be made from exploitation of commonality of process or economies of scale.

A clear understanding of the difference between your own and your competitors' value chains can also offer useful insights into competitive options. Value can easily be defined as: 'What the buyer will pay for product/service', and is clearly a key measure of competitive advantage. Likewise, profit can be defined as: 'The residue of value commanded less cost of supplying it'.

It has become common usage for the term 'horizontal integration' to be used for exploitation of commonality of process for a range of products or services. Correspondingly, 'vertical integration' refers to cases where there is primary focus on the 'end-to-end' processes for building, selling and delivering individual products or services. In the case of vertical integration, economies of scale or common process may be deliberately sacrificed, in the interest of maintaining clear product/service responsibility and accountability. Fashion on corporate organization appears to oscillate between the two over time.

Porter distinguishes between internal customer/supplier interfaces, which exist within a single organization, and across which notional value passes in exchange for internal money, and external customer/supplier interfaces, which obey rather stricter rules of economics. It is generally believed by many practitioners that the application of commercial market force thinking to internal customer/supplier relationships can be beneficial (up to some limit where the corporation may disintegrate into a set of warring robber-baron fiefdoms!). Further, if we wish to retain options, e.g. to 'outsource' or privatize what are today internal services, this easier to achieve if they are already operating on a quasi external market basis. It is less easy to see how, in a smoothly run organization, the notions of goodwill and willing co-operation can be reflected adequately in such tightly defined customer/supplier relationships.

In their efforts to minimize their internal bureaucracies, and to improve internal efficiency, some of the governments of the major states in the Western World are making heavy use of the above approaches. In the short term, the impact is high, and clear cost savings are becoming apparent. Only time and experience will tell whether the 'harder edged' customer/supplier interfaces will run smoothly in the longer term, and whether the restructured organizations and relationships will yield sustainable gains in efficiency and quality of service remains.

Types of value chain to investigate

Porter suggests that some fruitful sources of value chains for investigation include but are not limited to:

- Internal business units (often termed SBUs) and profit centres
- Key internal processes
- Outlets
- Competitors
- Suppliers
- Customers
- Regulatory/fiscal factors

Cost analysis using cost drivers

The manner in which analysis of cost drivers as defined above can influence business strategy is illustrated in the Figure 6-11, in which the behavior of two candidate cost drivers:

- number of products   ■ number of sales outlets

has been studied for a hypothetical organization.

In each case, the marginal change in cost incurred resulting from a relative change in the value of the cost driver has been plotted, both for positive and for negative changes. In the case of sales outlets, reducing their number below a certain level offers little saving – you need some form of sales organization to stay in business anyway. However, increasing their number appears to incur disproportionately high costs, presumably as we are having to introduce additional layers of management. It appears to suggest that we keep our total number of sales outlets small.

Figure 6-11:   *Cost drivers - example*

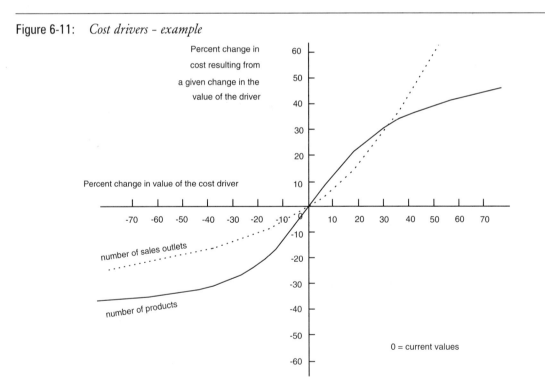

The curve for number of products has a different shape. Here, it appears that we are in an area of high marginal cost of increasing product range. We can either reduce our product range by around 30%, saving quite a lot of cost, or increase the range by 50% or more, at which level, the marginal cost of adding products becomes quite low. Clearly we need to explore the impact of these options on other factors such as market share and customer loyalty. This rather over-simplified example highlights two caveats over use of this technique:

1.   The inputs to the cost driver curves typically come from a survey of existing management, whose imagination and assessments may be limited by their own prejudices and experience. The shape of the curves thus owes a great deal to what detractors may call 'subjectivity', and proponents may call 'business judgement'.

2.   There is an implication that such factors can be considered in isolation. This is almost never true. Handling the interaction between our varying product range, and our growing or shrinking portfolio of sale outlets takes us firmly back into the judgemental arena.

Despite these reservations and shortcomings, organizations do make extensive use of these techniques. We will ourselves extend this concept later in Chapter 10 into the notion of 'value drivers', along the lines indicated by Parker and Benson (1989).

Business process (re)engineering

Introduction

Hammer (1990) and Davenport and Short (1990) are generally credited with originating the concept of Business Process Reengineering (BPR) – or Redesign as Davenport and Short call it, although the latter acknowledge many of the underlying roots of the concept in their references.

As described in the papers referenced, the BPR approach sets out to fundamentally re-think and re-structure both the processes carried out in a business and the way in the work is organized. The aim of this is to improve the way in which the desired business outcome is achieved, implicitly by saving costs, although alternative goals could be assumed (see comments below). The notion is hardly new – every O & M department ever set up was supposed to be attempting this, albeit with mixed success. However, Hammer's and Davenport and Short's formulations have captured the imagination of the Western Business world, according to the approach a glamour to which 'Organization and Methods' could never aspire. This is no bad thing; not all radical new business approaches are so eminently sensible, or have so much potential for delivering real business benefits.

BPR Goals

The key goal of BPR is to bring about radical improvement and simplification of the business processes required to achieve a desired end. Key features include:

1. Evolved from O & M approaches of the early 20th Century – but far more glamorous!

2. Basic thesis:
   - Re-focus on your desired business outcomes;
   - Question all assumptions and 'givens';
   - Step back from present organization, and present process detail;
   - Reconsider basic functionality needed to deliver business outcome;
   - Exploit key enablers, especially IT, to change patterns of working.

3. Good sources of 'how tos' in original papers by Hammer (1990) and Davenport and Short (1990).

4. Needs to be done top-down – risk of missed options and marginal benefits if done across too limited a scope.

5. Techniques have much in common with functional analysis used in early stages of SP4IS.

6. Ideally, should run concurrently with IS/IT strategy, so that viability of enablers can be evaluated interactively.

The relation between Business Process Reengineering (BPR) and IS/IT Planning

The relation between Business Process Reengineering (BPR) and IS/IT Strategic Planning is close. To be successful, IS/IT planning requires a willingness to scrutinise and fundamentally re-think the means used to achieve a desired business outcome, prior to considering the most effective means for its automation. This is precisely what should be delivered by BPR.

In IS/IT planning, we have used for many years approaches aimed at identifying relatively 'pure' functionally based business needs, as independent as possible of (and hence resilient to changes in) the way in which the business may be organized from time to time. The advent of BPR has encouraged and formalized this thinking. A properly conducted BPR study should make the conduct of an effective IS/IT strategy much easier – should even require it, in fact. Ideally, the two processes should run in parallel, after a short initial stage in which the very highest levels of business mission, goals and assumptions are reviewed from a BPR perspective. This paper explores this relationship more fully, and indicates some ways in which the scope of BPR could be extended.

Ways to add value to BPR

Just as the exponents of BPR have added value to the old O & M approach, so I believe we can extend their thinking, using their own principles, to gain further benefits. Aspects include:

- consider other enablers as well as IT
- start right at the top
- select goals and optimization criteria carefully and provide instrumentation
- consider radical scenarios

These are explored further below.

CONSIDER OTHER ENABLERS AS WELL AS IT

One of BPR's key insights is, rightly, to stress the enormous potential of IT, especially through access to shared, up to date databases, as an enabler in breaking down organizational barriers, and in opening up new ways of fulfilling the purpose of business activities. Davenport and Short use the phrase 'IT enabled', which offers a useful perspective, but they also refer to BPR as being 'IT driven', which risks putting the cart firmly before the horse.

The exponents of BPR fail to stress the need to examine the potential of other enablers, for example product substitution, in Michael Porter's terms (1985), where Customer needs can potentially be met by an alternative product requiring different, possibly simpler or cheaper business processes for its support. This is not always voluntary; external factors, such as fiscal change or developments in public opinion can also become powerful levers for change, leading to the need to alter, perhaps radically, the means by which a business goal is achieved. Those companies who identify and cope with or exploit such changes earliest or most effectively can gain major competitive advantage from doing so. In keeping with Hammer's advocacy of scrutinising ruthlessly all of our assumptions and preconceptions, we should extent the range of enablers considered in this way.

START RIGHT AT THE TOP

Another of Hammer's particular contributions is to stress that the process must be 'goal-directed, top-down'. Each piece of old baggage – customs, traditions, assumed rule or other 'given' which we carry forward into the re engineered organization is just another constraint which limits the range of alternative solutions which we will consider, and hence the degree of improvement possible. However, he neglects to apply this criterion at the very top level, by letting the overall business goals (generally assumed to be related to efficiency or service level) be implicit. Again here, we can extend the process whilst following its spirit by ensuring that we question and re-examine the top level mission and goals of an organization at the start of such an exercise. Davenport and Short are more explicit about selection of optimization criteria.

SELECT GOALS AND OPTIMIZATION CRITERIA CAREFULLY AND PROVIDE INSTRUMENTATION

Optimization goals and criteria are typically are related either to cost reduction or to improvement of service levels. Sometimes both are attempted at once; whilst this may be valid, it may not – an attempt to mix or compromise in these goals may lead to conflicts, and in any case needs care and clear thinking. There may be other goals, quite different but valid. The real point is that optimization goals need to be questioned, and must be clear, explicit and quantitative, otherwise success will be elusive – and may be hard to identify in any case if we haven't made provision to measure it! All of this stresses the need for improved instrumentation – information systems – so that we can tell how we are doing against the stated goals, and react in time to deviations and exceptions.

CONSIDER RADICAL SCENARIOS

In an environment which is volatile, or which embodies significant uncertainty, then BPR should be coupled with scenario planning (see above), or other appropriate techniques. It may well be that radical business options or approaches thrown up by consideration of extreme scenarios may prove to be fruitful starting points for BPR consideration.

Top down or bottom up?

There is a natural layering or sequencing of decisions required in the formulation and implementation of business strategy. Each stage is dependent on its predecessors, and represents the selection of options (with the closing off of others), along with addition of implementation detail and compromise.

The highest levels of abstraction are represented by the overall business mission and goals. Next come the strategies which are selected and pursued in the fulfilment of the mission. Thirdly, come the business functions and processes (defined as the lowest level functions) which need to be performed to carry out the strategies. These are still relatively abstract, in that they are not yet assigned to organizational groupings. If complex, such functions may need to be broken down through several levels, with appropriate objectives and performance measures being set at each level. Lastly, there come decisions as to the manner in which the functions and processes are arranged into roles or responsibility units – organization units and associated procedures. Note that the term 'functional' is sometimes used differently, e.g. by Davenport and Short, to mean 'organization unit based', i.e. different to processes. We shall use the more common terminology, described above, where functions are independent of organization, and become processes at their lowest level.

Whilst business process reengineering may be conducted at any of these levels, it is clear that the more radical and fundamental the scope of the reengineering, (i.e. the higher the level at which it is conducted), and the fewer the assumptions and givens preserved, the greater the opportunity for radical change and hence potentially for major improvement. Merely tinkering with low level processes or organization is about as relevant and beneficial as chrome plating the cylinder head nuts on our 1921 Model T Ford when what we really need is a different transport policy. Hammer (1990) makes this point very strongly, stressing the need for a cross-functional perspective. His graphic phrase for missing the point in this way is 'rearranging the deck chairs on the Titanic'. Davenport and Short (1990) found that: 'In most successful redesign examples we studied, the company's senior management had developed a broad strategic vision into which the process redesign activity fit.'

The above thinking rings alarm bells in those cases where organizations are seeking to apply the reengineering process at too low a level, or across too limited a scope. Hammer himself says in his paper: 'Reengineering cannot be planned meticulously and accomplished in small and cautious steps. It's an all or nothing proposition, with an uncertain result'. Going further, it is by no means guaranteed that, if we separately optimize a number of individual departments and business units, then the sum of the whole – the Corporation – will itself become optimized with no further action. I believe that, following a series of reengineering exercises within an organization, there needs to be some form of overall integration and global optimization process. To quote Davenport and Short (1990):

"...rationalisation of highly decomposed tasks may lead to a less efficient overall process. Instead of task rationalisation, redesign of entire processes should be undertaken with a specific business vision in mind."

Focus and priority – where to start

Whilst he offers a number of guide-lines for conduct of the BPR process, Hammer does not offer any clear guide in his original paper as to how to focus and prioritize our reengineering efforts. To tackle the whole organization to a consistent depth – a mistake made by proponents of other cure-alls in the past – will almost certainly take an unreasonably long time, and is likely to yield little or no benefit in the majority of areas.

It is generally accepted that some form of business prioritization of areas for attention is needed at a very early stage in the exercise. Sometimes the areas most in need of overhaul are clearly evident, and can easily be selected on the basis of common sense or business judgement. Davenport and Short recommend a 'high impact' approach *"which attempts to identify the most important processes or those most in conflict with the business vision and process objectives"*. They contrast this with what they call the 'exhaustive' approach, which they rather unfairly associate with James Martin's Information Engineering approaches (Martin 1982).

Practical interaction between BPR and IS/IT planning

The assumptions and rationale behind the reengineering or redesign process as described in the first two references are closely coincident with the early business analysis phase of most commonly used variants of IS/IT Strategic

Planning (ISP), which seeks to reassess and realign IS and IT strategy closely with the future directions and needs of the organization concerned. For ISP to be effective, it is clear that the broad and radical stages of business reengineering thinking should have been carried out prior to attempting to ascertain specific business objectives, functions and performance measures in the first ISSP phase. However, the latter stages of both processes may best proceed in parallel, as there is needed constant dialogue (termed 'recursive' by Davenport and Short) over:

- how IT capabilities may enable or constrain certain process redesign options;
- the impact of IS/IT delivery risks, costs and lead times;
- how the emerging IS and IT strategies and facilities can best be re-aligned to support the re engineered organization.

Davenport and Short assert that linking the BPR and IS/IT planning cycles in this way will preclude most application package solutions, lead to a higher level of need for custom written systems. Whilst this is so in terms of the potentially greater degree of achievable match with business needs, this ignores the lead time and implementation cost advantages of application packages based solutions. It is more likely that packages will continue to be preferred in cases where business pressures dictate that compromises must be made, e.g. a short lead time is critical or a 'utility' solution is acceptable. Packages are also valuable as tactical or stop gap solutions in many other cases. The increased cost and lead time of major custom system developments will tend to remain most clearly justifiable in cases where the marginal rate of return on the added functionality is greatest, e.g. strategic or competitive edge applications.

In a business where a mature IS/IT strategy planning cycle is already established, business process reengineering should prove somewhat easier to carry out, because there are already in place:

- a cultural readiness to think in functional terms, independent of present organization;
- documented analyses of the functions required to carry out the business mission, and the manner in which information systems support these at present;
- monitoring and maintenance systems designed to track and control progress against the plans;
- IS and IT infrastructures designed to be resilient to a fair range of organizational changes.

Even so, a radical, BPR review will undoubtedly prove sufficiently disruptive to require extensive overhaul of the existing IS/IT strategy, as well as the business plans, and provision for this should be made accordingly.

In conclusion, I see business process reengineering and IS/IT strategic planning as closely complementary. The early, radical business reengineering stages are clearly prerequisite for a successful IS/IT planning exercise, and the follow-on phases of reengineering require to be supported via a dialogue with the IS/IT planners as to viability, lead times and costs of the enabling systems and technology under consideration.

Evolution of control culture

Much is made nowadays of 'Quality', but the real point is often missed.

Being a 'Quality organization' is often interpreted as having achieved certification to certain aspects of BS 5750 and/or the ISO 9000 series. Achieving such standards has little to do with quality as perceived by the end customer, although increasingly it may required, for example, as an entry condition for participation in competitive tenders.

Similarly, many organizations feel that they need to have 'standards' for doing almost anything, but often the standards, once written, perhaps at great cost by a consultant, are placed in the archetypal glass-fronted bookcase and ignored thereafter. They salve a few consciences; their presence may be mandatory for quality inspections, etc., but they do no real good.

Observation of the above phenomenon has led myself and others to the following classification of stages of evolution of corporate control culture, for which I claim no originality:

STAGE 1

No standards, no awareness of the need for them. This is fine if you are really small, otherwise it is a recipe for anarchy.

STAGE 2

Standards exist, but are not followed; there are no controls to identify whether there is compliance. This is faking it.

STAGE 3

Standards exist and are followed in a reproducible manner. Tracking systems exist to ensure compliance. This is broadly the stage represented by BS 5750 or the corresponding ISO 9000 series, but, as indicated above, this means little in terms of quality perceived by the end customer. There can be many reasons, such as:

- *flawed standards*   - *flawed controls*   - *flawed culture*

Further, such a state can be a great handicap in achieving true quality, as once you are locked in to the straitjacket of a documented quality system, change can be prohibitively expensive, and can take far too long. And you dare not be seen to lose the hard won certification by abandoning the standards.

STAGE 4

Standards exist and are followed to good effect; i.e. all of stage 3, but the tracking systems monitor not only compliance but also outcome. At this stage, you are nearly there.

STAGE 5

All of stage 4, plus the observations of outcome and of customer perception are systematically fed back into a continuous improvement process. This is the only place worth being. It is much better to have a few simple, flexible standards backed by a continuous improvement process and ethos, than to have the world's biggest and glossiest fake standards manual.

CHAPTER 7

Determining business directions and requirements

Introduction

The needs of the business, as articulated by the senior management, are the only possible authentic foundation for viable IS and IT plans. The specific requirements, in terms of current plans, products, organization and intentions, along with their likely directions of development must be established and agreed before systems and technology solutions can be realistically assessed or considered. This chapter presents the process and techniques which are recommended to achieve this.

As well as being the basis for development of IS and IT strategy, this body of information also forms the basis for:

- establishing management commitment to the business needs, the potential benefits which are expected to arise from meeting them, and to the nature of their solutions;
- identifying and managing the effects of change to the needs, and in consequence to the strategies derived from them.

As well as what is needed by the business, and what is going to be needed, we also need to establish as clearly as possible what exists today, in terms of systems and IT infrastructure, and how well that supports the needs identified. That assessment will be covered in Chapter 10.

Phase 1 – Determine business information and support needs

Phase objective

Figure 7-1 illustrates the first phase proper of the SP4IS process, which includes the work which is the subject of this chapter. In this phase of the work, we are seeking to establish as complete as possible a basis of fact on which to build an IS/IT strategy. This should encompass:

- Present IS and IT achievements and assets.
- Where do we want to be – in terms of business plans and requirements.
- Other 'givens' and constraints including external.
- The nature and range of prevailing uncertainty – e.g. over business directions and/or volumes.

Figure 7-1:   *Determine business information and support needs*

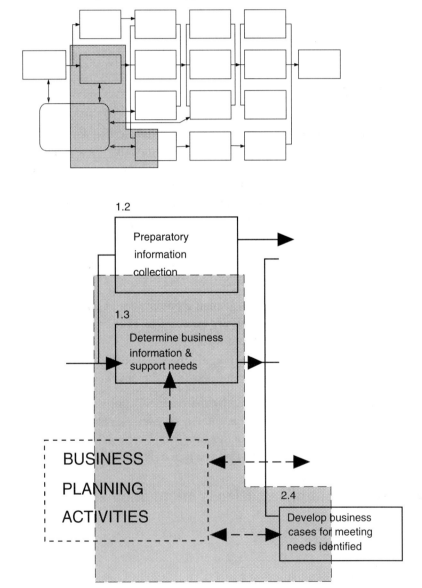

Business analysis – key aspects

- *Business plans*:
    - visibility
    - consistency
    - currency
    - commitment
    - quality
    - stability

- *Timing*:
    - study and planning cycles
    - other related initiatives

- *Management support/commitment*
- *Organizational structure*:
    - focus
    - stability

- *Uncertainty, rate of change*:
    - external
    - internal

Business analysis process

The overall process for business analysis is set out in Figure 7-2. How much work is involved, and how long it will take, depends on:

1. where you start from – including how much work has been done already by the business planners, or in preceding IS strategy cycles;

2. the point at which the results of further analysis cease to have material impact at the strategic level;

3. the tolerance of the organization for navel contemplation.

(2) will usually stop you first, you may feel too soon. This is still better than doing too much and losing credibility. You may sometimes have to cope with business planners who themselves have lost their way and overdone the analysis. Be guided primarily by the most senior operational line management who will talk to you.

If there is a considerable body of existing material, then a changes-only basis may be a very useful approach. Also, if you have on the team and industry expert in this type if business, they may have ready-made inputs to offer. However, these should always be reviewed carefully, and not imposed. Sometimes the phrases 'best of breed', or 'best practice' cover a multitude of sins. We should not become responsible for propagation of errors or poor solutions.

Figure 7-2:   *Process for business analysis*

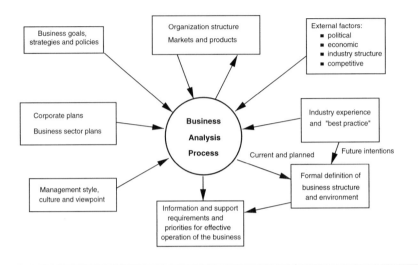

Figure 7-3:   *Variety in organizational structure*

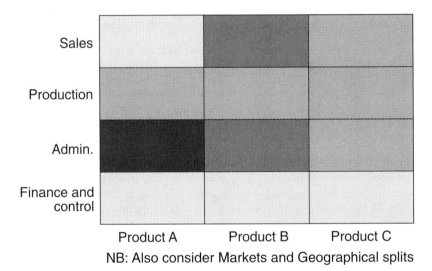

We often find that in a diverse organization, similar functions for different products or services prove to be covered by different procedures, organization units and/or systems. Figure 7-3 illustrates a simple case. There is often a clear reason why this has happened, e.g. the company may have grown by acquisition, and did not integrate the systems or administration as it did so. In the case above, support for product C is vertically structured, whereas there is common support for all products in the case of Production and Finance. This company may have initially been built on product C, and then grown by acquisition. There are often major savings to be taken in such cases through reduction in diversity.

BUSINESS ANALYSIS – KEY ACTIVITIES

- Desk research and pre-interview analysis
- Plan and organize main interview program
- Conduct main interview program
- Analyze interviews and verify results
- Derive and consolidate conclusions; obtain agreement and commitment from management
- Desk research and pre-interview analysis – objectives

GET INTO A POSITION TO MAKE MAXIMUM EFFECTIVE USE OF THE INTERVIEWS

- Understand business structure
- Understand business organization
- Acquire 'public domain' knowledge
- Understand current plans
- Obtain job definitions
- Initial view of business objectives
- Develop an initial view of systems and IT needs

MAIN SOURCES OF BUSINESS INFORMATION

Some of the most fruitful sources of information on the business include:

- *Business Plans*
- *Organization Charts*
- *Past Studies/Reports*
- *Annual Reports*
- *Job Definitions*
- *Policy Statements*
- *Procedure manuals*

INPUT INFORMATION CHECKLIST

In more detail, we should assemble or consult information on as much as possible of the following:

- *Business Structure:*

    - Companies ■ Divisions ■ Departments ■ Sections

- *Business plans:*
    - Current versions, however mixed the quality
    - Evidence of status versus plans
    - Views on future planning initiatives
- *Management Personnel*
    - Job Titles
    - Reporting Lines
    - Responsibilities (written job descriptions are ideal if valid and up to date)

- *Company overall and business units*

  - Objectives/Targets
  - Key Policies
  - Products and Markets
  - Market Strategy
  - Main functional areas
  - Major Current Programs – including indications of restructure

- *Key external events*

  - Legislation
  - Competitive activity
  - Market changes
  - Economic factors

- *Results from previous planning activities/cycles*
  - However old (within reason)
  - Whether regarded as a success or not – there are lessons to be learned from past failures

Wherever possible this should be accepted in computer processable form – but do not reject any evidence initially.

Typical causes of business uncertainty

One of the most important aspects of the current business status will be identification of those areas where uncertainty is perceived to be greatest, and some indication of the parameters or degrees of freedom which delimit the types of change which may occur. This applies both to threats to the company's success or even its existence, and those events which may present business opportunities if exploited effectively. By definition, the unexpected is sometimes difficult to pin down, but it is sometimes possible to flush out issues by considering categories. Some relevant categories include:

- *Strategic:* e.g. options for tackling expanded markets
  - buy local subsidiaries;
  - make agency arrangements;
  - run subsidiaries directly out of the home country.
- *Organizational:* e.g. centralization/devolution.
- *Operational:* e.g. sales volumes:
  - beating/missing targets;
  - small/large change.
- *Industry:*
  - new entrants
  - product revolution
  - price war
- *Environmental:*
  - war/peace
  - boom/recession
  - political overthrow
  - banking/economic collapse

Results of pre-interview analysis

- Clarification of business plan definition and status
- Highlighting key areas for attention
- List of meetings and interviews needed
- Preliminary materials for interviews
  - job definitions, responsibilities etc.
  - lists of main functions
  - check lists of key points/issues by area
- Basic understanding of business and area plans and objectives

Organize and conduct the interview program

Objectives

- To determine business information and support needs in a structured manner that directly relates IS and IT needs to business objectives
- The program should ensure that the needs identified are:
  - capable of formal analysis
  - demonstrably complete
  - in a form suitable for future maintenance
  - understood and agreed by business management

Key factors

- Selecting interviewees – balance versus focus
- Must involve all management who operate at a strategic level (e.g. over 2 years horizon for decisions)
  - include all executive Directors and Divisional Heads
  - vary the participant levels depending on role e.g. marketing, product planning etc.
- Participation of IT Management
- Full support of Board and Chief Executive
- Well organized and professional approach

Interview organization

PRELIMINARY TASKS

- Analyze functions and organization
- Briefing letter from Managing Director
- Set up control system

FOR EACH INTERVIEW OR GROUP SESSION

- Arrange date
- Send agenda and pre-interview analysis
- Conduct interview
- Analyze detail of interview
- Review and confirm corrections
- Preliminary tasks for each interview

- Confirm date
- Prepare team members for meeting

- Quick response of key issues
- Send analysis for comments
- Determine list of interviewees

Target products

- Summary of key issues arising from the interview.
- Full analysis – first draft – to the format in Figure 7-4.
- Full interview analysis – approved by interviewee – see Table 7-1.
- Interviewee respect and commitment as a basis for sponsorship role.

Figure 7-4:   *Business interview analysis format*

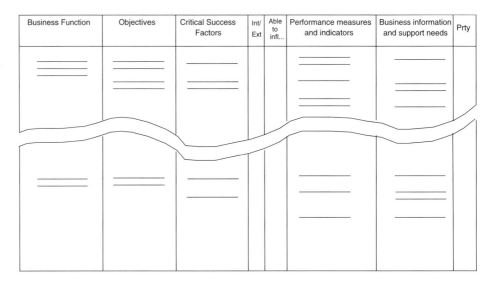

Description of the interview analysis layout

This description is typically attached to the first draft interview analysis to assist the interviewee in his review of it.

FUNCTIONS

These represent the understanding gained of each of the interviewee's main areas of functional responsibility. They will often not align exactly with present organizational boundaries. This identification of 'pure' business functions can be of immense value in unraveling complex and eccentric organizations, and is a key foundation for:

- effective business process re-engineering;
- identification of opportunities for treating similar problems with common solutions.

OBJECTIVES

This section records each objective pursued, both at the overall level, and in each specific area of functional responsibility. We need to determine where quantified goals are set at present, or where there is potential for them to be set, as well as the ways in which they could alter. It is useful, but not critical, to determine the present targets in quantitative terms.

CRITICAL SUCCESS FACTORS (CSF)

These represent factors, of whatever nature, which may have a critical influence on success or failure in management of a function or the pursuit of objectives. These are recorded regardless of whether or not the interviewee believes that they are well controlled at present, as we wish to avoid proposing changes which may be prejudicial to areas which are already well under control. However, we are particularly interested in those CSFs which are most troublesome at present, or which may become so in the future.

- *Internal/external* – This indicates whether or not a CSF relates solely to matters internal to the organization.
- *Able to influence* – This indicates whether the interviewee is able directly to influence the CSF itself, as opposed to being limited to monitoring its behavior.

CSF analysis is addressed in more detail later in this chapter.

PERFORMANCE MEASURES

These are measures or indicators which would give most help in assessing:

- the performance of a function directly;
- the degree of success in attaining a business goal or objective;
- the behavior of a CSF.

Again, we are interested both in those which are satisfactorily provided today, and others which are needed to meet present or future needs, regardless of the current status of their provision.

BUSINESS INFORMATION AND SUPPORT NEEDS

In this section, we present what we believe from the interview to be the relevant business information or support needs, based on our analysis of the above categories. These will be the focal point of the next stages of consolidation and consensus. We are at this stage seeking the interviewee's views on the rationale behind our conclusions.

FUNCTION	OBJECTIVE/GOAL	CRITICAL SUCCESS FACTORS	Ext/ Int	Can infl	PERFORMANCE MEASURES	BUSINESS INFORMATION & SUPPORT NEEDS	PRTY
Set up and run Trendy's retail operation.	Get retail acquisition back to break even by 1Q '93	Ability to identify and cut key costs fast	I	Y	Store performance reported accurately and promptly	Revenue and profit volumes overall and by: ■ item ■ square foot for each: ■ store ■ region actual versus plan, this year versus last.	VH
		Ability to prune store portfolio	I	Y			
	Make 30% gross margin on turnover in 1993 i.e. 15% net profit	Have the right goods in stock at the right price and margin, in the right stores at the right time.	I	Y	Sales item performance overall and by store reported accurately and promptly		
	Grow square footage by 25% p.a. compound from 1993 onwards	Ability to find the right sites for new strore and to exploit them.	E	Y	Site evaluation support.		
					New store performance high-lighted.		
		Ability to staff new stores	I	Y	Staffing achieved vs targets.		
		Size of new stores (need to be larger on average).	I	Y			
Stabilise current operation – 'stop the haemorrhage'	Turn around or close non-performing stores	Ability to spot poor performers	I	Y			
		Accurate identification of causes	I	Y			
		Ability to shed poor sites; close stores & sell	I	Y			
	Cut 'shrinkage' from 2.5% at least to the industry average – 1.5%	Improved controls at all points in the chain.	I	Y	Average shrinkage by location, goods type by time.		
	Make store managers more responsible as managers – mini-business concept, with each store in effect a profit centre, by mid 1993	Effective in-store systems to support the store manager	I	Y		In-store systems to enable the store to run as a business unit	H
	Highlight non-performing store managers and release them.	Effective training programmes	I	Y	Store manager performance		
		Ability to recruit enough store managers of the necessary calibre	I	Y			

Table 7-1: *Trendy Product PLC – information systems strategy – analysis of Gerry Floggitt interview*

FUNCTION	OBJECTIVE/GOAL	CRITICAL SUCCESS FACTORS	Ext/ Int	Can infl	PERFORMANCE MEASURES	BUSINESS INFORMATION & SUPPORT NEEDS	PRTY
Plan and open new stores	Find the right new sites to meet growth objectives. 10 new stores in 1993; 15 p.a. during '94 to '96.	Capital availability to invest in new stores	I	Y		Effective cash management systems, so as to free up the working capital needed.	M
		Accurate evaluation of potential sites	I	Y			
		Accurate tracking of new stores in the critical early stages	I	Y			
Stock the right items	Know accurately what we're really selling soon after we sold it.	Goods identified at point of sale	I	Y	Sales volume by stock item Level of stock outs or over-stocking by store & item	EPOS at all points in all stores.	H
		Easy to operate fail safe recording of goods sold linked to cash records.	I	Y			
	Translate sales data into shipment orders.	Sales data automatically fed back into ordering cycle.	I	Y		Good information systems running all the way through: ■ the point of sale ■ in-store inventory and ordering ■ distribution chain ■ buying and warehousing	VH
	Ability to buy at the right price & lead time.						
Get the goods into the stores on time	Cut distribution costs as a percentage of revenue from 12% to 7%.	Ability to identify and ctl store costs.	I	Y	Distribution costs by: ■ region; ■ carrier type.		
	Cut late deliveries from 30% to under 5%.	Enforcement of scheduling disciplines in distribution operation	I	Y	Delivery performance versus schedule by region & carrier		
Monitor sales and other store performance measures effectively.	Know accurately what we're really selling soon after we sold it, and be in position to act on the information.	Good information systems running all the way through: ■ the point of sale ■ in-store inventory and ordering ■ distribution chain ■ buying and warehousing	I	Y		Revenue and profit volumes overall and by: ■ item ■ square foot for each: ■ store ■ region actual versus plan, this year versus last.	VH
		Good information on and control over store performance and costs.	I	Y		Costs overall and by type for each: ■ store ■ region Staff turnover by store and grade.	H M

Table 7-1: (continued): *Trendy Product PLC – information systems strategy – analysis of Gerry Floggitt interview*

PRIORITY

In the first draft, the interviewee is invited to allocate a priority to each identified business information and support need (or to re-consider the priorities already stated). The categories are High, Medium and Low. At this stage, the priority of the business needs is required strictly from a business viewpoint, and independently of any existing or potential means for its provision. The extent to which current systems meet the needs identified will be addressed in the next stage of the work analysis, along with the cost and viability of their provision.

Interview conduct

MENTAL MODEL

Unless your organization has a very unusual business planning style, it is highly likely that the model illustrated in Figure 6-2 (page 131) will prove useful as a basis for discussion and investigation of business plans. This view is refined in Figure 7-5 below.

Figure 7-5:   *Analysis of business plans and strategies*

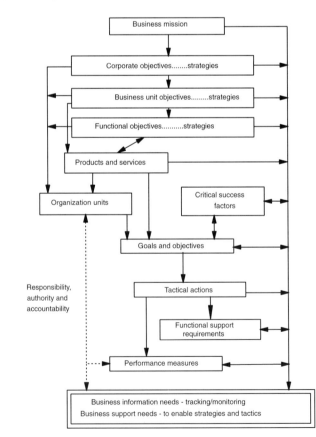

It is vital that quantified goals and other performance measures should not be considered purely from a financial standpoint, nor even from the most superficially obvious performance basis, especially when considering service organizations and public sector. The cry is often heard from reluctant candidate measures: "*You can't measure what I do*". This is usually incorrect, but is sometimes the fall-out from a ham-fisted attempt to impose inappropriate measures in a climate of fear.

Typical recent examples include:

- The Chicago Fire Department: "*Whaddya want - more fires*" – when of course a better answer may be fewer fires, as a measure of effective fire prevention;
- The Sheehey report on the UK Police, where the concern expressed by the Police Federation was that simple performance measures such as numbers of arrests and tickets issued would lead to serious distortion of police officers' behavior and priorities, and especially make it harder to maintain effective contact with the public;
- The persistent reluctance of primary and secondary school teachers in the UK to be measured is sometimes expressed, for example, as concern over excessive weight being given to external examination results. This has been exacerbated by recent poorly planned attempts to impose standardized pupil testing based on the UK National Curriculum.

Meaningful and useful performance measures must come from a top down consideration of business goals. The claim that the performance of a function is not measurable can often be countered by the argument that if this is the case, ceasing to do it at all would not be detectable, and therefore the job is a candidate for elimination!

INTERVIEW TEAM ROLES

- Two members of team, alternating roles of questioner and note taker
- Thorough pre-interview review of documentation and interviewee background
- Send relevant material before interview
- Listen, but prompt when necessary:

  - *to maintain flow*
  - *to ensure completeness*
  - *to avoid digressions*
  - *use check-list*

- Closing – be clear on next steps

There follows a detailed procedure guide for interview planning and conduct. This guide, and several papers of a similar nature which follow may appear to some readers to be rather 'Mickey Mouse' in nature, in some cases appearing so obvious as to verge on being an insult to experienced project team personnel who we would normally expect to have their own procedures for such work. I used to think this myself, until persuaded otherwise by those very same experienced personnel whom I was wary of insulting that they really wanted guide lines this specific. Ignore these papers if you wish, or improve on them. Your project teams will probably demand something very similar in the end.

Procedure for interview planning and conduct

Overall

1. Identify likely interview candidates; discuss and validate the list.

2. Hold a pre-briefing for all likely participants – either a short presentation, or an introductory letter.

3. Identify which candidates form natural groups for group interviews.

4. Build and maintain interview schedule; include scheduling of interview teams.

5. Obtain and review business planning and background materials.

For each interview

6. Send pre-interview briefing note and questionnaire

7. Re-confirm date if necessary

8. A few days before:

    -   discuss interviewee's job scope and personal style with knowledgeable advisors;
    -   adjust preparation and team if appropriate;
    -   draw up preliminary view of functional structure of the area;
    -   review any recent information, such as relevant key issues summaries from other interviews;
    -   identify any further preparation needed.

9. Interview pre-planning

Agree which interviewee(s) will get a pre-interview pack together to aid coverage and gain credibility at the interview:

    -   Document relevant parts of the Strategic and Tactical Plans on pre-interview notes;
    -   Estimate key functions and objectives, guess at KPIs and CSFs for each and document on Interview Analysis sheet;
    -   Compile list of systems owned (name, principal functions);
    -   Compile list of direct reports and their areas of responsibility.

10.   Team to assemble 30 mins before the interview:

- substitutes if anyone's missing;
- circulate and discuss pack;
- last minute updates;
- agree roles.

11.   Conduct the interview

- *One front man* – 'eyeball-to-eyeball' with interviewee, leading the questioning, and writing necessary notes e.g. main functions etc.
- One principal note-taker
- *One 'checklister'* with a blank Interview Analysis sheet, checking off at least some coverage of all sections, and asking questions to ensure coverage, as necessary and writing a few notes.

Where there are only two interviewers, the scribbler and checklister functions will have to be done by one person, who will usually need to take over the front man role to tidy up around the edges about half way through.

12.   Interview structure

a. Agree functional responsibilities and reporting lines

b. Identify objectives for each function – pursue quantification tactfully but persistently

c. Explore/determine Critical Success Factors for each objective:

- internal/external;
- able to influence.

d. Identify tracking measures for each CSF. (See the separate CSF Tutorial which follows).

e. Identify performance measures from other sources.

f. Discuss Business Information and support needs

g. Allocate preliminary priorities.

NB: If time runs desperately short during the interview, two alternative strategies can be adopted:

- Agree to postpone discussion of some functions to another session, and then complete a–g for the core functions.
- Complete a–e only, for all functions, document this and agree with the interviewee, then schedule a follow-up session to cover f and g. Interviewees often appreciate an opportunity to review and reconsider priorities especially once the main body of the analysis is stable.

13. Agree and schedule any further interviews or group sessions arising, e.g. with a group of his reports. (But keep the number of interviews reasonably low).

14. Preferably the same day: – write up and issue key issues summary. NB: This should not be 'over-worked' – it should remain brief, focused and pithy. For style, see the sample which follows.

15. Within 3 working days: – complete, review internally and issue the interview analysis. Covering note (see the sample which follows) to explain what is expected of the interviewee – i.e. review, annotate where appropriate, add priorities, approval if possible, and what will happen next – i.e. we will fix and iterate until he approves.

16. During 14 and 15, only if necessary, make follow-up call(s) to the interviewee to clarify any obscure areas. In the worst case, schedule a brief walk-through of the partially completed analysis with the interviewee to fill in gaps.

17. During interview analysis and documentation, the following apply:

    a. refer back to the key issues summary – ensure that explicit IS/IT opportunities and other 'hot topics' hot topics are reflected in explicit needs wherever appropriate;

    b. review functions and objectives against the most up to date materials available, such as tactical plan, explicit objectives statements, etc.;

    c. bear in mind that KPIs are a state of mind, not carved in stone;

    d. where common-sense, knowledge of 'best practice' or prior experience indicates issues which have not surfaced explicitly, embody them to an appropriate degree in the interpretation, highlighted so that the interviewee does not feel we're putting words into his mouth.

    e. It is quite acceptable to add a degree of creative interpretation to what the interviewee actually said. However, if you do so, it is critical that this is easy for the interviewee to identify and validate. Therefore flag such areas as follows:

        ■ Use *italics* for inferred CSFs / KPIs etc.

        ■ use *??question marks plus italics??* to identify questions, gaps or uncertainties of understanding.

18. Chase interviewee responses tactfully but firmly.

19. When the interviewee has approved the key issues summary and the full analysis, pass them forward for consolidation.

A sample pre-interview memo to interviewees

To be issued to all interviewees as soon as they have agreed a date.

This is to confirm the date and time of your interview as part of the IS/IT strategy initiative.

Date: _____

Time: _____

Location: _____

We understand that you will be accompanied by:_____ (if relevant)

Our interview team will consist of:_____

The interview will last a maximum of 1 1/2 hours (for a single interviewee), 2 hours (for a group).

The objective of the interview is to determine your most important needs for business information and support, and to ensure that we understand the rationale behind these needs.

The scope of the interview will encompass:

- your functional responsibilities;
- the goals and objectives which you are pursuing in each case;
- key constraints;
- relevant performance measures and other information needs;
- business process support needs;
- the manner in which any of the above are likely to alter in the future, and
- the factors which you believe will be most influential in bringing about such change.

In the case of business information and support needs, we need know your most important needs independently of the quality of present support. However, we would also appreciate your views on the degree to which they are met at present.

The approach which we plan to follow in the interview is illustrated in more detail by the sample questionnaire which is attached to this note. This questionnaire is intended as an aid to the structuring of the interview, and to your preparation; it should not unduly constrain the scope of the interview.

As soon as possible following the interview, we will return to you for review and approval a brief bulletin summarizing the key issues which emerged. This will be followed shortly by a fuller analysis, on which we shall also be seeing your agreement.

By ****, we plan to consolidate the results of this interview cycle into a joint **** wide statement of business information and support needs, including priorities. We will then seek consensus on this document across the **** management team, after which it will form the primary basis for:

- directing the remainder of the work of the IS/IT strategy review;
- detecting and managing future change in business intentions and needs;
- subsequent review and maintenance of ****'s IS/IT strategy and plans.

Attachment: Interview questionnaire (see Appendix III).

Estimating guidelines for interviewing

How long should it take to conduct a 2 hour interview?

- *Preparation:* $2 \times 2 = 4$ man hrs
- *Conduct:* $2 \times 2 = 4$ man hrs
- *Analysis:* $2 \times 4 = 8$ man hrs
- *Agreement/approval:* 1–3 man hrs

Rule of thumb – 3 man days per lone interviewee; 5 man days per group session

A sample memo covering key issues summary

Trendy Products Plc – IS strategy study

To: Interviewee

From: Interview team

cc:

Date:

Re: Interview on ——————————————————————

Thank you for giving us your time on ——————————————————————

We now attach our preliminary summary of the key issues which were raised in the interview. We would be glad if you would review this, and return any comments to … where appropriate.

As previously discussed, we are at present preparing a fuller analysis of the results of the interview, which will focus on derivation of information and support requirements. We will be sending you a draft of this in a few days, also for review and comment.

For examples of style of key issues summaries, see the material at the end of this chapter under 'exercises for the reader'.

Techniques for analysis and documentation of interviews with special reference to critical success factors (CSFs)

COMMUNICATION STYLE

It is important to retain the interviewees' confidence and regard by always appearing well organized and well prepared. Remember that we are asking busy people to allocate quite large units of time – one to two hours at a stretch – to the interviews, plus significant effort to review and tidy up the result. Also, we wish to raise their expectation of what will result, and avoid the 'crisis of confidence' which will result if they see no result soon.

Therefore, it is vital to reflect back to the interviewee the key issues summary (see below) within, say, two working days, regardless of the rest of the project schedule. This should be accompanied by a brief note stating that the full

Interviewee	Interview date set & memo sent	Interview					Interview analysis						Extracts taken for consolid'n	comments
		date/ time	team	date conf.	held	key issues fed back	resp. to KIS	analysis issued	an. 1st resp.	analysis final	an. appro by intvwe			

Table 7-2: *Trendy products PLC – IS strategy study – interview progress control*

interview analysis will follow within, a further two days, and that we will telephone soon after to check preliminary reactions, and to arrange follow-up discussions if needed.

KEY ISSUES FROM THE INTERVIEW

Immediately after the interview, a brief note of the key issues raised is reflected back to the interviewee for information and confirmation. These 'hot off the press' bulletins form an excellent medium for communication within the project team, and also, in summarized/integrated form, with the project steering committee. Typically there is material of great business sensitivity and confidentiality in these, and so care must be taken over security, balancing the merits of full and clear communication against the needs of real confidentiality, and also, of retention of the confidence of the interviewees. Examples of key issues summaries are shown in at the end of the chapter.

INTERVIEW ANALYSIS AND DOCUMENTATION

Following this, the interview is documented using the 'Interview Analysis Worksheet' illustrated in Table 7-1, and reviewed and approved by the interviewee in that format. Often, there may be a cycle of discussion with the interviewee, using this document as a basis, concerning precise definition of key objectives and priorities.

The formal analysis of the information gained in the interview is carried out on the basis of the following assumptions. It is assumed that the interviewee is responsible for a *business area* or *organization unit*. In response to some form of directive or terms of reference, he or she performs a number of *business functions*, which jointly contribute to the achievement of a set of objectives which have been chosen so as to assist in the execution of the business strategy of this area.

The functions may well be broken down into a series of smaller functions; these may be allocated to subordinates, who may be interviewed in a similar manner. This process may be repeated through as many levels of the organization as is productive.

Where possible, the objectives are transformed into specific quantified goals, which represent measurable factors known as *critical success factors* (CSFs), or *key performance indicators*, which can be used to assess the degree of success which is being achieved in meeting the objectives. These are tracked through *performance measures*, which lead in a simple manner to *business information needs*. It must be stressed, both in the interview, and to those conducting the analysis, that the information needs must be considered regardless of:

- whether they are met at present or not
- whether they are regarded as being capable of being met through automated means.

Priorities are assigned to these information needs in terms of their value in running the business. The degree to which they are met at present is for separate consideration.

Interview analysis tips and techniques

There are a variety of common patterns and problems which may be encountered whilst analyzing the interview. Some of these are discussed below.

1. Top management may only have one function (or at least main one). This doesn't matter, as long as you get good objectives for it.

2. It is a good idea to ensure that you have a clear picture of the functions (and the way in which they break down) before looking for CSFs etc. As we interview further levels of management, the functional breakdown of the senior managers needs to be reconciled with the stated functions of their subordinates – don't expect this to always be tidy in the first place – we may need to work at it in places.

3. Every function should have at least one tangible objective – but you may find that this was not explicitly mentioned by the interviewee in the first case. This is a clear indicator of a need to check back with the interviewee for clarification of 'foggy' areas.

    Checking back to clarify issues is quite valid – if you hit obscure patches when analyzing an interview, it's best to go on and complete as much of the rest as possible, so that you define more clearly the scope of what you need to go back for, and can get it in one go.

4. Before looking for CSFs check whether an objective has a 'direct' performance measure or information need, they often do, as in the following example. Where they do so, it is clearest to show this association by aligning the entries horizontally, prior to setting out the CSFs, e.g.:

OBJECTIVES	C.S.F.	PERF. MEASURE	B.I.N.
Achieve target profitability	–	Profitability achieved	Profit by:
			■ dept
			■ product
			■ customer
			actual vs. plan
	CSFs will follow here		

5. Each CSF should have a performance measure (except in rare cases, see below), or at least a business information need. CSFs may be external, or internal, and they may be controllable completely, partly, or not at all by

the manager. What matters is what he needs to monitor, whether it is to check how successful he is being at controlling the factor, or just in order to track it, so that he can take some other action. e.g.:

OBJECTIVE	C.S.F.	PERF. MEASURE	B.I.N.
Penetrate new markets	Ability to identify and exploit opportunities (IC)	–	General market intelligence of all kinds needed to identify (a) opportunities (b)
	Having good products for the market (I,C)	Market share achieved by products	Market share achieved by: ■ product ■ industry (c) sector (a)
	Activity of competitors	Competitors' market share	Market share by: ■ competitor ■ product type (a) ■ industry sector (d)

Notes:

(a)   CSFs flagged as external/internal and controllable/uncontrollable as a reminder of the purpose of the resulting information needs.

(b)   CSF causing a direct information need – which, incidentally, at this stage may be left very general (it is) but acts as an indicator of considerable work, probably mostly within a functional design project.

(c)   An 'active' information need – something we can directly affect

(d)   A passive information need – tracking the outcome of competitor activity. Reaction to trends of this sort must be less direct – e.g. alter our pricing, or attack another market area.

6.   Only very rarely may CSFs not have any performance measures – always think hard before accepting this. One possible example is as follows, but even here, one would expect there to be some quantified goal framed in terms of net value and/or specific counterparties:

OBJECTIVES /GOAL	C.S.F.	PERF. MEASURE	B.I.N.
Become a net borrower in the inter-bank market	Group policy changes to accommodate this goal	–	–

7.   Business information needs may reflect performance measures direct, or they may reflect a train of thought, based on the topics raised by the analysis. Where the interviewers, during subsequent analysis, find that they need to become somewhat creative, as in the example below, it is fair to do this, and to document the result, but we need to check back to the interviewee in order to check that he subscribes to the result.

OBJECTIVES	C.S.F.	PERF. MEASURE	B.I.N.
Service products efficiently at minimum cost	Availability of the right people/skills	Skill/resource levels actuals versus plan	Manpower / skills resource inventory Manpower scheduling and planning model Background info concerning availability of required skills in the job market

Sample interview analysis cover memo

To: [Interviewee, job title]
cc: [other attendees]

Information Systems Strategic Planning Project Draft Interview Analysis

[Interview reference/date]

[If appropriate, otherwise a reminder to send back comments] Thank you for your comments on the summary of key issues. [Revised edition enclosed if appropriate].

We now enclose a draft of our full analysis of the interview, and we are seeking your review and feedback on this material. The meaning and purpose of the column layout of the analysis are summarized in the attachment . Inevitably, the analysis presented embodies a degree of interpretation of the subject matter covered in the interview, and we are specifically seeking your approval of this. Items which are highlighted or which are framed as questions indicate areas where our interpretation may be most open to question or where we would appreciate further clarification. We also need you to allocate priorities to individual Information and Support needs at this stage.

- Either (for a 'gappy' analysis):
    - It is important that we capture your high priority needs accurately at this stage; we feel that there are several areas where further clarification would be beneficial, and we have arranged with your secretary a 15 to 30 minute appointment on [date/time] for this purpose. During this session we plan to:
        - walk through the material and its structure with you;
        - seek your views on priorities;
        - cover any supplementary issues which you feel are relevant.
- or (for a fairly complete version):
    - If you have any queries or need any clarification, please call [name] on the above number. Alternatively, we will be happy to spend a short time walking through this document, its purpose and uses with you if you wish.

We would appreciate your response, in terms of an annotated copy of our analysis, by [date]. Following agreement of your input in this format, we plan subsequently to compare and consolidate individual managers' requirements into one prioritized business statement. We shall then be seeking to obtain agreement as to the relative priorities and impact at this consolidated level. In order to achieve this consensus across the business it will be necessary for us to hold a group working session early towards the end of July. I shall contact your secretary to arrange the date, time and venue.

Signed: Project Director

Attachment – description of the columnar layout

Functions

These represent our understanding of each of your main areas of functional responsibility; they may not always align exactly with present organizational boundaries.

OBJECTIVES

This section records each objective pursued, both at the overall level, and in each specific area of functional responsibility. We need to know where quantified goals are set at present, or where you feel that they could be set, and the ways in which they could alter, although we do not need to know the present targets.

CRITICAL SUCCESS FACTORS (CSF)

These represent factors, of whatever nature, which may have a critical influence on success or failure in management of a function or the pursuit of objectives. These are recorded regardless of whether or not you believe that they are well controlled at present, as we wish to avoid proposing changes which may be prejudicial to areas which are already well under control. However, we are particularly interested in those CSFs which are most troublesome at present, or which may become so in the future.

- *Internal/external* – This indicates whether or not a CSF relates solely to matters internal to the Association.
- *Able to influence* – This indicates whether you are able directly to influence the CSF itself, as opposed to being limited to monitoring its behavior.

PERFORMANCE MEASURES

These are measures or indicators which would give most help in assessing:

- the performance of a function directly;
- the degree of success in attaining a business goal or objective;
- the behavior of a CSF.

Again, we are interested both in those which are satisfactorily provided today, and others which are needed to meet present or future needs, regardless of the current status of their provision.

BUSINESS INFORMATION AND SUPPORT NEEDS

In this section, we have derived what we believe are the relevant systems related information or support needs, based on our analysis of the above categories. These will be the focal point of the next stages of consolidation and consensus. We are seeking your views on the rationale behind our conclusions.

PRIORITY

Please allocate a priority to each identified business information and support need. The categories are High, Medium and Low. At this stage, the priority of the business needs is required strictly from a business viewpoint, and independently of any existing or potential means for its provision. The extent to which current systems meet the needs identified will be addressed in the next stage of our analysis, along with the cost and viability of their provision.

Alternative interviewing styles

Group interviews

This is a common and valuable variant in the process, and is illustrated in Figure 7-6.

- Some interviews are best conducted with a manager and his direct reports together
- Others may be best carried out with a group or sample of peers, e.g. branch managers
- Need more preparation and management
- Can bring significant savings in time and resource
- Pitfalls if not done carefully, or with unsuitable groups

Figure 7-6:   *Group methods*

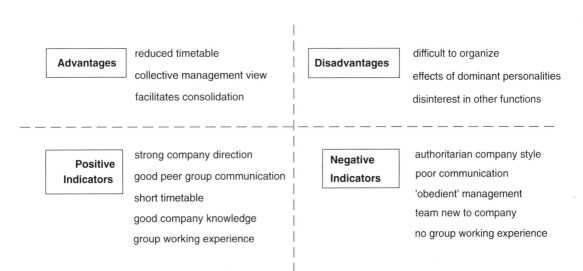

Two-stage interviews

In this process, the first interview comprises identification of functions, objectives and CSFs; these are documented and agreed, and the second session covers performance measures, information and support needs and priorities.

ADVANTAGES

- Difficult to cover full range at one interview
- Analysis partly confirmed at second interview
- Sessions are shorter
- Interviewee can prepare differently for the second interview

DISADVANTAGES

- Need twice as many sessions
- Team effort needed
- Availability of managers
- Extends timetable – but not twofold

This approach often offers a useful fallback in case of an interview which overruns in time, or in which complexity gets out of control. In such cases, follow-ups should be kept as focused as possible.

A more radical alternative – the 'single session' process

A single 2 or 3-day intensive 'off-site' process involving senior line and IS/IT managers can be most effective in a fairly close knit business of moderate complexity. It works best where there is:

- strong commitment at all levels
- a relatively simple, well defined business scope
- a small company or medium sized fairly autonomous business unit
- strong, experienced process leaders

It needs meticulous preparation, and the follow-up solutions phase is critical. There are commercially available processes based on this approach, such as Boeings 'Consensus' process. This has been used with success for more detailed tasks, such requirements definition for key systems. The approaches outlined in the addenda to chapter 3 to aid in 'fast tracking' of key stages contain elements of this type of approach.

Activities concurrent with interviews

A variety of activities need to take place concurrently with the interviews themselves:

1. Rapid communication between team members on key items picked up during interviews is vital. Key issue summaries produced immediately after the interview are especially useful as intra-team bulletins for this purpose.

2. As understanding of the business structure and allocation of manage-
    ment responsibilities grows, this is best embodied in a progressively
    developing draft of the business function hierarchy. As this may yet be
    wrong in places, it should not receive early circulation outside the team.

3. In a similar way, assembly of an early draft data entity model can be
    beneficial.

4. Interested senior management will inevitably be breathing down the
    team's collective neck asking what you've found so far, and what the
    answer is. '*Go away we haven't finished yet*' is not a tactful or productive
    response at this time. It is useful if there is a rolling list of the 'top ten'
    or so key issues identified to date. If some of these require management
    action, so much the better. If they get given tasks to do, they may stop
    bothering us until we have something more constructive to say!
    Seriously though, these informal dialogues, if used constructively, can be
    of immense value in maintaining management confidence, and in
    initiating management action on items which would otherwise impede
    progress. They also help the team maintain focus.

The post interview process

Analyze interviews and verify results

- Interviewing teams must keep up with documentation
- Summary of key points next day
- Briefing bulletins within team
- Follow-up telephone calls or brief discussions on key points
- Documented analysis to interviewee within 4 working days, with agreed
  deadline for turn-round
- Firm up on derived needs and priorities during the verification cycle
- Acknowledge and action his/her comments
- Iterate until all are satisfied

Prepare for the consolidation process

At thus stage, our objectives are to:

- obtain consensus across the business on key needs and priorities;
- develop 'critical mass' of support for the most important initiatives;
- achieve an agreed basis on which to move forwards.

The key product around which this process centres is the consolidated
statement of business information needs (CBINS), whose assembly is discussed

below. The process flow in its production is illustrated in Figure 7-7, and its format is illustrated in Figure 7-8.

Figure 7-7:   *Process flow to derive information and support needs*

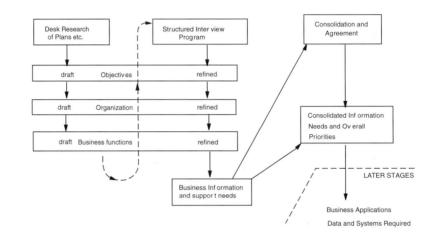

Derive and consolidate the business information and support needs statement

Obtain agreement and commitment from management

OBJECTIVES

- Consolidate interview results
- Collate into related groups
- Derive and validate key performance indicators (KPIs)
- Obtain overall priorities by consensus process
- Outline business case
- Assign sponsor for each group

PRE-REQUISITE MATERIALS FOR CONSOLIDATION

- Categories for analysis:

  - main business areas
  - Defined team responsibilities
  - levels of functions
  - Agreed interview analyses – a critical mass of stable material

Products of the consolidation process

We now have to produce a 'Consolidated business information and support needs Statement'. Most project team members quickly lose patience with this mouthful, and the acronym CBINS has become commonly used in its place. We will do so from here on. The overall structure of a CBINS is shown in Figure 7-8; a realistically populated example was shown in chapter 5 Table 5-4.

Figure 7-8:   *Consolidated statement of business information and support needs*

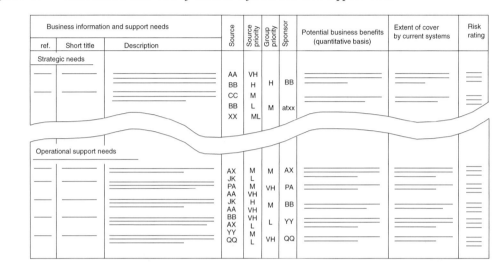

Information needs consolidation – getting started

Like many tasks, building a CBINS is a lot easier if you have a plausible one to start with. Building a CBINS for the first time in an organization is the hardest, especially if you have no example of style from the same type of industry to work from.

The first step for a 'green-fields' CBINS is the overall structure. As illustrated in the typical 'shell' for a CBINS in Figure 7-9, I have found it most useful to start with a set of categories or pigeon holes where the (logical) the columns are based on broad business functional areas, and the (logical) rows are based on the layers from the Anthony triangle which we met in Chapter 1. There is no doctrinal reason for this: the goals are to have a sensible topology whilst consolidating, so as to facilitate juxtaposing similar needs so as to prompt creative consolidation. It is also useful to have a structure which lends itself to partitioning of the work-space in a manner which is sensible in business terms. As the consolidation proceeds, the finished document typically retains the Anthony triangle rows as major partitions, whereas the association with business functional areas tends to become less hard and fast as cross-business area consolidation proceeds. However, the identities of the relevant business function(s) should be retained, however, as keys for traceability and for selection in preparing sub-sets for management group review. Some typical partitioning categories are suggested below:

CBINS ROWS – BASED ON LEVELS OF INFORMATION NEED

- *Strategic*   ■ *Planning and Analysis*   ■ *Operational Control*
- *Transaction Systems*   ■ *Administrative support Systems*

COLUMNS – FOR THE ORGANIZATION OVERALL

- Overall planning and control
- Services:
    - *personnel*   ■ *premises*   ■ *IS functions*   ■ *Finance*

COLUMNS – FOR EACH BUSINESS AREA – BUT BEWARE TOO MUCH FRAGMENTATION

- *Marketing*   ■ *Product development*   ■ *Sales*
- *Manufacturing*   ■ *Distribution*   ■ *Customer Relationship*
- *Purchasing*

Figure 7-9:   *Business information and support needs - indicative set of categories for consolidation*

Typical business functional areas

Information level	Plan & control	Finance	Resources and infrastr.	Customer rel'ship	Product/ service def'n	Marketing	Selling	Distrib'n/ delivery	Product support	Risk Mg'mt & Control
Strategic										
Planning & analysis										
Monitoring & control										
Transaction										
Operational support										

The consolidation process – big bang or incremental?

Still considering the most difficult 'green fields' case, over the years I have tried several approaches to populating the initial version of the CBINS. The two commonest approaches are 'big bang' and incremental.

BIG BANG

- Quasi DP process - allocate keys, then a big sort
- Needs all interviews in a single file, one row pre stated need
- Serious risk of being swamped by sheer volume, loss of business focus
- May gain insights from unexpected juxtapositions
- More automatable - time scale can be short - 'wide coal face'

This approach has great appeal, as it offers benefits of speed and automatability. However, I haven't found a way to make it work effectively yet - there usually arises a mass of complexity and interpretation issues, and there is a risk of the project team becoming preoccupied with the process, rather than with business and IS strategy.

INCREMENTAL

- Take one 'good' interview, which will serve as a starter, and 'drop' it into the CBINS format
- Take each of the remaining interviews in turn and process as increments

This approach is more 'linear'; it takes longer, and involves more manual effort. However, it seems to foster a better sense of focus, and it is also good for demonstrating the subsequent process of CBINS maintenance. Work can proceed initially in parallel; if time is short, several concurrent starts can be made in well-separated business areas. But they must be combined quite quickly, otherwise full cross-functional consolidation will not be achieved.

The consolidation processes – summary

- Define analysis structure and categories
- Define business areas, business functions, levels of detail
- Allocate information and support needs from approved interview and other analysis documents
  - manual – *reference cards*
  - computer supported – *spreadsheet, database, free text analyzer*
- Consolidate/de-duplicate – free text analyzer
  - *clarify descriptions*   *note cross-references*
  - *derive key performance indicators (KPIs) and preliminary priorities*

It's time for more about KPIs.

Key Performance Indicators (KPIs)

What they are, why they are needed

- The derivation of KPIs was alluded to in the lower section of Figure 6-2 in chapter 6, and in Figure 7-5.
- Many information needs may be:
  - *closely similar*   *unrealistic to produce directly*
- There may just be too many needs stated
- KPIs are a derived composite of several measures:
  - *key information only*   *not too many*

- *derivable from the available data*
- *present users with a controllable environment*
- KPIs are a compromise, and may need to change
- Judicious use of KPIs can help to condense complex CBINS further.

KPIs – support and usage

KPIs need to relate to the manager's decision making process

- What is it *really* telling me?
- What does deviation from the plan or norm mean – is it necessarily 'good' or 'bad'?
- Is the KPI behavior linear, or are there thresholds?
- Can it be 'rigged' by those being monitored – how easily, how can I tell?
- How will being monitored by the KPIs in question influence the overall environment and the user's behavior – how can these change be monitored?

Relation to responsibility level

- What decisions does the manager need to make:
  - *how fast?*   *in what priority sequence?*   *on what criteria?*
- What information is needed to make them?
- What questions will be asked when a KPI deviation is noticed?
- What information is needed to answer them – what are the sources?
- What form of diagnostic support is needed?

Process for formulating Key Performance Indicators

- Identify the decisions being made
- Investigate the nature of the decision making environment:
  - *pressures*   *time-span*   *threshold/trigger values*
  - *hierarchy of needs*   *what a change in value means*
  - *chain of decision logic, and associated secondary information needs*
- Assess the range of information required:
  - *scope*   *time period covered*   *degree of accuracy/tolerance*
- Investigate the decision making process:
  - acceptable time lag for effective reaction
  - deductive process and criteria in arriving at a management decision
  - determine the nature of the reporting baseline
  - assess potential impact of KPIs on the decision making process

- Conduct sensitivity analysis – impact of inaccuracies or time delays
- Agree the definition of a significant deviation from plan or norm, and how it is recognized
- Develop appropriate presentation format(s):
  - *paper, screen, sound etc.*   ▪ *table*   ▪ *graphs*   ▪ *lights/alarm bells*
- Work through the layers of supporting process and information

KPI health warnings

- Can affect behavior of system and of people:
  - *need meta-KPIs*   ▪ *will need to be altered.*
- Need a user guide – *"What do I do when the index goes over nn?"*

Consolidated needs – the agreement processes

Now we have a first draft CBINS, all we have to do is to present it to management and obtain their agreement! This may sound easy, but potential for failure always lurks close at hand, and we must be very careful. Success at this stage is critical to the entire IS/IT planning process. An agreed CBINS, supported by committee sponsors constitutes an essential foundation both for the remainder of the planning cycle, and as a baseline for future change management.

If we have gained the respect of interviewees during the interviewing and analysis process, and if we have handled the concerns and challenges presented during the process well, this can be a straightforward and stimulating process. Typically, though, there will be pockets of concern, reluctance or even outright hostility among our interviewees. Hopefully, these will be balanced by areas where key individuals have begun to sign up strongly to what they perceive as a genuine opportunity to dramatically improve their business performance through better focused systems.

Experience has shown that to get a reaction, even of hostility or deep concern, (although genuine support and interest is best) is far preferable to being ignored. Widespread perception of IS/IT strategy as being irrelevant to the business is a key, albeit common, symptom of deep malaise, either of the existing IT operation or of the senior management team, or both. It should have been picked up at Phase 0, scoping study time, but if it was not, or if it was ignored then, it must now be addressed as a matter of top priority before proceeding with the CBINS process.

We may well be at fault. Doubters and opponents usually have valid concerns, which we may well have not grasped straight away. They must be understood and negotiated or accommodated before we proceed. Apparent opponents may care passionately about having certain business needs met, or existing shortfalls rectified. They may have become jaundiced and cynical as a result of past IS/IT failures, but if they come to see the IS/IT planning initiative as a vehicle for overcoming the problems, they can become the strongest supporters. No recipe book approach can guarantee success here – we need to use all of our skills, and experience, and must remain alert and open minded as to real needs and motivations.

Do not necessarily expect 100% success – many organizations have one or two 'rogue elephants' who are valued for their business focus and forceful persona, rather than for their open mindedness, charm or charisma. In extremis, we may have to negotiate a truce with someone, rather than risk a fatal mauling. In any case, serious intransigence at Board level is really matter for the Steering group, and must be escalated rapidly to that level, (but framed in as objective a manner as the circumstances permit).

Stages in the agreement process

1. Circulate relevant sections of the first draft CBINS, supported by appropriate briefing materials.

2. Schedule and hold a group working session for each business area (allow for specific follow-up sessions on key topics).

3. In the group session, undertake overall assessment of the group's priorities.

    -   agree the full analysis;
    -   agree overall priorities;
    -   review impacts of priorities, including the need to cross-functional priorities;
    -   review and confirm derived KPIs;
    -   identify key sources of benefit for each agreed need;
    -   identify candidate sponsors.

4. Following the group session, work with the business sponsors in building the business cases.

A general purpose process for prioritization and consensus

This process may be applied wherever there are several peer parties or groups who need to agree on a joint set of priorities. In particular, it is relevant to:

-   group and overall consensus on CBINS priorities;
-   application needs priorities;
-   application and technical project priorities;
-   allocation of human resources and funds.

Assumptions

1. Requisite business or technical analysis has been done, and the items to be prioritized are clearly identified.

2. The participating sponsors or fund-holders have assigned their individual priorities (H/M/L) and have identified and quantified anticipated benefits.

3. Costings are available.

Approach/characteristics

1. Business driven.

2. Efficient in elapsed time and management resource.

3. Repeatable – analysis can quickly be re-worked if inputs, budgets or criteria change.

4. Includes all inputs – tactical as well as strategic, significant enhancements as well as new developments.

5. Facilitated by independent parties, but carried out by participants (co-ordinators) who represent the interests of an area. Co-ordinators are responsible for delivering a joint set of priorities for their area; they may cascade this process downwards if they see fit.

6. Two-pass process:

    - *rough-cut, parochial*   - *systematic, cross-area, with impact analysis*

7. Consensus process to obtain agreement.

8. Specific scoring/ranking algorithms can be selected to be more or less rigorous/pragmatic.

9. Supported by quantitative evidence and analysis.

10. Results go under a formal change control process.

The process

1. Agree goals and identify co-ordinators for each area

2. Assemble pack of raw materials:

    - current systems/project status, including quality assessments;
    - any relevant previous strategic and tactical plans, including short term fixes and significant current system enhancements;
    - results of underlying analysis, e.g. business or technical requirements plus agreed priorities for current plan and new entries, quantified costs and benefit profiles;

- key constraints and dependencies, including business timings, budget limits etc.

3. Identify clearly the scope of each co-ordinator's interest, and the preparation which they need to do.

4. Invite participants to briefing session with introductory note – each bring your up to date 'top ten' hit list of priorities.

5. Hold briefing session for all participants:

   - the whole pack to each coordinator;
   - walk through contents;
   - make clear what is expected (see 6) by when;
   - ensure they understand the process, including ranking algorithms, and are committed to it;
   - round robin discussion of key priorities – basis for cross-area negotiations;
   - establish contact points in each area;
   - set up an impartial 'referee' group to aid the process and moderate in disputes.

6. First prioritization period – 2 weeks 'off-line'. Each coordinator develops his/her area's 'nearly ideal' delivery sequence, with options if necessary, taking account only of very hard limits and dependencies. Consultation as necessary within his/her area. Cross-area negotiation at their discretion. Documentation of rationale, impacts.

7. Coordinator inputs are consolidated and circulated without modification to all, with briefing note stating what is expected – come to second prioritization with the following, and the authority/capability to negotiate compromises:

   - impact/dependency assessment from your viewpoint;
   - priority conflicts/clashes;
   - suggested approaches to resolve.

8. Second prioritization – plenary session – be prepared for 'blood on the carpet'. Detailed walkthrough top down, of priorities. On-the-spot exploration of impacts, dependencies, clashes, options and compromises. Session continues until all high and medium priorities are placed in a joint list. Referee team present (essential), helping to ensure completeness. On-the-spot help with quantified ranking via a computerised spreadsheet plus driver.

9. Agree and publish the results.

Conduct of the group 'consensus' process

This process can be applied to initial group interviews, and/or the subsequent consolidation/consensus process. Organization and preparation are critical.

1. Identify a suitable environment – eliminate interruptions.

2. Allow typically requires 1/2 day per session.

3. For the sessions:

    ▪ prepare relevant briefing and materials;
    ▪ allow time for inter-session analysis.

4. Provide for effective leadership of the session.

5. Arrange sufficient clerical and documentation support is needed on-line in the session.

Formulating business cases

The business case for building an information system – or for any other form of significant expenditure for that matter – is critical. As soon as business sponsors begin to identify themselves, they should be encouraged to think in business case terms – i.e. to consider how best to compete for funding and resources to have their needs met.

Business cases do not emerge ready made, they develop and are refined at several stages of the IS/IT planning process. We will re-visit the process of business case development at several points, but especially in Chapters 11 and 14, but the process starts here. There follow below an outline template for a business case, and a very simple approach to assessment of benefits and risk. Parker and Benson, (1989) offer valuable techniques, under the banner of 'Information Economics' for refining this approach.

Outline template for a business case

Key questions:

▪ What is recommended?
▪ Why should we do it – what will it do for the business?
▪ What happens if we don't do it – what are the alternatives?
▪ How much will it cost?
▪ When will you deliver it?
▪ How will it be achieved?

What? – Title and one paragraph. description of what is proposed.

Cross-references to acknowledged business needs, e.g. CBINs or other specific user sponsored initiatives.

Why? – Business rationale for the development – qualitative

Business benefits – costs/headcount saved

- *risks controlled or losses avoided*   - *revenue or profit improvement*

Impact/risk of not doing it

Alternatives considered, and why they were rejected.

How much? – Total costs, split by:

- *internal staff*
- *external contractors*
- *software licenses or services*
- *equipment*

When? – By date:

- *£ spend, by*   - *£ amount of benefit delivered*   - *deliverable*

How? – Who will do it

- With what training or other purchased assistance
- With what technology
- Key risks and control measures
- What are the dependencies, impacts and side effects, and how are they to be controlled.

A method for assessment of benefits and risk

1. Benefits

1.1   Identify significant business benefits which the sponsors can quantify, and which they believe they can deliver if the need is met. Suggested categories include but are not limited to:

a. reduction of costs;

b. improvement of service quality;

c. enhancement of income revenue.

1.2   Allocate points B based on total value: Points

a. up to £100,000 p.a.   0

b. over £100,000 p.a., up to £250,000 p.a.   1

c. over £250,000 p.a., up to £500,000 p.a.   2

d. over £500,000 p.a., up to £1M p.a.   3

e. over £1M p.a., up to £2M p.a.   4

    f. over £2M p.a.   5

2. RISKS

2.1   Identify risks, impact and potential business or market share loss which may result if the need is not met within, say, 2 years.

2.2   Allocate points R based on total value:Points

    a. up to £100,000 p.a.   0
    b. over £100,000 p.a., up to £250,000 p.a.   1
    c. over £250,000 p.a., up to £500,000 p.a.   2
    d. over £500,000 p.a., up to £1M p.a.   3
    e. over £1M p.a., up to £2M p.a.   4
    f. over £2M p.a. or any severe impact   5

(e.g. audit qualification)

3. URGENCY

3.1   Allocate an urgency rating U:*Points*

    a. must be done immediately, e.g. legal compliance   3
    b. must be done within 12 months   2
    c. needed within 2 years   1

4. CALCULATE AN OVERALL RATING $= U * (B + R)$

5. Banding

5.1   The maximum score is 30 points. CBINs can be grouped into one of three bands, according to the number of points scored, as follows:

    a. over 26   Very high; the topmost priority;
    b. 16 to 25   High;
    c. 8 – 15   Medium;
    d. under 8   Low; unlikely to be considered.

A sample cover note to CBINS near final drafts

To:	[sponsor]
From:	[Project Manager]
cc:	[co-sponsor, co attendee]
Date:	*******
Subject:	IS/IT Strategy Project Review of consolidated business requirements on ********** at *******

Following this review and the associated agreements concerning sponsorship and priorities, we now enclose:

1.   A brief extract from the consolidated requirements document, which shows, in priority order, those items which you have agreed to sponsor.

2.   For reference, a copy of the complete consolidated business requirements document from which your extract has been taken. This embodies all items agreed in subsidiary working groups, which have been grouped by priority.

Notes about the enclosed documents

1.   Where your initials are in brackets means that you will be acting as sponsor, but as requested your Board director's name has been listed as well.

2.   Where priorities were set in more than one working group, the highest has been presented.

3.   Where requested, there have been changes to the original definitions and groupings of business needs.

4.   You may have been asked to sponsor items by a working group which you did not attend.

For these reasons, it is important that you validate the results presented under item 1 above. Please contact us immediately if there are items with which you do not agree.

Short-term sponsorship responsibilities

We now plan to assist you as follows:

1.   Identify and quantify business benefits:

- identification by [date];
- refinement and quantification by ****;

2.   Ascertain business views as to the quality of coverage and development potential offered by current systems (by [date]).

3.   Seek to exploit any opportunities which there may be for very early delivery of simple solutions to high priority needs (by [date]).

Subsequent activities

Subsequently, you should expect to become involved in the following processes as part of the project:

1.   Overseeing the assessment and selection of candidate systems solutions, and their subsequent grouping into project proposals.

2.   Negotiations as to how best to reflect business priorities in project phasing and sequencing — taking account of business and technical constraints and dependencies.

3.   Translation of business cases, initially into support for systems solutions, and then into specific development projects. Specifically, we anticipate that sponsors will take the lead in providing the benefits elements of the business case; we will provide options (and costs) for systems solutions. Overall integration into a financial case will be a joint activity.

We have not copied this material to other managers who were interviewed with you, but please feel free to involve any of them in this process. We will call you in a few days to determine how best to progress this work with you.

Useful answers to awkward questions from sponsors

This section addresses a number of the more awkward questions – taken from real situations – asked by interviewees at some stage during the interview/ analysis process, or further down the track during the formulation of business cases. Such questions generally represent something of a cry for help, and frequently present an opportunity (at times hard to recognize admittedly) to sell to the interviewee the real benefits of the study and of his/her active participation in it. The sample answers suggested should be treated as a starting point for customization and creative embellishment, rather than the last word.

WHY DO YOU WANT TO KNOW ALL ABOUT THE BUSINESS, WHEN IT'S IT THAT YOU'RE SUPPOSED TO BE LOOKING AT?

'IT' in this sense means both the systems (IS) to meet business needs and the technology (IT) which they run on. The systems which we implement must be driven by the needs of the business; the technology can then be selected and configured to meet the systems and business needs and volumes. Doing it the other way round – technology first – is wrong because we would be trying to impose solutions to problems which we didn't understand. In the past, elsewhere, this has frequently led to failure to meet business needs and/or excessive IS/IT costs.

We don't expect you to design systems, but we do need to know from you as much as possible about your current and future business needs and intentions so that we can ensure that the systems solutions which we recommend are positioned to meet those needs. If we only talk with you about systems, there is a risk that your expectations may be limited by what has been offered before, or what you have seen done by customers or competitors.

In certain areas, such as the ability to offer systems which can support the clients' operations, the Corporation's IS/IT capability can constitute a real competitive edge. We need to know the business background to such areas to ensure that this edge is maintained and heightened, and to help identify new opportunities, perhaps in unexpected areas.

WHY DO I NEED TO GET INVOLVED?

Who else do you trust to tell us about your key business needs and priorities? Please, can we see them, too?

WHAT HAPPENS IF I DON'T PARTICIPATE?

If you don't participate now, your views are unlikely to be represented effectively in the next stages when we are pulling together the overall systems vision and strategy for the next 3 to 5 years. Views and priorities from other participants will pre-empt yours. Although you may be able to continue to play 'catch-up', and meet some of your needs on a 'cottage industry' basis, it will take more of your time and attention in the end, the results will be less satisfactory and less resilient to future change, and the Corporation as a whole will suffer from having systems which are not cohesive, and which are hard to adapt quickly.

WHAT IS EXPECTED OF ME?

1. Represent your current and future business needs and intentions as clearly as possible; ensure that your key line reports do the same.

2. Participate in the cross-functional discussions aimed at attaining consensus on the joint set of needs and priorities. Ensure that the results of these sessions accurately reflect your views and needs.

3. Help to construct sound business cases (see below) for having your business needs met.

4. As recommended systems solutions emerge, and are framed as specific projects, ensure that you are clear that the solutions will deliver the key business benefits which you are seeking. Insist on understanding the proposals in business terms, and on the reasons for rejection of alternatives which you might have preferred being clear to you. Don't put up with any technical 'mumbo-jumbo'.

WHY SHOULD WE BOTHER? – IT'S ALWAYS BEEN OK UP TO NOW

This question tends not to arise in a large, mature organization, where there is usually an extensive history of information systems lagging badly behind business needs, interspersed by partially successful efforts to overhaul them. Instead, another question arises – see below.

- *For a small-to-medium sized, fast growing organization:*

The Corporation has grown very quickly, and needs to continue to grow. It has now outstripped the capability both of its management structure and its existing information systems to sustain this further growth rate. Both need a major overhaul.

The current generation of systems have been assembled over the years on a pragmatic basis, and although they have served your needs to date very well, in recent times this has only been through increasingly strenuous efforts and improvisation by the IT department. The recent scoping review showed clearly that what potential there was in many current systems to go on adapting on an ad-hoc basis to changing business needs is rapidly being used up, and that very soon the current IS/IT basis for supporting the business could become a straitjacket.

There is time now, before the straitjacket starts to hurt too much, to re-establish an open-ended systems platform for the next stages of business growth. If this opportunity is missed, the risks of systems limitations cramping future business development and competitive agility are very real, and will increase sharply.

PREVIOUS ATTEMPTS AT SETTING IS/IT STRATEGY TOOK TOO LONG, WERE TOO ESOTERIC, AND DIDN'T PRODUCE RESULTS OF LASTING VALIDITY. WHAT'S DIFFERENT THIS TIME?

1. The process in use is top-down, business-driven. There is strong commitment from senior management to its succeeding. Previous efforts were driven partly from within IT, and dwelt heavily on IT based analysis methods. The previous results were insufficiently relevant to the business.

2. Success isn't optional – IS/IT are increasingly critical to competitive success and even survival.

3. Previous efforts attempted to secure commitment to long term static strategies. Strategy doesn't mean long term lock-in. It means the capability to adapt and change; to survive the unexpected.

4. The methods now in use are proven. They are aimed at yielding a business oriented result within a realistic time-scale.

5. Part of the outcome of this process will be clear organizational and procedural provision for the IS/IT planning process to be effectively integrated with the business and product planning cycles.

6. There will be effective provision for plan monitoring and maintenance:

    ▪ on a regular and exceptional basis;

    ▪ based on changes detected to business needs;

    ▪ by means of an efficient process, based on largely automated documentation.

(WHEN FACED WITH A FORMAL INTERVIEW ANALYSIS.) THIS IS TOO COMPLICATED AND TOO DETAILED. IT SHOULD BE SIMPLE AND EASY, WITH A FEW KEY FACTORS IDENTIFIED.

This is an (imperfect) attempt to derive from your functional responsibilities and strategic goals and objectives the information and support which you need to fulfil them. We need your help to focus on the high priority items and issues; the lesser priorities can be ignored.

The business rationale behind the high priority items needs to be recorded, because it may alter, and we will then need to assess the impact of such a change. Also you may need to justify your priorities to your colleagues when competing for funding for systems projects.

We need to be specific in these statements, because considerable investment in systems may be required to meet the needs, and this will need to be justified.

WHY DO I NEED TO ALLOCATE PRIORITIES TO ITEMS WHICH ARE OK ALREADY?

We are looking at all systems, current as well as future, and the basis for their features. When we allocate priorities for systems enhancement or replacement, we must not throw out the baby with the bath water, so we must ensure that all of the important existing system features are retained across any recommended changes. So we need to know about them. This applies particularly to features of any local PC systems which you may have had built. In some cases, these indicate key needs which should be supported in the future on a consistent basis by core systems.

WHY SHOULD I SPONSOR THINGS WHICH THE SYSTEMS CAN'T DO?

How do you know they can't? IT capabilities and costs are changing so fast that some things which were impossible or too costly even a few years ago are now relatively straightforward. If you don't tell us about the needs, we can't even begin to consider the potential for their automation. Telephone Banking, as offered by First Direct, is an example from the recent past. The ability to store and manipulate large volumes of document images is another.

WHAT CAN I DELEGATE?

- *To us*

1.   To devise and recommend systems solutions to meet your needs.

2.   To assemble the IS/IT cost line items of the business cases.

- *To your line reports*

1.   To support your statements of high level needs and direction with more specific statements of what they need to help them achieve your goals.

2.   To negotiate across the business with their peers as to the relative priorities for meeting these needs.

HOW DO I BUILD A BUSINESS CASE FOR WHAT I NEED DONE?

Business cases for development projects will follow the Corporate standard. Their assembly will be a joint task. The project team will contribute cost line items, and you will be responsible for identification of business benefits.

State as clearly as possible the business benefits which you expect to be able to achieve if the relevant information or support needs are met. It is important that these be quantified wherever possible – money is more persuasive than rhetoric. We can offer criteria which will assist in the identification and quantification of benefits, but you will be ultimately responsible for delivering the benefits themselves once you have the systems support.

HOW WILL CONFLICTS OVER PRIORITY FOR SYSTEM DEVELOPMENTS OR ENHANCEMENTS BE RESOLVED?

During the next few weeks, we plan to run a series of sessions in which the emerging set of joint needs and views is reviewed, initially within business areas, and then across the whole of the business. In this way, we expect to arrive at stable consensus as to the relative priorities of needs requiring strategic systems solutions. By the end of this stage, we plan to have preliminary IS/IT costs identified for meeting these needs, and it will then become apparent to what extent there is conflict over IS/IT development resource or capital expenditure. Where this conflict cannot be met by increasing the rate of spend, then we expect that the sponsors involved will negotiate a resolution on the basis of the relative merits of the business cases. Where agreement cannot be reached, the conflict will need to be escalated, up to Board level where necessary.

WHAT HAPPENS WHEN BUSINESS NEEDS CHANGE IN THE FUTURE?

We will be recommending that there be established an IT Steering Committee, composed of Board members and selected senior managers, who will be responsible for reviewing on both a regular basis and, exceptionally, on an ad hoc basis, the degree of achievement versus the IS/IT strategic plan, and the extent to which the plan is still in line with business goals, needs and intentions.

We envisage that this Committee will be aware of (or responsible for formulating) current business plans and intentions, as well knowing about as imminent changes, both to the plans themselves and to factors affecting them, such as the competitive climate, and will review these against the joint statement of business information and support needs produced by the current IS/IT strategy study. The Committee's work will need to be supported by a team who will:

- monitor changes to business plans and the resulting needs;
- maintain the joint statement of business information and support needs;
- examine the impact of any changes on IS/IT strategic and tactical plans;
- determine where changes are needed to the plans, develop proposed solutions and recommend changes to the IT Steering Committee where appropriate.

This team will need to know their way around the IS/IT strategy working papers and files, but will probably only be constituted for the limited period needed to review and amend the plans.

HOW DO I CONTROL THE EFFECTS ON SYSTEMS AND PROJECTS? WHAT HAPPENS WHEN OTHER COMPETING BUSINESS PRIORITIES THREATEN MY NEEDS?

1. Ensure that your business area is represented effectively on the IT Steering Committee.

2. Ensure that you understand the business reasons for any proposed changes to the IS/IT strategic or tactical plans.

3. Have your line reports do their homework on the impact, risks, costs and benefits of any changes to the plan.

4. Where appropriate, press for re-distribution of funds or variation in system development priorities so as to ensure that the interests of your business area are furthered.

GETTING AND RETAINING BUSINESS: 'BUY-IN'

Buy-in and commitment from business sponsors are only achieved with care, and their retention is not guaranteed; it has to be constantly re-earned. Even when well established, they can easily slip away if we are not alert to the risks. Management attention is easily distracted, especially if we are seen as lethargic, or if we appear to have taken our eye off the ball. Overriding business priorities or crises can arise which will divert the attention of even the most committed sponsor.

For all of these reasons, we will sometimes have to re-open the dialogue with key business areas, e.g. after a reorganization or other distraction.

At this time, it is critical to have a plan and a focused approach. One such is set out below.

A template for business 'buy-in' sessions

Structure

1.   Planning

2.   Preparation for buy-in sessions

3.   Session follow-ups

4.   Integration of strategic and tactical plans

OBJECTIVES

1.   Establish or re-establish contact and interest on the part of senior and middle management in:

- their high priority information needs;
- the business benefits of having them met;
- the systems initiatives needed to meet them.

2.   Identify cases where business needs and priorities have changed since the interviews or previous cycles.

3.   Ensure that sponsors are identified and committed, and that they understand what they need to do to fund and champion their projects.

4.   Determine the work needed to

- respond to changes and current management priorities;
- re-assess costs and benefits of recommended projects;
- finalize and launch the revised IS/IT plans.

5.   Agree the way forward needed to re-focus the strategic IS/IT plans on the current and likely future business needs.

Planning

1. Resourcing before, during and after buy-in sessions.

2. Scheduling of the first key buy-in sessions.

3. Most effective approach for each key session.

4. Most effective use of specialists' time.

Preparation

1. Schedule first buy-in sessions – senior management diaries are hard to get into – and work back from these dates.

2. Review CBINs and recommended projects internally for obvious changes since last contact; modify as appropriate (high level only). Note where projects are already under way, or where tactical plan projects are now committed.

3. For high priority projects only, draw up outline synopses if not already present (see the pro-forma template in Figure 3-17 in chapter 3).

4. Partition CBINs and projects into packs for each buy-in session group.

5. Circulate packs to group attendees in good time with covering briefing note.

6. Agree all session participants and roles.

Session Structure

1. Introduction (should be summarized in the packs covering note):

   - brief, targeted verbal summary of the key messages to date;
   - review of fall-out (impact on attitudes and events since last contact);
   - 'W.I.I.F.M.' (What's in it for me?);
   - what business sponsors need to do now to realize the benefits of the IS/IT plan;
   - what happens if I participate in the buy-ins?
   - what happens if I don't participate?

2. Summarize intended results from the buy in sessions:

   - sponsorship commitments
   - issues
   - responsibilities
   - business case development
   - agreed actions
   - time scales

3. Work through CBINs and project synopses, raising/clearing issues. *(most of time here)*

4.   Agreement of next steps – actions, dates and responsibilities.

Session Groupings

Define based on business functional responsibilities. **NB:** All sessions to include relevant functional MIS.

Follow up

1.   Seek to ensure that actions from the buy-in sessions cover:

   - revisions to be made to CBINs and/or project definitions;
   - actions to resolve any outstanding issues;
   - clear identification of business sponsorship, and a revised priority rating;
   - (items without sponsors or high priorities will not get done)
   - sponsor responsibilities for business case preparation.

2.   Re-plan and allocate resources to carry out actions agreed.

3.   Issue preliminary revised CBINs and project synopses partitioned by sponsor for review and approval.

4.   Parallel to 2:

   - carry out agreed actions/work on projects/business cases;
   - analyze revised project prerequisites and dependencies and negotiate with sponsors as necessary;
   - review and action impact on tactical plans

5.   Agree dates, resourcing and funding of work with sponsors.

6.   Carry out IT Department internal work needed to develop full manpower, computer and network resource plans.

7.   In due course, issue and maintain revised combined strategic and tactical plan.

What we do with the results

- The consolidated statement of business information and support needs ('CBINS') acts as the 'charter' for the IS and IT strategy setting and maintenance process.
- CBINS and sponsorship commitments acts as the focus for sponsorship and business case development.
- Analysis of CBINS yields detailed material for building and cross-checking the information architectures – see chapter 8.

- Especial focus on the business process model – insights from interviews and CBINS are key to deriving a clean, general:
  - business function hierarchy;
  - business process schematic.
- The sight of business priorities offers the first opportunity to identify and pursue urgent, high value 'quick fixes'.

Exercises for the reader

Based on the available interview materials (below) from the 1991/92 review, plus the Floggitt interview in Table 7-1:

1. Consider how you would amend the consolidated statement of business information needs (CBINS), in Table 5-4 (page 100) in the light of the 1991/92 review materials.

2. Prepare a list of follow-up issues arising.

3. Plan the conduct of the new IS Strategy review now to be carried out, including the interview process and style, and the subsequent consensus process needed to achieve overall agreement to the CBINS by Trendy's senior management team.

4. Prepare for interviews with Bill Jones and Gerry Floggitt as part of the new study.

Bill Jones – key issues summary – October 1992

GOALS

1. UK base – getting it in shape as a sound basis for the push into Europe. Break even in 1992, back to 15% profit on turnover in 1993.

2. Europe – it is a matter of survival to extend the base of operations to a broader European profile. The Group split between UK and rest of Europe is no longer appropriate.

3. Re-building management team:
   - distribution – replace the contractor; hire a strong GM;
   - marketing – start doing it!
   - sales;
   - IS/IT function – now covered with Barnes joining.

4. Cost cutting – basic housekeeping spend is still too high it is a threat to our short term survival.
   - we must save/strengthen good areas;

- prune weak areas very hard.

5.   Meet the required contribution to Group profitability and internal service delivery.

6.   Ensure that our expectations from Group are met:

- functional support – e.g. expertise in areas where we are weak;
- marketing;
- coordination of activities and business with multi-national customers;
- capital provision.

ACHIEVEMENT AGAINST PLANS

1.   UK retail – Jones was the architect of the venture into retail. Unfortunately, it has proved a cash sink, rather than a generator so far. We thought we had the proven expertise – Floggitt joined in Jan '91 – but he hasn't delivered yet. He quite rightly points out that it was the worst possible timing re the UK economy – but he took it on. The Group now wants Floggitt for a European role, but I need him to prove he can finish the job he came to do first. Retail also needs heavy investment in sites and a common set of systems and processes – a 'template' for flagship stores – this sort of capital is hard to provide at present.

2.   Distribution – this is bogged down by poor service. We need to fire the contractor, get a larger, more professional outfit in – or maybe two and have them compete. This needs a procurement exercise – I need to find time to initiate it.

3.   IS/IT – the last plan ('88) looked OK, but never really got under way at the right pace, and has become increasingly irrelevant, as shown by the '90/91 review, which really only scratched the surface. It needs a complete re-build, but we must make sure that it really happens, and that it stays in touch with the business. As a result of that review, Jones took IS/IT off Ed Brown, fired the DPM, and has now hired Andy Barnes to head up the function reporting direct to him. His first job is to re-do the IT Strategy. He is a Director designate, but Jones wants him to prove he's worth the Board position by building a Board consensus for his new IS/IT plan and then delivering the first few phases on target first.

VIEWS ON UK PROSPECTS

Pessimistic on the business climate – flat in '92, with some growth in '93 if we're lucky. The return to profitability will have to come from:

- squeezing costs;
- pushing up sales volume through better sales and marketing, and by aggressive pricing.

This all means the ability to finely tune margins – which means better information systems.

PRIORITIES AND CONCERNS

1. Getting better operational control information for fine-tuned decisions.

2. Getting the retail operation on its feet despite the climate.

3. Where to find a Treasure chest for strategic investment – will the Group act as the Good Fairy?

4. Getting a slice for the UK of expansion into the EC and Eastern Europe

5. Avoiding terminal damage to the UK operation during UK recession.

6. How to fight off predators on UK company.

7. Strengthening key functions:

    - Marketing
    - Distribution
    - IS/IT

Gerry Floggitt – interviewed in 1991

1. Only on board 3 weeks – not yet 'institutionalized'. Doesn't think Trendy thought through the retail venture properly – they saw it as an easy kill, but retail is really a very tough and finely tuned business. And especially difficult at present!

2. GF is committed to making the retail venture work – but not yet convinced that other Board members understand what is needed.

3. The retail operation needs flexibility to select the most appropriate suppliers and distribution capability – better to be 'hands off' from the rest of Trendy.

4. Current information systems and much of the management infrastructure of the newly acquired retail chain are obsolete or non-existent.

5. The operation was 'on the rocks' when Trendy bought it. In store systems are archaic, sales are monitored on a sample basis only, and only by cash – they literally don't know what they are selling!

6. Takings are down at present, just like everyone else.

7. 'Shrinkage' is way above the retail industry norms – and there is no basis for telling where the goods are going.

8. Key priorities are:

    - 'stop the rot'; get the current operation back under control and at least past break even;

- a spring clean of store managers – release those not up to it, then replace them and restore staff motivation and incentive;
- get takings up by fair means or foul;
- capital investment – more, better sites;
- overhaul the catalogue – and buy in where Trendy can't supply it;
- cut out the slack in the chain. This needs effective systems, especially inventory and more fine-tuned distribution;
- know more accurately what we're selling. Needs better store-level operational systems and more prompt linkage into distribution and consolidation;
- re-vamped distribution operation – current is too slack, and too costly;
- effective market analysis and intelligence – also currently non-existent;
- flexibility in remuneration/reward package to hire and keep top rate store managers;
- 'idiot-proof' in store systems, as the staff turnover is so high there's not time to train them in anything complex;
- ability to feed right back into Trendy's manufacturing plans and even into the product development/purchasing cycle.

Gerry Floggitt – key issues summary October 1992

GOALS

1. UK retail sector:

    - get retail operation on to a basis of 15% net profit on turnover by mid-'93;
    - growth – open 10 new sites p.a. each in SE and the North – £50M t/o p.a.

2. UK sales:

    - fulfil caretaker role
    - hire an effective Sales Director by end '92

3. Distribution:

    - hire an effective Distribution GM;
    - replace weak contractor by end 92;
    - get the service levels up to target by 2Q '93.

4. EC single market – deliver a specific plan and investment case to group by end '92;

5. Eastern Europe – support Group planning – produce outline proposals by 2Q '93.

ACHIEVEMENT AGAINST PLANS

1. *UK retail sector.* Profitability is not yet coming back, due to limited takings and the cost base already being pared to the bone. We have identified several excellent sites for new stores, and have the development plans in place to maintain store growth targets, but we are not allowed to proceed at present. The Board say there is there is no investment capital, and there is no guarantee that the new stores will hit their revenue targets in the present climate.

2. *UK sales director* – interviewing candidates currently.

3. *Distribution* – awaiting time with Bill Jones to initiate the procurement for a new distribution contract. New Distribution GM recruitment is at short-list level.

4. *EC single market.* Production of the plan is on target. It will need investment and good support services.

5. *Eastern Europe.* First draft paper has been delivered early. Now working with a Group level committee on it.

VIEWS ON UK PROSPECTS

Currently lousy; little hope in rest of 1992; goal must be to survive into 1993.

FRUSTRATIONS

1. Knowing what's going on – in his previous position was used to an up to date, accurate information flow. Now feels blindfolded.

2. UK recession – has done all the right things, but they don't work in this climate.

3. Fred Rogers – why is he so sticky over Eastern Europe, when the opportunities are so great?

EXCUSES

- UK recession;
- lack of good, prompt information on store and product performance;
- lack of investment in the new sites (e.g. in the less depressed North), which would bring in the cash, even in this climate;

CONCERNS

- Group commitment to Europe – still wavering
- UK support for European ventures
- UK recession
- Investment
- IS support

For Floggitt's full interview analysis see Table 7-1.

Ed Brown – key issues summary – September 1992

GOALS

1. UK survival – cost base still too high

   - cut costs another 20% on average by 2Q '93;
   - protect the good areas but prune soft areas harder;

2. Contribution to Group:

   - UK to break even in 1991 overall;
   - get UK profitability back to 15% net on t/o in f.y. 1993;
   - get the UK consolidated financial reporting accurate and within 3 days of period end;

3. Expectations from Group:

   - provision of effective overall Treasury Management;
   - source of cheap investment capital to fuel exit from UK recession.

ACHIEVEMENT AGAINST PLANS

1. UK recession has deepened; we're currently heading for £10M plus loss in '92. Cost cutting is so deep it's causing lasting damage, but is still not enough. We simply will have to cut more. Better takings from the retail stores are needed, quickly.

2. Cash management (currently debt management mostly!) is still not very good. Group treasury need to get their act together – but they also need prompter reporting of cash positions from the companies.

3. Group also don't seem to have any cheap investment capital to offer us.

FRUSTRATIONS

1. Continuing lack of effective high level financial control systems.

2. Carried the can for the failure of the 1988 IS strategy – unfairly, he feels, as he wasn't allowed to sort out the IS/IT function when he had responsibility for it.

3. The retail operation is still totally out of control – apparently impenetrable to sound financial practices. This is tragic, as it could be our lifeline in 1993 as the worst of the consumer gloom lifts.

EXCUSES

1. Poor control systems.

2. UK recession.

3. Lack of financial discipline in the subsidiaries and operating divisions.

CONCERNS

1. Effective accountability and control of the retail operation.

2. Meeting UK and Group requirements for consolidated financial reporting with continuing weak IS.

3. How to fight off take-over predators in the post UK recession climate.

4. How to do business in Eastern Europe – if we get involved – in terms of contracts and currency management.

The full interview analysis for Ed Brown is shown in Table 7-3 (starts on page 214).

FUNCTION	OBJECTIVE/GOAL	CRITICAL SUCCESS FACTORS	Ext/ int	Able to infl	PERFORMANCE MEASURES	BUSINESS INFORMATION & SUPPORT NEEDS	Prty
Perform overall financial control of Trendy Plc Group	Get Trendy (UK) under control financially	Adequate flow of timely, consistent and accurate financial information	I	Y	Degree of financial control achieved / Timeliness and accuracy of financial reporting	Cost and revenue figures by cost centre, product and activity type	H
		Ability to overcome inertia in information systems development which has stalled efforts to deliver effective management information	I	(P)	Timeliness and accuracy of financial reporting	Rapid re-vamp of operational accounting systems and mgmt accounting feeds from them.	VH
	Achieve consistent & uniform accounting conventions & policies	Effective accounting policies and coding structures, along with means for implementation.				Urgent rationalization of coding structures and accounting conventions to be harmonized across the Group.	VH
	Upgrade information systems as needed	Effective information systems plan, which reflects the agreed business needs & priorities	I	Y		Effective plan to achieve the above started a.s.a.p. – must deliver results this time.	VH
	Provide control systems to support management efforts to meet targets for revenue and profitability.	Availability of accurate, consistent underlying sources of information	I	Y	Degree of reconcilability of information	Underlying systems must be complete enough and compatible enough to give the information promptly and accurately.	H
		Willingness of information sources to follow orderly financial disciplines	I	Y	Timeliness of information / Promptness of information flows		
	Meet statutory reporting obligations promptly and accurately.	Availability of accurate, consistent base information.	I	Y	Accuracy of information / Incidence of difficulties over statutory reporting.	Accurate, consistent base information.	M / H
	Effective high level reporting systems.	Effective high level reporting systems.	I	Y		Effective high level reporting systems.	M
Provide capability for effective financial control at sector and business unit level.	Establish compatible measures of performance across BUs				Ability of senior mgmt to really see what's going on and influence it.		
	Educate Business Unit Management to think and act in terms of these measures.	Receptiveness of BUMs to recommendations.	I	N			

Table 7-3: *Trendy Products PLC – Information systems strategy plan – analysis of Ed Brown interview*

FUNCTION	OBJECTIVE/GOAL	CRITICAL SUCCESS FACTORS	Ext/ int	Able to infl	PERFORMANCE MEASURES	BUSINESS INFORMATION & SUPPORT NEEDS	Prty
	Establish a commitment and culture in which achievement is tracked against measures and action taken to effect control.	Skills/caliber.	I	(P)		Efficient and clear management communications.	M
						Training in basic skills for middle management.	H
	Establish at BU level information feeds to provide these measures	Quality/completeness of BU operational systems.	I	(P)		Underlying systems must be complete enough and compatible enough to give the information promptly and accurately.	H
		Consistency/compatibility of information content.	I	(P)			
	Plan and implement the most appropriate set of information systems to meet the needs of Trendy UK	Accurate perception of business needs & priorities.	I	Y			
		Availability of skilled staff to do the job.	I	(P)			
Provide budgeting & planning services	Meet service needs of user departments	Effective planning support systems	I	Y	User perception of quality of service	Effective budgeting and planning systems linked to underlying management accounting information.	M
		Sufficient & appropriate skills & resources Information to be up to date	I	P			
Monitor and report actual performance against plan	Track performance in a manner which enables effective action to be taken in time to identified problems		I	Y	Degree of effective control which the Board are able to exert over Trendy	Actual versus plan for the chosen key factors: ■ profitability by department, product and market area ■ productivity by dept and cost centre ■ others to be defined	H
		Information to be accurate	I	Y			

Table 7-3: *(continued) Trendy Products PLC – Information systems strategy plan – analysis of Ed Brown interview*

Table 7-3: (continued) Trendy Products PLC – Information systems strategy plan – analysis of Ed Brown interview

FUNCTION	OBJECTIVE/GOAL	CRITICAL SUCCESS FACTORS	Ext/int	Able to infl	PERFORMANCE MEASURES	BUSINESS INFORMATION & SUPPORT NEEDS	Prty
		Information to be presented in a manner which facilitates rapid evaluation	I	Y		Updated forecasts & projections	M
Plan finances of Trendy Corp	Establish sound basis and plans for 2–3 year horizon	Clear forward picture of:			Acceptance of plan by Board and Group	Changes to plan at Board and group level	M
		▪ expenditure plans	I	I	Degree of success in meeting plan		
		▪ revenue patterns	Y	N	Level of 'surprises' due to unexpected external events		
		▪ external financial factors	E	N		Actual results against plan	H
						External information on:	M
						▪ economic climate	
						▪ consumer spending patterns	
						▪ likely trade and fiscal changes	
Manage cash and Treasury for the Trendy Group	Obtain funding for the Trendy Group's operations at the most favourable combination of rates and terms.	Clear forward picture of:			Cost of funds	Investment project plans & proposals	H
		▪ expenditure plans	I	Y			
		▪ revenue patterns	I	Y	Ability to carry out investm'nt plans	Cash flow & revenue forecasts	VH
	Make our spare cash work to best effect.	Prompt visibility of cash peaks and troughs	I	(P)	Rate of return on cash deposits	Current and projected Bank account positions	M
					Rates paid for short term finance		
					Frequency of cash crises and other surprises.	Prompt information on cash peaks and troughs.	H
		Comprehensive view of external financial factors	E	N		External information on financial markets	M
						On-line links to trusted financial advisors.	L
	Provide protection against exposure to interest and FX rate fluctuations	Accurate knowledge of cash flows & needs by currency	I	Y	Profit/loss by currency	Cash flows & needs by currency	H
		Access to up to date FX market information	I	Y		Up to date FX market information	M
						Currency exposure and exchange	M

CHAPTER 8

Developing and using information architectures

Phase 2 – Establish information architectures and options for solutions

Having clearly identified the business information and support needs, and having also hopefully got some business sponsors thoroughly interested in having those needs met, we can now move into the second phase of the overall process, which has the following aims:

1. To assess the extent to which the present systems and development projects meet the current perception of business needs and priorities, and the extent which they are likely to continue to do so if things are left as they are (covered in this chapter).

2. To determine strategic IS and IT goals for the organization, and specifically to formulate these in terms of strategic IS and IT architectures which will offer the best future match to business needs. (Covered in this chapter).

3. To establish a range of options for achieving the goals identified, along with criteria for selecting between them. (Covered in Chapter 10).

The overall context is shown in Figure 8-1, where the shading relates specifically to the architectural work covered in this chapter. In more detail, this involves the following steps:

- Determine 'where we want to be':
  - business information and support capability
  - target IS/IT 'vision'
  - strategic information architectures
- Evaluate the scope and quality of coverage of business requirements offered by current IS and IT
- Assess the value and relevance of current IS and IT infrastructure
- Establish priorities for delivering business information and support

- Identify application options for meeting business priorities
- Foster development of business cases to support key initiatives

Figure 8-1:   *Develop information architectures*

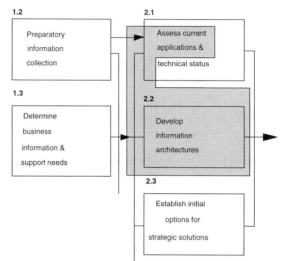

Information architectures

Definition

Before we go any further, a definition of 'architecture' is in order. In IS/IT terms, a piece of architecture is some or all of the following:

- An outline master plan.
- A blueprint, covering current and future systems and associated information.
- A definition of those elements which are least likely to change in the face of change in business priorities or technology facilities.
- A basis for future flexibility.

i.e. something which you are much better off with than without.

Architectures, as we will define and use them, have certain quite specific characteristics. They are:

- Cheap to develop and maintain ■ Expensive to omit ■ 'Layered'

- Demanding of quite specific skills and techniques in their formulation.

The layering is necessary to keep the amount of detail presented in any one view within that which the average human can cope with. The aim is that the 'rightness' of architectures should be self-evident, which is impossible if the manner of their presentation is too complex. The following diagram illustrates this. In Figure 8-2, our Galactic Gazetteer, if we had one, could not possibly present us simultaneously with all of the details of all public transport systems on all of the planets in the galaxy at once – we would first have to select the stellar system, the planet, the continent and country, and the city, in that order, working down through layers of detail as we did so. So it is with information architectures.

Figure 8-2: *Architecture levels*

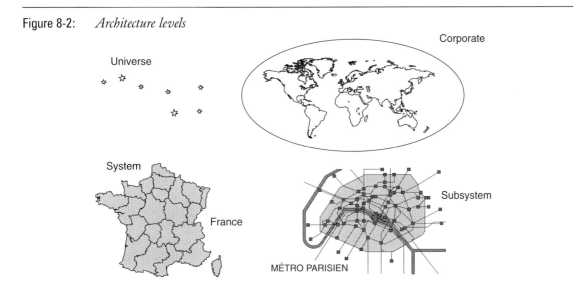

Architecture objective

The objective IS/IT of architecture work is to define in advance of implementation, sufficient framework/context to ensure that applications can be:

- Designed as simply as possible, and at low risk of side-effects;
- Implemented quickly using the most appropriate tools;
- Operated correctly and reliably;
- Enhanced quickly as needed to meet business developments

Issues involving information architectures at the strategic level

SOME OF THE KEY ISSUES INCLUDE:

- How much work to do, and when...
- Functions and benefits;
- Architecture components
- Working styles
- Controlling the level of detail

TOO LITTLE ARCHITECTURE CAN LEAD US INTO:

- False economies
- Data not available, or inconsistent
- Unforeseen or uncontrollable side-effects
- It can't be done
- Massive replacement costs for key systems
- Information systems fall behind business needs

TOO MUCH ARCHITECTURE CAN LEAD US INTO:

- 'Paralysis by analysis'
- Design (or even worse, analysis), seen as an end in itself
- Management impatience/despair
- Applications obsolete before delivery

Benefits of Architectures

Some of the benefits of having conducted the right level of architectural work include:

- We are able to base databases and applications on data structures which we know will remain relatively stable
- Control over information completeness, consistency and timeliness
- Basis for analyzing dependencies and constraints
- Vehicle for identifying and controlling user responsibilities for data
- Basis for infrastructure investment decisions
- Change control and impact analysis
- Basis for assessing current status against needs
- Good value – cheap to draw up blueprint
- Basis for identifying simple, separable problems
- Basis for incremental delivery

Relative stability of business features

There is a hierarchy of stability of different types of business feature, as follows:

1. Data structures – the most stable, sensitive only to fundamental changes in the nature of the business.

2. Business functions and process, which only change significantly when we do different things in the business.

3. Business products and services, which have to change in order to meet evolving customer needs if we are to remain in business.

4.   Organization structure, which is more volatile, and which can appear to fluctuate unnecessarily, especially if we disagree with the latest organization chart.

5.   Information presentation formats, which vary widely with the style of the manager requesting them and the willingness of the information providers.

The art is, by exploiting the inherent stability of the items early in the above list, to make it easier and cheaper to cope with the volatility of the items lower in it.

Architecture components and purpose

The main types of architecture are as follows:

1.   Business model

2.   Application systems architecture

3.   Data architecture

4.   IT technical architecture: IT Technical Architecture embodies policies and standards for IT solutions and interfaces. It forms the basis for:

   - managing IT supplier relationships
   - controlling complexity and diversity of IT solutions
   - minimizing mismatches and cost/performance barriers
   - evaluating the fit of candidate solutions
   - open ended growth path

IT Technical Architecture is dealt with in Chapter 12. Development of the first three categories, which are often collectively referred to as Information Architectures, is covered in some detail in this chapter. These information architectures are necessary tools for assessing the quality of coverage offered by current systems and projects; this is addressed later in this chapter.

BUSINESS MODEL

This is a definition of the inherent structure and characteristics of the business and industry. It forms a basis for assessing the match of the business to its environment, and for exploration of alternatives, in terms of:

   - opportunities to differentiate our organization and its products or services from the competition;
   - product/market strategies;
   - business process structures/options;
   - IS/IT support opportunities;
   - organization structures.

Business model products result from a business analysis or similar process. They typically consist of definitions of:

- the 'natural' functional structure of the business, which acts as the skeleton for assessment of options for process support – e.g. for business process reengineering;
- an understanding of the cost structure and value chains;
- process schematic;
- organization and responsibility definitions;
- information and resources flows.

APPLICATION SYSTEMS ARCHITECTURE

At one level, this is the ideal 'template' or conceptual blueprint for applications flows of information systems in the organization – the 'directional vision'. It illustrates the manner in which the information systems components and flows support the business structure, and forms the basis for:

- assessment of current IS status, strengths and weaknesses and their coverage of business needs;
- evaluating the competitive strength of the IS portfolios of competitors or potential acquisitions;
- comparing alternative IS evolution strategies;
- assessing options for grouping systems developments into deliverable units
- evaluating the business fit offered by candidate solutions – package and custom.

The application systems architecture consists of a layered series of charts which:

- illustrate the key applications and their interactions;
- identify the relation both to business processes, and to current IS support;
- can be annotated, e.g. in color, to highlight both areas of high business need, and of current weakness.

DATA ARCHITECTURE

The data architecture expresses the logical information structure of the business and industry, independent of implementation media or decisions. It forms the basis for:

- ensuring generality/flexibility of solutions;
- evaluating scope and fit of particular solutions;
- managing dependencies for implementation and migration.
- The data architecture is expressed in terms of:
- broad data classes/groupings;

- data entities, relationships;
- basis for subject database groupings;
- application dependencies for delivery phasing;
- current databases and files mapping.

Affinities – interactions between architecture components

Analysis of the interactions between architecture components can be of immense assistance in cutting through the fog of confusion, and in directing the search for powerful, long lived solutions. For example:

1. analysis of how similar functions are performed for different business products or services can highlight wasteful duplication of effort and infrastructure;

2. analysis of how business functions are mapped into organization units can help identify opportunities for streamlining the organization and for forming cleaner, more accountable business units;

3. identification of usage patterns between applications and database elements can provide a firm basis for organizing databases and application flows for smoother operation.

Some of the potential benefits from this process, which is termed affinity analysis include the following. Specific techniques for affinity analysis will be discussed later in this chapter.

- improved basis for groupings and sequencing;
- clarity of vision over who is, and who should be made responsible for what,
- who uses which resource, for what purpose;
- application/data usage;
- identification of common patterns, and hence potential economies of scale;
- identification and elimination of needless diversity.

The architecture development process

Getting the level of detail right

STRATEGIC MATERIALITY

- emphasis on long term and other strategic aspects
- avoid tactical side-tracks – let them rum, catch them on migration

SUFFICIENT

- thorough, but free from spurious detail
- one layer below results reported to management – to ensure justification

(2 levels in critical areas)

NECESSARY

- avoid work on areas which are not significant
- use stated business priorities to guide allocation/balance of effort – but don't hide behind them to excuse lack of common sense

Fitting detail to scope

Scope		Level of Detail
Corporate	Macro	■ Major functions
		■ Application areas
		■ Subject data areas
Business area	Middle	■ Function
and function		■ Process
		■ Data entity
Business operation/	Detail	■ Task
transaction		■ Process detail
		■ Data element

Guidelines for level of detail

RELATE TO DETAIL IN RESULTS

e.g. typical plan covers about:

- 40 to 80 projects, each about 2 to 10 man years
- 10 to 20 subject databases

Analysis probably gives sufficient supporting detail if it covers:

- 60 to 100 data entities
- 100 to 300 groups of information and support needs

This is equivalent to about 4 levels of decomposition, each about 10 functions wide, for each of 6 business areas

Add extra detail in key areas if necessary, e.g. customer database may need subdivision.

Balance effort/detail continuously:

- hierarchical analyses – at each level

- iterative processes – at each iteration

BUSINESS ASPECTS

- Keep to strategic level; note tactical points, current minor problems etc. but exclude from analyses
- Keep documents concise and structured

The key – quit while you're ahead

'Is the work now being done material to the design decisions at this level?'

'Never make a design decision at this level which you can put off to the next'

Top-down analysis and design versus bottom-up

TOP-DOWN

- *Advantages:*
  - Clear view/context ■ Stop early if answer is clear ■ Cheap and quick
- *Disadvantages:*
  - Risk of wasted work due to blind alleys ■ Problems found late

BOTTOM-UP

- *Advantages:*
  - Decisions completely ■ Problem areas well ■ Guaranteed to 'work' validated as you go   identified
- *Disadvantages:*
  - Slow and laborious ■ May miss radical but effective options
  - May do much unnecessary ■ Premature decisions may limit options detail work

THE ANSWER

- Start top-down
- Identify key areas and priorities
- Selectively validate bottom-up – use of automated aids
- Integrate and iterate
- Apply judgement
- Inside-out is useful, too!

Architecture development – main tasks and flows

Figure 8-3 illustrates the overall process in which architecture products are developed and used as an initial basis for construction of the first draft of the overall application and database vision.

Figure 8-3:   *Business models and information architecture development process and flows*

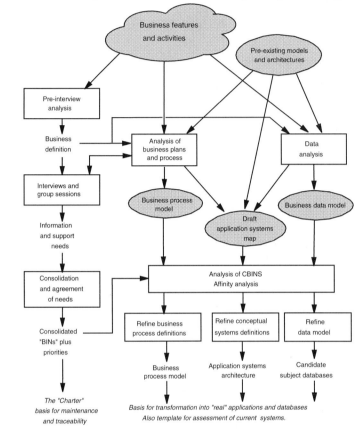

Key points at this stage are:

- Architecture products are developed progressively from the very first point of contact with the business.

- Early on, they help the team's understanding of the business structure, and aid in identifying organizational weaknesses and shortcomings and hence opportunities for business improvement.

- Making 'raw' architecture products visible to senior management may be counter productive, and may mask the acceptance of key business conclusions which we draw from them. Senior management are often impatient of what they perceive as IT jargon and esoteric systems methodology. Even if you are convinced that your data entity model is a paragon of elegance, this may not be the time to try to enlighten the Production Director to this fact! But he may get very excited if you can show how common functions can be supported more efficiently.

- Architecture products will evolve progressively during the IS/IT planning study and afterwards. Do not expect to finish them at this stage – it is too easy to get into too much detail and spend too long on them.

- There may well have been important work done previously in this area. It is vital that our architecture products are reconciled with this, and that the custodians of existing architectures are comfortable with our revisions. Considerable tact may be required here – sensibilities can be delicate.

The range of architecture development techniques which may be used is very great, and is growing all the time. The range and scope of the available options was illustrated in Figure 6-4 in chapter 6. The reader is encouraged to investigate and evaluate these and other techniques, in order to identify those which are most productive for his or her needs. But the caution is repeated that it is all to easy to over-use such techniques, and it is vital to be sparing in use of analysis effort at this level.

The Soft Systems Methodology (CCTA 1993, Checkland 1981) is of particular value in circumstances where the nature of the business problem or requirements are ill defined, or in contention. Contrary to widespread belief, it is not at odds with the 'harder' analytic disciplines discussed in this chapter, but complementary if used with care. The tables which follow indicate its broad relevance, but readers wishing for specific information should consult the references. The tables which follow summarize the relevance of a core set of architectural techniques which are of greatest relevance at the strategic level to:

- different architecture products (Table 8-1)
- appropriate levels of detail in later stages in the systems life cycle (Table 8-2)

Table 8-1: *Relevance of analysis techniques to types of architecture*

Technique	Architecture types				
	Business	Data	Application	Technical	Organisation
Information needs analysis	High	High	High		Medium
Soft systems analysis	High	Medium	High		Medium
Data analysis (entity modelling) (same emphasis will apply to object analysis)	Medium	High	Medium	Medium	
Functional analysis (functional decomposition)	High	Medium	High		High
Affinity analysis		High	High	Medium	
Entity life cycles	Limited	High, at detailed level only	High, at detailed level only		
Data flow analysis	Limited		High, at detailed level only		
Portfolio analysis	High		High	Medium	

Table 8-2:   *The level of detail appropriate to architectural work varies according to the scope and depth of the analysis required*

| Technique | Scope of architectural analysis | | | |
	Corporate business strategy	Business area	Application system	Application subsystem
Information needs analysis	Key management information needs	All management information needs		
Soft systems analysis	Macro level business view	Clarifying obscure aspects of business purpose, structure or processes	Application processes to meet business needs	
Data analysis (entity modelling, and object analysis in due course)	Broad subject data bases only	In-depth analysis of data entities and relationships. (Extension of this discipline to object analysis will cause work here to include object classes and methods)	Mapping of data entities /objects to databases; methods to procedures. Extended to data item/ element level.	Process logic analysis to level of transaction profiles.
Functional analysis (functional decomposition)	Business areas, key functions and business operating units	Business functions and processes. Relationship to application processes which are required to support them. Exploration of organisational responsibility issues.	In depth analysis of application processes. Increasingly close relation to object class hierarchies.	Process logic analysis to level of transaction profiles.
Affinity analysis	Restrained use of cluster analysis to help determine subject data areas and business ownership.	Cluster analysis to help determine most natural groupings of data entities into databases and processes into organisation units.	Cluster analysis to help determine most natural groupings of data entities into databases and application processes into systems.	
Entity life cycles			Limited strategic relevance	
Data flow analysis			Limited strategic relevance	
Portfolio analysis	Macro level view of products, markets and business units	Rigorous assessment of the portfolio of products, markets and business assets held.	Rigorous assessment of the strategic relevance of the present and future application portfolio.	

Developing the business model and information architectures

Scope

We have analyzed the following characteristics of the business:

- Plans, goals, objectives – corporate and by sector
- Industry and competitive positioning
- Specific strategies being followed.

We will in parallel have been identifying the management's view of their functional responsibilities, and their views on the information and support needs to run the business documented in the consolidated statement of business information needs (CBINs).

We now need to develop a much tighter and more systematic view of the 'business architecture', especially:

- the functional structure of the business;
- its cost structure and value chains;
- the products and services;
- the rationale behind the organizational structure, and the manner in which it supports the functions;
- the responsibility structure – organizational placement of functional responsibility for product/service support and internal services;
- the overall planning and control approaches and framework.

We will develop these 'business models' preparatory to attempting to build the corresponding information systems architectures which are required to support them. Although this is presented here as a linear process, in fact a great deal of this work takes place in parallel with the interview and analysis cycle discussed in Chapter 7. This is both most efficient way, and is also necessary on the grounds that we need to understand the inherent structure of the business as quickly as possible during the interview cycle, so that the most effective possible communication takes place with senior management at this time.

Approach

There are always two routes to identification of key elements of the business model and related information architectures:

- 'top down', i.e. generally based on experience and judgement, especially having analyzed similar types of business before;
- 'bottom-up' – i.e. based on some form of formal analysis of the available materials.

Both are relevant and valid in this situation – indeed, either alone will lead to unsatisfactory results. Generally, a high level top-down view is the best starting point, especially if it can be based on the results of similar work done elsewhere. But it is critical to remember that every organization is different, and it is too easy to carry over false preconceptions and assumptions from elsewhere. So care is needed.

Once an overall skeleton is available for any of the business model or architecture products, it must be fleshed out and validated in a more bottom-up manner, based on reasonably rigorous analysis. At this stage, it is too easy to dive straight into detail, and lose all strategic perspective; so the level of detail must be rigorously controlled. Means for this are discussed later.

A key source of raw material for this more rigorous analysis is any piece of written prose describing the business – assuming that it is reasonably objective, carefully written, and relatively free from sales-oriented exaggeration. Into this category come business plans, and, especially, the descriptions of business needs embodied in the CBINS document (Figure 8-4), which we have been to so much pains to produce in Chapter 7.

Figure 8-4:   *Consolidated statement of business information and support needs*

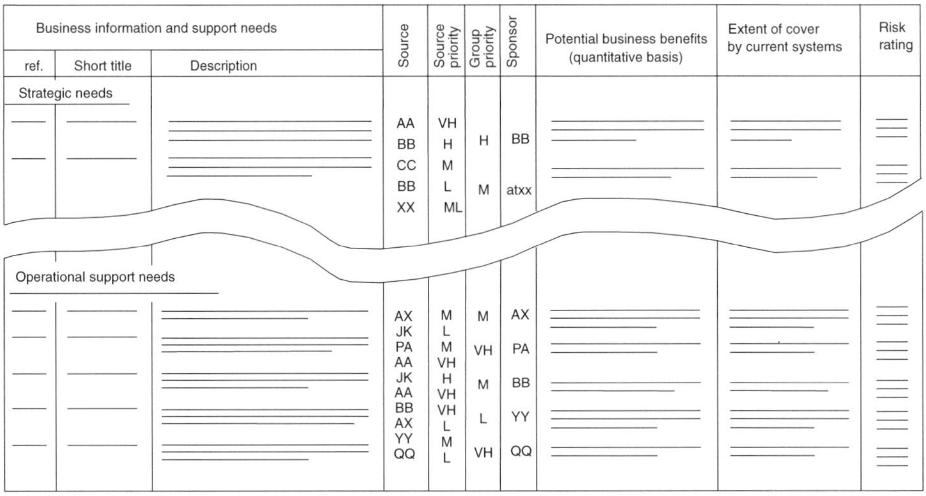

In building the CBINS, we have already analyzed the business mission, goals and plans, along the lines indicated in the next diagram. We can now, in the manner illustrated below, analyze the concepts and even the syntax of elements of CBINS statement (or any other suitable piece of text), and derive from it business processes and relevant data entities. These become valuable raw material for building the business models and information architectures which are described in the remainder of this chapter.

Figure 8-5:   *Analysis of business plans and strategies*

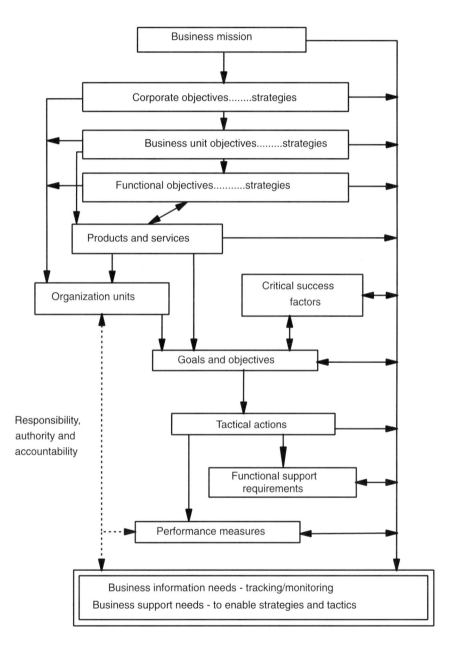

Figure 8-6:   *Derivation of architecture elements*

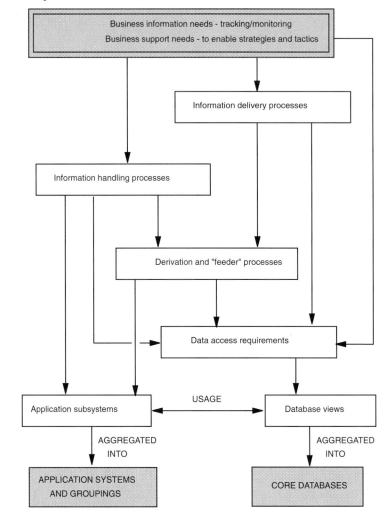

Building the business model

Components

- Functional groupings
- Business Function Hierarchy
- Business information flows
- Business Process Schematic

Together these provide the basis for analyzing value chains (internal and external), and for establishing the framework for IS support.

The Business Function Hierarchy

What it is

The Business Function Hierarchy sets out the main functions required to be performed to run the business, and indicates the manner in which the large functions break down into the smaller. It seeks to remain independent of the manner in which the functional responsibilities are mapped on to jobs, roles, or organization units, as this is often dependent on many transient, local factors, including personal taste, whereas the inherent functional structure is usually quite stable unless the scope of the business changes radically. The lowest level functions are commonly referred to as processes.

What it is for

The set of business functions so identified may be used in many ways:

- it provides an unambiguous vocabulary for describing business actions and processes;
- a clear view of the functions enables a clearer understanding of the organizational structure to be attained, and is a powerful tool for identifying redundancy, duplication and other opportunities for simplification;
- comparisons with other organisations – customers, suppliers, competitors – is facilitated;
- it is an essential prerequisite for any form of business process engineering;
- the functions and their interrelationships form a particularly strong framework for developing and effective IS architecture.

How to build it

The strategic analyst develops a 'feel' for what is and what is not a natural business function. Business functions should be regarded as actions, or verbs, with inputs and outputs. They are not organization units, but they will be performed by organization units. At each level, the set of functions should express the scope of the level completely, but may leave matters of detail open. Each may then be broken down, so that its scope is described more fully by the next level.

The style is best illustrated by looking at the Business Function Hierarchy for Trendy Products Plc. The overall function, 'Run Trendy Products', which describe the entire scope of Trendy (albeit vaguely) is broken down into:

1.   Market products and services

2. Develop products and services

3. Sell products and services

4. Distribute products and services

5. Buy products, services and raw materials

6. Produce products and services

7. Plan and control the business

8. Manage finance

9. Operate support services

which together cover the same scope. Each of these functions is broken down further - see the sample function hierarchy for Trendy Products, Appendix 2 at the end of this chapter.

The Business Process Schematic

What it is

The Business Process Schematic is a diagrammatic representation of selected layers of the business functional structure identified in the Business Function Hierarchy, but with a 'horizontal' business flows perspective added. These flows include both linkages to external customer and supplier chains, and their internal equivalents, or 'value chains'.

It is closely based on, and should be reconcilable with, the Business Function Hierarchy.

What it is for

1. Base for identification, analysis and consolidation of the 'pure' view of business functions and processes, independent of organization, as a basis for:

    - consideration of opportunities for improving the organization, in terms of:
        - scope of accountabilities;
        - elimination of duplication of effort;
        - rationalization of the manner in which the processes are carried out organizationally
        - identification and rationalization of the Customer/Supplier interfaces, both internal and with the external world;
    - evaluating opportunities for gaining economies of scale and synergy

gains through commonality of processing;
- identification of types of IS support required.

2.   Basis for construction of the Application Systems Map

How to build it

The Business Process Schematic illustrates a number of business functions which are at approximately the same level, along with their input and output flows. The most important consideration initially is that of clarity and accessibility. For this reason, the Business Process Schematic needs to be 'layered', i.e. there should be a single relatively simple overall diagram covering the whole organization. This should embody 10 to 20 high level functions, and should be easy to relate to the business as a whole.

There should then be a series of charts, one for each major functional area of the business, where the level of function illustrated is limited by considerations of clarity and of materiality. In a small to medium business of moderate complexity, the functional areas may be combined on a single page, as in the examples which follow. In cases involving greater complexity, the charts may be divided according to taste and presentational need.

Getting the level of detail right is an art. Detail should be omitted by default, especially where the processes are getting too small for their inputs and outputs to be of strategic significance. Further detail may be added in later stages of the systems design life cycle – at these lower levels, there are close parallels with Data Flow Diagrams (DFDs) and Entity Life Cycle diagrams.

Like building the CBINS (Chapter 7), building a Business Process Schematic is a lot easier if you have a plausible one to start with. Building a Business Process Schematic for the first time in an organization is the hardest, especially if you have no example of style from the same type of industry to work from.

The first step for a 'green-fields' Business Process Schematic is the overall structure. Except where there are overriding reasons for doing otherwise, I have generally found it most useful to follow the same sets of categories for rows and columns as used for the CBINS (see Chapter 7), but now giving the logical rows direct physical manifestation on the charts. This makes the two documents much easier to cross-relate. As indicated in Chapter 7, we should base the columns on broad business functional areas, and the rows on the layers from the Anthony Triangle which we met in earlier chapters. As with CBINs, there is no doctrinal reason for this: the goals are to have a sensible topology to enable allocation of business functions or systems processes in a straightforward manner, and as the complexity grows, to enable the analyst to find his or her way around the diagram easily. It is also useful to have a structure which lends itself to partitioning of the diagram, if it becomes over complex, in a manner which is sensible in business terms. Typical partitioning categories, which should be used as a starting point for customization, are suggested below:

ROWS – BASED ON LEVELS OF INFORMATION NEED

- Strategic
- Planning and Analysis
- Operational Control
- Transaction Systems
- Administrative or operational support systems

COLUMNS – FOR THE ORGANIZATION OVERALL

- Overall planning and control
- Services:
  - *personnel*   - *premises*   - *IS functions*
- Finance

COLUMNS – FOR EACH BUSINESS AREA – BUT BEWARE TOO MUCH FRAGMENTATION

- *Marketing*   - *Product development*   - *Sales*
- *Manufacturing*   - *Distribution*   - *Customer relationship*
- *Purchasing*

These result in an overall grid – along the lines illustrated in Figure 8-7.

Figure 8-7:   *Business process schematic or application systems map typical overall structure*

Typical business functional areas

Information level	Plan & control	Finance	Resources and infrastr.	Customer rel'ship	Product/ service def'n	Marketing	Selling	Distrib'n/ delivery	Product support	Risk Mg'mt & Control
Strategic										
Planning & analysis										
Monitoring & control										
Transaction										
Operational support										

Starting with the obvious candidates from the Function Hierarchy, but with a heavy helping of common sense and business perspective, selected functions are then placed in the appropriate boxes, and their business inputs and outputs identified and joined up. It is best to start at the overall level, and then to decompose only those areas which are found to be both complex and material. It is usual to iterate significantly in areas of business novelty, and significant revision to the function hierarchy may also result. As detail proceeds, the function hierarchy will become exhausted as a source of raw material, and then even business knowledge. The CBINS will prove a fruitful source of inspiration, but restraint needs to be exercised in its use, as the tendency will be to be driven to too low a level if care is not taken.

Versions

Several different versions of the BPS can prove useful, and will be critical to any business process engineering activity:

1.   The 'pure' logical version, which shows in idealized form the business functions and processes in as clean a form as possible, independent of present organizational arrangements, which acts as the template for all of the other versions.

2.   A version which reflects present organizational grouping and boundaries.

3.   Potential future variants. There may be several – one for each of several key milestone dates, indicating potential evolutionary stages. There may be several for some milestones, indicating key organizational options or potential extensions or contractions of business scope.

It is best if versions other than 1 are represented either by a copy of 1 with annotations or boundaries marked, or by a matrix which links the functions and processes of 1 with organizational units.

Layering of business process and applications

As a guide to of allocation business processes (and subsequently the applications layers) to the adapted Anthony layers, the following charts (Table 8-3), may be useful. For each layer, they illustrate the general characteristics, under several headings.

CUSTOMER/SUPPLIER CHAIN ANALYSIS

Analysis of Customer/Supplier chains, or value chains, is becoming of increasing importance in business process engineering, and in any approach aimed at streamlining an organization and making the business units more manageable and accountable. The following questionnaire has been found useful in collecting information for this purpose.

Table: 8-3: *Summary of business process and application layers*

	GENERAL CHARACTERISTICS	EVENT HORIZON	DATA CHARACTERISTICS	PROCESSING VOLUMES AND TYPE	DELIVERY AND PRESENTATIONAL FACILITIES REQUIRED	DEVELOPMENT VEHICLE REQUIREMENTS
STRATEGIC (DECISION SUPPORT)	■ Highly unpredictable ■ Extensive 'what if' and judgemental content ■ Many one-off tasks ■ Inputs from many external sources ■ Concerned with refining or changing goals ■ Always likely to be subservient to human judgemental process ■ Workload type/patterns linked to personalities/preferences of key managers	■ Often five years or more ■ More concerned with future than past.	■ Wide variety – intelligence, summaries, image, text, as well as MIS, models etc. ■ Possibly high uncertainty - assumptions & approximations heresay, probabilities, scenarios. ■ 'Wide angle', in scope, type and subject area	■ Low volumes, often via intermediaries. ■ Access may be heavily clustered when senior management are concerned with a problem area. ■ Closely interactive, with potentially heavy compute load. ■ Demand patterns unpredictable and erratic.	■ High stress on clarity – verbal, graphic, highly summarized ■ Rapid flexible preparation facilities needed for presentation material. ■ Text-orientation ■ Human intermediary role in interpreting requests and responses important	■ Statistical & modelling packages incl spreadsheets ■ Human intermediary for interpretation ■ End-user ad hoc languages with natural language. ■ Free text analysis increasingly important. ■ Significant sub-class of expert/knowledge-based types.
PLANNING AND ANALYSIS (DECISION SUPPORT)	■ Unpredictable in detail, but based on a limited framework ■ Extensive statistical & modelling content ■ Concentration on assessing trends & identifying exceptions ■ Multiple, frequent 'what if' iterations ■ Frequent modification, medium lifetime ■ Intangible benefits	■ Usually 1–2 years ■ Need for extensive historic information as basis for extrapolation	■ Numeric (modelling) ■ Text reports & intelligence ■ Ability to process & generate graphics ■ Aggregates & extracts from operational data ■ Need for 'browse' type access to detail	■ Relatively low volumes of requests, but each may lead to heavy work ■ Some high volume scans of databases on exception basis ■ Extensive ability needed to generate & process extracts	■ Screen based text & graphics ■ Low volume printed summaries ■ Interface to document management important ■ Extensive ad hoc needs – easy, rapid change to processes is important ■ Help for casual users	■ Statistical & modelling packages incl spreadsheets ■ End-user ad hoc languages ■ Free text analysis becoming increasingly important. ■ Significant sub-class of expert/knowledge-based types.
MONITORING AND CONTROL (OPERATIONAL SYSTEMS)	■ Routine analysis & reporting ■ Timeliness relates to day/week/month/annual cycles ■ Suitable for replacement of many reports by online online enquiry ■ Long lifetime ■ Tangible but moderate benefits	■ Current control cycle day/week/month/year ■ Need for recent history for trends, indices, plans to compare actuals ■ Need for up to date actuals	■ Predefined, structured operational data accessed 'en masse' ■ Critical timeliness /cut-offs	■ High volume data analysis at peak periods ■ Need for high performance database scan.	■ 'Bland' printed reports ■ Pre-formatted screen enquiry ■ Increasing trend towards 'smarter' analysis leading to reporting triggers on exceptions only.	■ Packages ■ Application generators ■ 4 GL Report writers/enquiry facilities ■ Traditional custom dev't as a last resort

	GENERAL CHARACTERISTICS	EVENT HORIZON	DATA CHARACTERISTICS	PROCESSING VOLUMES AND TYPE	DELIVERY AND PRESENTATIONAL FACILITIES REQUIRED	DEVELOPMENT VEHICLE REQUIREMENTS
TRANSACTION	■ High volume, predefined ■ Online processing ■ Few, heavily used transaction types ■ Clerical users ■ Time-critical ■ Long lifetime ■ Headcount reduction justification ■ Users may be widely dispersed	■ Today's business transactions with a proportion carry-forward	■ Predefined, structured operational data accessed item by item ■ Responsibility for creating & maintaining base data ■ Very heavy data access can arise from high transaction rates ■ Integrity/availability requirements can be very high ■ Large volume long term archival may be needed	■ High, but peaky ■ Some transactions may need fast response ■ High communications load ■ Availability requirement may be very high ■ Relatively low compute load per transaction.	■ Pre-formatted screen-based enquiry & update ■ Needs to be oriented to efficient use by trained users	■ Packages ■ Application generators ■ Traditional custom dev't as a last resort ■ 4GL development for low volumes
OPERATIONAL SUPPORT	■ Text & communications oriented, but higher decision support content becoming common ■ High request & data volumes ■ Wide range of data classes ■ Rapidly increasing automation of routine office procedures ■ Use needs to be universal to be effective, therefore very easy user interface ■ Often highly interactive, especially decision support classes ■ Users may be widely dispersed	■ Current day/week/period ■ Current operational concern. ■ May need data archive for transaction/data feed history	■ Large volumes of text documents ■ High volume of messages ■ Extensive connectivity across data types & services ■ Stress on human interface ■ Rule & assertion content for expert systems sub-class. ■ Raw bit-stream in some cases	■ High, but peaky ■ Communications load may be especially high, due to voice content, interactive responses needed and bitmapped graphics. ■ Direct computer-computer data feeds in some cases	■ Simple interface to a wide range of services ■ Built-in help for casual users ■ Fail-soft for mis-use ■ Highly visual; increasingly wider range of I/O types, audio/tactile. ■ Stress on man/machine interface	■ High proportion of pre-written functional software, e.g. document/text mgmt, messaging, diaries, modelling, decision support etc. ■ Significant sub-class of expert/knowledge-based types. ■ Real time processing, e.g. for data feeds, etc.

Table: 8-3: (continued) Summary of business process and application layers

Questionnaire for service orientated business analysis

1. CUSTOMERS

Who are your primary Customers?

❏ *internal*   ❏ *external*

2. SERVICES

1.   For each Customer, what service(s) do you provide?

❏ *primary services*   ❏ *secondary services*

2.   For each service:

i.   What is the nature – qualitative description?
ii.   What is the frequency?
iii.   What are the volumes or other workload measured?
iv.   How volatile and/or forecastable is the workload?
v.   On what factors do the volumes depend?
vi.   What are the availability and/or turnaround requirements?
vii.   What are the accuracy and/or other quality requirements and criteria?
viii.   Which resources (see below) are utilized in providing the service?
ix.   On what basis is the service costed, charged or other wise accounted?
x.   What form, if any, does inter-unit billing or accounting take?

3. SERVICE PERFORMANCE

For each service:

i.   Is there a documented SLA or other form of service agreement (please supply a copy if so)?
ii.   On what other criteria is service performance judged?
iii.   On what factors does your success in meeting service requirements depend?   ❏ external ❏ internal
iv.   How is performance measured?

4. INPUTS

What are the primary inputs of your organization?

❏ *internal:* ▪ resources ▪ services

❏ *external:* ▪ resources ▪ services

For each input:

i.   Who is/are the supplier(s)?
ii.   What are your service requirements? (frequency, volumes

iii.   On what basis is the service costed, charged or other wise accounted?

iv.   Is there a documented SLA or other form of service agreement (please supply a copy if so)?

v.   On what other criteria is service performance judged?

vi.   How is the supplier's performance measured?

5. ORGANIZATION, PROCESS AND RESOURCES

i.   What is the organizational structure, with headcount?

ii.   What equipment, software and other resources are used?

iii.   What staff skills, experience and qualifications are required for each relevant post?

iv.   What functions and processes are performed in meeting the service?

v.   What other activities take place?

vi.   How are the functions mapped onto organizational responsibilities?

vii.   What performance objectives are set for the organization units?

viii.   What are the primary inputs and outputs of the organization units?

ix.   How is the performance of the organization units measured?

6. SERVICE IMPROVEMENT

i.   In what ways could your delivery of primary services be improved?

ii.   On what factors does this depend?

7. SERVICE SUBSTITUTION

i.   Are you aware of any alternative means for meeting the service outcomes required by your customers?

ii.   To what extent has the potential of any of these been investigated?

iii.   If so, what are the primary considerations, and on what factors do you believe that the viability of these alternatives depend?

Building the applications architecture

Components

- Application Systems 'Map' (ASM) ▪ *ideal* ▪ *current* ▪ *attainable*
- Migration plans
- Application development project definitions

Issues

- Layering
- Interfaces and integration
- Limitations of vehicles
- Functional groupings
- Degree of automation

The Application Systems Map

What it is

The Application Systems Map is a diagrammatic representation of the ideal conceptual set of applications to meet all business needs identified. It is closely based on the Business Process Schematic (above).

What it is for

1. Basis for mapping from business functions so as to identify their needs for IS support.

2. Basis for mapping of current applications so as to support assessment of coverage offered.

3. Basis for identifying candidate applications, and their interactions, prior to considering their scope and implementation priority.

4. Basis for designing the interactions of recommended future systems.

How to build it

The Application Systems Map (ASM) has the same underlying topology as the Business Process Schematic, and is constructed in a similar manner. There is a greater degree of interpretation involved, as we are designing an ideal portfolio of applications, rather than just recording business processes.

The ASM should show all likely applications, not just those existing or even currently planned. It is important that the applications identified should remain idealized in the core version, as this should remain as independent as possible from particular implementations.

Versions

Several versions of the ASM are required:

1. The 'pure' logical version, which shows in idealized form all potential applications, regardless of priority, and which acts as the template for all of the other versions.

2. The current version – what actually exists today.

3. Future versions. There may be several – one for each of several key milestone dates, indicating potential evolutionary stages. There may be several for some milestones, indicating key options.

Information content

The ASM is required to convey a great deal of information, especially in its more detailed and more developed forms. This includes:

- idealized applications;
- cross-references to business functions in the Business Function Hierarchy;
- inter-system flows;
- underlying business priorities;
- cross-references to particular CBINS entries;
- cross-references to current systems or projects;
- the extent and quality of coverage offered.

Showing all of this on a single diagram, or even a series of diagrams, is a tall order, but the resultant gain in presentational clarity is worth it. A notation for achieving this is illustrated after the initial examples.

ASM examples

In the examples which follow, the first, Figure 8-8, is an early draft of the overall ASM for Trendy Products. It is still close to a Business Process Schematic, and in a real life situation would have a considerable way to go to completion. In the completion process, the overall chart would be retained, but in a simplified form, and a series of detailed charts prepared, one for each functional area – i.e. a vertical slice of the overall chart.

The second example, Figure 8-9, is a typical template which may be used for generating each of the detailed functional charts in turn. It addresses all five layers of the modified Anthony triangle, and embodies generic forms of the type of processing likely to be required at each level.

Application coverage assessment

Once we have constructed the idealized Application Systems Map, we can use it to examine each of two sets of information in turn:

1. The relevance of each entry in the CBINS can be identified, and its existence logged on the ASM, e.g. by means of a reference number – see the example below. At this stage, the idealized application boxes may be

Figure 8-8: *Trendy Products PLC application systems map with priorities added*

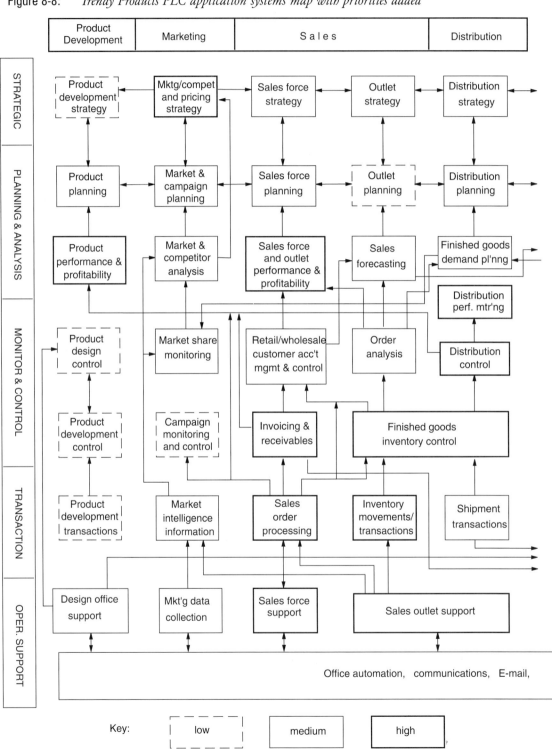

Figure 8-8:   *(continued) Trendy Products PLC application systems map with priorities added*

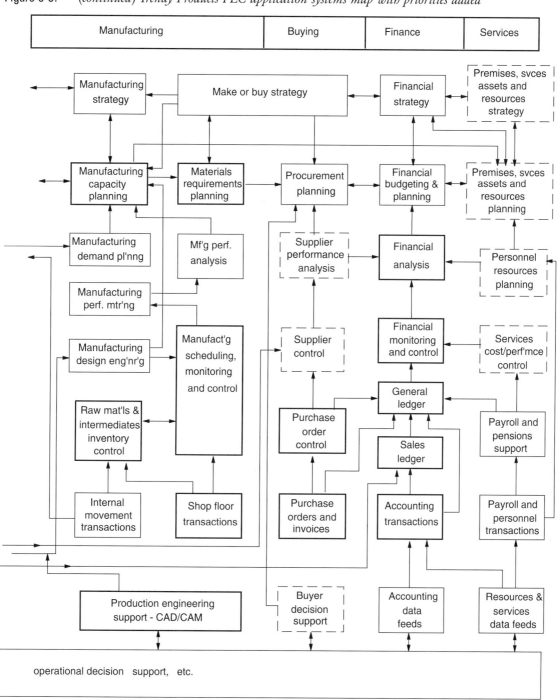

Figure 8-9:   *Generic application flows*

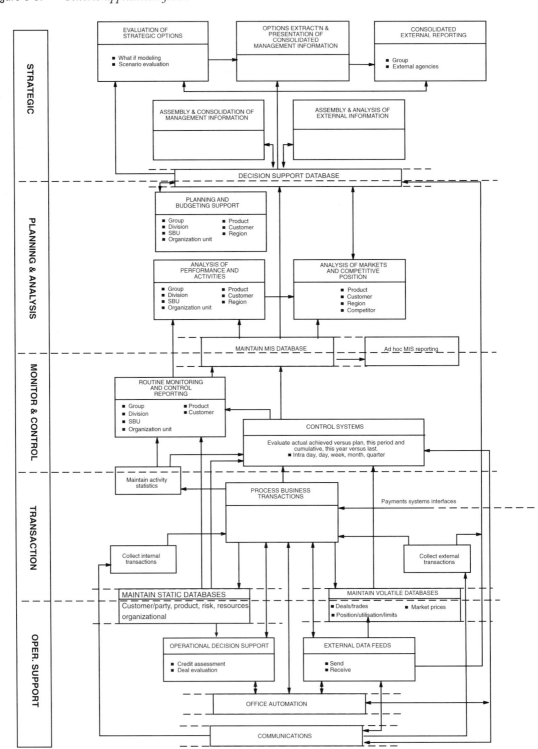

coded, as illustrated, to indicate business priority – this is regardless of whether or not the need is well met at present.

2. The relevance of each existing or planned application may likewise be identified and logged on the ASM – the examples below use the system name in italics for this purpose.

3. Thirdly, the quality of coverage offered by the existing or planned application can be indicated – here, by shading, but for real, highlight pens are best.

We can then record the results in a manner which highlights the strengths, weaknesses and gaps in the IS coverage offered by current systems and plans. This work is best carried out on the fine scale detailed charts, which should be retained as an audit trail, as it is only there that specific correspondence between CBINS and applications is relevant. The full notation, with suggestions for use of color, is shown in Figure 8-10 below. The final result may be summarized in glorious Technicolor back onto the summary level ASM for presentational use – as in Figure 8-11.

Figure 8-10: *Application coverage assessment – detailed notation*

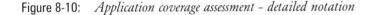
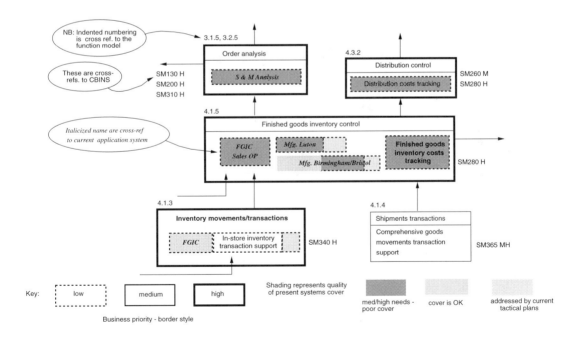

Figure 8-11:   *Trendy Products PLC application systems map with coverage notation*

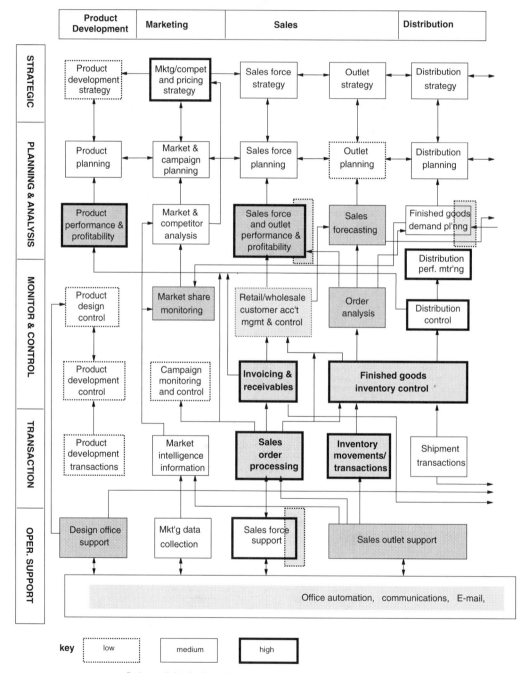

Figure 8-11: *(continued) Trendy Products PLC Application systems map with coverage notation*

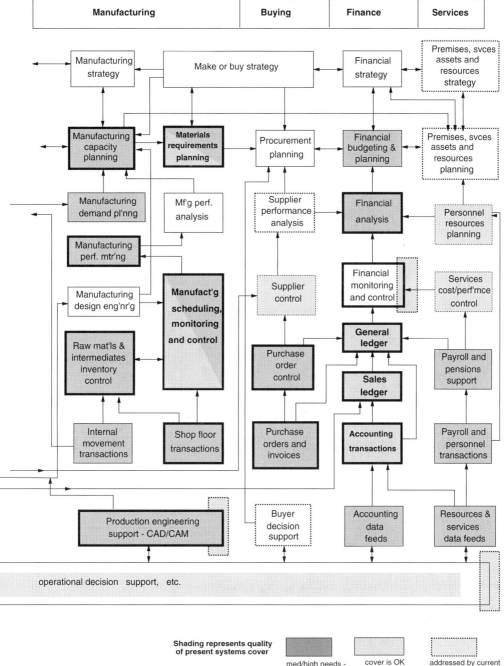

The Application Portfolio approach – McFarlan

The Portfolio Analysis approach, due to McFarlan (1981, 1984), and developed by Ward, Griffiths and Whitemore (1990) is based on a McKenny Square analysis in which applications' importance to the future business is plotted against the importance to past/present business.

The goal is to rate IS as candidates for level and type of investment into one of four categories:

- *Strategic* – clearly critical to future success
- *Turnaround* – high potential to become strategic – but risk that it may not
- *Key operational* – currently critical, becoming less so
- *Support* – not critical, but still needed – low potential
  - **Note** – these are not coincident with the application layers previously described – the partial overlap in names can be misleading

Figure 8-12:   *Application portfolio approach - McFarlan*

	high staying high	low maybe becoming high
Critical systems	**STRATEGIC** * Clearly critical to business success * Current source of competitive edge if done right * Premium investment is justified	**HIGH POTENTIAL - "Turnaround"** * Potentially critical in the future * Potential source of competitive edge * Potential candidates for innovative, high risk solutions * Speculative investment may be justified * Beware a low hit-rate
"Hygiene" systems	**KEY OPERATIONAL** * Must be kept running effectively * Strategic premium levels of investment are probably not justified * Cost reduction candidates * Low cost upgrade or replacement if needed	**SUPPORT** * Disinvest - "when can we turn it off" * Candidates for cost elimination
	high becoming lower	low staying low

Vertical axis: Importance to future business (high → low)
Horizontal axis: high ← Importance to past and present business → low

Application portfolios – risks and considerations

- Over emphasis on a single technique – CCTA, Cranfield
- Over-simplification:
  - only four categories – need for finer discrimination
  - need to think about specific needs

- risk of missed dependencies – e.g. an application categorized as Support may be a key enabler for a Strategic system
- Type-casting
- Misleading labels – especially 'Strategic', 'Key Operational' and 'Support' – these are not application types

Application portfolios – uses and relevance

- Alternative categorization scheme for assessment of coverage of needs
- Confidence factor – two alternatives indicate similar answers
- Identification of options
- Valuable guide to:
  - *allocation of emphasis* ▪ *investment policy* ▪ *style of candidate solutions*

Building the data architecture

Key elements

- Entity models:
  - *corporate* ▪ *by business area*
- Entity definitions ▪ Coding structures
- Mapping of entities to real files/databases
- MIS database ▪ Migration plans

Data architecture issues

- Level:
  - *corporate* ▪ *business area* ▪ *user/process*
- Responsibility/control
- Sharing
- Consistency, integrity, timeliness
- Distribution control and synchronization

Entity/relationship model components

- Entity – an object of relevance to the enterprise
  - *definition* ▪ *population* ▪ *existence rules* ▪ *identifying keys*
- Relationship – the nature of an association between entity types e.g. '*commodity*' is supplied under *supply contract*'
  - *conditions* ▪ *cardinality*

■   Attribute – a data item which pertains to an entity type; this may be an entity key – i.e. one or more attributes may, together identify an entity occurrence by virtue of their values.

Process for building an entity/relationship model

There have been many books and treatises written on the process for building and using data entity models. These usually dwell on techniques for 'normalization' and the like. We will not add to these here. It is sufficient to point put that the approach to use of raw materials suggested for building the function models applies equally to the data models. Likewise the considerations for controlling the levels of detail.

Data entities in many way provide the nouns in sentences about the business, where the verbs are the functions. The feasibility of creating meaningful and unambiguous sentences about the business in this way is one of the better tests for sound entities and functions.

The first of the examples which follows (Figure 8-13) is for Trendy Products. The second (Figure 8-14) is included for sentimental reasons, as a memento of one of the Author's more congenial consulting assignments.

Affinity analysis

As its name suggests, Affinity analysis in concerned with examination of the 'natural' affinities between objects or concepts in a business or systems environment. Its use is based on the thesis that, if we can identify natural clusters of associations between such objects, then we can use these to guide us to better design decisions. For example, study of the clustering of associations between data entities and business functions may be expected lead to better database designs, and may indicate the ways in which applications and subsystems should be partitioned.

It has to be said that, whilst attractive, this thesis is not necessarily proven, and the technique should not be relied upon to make sense out of a mass of unstructured detail which you do not otherwise understand. However, its use is sometimes useful in a sort of reductio ad absurdum manner, in that if cluster analysis indicates results which are palpably absurd, then it is almost certain that there are gross flaws in the inputs, i.e. your detailed analysis work.

Because many of us still feel that there is more to be gained from Affinity Analysis than has been delivered so far, it is covered in outline below.

The types of affinity whose investigation is likely to prove most informative are shown (in no particular order) in the following table.

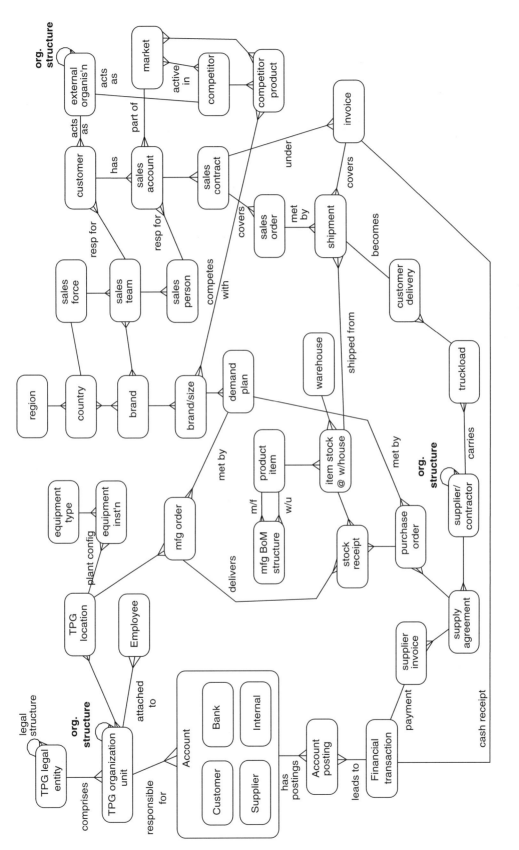

Figure 8-13: *Trendy Products PLC overall entity/relationship diagram*

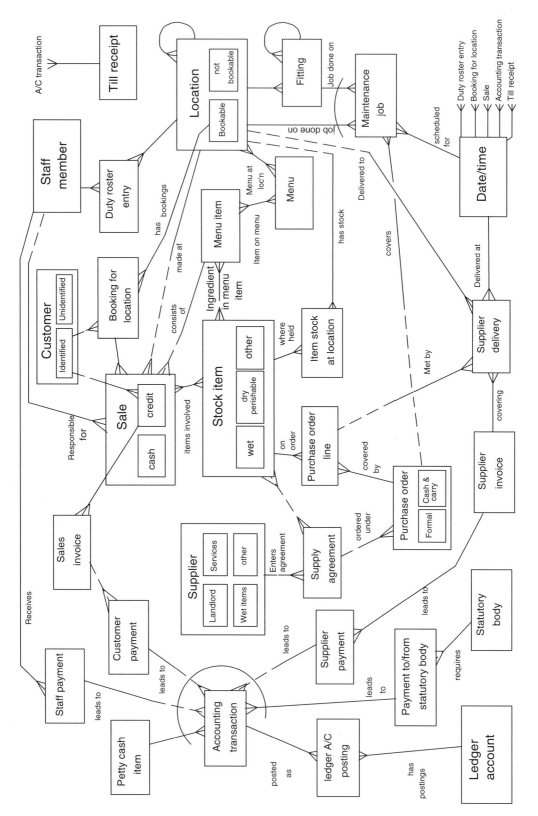

Figure 8-14: *Public House entity model*

Association	Relevance
■ Business product/service to business function	*potential economies of scale*
■ Business product/service to organization unit	*rationale and focus of organization*
■ Data entity to business function	*data ownership and responsibilities*
■ Data entity to organization unit	*data ownership and responsibilities*
■ Business function to organization unit	*rationale and focus of organization*
■ Data to application area	*guide lines for database and application design*
■ Application area to organization unit	*application usage and sponsorship*
■ Application area to business function unit	*application usage and sponsorship*

Affinity Analysis is always best used in a manner in which there is possible a degree of parallel 'top down' validity checking. This mode of use is illustrated in Figure 8-15.

Figure 8-15: *Effective use of cluster analysis*

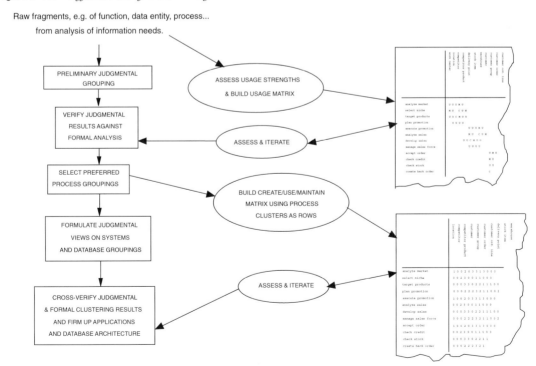

Cluster analysis results

There follows a series of sample results from the use of cluster analysis software. In the first example, Figure 8-16 an affinity matrix has been analysed to determine and recommend the most useful groupings of data entities and of business functions. In the second, Figure 8-17, a data usage matrix (commonly known as a CRUD matrix, from Create Read Use Delete) has been analysed so as to identify natural clusters which suggest themselves an application systems. In both cases. it is fairly clear that:

- the results of cluster analysis are wholly dependent on the input data;
- the results are extremely sensitive to small errors in the input data;
- the whole process is strongly reminiscent of reading tea leaves.

The reader is therefore cautioned not to spend too long in carrying out cluster analysis nor in analysing its results. However, it has its place. In a process which is strongly top-down, and heavily judgemental, it is useful to be able to conduct a limited amount of bottom up verification. Just don't run away with the idea that what you are doing is particularly objective, or that it will find eternal truths buried in your detailed data.

Figure 8-16: *ENTITY/BUSINESS FUNCTION MATRIX – with usage strengths reflecting affinity. Further header lines are permitted, with/without leading blanks – but only the text in column A is used. NB: the analyser takes the first row with an empty cell in col A as the row of column titles. Row titles must be in column A; cell entries must be null, or one of: 1, 2, 3, or zero, which is equivalent to null*

	customer	customer group	customer order	delivery point	cust order line	backorder item	customer invoice	cust invoice line	stock item	warehouse	supplier	suppl'r agreem't	supplier del'y	purchase order	purch. invoice	purch inv. line	product structr	factory	work centre	mfg. process	product group	financial txn.	ledger acc't	salesman	sales area	org. unit	employee	outlet	distrib'n channel	del'y shipment	cash receipt	cash paym.ent	job	skill	market sector	geog. region	competitor	compet. product
analyse market	3	2	0	2			2	2	0			0							0	2	3					2	2									3	3	3	3
select niche	1	3							2	2										2	3					3	2								3	3	3	3
target products	2	3		0	2				3	3	0			0				2	1	3	3		1	1	2	1			3	2	1				3	3	3	3
plan promotion	2	3		1					3			0						1	1		3		2	1	1	1			3	2	2				3	3	1	2
execute promotion	2	3	2	1			2	3	1					1	2				2		1	2	3	2	2	2			1	2			2		2	2	2	
analyse sales		3	3	3	3	2		2	2				0					0		2	3				2	2			3	2	3				1	2		
develop sales force										0														3	2	2	3						3	3				
manage sales force	1		2		2			2					0						2	3					2	3		2					2	3				
qualify credit customer	3		2	2		2													1	2	2	1							2	2								
motivate sales force				1	2			3			2	1						1	3	3		1	2	1	1	3	3		2				2	2				
accept order	3		3	3	3	3		2	3	2			1						1	2	2	2	1		2	1	2	1										
check credit	3		2	2	3			2											2	3		2					3		1	2	3							
check stock		3		3	2			3	2			2		0	2			1					1	2		2		2										
create back order	1		2	3	3			3	2					1				2							2	3	1											
plan distribution routing	1		2	2		1		1	3			2					1	1						1	1	3	3								2			
schedule trucks			2	2	1			1	3		1	1			2		1	1						1	1	1		3	2	2					2			
load trucks			2	2	3		2		2		3	2	2		1		3	2	2		1	2	3	2	2	2		1	2									
issue goods		3			3		2	3	3				2				2	2	3	2			2	2	2	3	2	3										
ship goods	2	3	2	3	3	2		2	3	3			2					2	3						2	3		3								2		
invoice customer	3	3	2	1	2	1	3	3	3									1	1	1	3	3	1	1	3	1			2									
chase cash	3	3		2	1		3												3	3	2				2	2	1	3										
review product catalogue									3		2	2					2			2					1			1	1									
plan demand	1		2	2	3	2		2		1	1	2			1	2	3	2	2		1	2	3	2	2	2			1	2					2	2		
develop make/buy schedule		1					2	3		2			2	2	2			2	2	3	2			2	2	2	3	2										
control stocks		2		3	2		2				3	3					2	2	2	3				2	3		2											
plan delivery schedule	2		2	1	3	2		3	3	2	2	2	1	3			2	1	3	3		1	2	1	1	3	2		2									
qualify supplier									2		3	1	1		1	2	1	1	1		3	2	2	1	1		2			2								
negotiate supply agreement								2	3	1	3	3	2	2	2	1	1	2		2	1	2		2	2	2			1									
place supply orders								2	3	2	3	2	3	2	3	3	2	2		2	2	3	2		2	2	2		2									
accept goods receipt								2	3	2	1	2	3	3	3	3			2	3					2													
pay supplier								3	2			3	2	3	3	3	3		2	1	3	3		1	2	1	1	3			2	3						
plan manuf'g capacity					2			3	1	2	1	1		3	2	3	1	1		3	2	2	1	1			2									2		
make goods					2		2	3	1		3	2	2		1	3	3	2	2		1	2	3	2	2	2		1				2						
plan raw mat'ls needs					2		2	3	1	2		2	2	3	2	3	1	2	2	3	2		2	2	2	2		2										
plan human resource					2									2	3			2	2	2	3			2	2	2	3						3	3				
recruit								1	2	1						2	1	3					2	2	2	3							3	3				
develop/train staff								1	1			1				1	1			1			3	2		2	1	2	3				3	3				
reward staff					2						2	2					2	2		1	2	3	2	2	2		2	2	2	2	2							
plan cash flow	1				2						2	2	2	1			2	2	3	3	3			1	1	1	3	3										
assess capital requm'ts					2	3					2	3			2			2				3	3			2	3											
manage cash					2	1	1		1	2	1	3	2			2	1	3	3		1	2	1	1	3	3		1										
produce operating stm't								3		2	1	1		2	1		1	1		3	2	2	1	1		3	2	2										

Figure 8-16:   *(continued) Cluster analysis program output*

cluster analysis program output
input matrix I
strengths of usage of data by functions

```
                            c c c d c c c s w s s s p p p p f w m p f l s s o e o d d c c j s m g c c
                            u u u e u u u t a u u u u u u r a o a r i e a a r m u i e a a o k a e o o
                            s s s l s s s o r p p p r r r o c r n o n d l l g p t s l s s b i r o m m
                            t t t i t t t c e p p p c c c d t k u d a g e e a l l t i h h   l k g p p
                            o o o v o o o k h l l l h h h u o   f u n e s s n o e r v         l e r e e
                            m m m e m m m   o i i i a a a c r c a c c r m   i y t i e         t a t t
                            e e e r e e e i u e e e s s s t y e c t i   a a s e   b r r p       p i i
                            r r r y r r r t s r r r e e e   n t   a a n r a e   u y e a         h t t
                                    e e       s   t u g l c   e t   t   c y         s i o o
                            g o p o i i m   a d o i i t   r r r   c   a i         i s i m       e c r r
                            r r o r n n       g e r n n r   e i o t o       o   o h e e         c   s
                            o d i d v v       r l d v v u   n u r u       n   n i p n         t r   p
                            u e n e o o       e i e o o c   g p a n           p t t         o e   r
                            p r t r i i       e v r i i t       n t       u   c m         r g   o
                                    c c       m e   c c u   p   s       n   h e         i   d
                                l e e       e r   e e r   r   a       i   a n         o   u
                                i           n y     e   o   c       t   n t         n   c
                                n   l       t       l   c   t       n                     t
                                e   i               i   e   i       e
                                    n               n   s   o       l
                                    e               e   s   n
                          |-------------------------------------------------------------------------
analyse market            | 0 3 2 0 2 0 2 2 0 0 0 0 0 0 0 0 0 2 3 0 0 0 2 2 0 3 2 2 0 0 0 0 3 3 3 3
select niche              | 1 3 0 0 0 0 2 2 0 0 0 0 0 0 0 0 0 2 3 0 0 0 0 0 3 2 0 0 0 0 0 3 3 3 3
target products           | 2 3 0 0 2 0 3 3 0 0 0 0 0 0 0 0 2 1 3 3 0 1 2 1 0 3 2 1 0 0 0 0 3 3 3
plan promotion            | 2 3 0 0 1 0 0 3 0 0 0 0 0 0 0 1 1 0 3 0 2 1 1 1 0 3 2 2 0 0 0 0 3 3 1 2
execute promotion         | 2 3 2 0 1 0 2 3 1 0 0 0 0 0 1 2 0 0 2 0 1 2 3 2 2 2 0 1 2 0 0 2 0 2 2 0 0
analyse sales             | 0 3 3 3 3 0 2 2 0 0 0 0 0 0 0 0 0 2 3 0 0 0 2 2 0 3 2 3 0 0 0 0 1 2 0 0
develop sales force       | 0 0 0 0 0 0 0 0 0 0 0 0 0 0 0 0 0 0 0 0 0 0 3 2 2 3 0 0 0 0 0 3 3 0 0 0
manage sales force        | 1 0 2 0 2 0 0 2 0 0 0 0 0 0 0 0 0 2 3 0 0 0 0 2 3 0 2 0 0 0 0 0 0 0 0 0
motivate sales force      | 0 0 0 1 2 0 3 0 0 0 2 1 0 0 0 0 0 1 3 3 0 1 2 1 1 3 3 0 2 0 2 2 0 0 0 0
accept order              | 3 0 3 3 3 0 2 3 2 0 0 1 0 0 0 0 0 0 0 0 1 2 2 2 1 0 2 1 2 1 0 0 0 0 0 0
check credit              | 3 0 2 2 3 0 2 0 0 0 0 0 0 0 0 0 0 0 0 2 3 0 2 0 0 0 1 2 3 0 0 0 0 0 0 0
check stock               | 0 0 3 0 3 0 0 3 2 0 0 2 0 0 2 0 0 1 0 0 0 0 0 1 2 0 2 0 0 0 0 0 0 0 0 0
create back order         | 1 0 2 0 0 0 3 2 0 0 0 0 1 0 0 0 2 0 0 0 0 0 2 3 0 1 0 0 0 0 0 0 0 0 0
plan distribution routing | 1 0 2 2 0 0 0 1 3 0 0 2 0 0 0 0 1 1 0 0 0 0 0 1 1 3 3 0 2 0 0 0 0 0 2 0
schedule trucks           | 0 0 2 2 1 0 0 1 3 0 1 1 0 0 2 0 1 1 0 0 0 0 1 1 1 0 3 2 2 0 0 0 0 0 2 0
load trucks               | 0 0 2 2 3 0 2 0 2 0 3 2 2 0 1 0 3 2 2 0 1 2 3 2 2 2 0 1 2 0 0 0 0 0 0 0
issue goods               | 0 0 3 0 0 0 3 3 0 0 2 2 0 0 2 2 0 2 2 3 2 0 0 2 2 2 3 2 3 0 0 0 0 0 0 0
ship goods                | 2 3 2 3 3 0 2 3 3 0 0 0 2 0 0 0 0 0 2 3 0 0 0 0 2 3 0 3 0 0 0 0 0 2 0
invoice customer          | 3 3 2 1 2 3 3 3 0 0 0 0 0 0 0 0 0 1 1 1 3 3 1 1 1 3 1 0 2 0 0 0 0 0 0 0
chase cash                | 3 3 0 2 1 3 0 0 0 0 0 0 0 0 0 0 0 3 3 2 0 0 0 2 2 1 3 0 0 0 0 0 0 0 0 0
plan demand               | 1 0 2 2 3 0 2 0 1 1 2 0 0 0 1 2 3 2 2 0 1 2 3 2 2 2 0 1 2 0 0 0 0 2 2 0
develop make/buy schedule | 0 0 1 0 0 0 2 3 0 2 0 2 2 0 0 2 0 2 2 3 2 0 0 2 2 2 3 2 0 0 0 0 0 0 0 0
control stocks            | 0 0 2 0 3 0 2 0 0 0 0 3 3 0 0 0 2 2 2 3 0 0 0 0 2 3 0 2 0 0 0 0 0 0 0 0
plan delivery schedule    | 2 0 2 1 3 0 3 3 2 2 2 1 3 0 0 0 2 1 3 3 0 1 2 1 1 3 2 0 2 0 0 0 0 0 0 0
qualify supplier          | 0 0 0 0 0 0 2 0 3 1 1 0 1 2 1 1 1 0 3 2 1 1 1 0 0 2 0 0 2 0 0 0 0 0 0 0
negotiate supply agreement| 0 0 0 0 0 0 2 3 1 3 3 2 2 2 1 1 2 0 2 0 1 2 0 2 2 2 0 1 0 0 0 0 0 0 0 0
place supply orders       | 0 0 0 0 0 0 2 3 2 3 3 2 3 3 2 2 0 2 2 3 2 0 0 2 2 2 0 2 0 0 0 0 0 0 0 0
accept goods receipt      | 0 0 0 0 0 0 2 3 2 1 2 3 3 3 3 0 0 2 3 0 0 0 2 0 0 0 0 2 0 0 0 0 0 0 0 0
pay supplier              | 0 0 0 0 0 0 3 2 0 3 2 3 3 3 3 0 2 1 3 3 0 1 2 1 1 3 0 0 0 2 3 0 0 0 0 0
plan manuf'g capacity     | 0 0 0 0 0 0 3 1 2 1 1 0 3 2 3 1 1 0 3 2 2 1 1 1 0 0 2 0 0 0 0 0 0 2 0 0
make goods                | 0 0 0 0 0 0 2 3 1 0 3 2 2 0 1 3 3 2 2 0 1 2 3 2 2 2 0 1 0 0 0 2 0 0 0 0
plan raw mat'ls needs     | 0 0 0 0 0 0 2 3 1 2 0 2 2 3 2 3 1 2 2 3 2 0 0 2 2 2 0 2 0 0 0 0 0 0 0 0
plan human resource       | 0 0 0 0 0 0 2 0 0 0 0 2 3 0 0 2 2 2 3 0 0 0 2 2 3 0 0 0 0 3 3 0 0 0
recruit                   | 0 0 0 0 0 0 0 1 2 1 0 0 0 0 2 1 3 3 0 0 2 2 3 0 0 0 0 0 3 3 0 0 0
develop/train staff       | 0 0 0 0 0 0 0 0 0 1 1 0 0 1 0 1 1 0 3 2 0 2 1 2 3 0 0 0 0 3 3 0 0 0
reward staff              | 0 0 0 0 0 2 0 0 0 0 2 2 0 0 0 0 2 2 0 1 2 3 2 2 2 0 0 2 2 2 2 0 0 0 0
plan cash flow            | 1 0 0 0 0 0 2 0 0 0 0 2 2 2 1 0 2 2 3 3 3 0 0 0 1 1 1 3 3 0 0 0 0 0
assess capital requm'ts   | 0 0 0 0 0 2 3 0 0 0 0 2 3 0 0 2 0 0 0 3 3 0 0 0 2 3 0 0 0 0 0 0 0 0
manage cash               | 0 0 0 0 0 2 1 1 0 1 2 1 3 2 0 0 2 1 3 3 0 1 2 1 1 3 3 0 1 0 0 0 0 0 0
produce operating stm't   | 0 0 0 0 0 0 0 3 0 2 1 1 0 2 1 0 1 1 0 3 2 2 1 1 1 0 3 2 2 0 0 0 0 0 0
```

Figure 8-16: *(continued) Data Entity Groupings*

```
Option selected to cluster on Columns (data entities).
customer
---------------------
        customer order
                customer invoice
                        customer group
                        delivery point
                                customer order line
                                work centre
                                        factory
                                        manufacturing process
                                        financial transaction
                                        sales area
                                                warehouse
                                                supplier
                                                purchase invoice line
                                                ledger account
                                                salesman
                                                        stock item
                                                        supplier delivery
                                                        purchase order
                                                        purchase invoice
                                                        product structure
                                                        outlet
                                                        delivery shipment
                                                        cash  receipt
                                                        job
                                                                supplier agreement
                                                                product group
                                                                organisation unit
                                                                employee
                                                                distribution channel
                                                                cash  payment
                                                                skill
                                                                market  sector
                                                                competitor
                                                                competitors product
customer group
---------------------
                        customer
                        customer order
                                delivery point
                                        customer invoice
                                                customer order line
                                                work centre
                                                        factory
                                                        manufacturing process
                                                        ledger account
                                                        sales area
                                                                stock item
                                                                warehouse
                                                                supplier
                                                                purchase order
                                                                purchase invoice line
                                                                product group
                                                                financial transaction
                                                                salesman
                                                                outlet
                                                                distribution channel
                                                                delivery shipment
                                                                cash  receipt
                                                                job
                                                                competitors product
customer order
---------------------
        customer
        delivery point
                        customer group
                        customer order line
                        customer invoice
                        sales area
                                work centre
                                manufacturing process
                                financial transaction
                                        warehouse
                                        supplier
                                        product structure
                                        factory
```

```
                                        ledger account
                                        cash  payment
                                                purchase invoice line
                                                salesman
                                                employee
                                                outlet
                                                delivery shipment
                                                cash  receipt
                                                job
                                                skill
                                                competitors product
                                                        stock item
                                                        supplier agreement
                                                        supplier delivery
                                                        purchase order
                                                        purchase invoice
                                                        product group
                                                        organisation unit
                                                        market  sector
                                                        competitor
                                                                distribution channel
                                                                geographic region
                                                                        customer invoice line
```

Figure 8-16:   *(continued) Business Function Groupings*

```
Option selected to cluster on Rows (business functions).

analyse market
---------------------
        target products
                analyse sales
                        select niche
                        plan promotion
                                execute promotion
                                ship goods
                                        issue goods
                                        invoice customer
                                        plan demand
                                        plan delivery schedule
                                                motivate sales force
                                                accept order
                                                schedule trucks
                                                develop make/buy schedule
                                                control stocks
                                                        manage sales force
                                                        check stock
                                                        create back order
                                                        plan distribution routing
                                                        load trucks
                                                        place supply orders
                                                        pay supplier
                                                        produce operating statement
                                                                accept goods receipt
                                                                make goods
                                                                plan human resource
                                                                plan cash flow
select niche
---------------------
                        analyse market
                        target products
                                plan promotion
                                        analyse sales
                                        execute promotion
                                        ship goods
                                                issue goods
                                                invoice customer
                                                develop make/buy schedule
                                                plan delivery schedule
                                                        manage sales force
                                                        motivate sales force
                                                        accept order
                                                        create back order
                                                        schedule trucks
                                                        chase cash
                                                        plan demand
                                                        plan manuf'g capacity
                                                        plan raw mat'ls needs
                                                        plan cash flow
                                                        manage cash
                                                        produce operating statement
```

```
                                                  check credit
                                                  check stock
                                                  plan distribution routing
                                                  load trucks

target products
---------------------
        analyse market
        plan promotion
                    select niche
                    execute promotion
                    analyse sales
                    plan delivery schedule
                            ship goods
                            invoice customer
                            plan demand
                                    motivate sales force
                                    accept order
                                    load trucks
                                    issue goods
                                    develop make/buy schedule
                                    make goods
                                    manage cash
                                            schedule trucks
                                            control stocks
                                            negotiate supply agreement
                                            place supply orders
                                            pay supplier
                                            plan manuf'g capacity
                                            plan raw mat'ls needs
                                            plan human resource
                                            plan cash flow
                                            produce operating statement
                                                    manage sales force
                                                    check credit
                                                    check stock
                                                    create back order
                                                    plan distribution routing
                                                    chase cash
                                                    qualify supplier
                                                    recruit
                                                    reward staff
                                                    assess capital requm'ts
                                                            accept goods receipt
                                                            develop/train staff
                                                                    develop sales force
```

Figure 8-17:   *ENTITY/SYSTEM PROCESS MATRIX – showing Create/Reads/Updates/Modifies/Deletes activity*

	customer	customer group	customer order	delivery point	cust order line	backorder item	customer invoice	cost invoice line	stock item	warehouse	supplier	suppl'r agreem't	supplier del'y	purchase order	purch. invoice	purch inv. line	product structr	factory	work center	mfg. process	product group	financial txn.	ledger acc't	salesman	sales area	org. unit	employee	outlet	distrib'n channel	del'y shipment	cash receipt	cash paym,ent	job	skill	market sector	geog. region	competitor	compet. product
analyze market	R	U	R		R				R												M	R	R		M			R	R						R	R	R	R
select niche	R	R	R			R	R														R			R				R	R						R	R	R	R
target products	R	R	R		R			R	R												R			R				R	R						R	R	R	R
plan promotion	R	R	R		R			R	R												R			R	R	R	R	R	R						R	R	R	R
execute promotion	M	R					R	R	R												R			R	R	R	R	R	R						R	R	R	R
analyze sales	R	R	R		R	R			R												R	R	R	R	R	R	R	R	R						R	R	R	R
develop sales force																					R			M	R	R	R	M	R								R	R
manage sales force			R		R				R												R			M	R	R	M	R	R								R	R
motivate sales force		R	R		R																R	R	R	R	R	R	R	R	R						R	R		
qualify credit customer	C		D	D		R															R	R	R	R				R	R						R	R		
accept order	M		C	U	C	C			M	R											M	R	R					R	R		M	M						
check credit	R		M		M		R	R													R	R						R	R		R	R						
check stock			M		M	R			R	R				R	R																							
create back order	R		M		M	C			M	R	R	R	R	R			R	R												R								
plan distribution routing	R	R	M	R	R	R					R			R				R										R	R									
schedule trucks		R	R	R							R							R										R	R									
load trucks		R	R	R	R				R	R																												
issue goods		R	R	R	D				R	R																												
ship goods	R	U	R		U	R	M	U	U	R	R											U	R							U	U							
invoice customer	M	R	U		R		C	C	R													C	R					R	R		C	C						
chase cash	M						R	R														R	R					R	R		R	R						
review product catalogue									C			R	M				C				U			R				R	R									
plan demand		R		R	R				R	R	R	R					R	R			R			R				R	R	R					R	R	R	R
develop make/buy schedule		R								M		M	M	R	R		M	R	R	R				R			R											
control stocks		R		R	R				R	M				R	R			R									R											
plan delivery schedule		R	R	R					M	R	R	M	R	R			R	R						R				R	R	R								
qualify supplier									R	R	R	C	C	R	R	R					R	R	R												R	R	R	
negotiate supply agreement									M	M	M	C	R	C			R				U	R		R				R	R				U	U	R	R		
place supply orders									R	R	R	M	R	C			R				U	R		R				R	R	R			U	U	R	R		
accept goods receipt									R	M	R		R	R	R	R	M	M			R			R				R	R	R	C							
pay supplier									R				M	R	R	R	M	R				C	R							R	C	C						
plan manuf'g capacity									R	R	R	R		R			R	R	U	U	R			R	R			R	R						R	R	R	R
make goods						R			R	R				R	R		R	R	R	R				R														
plan raw mat'ls needs						R			R	R	R	R	R			M	R	R	R	R				R				R	R	R								
plan human resource									R									R	R	R				R	R	R	R						R	R	R	R	R	R
recruit																								C	R		C						R	R				
develop/train staff																								R	R	R	R						U	U				
reward staff					R													R	R	R		C	R	R	R	R	R						C	C	R	R		
plan cash flow									R					R	R	R		R				R	R		R			R	R		R	R			R	R		
assess capital requm'ts											R			R	R			R	R			R	R		R			R	R		R	R			R	R		
manage cash					R				R					R	R	R		R				R	R		R			R	R		R	R			R	R		
produce operating stm't									R									R				R	R		R			R	R		R	R			R	R		

Figure 8-17:   *(continued) Output from cluster program 2 - input matrix II - Data Create/Use/Modify*

```
                     c c c d c c c s w s s s p p p p f w m p f l s s o e o d d c c j s m g c c
                     u u u e u u u t a u u u u u u r a o a r i e a a r m u i e a a o k a e o o
                     s s s l s s s o r p p p r r r o c r n o n d l l g p t s l s s b i r o m m
                     t t t i t t t c e p p p c c c d t k u d a g e e a l l t i h h   l k g p p
                     o o o v o o o k h l l l h h h u o   f u n e s s n o e r v       l e r e e
                     m m m e m m m   o i i i a a a c r c a c c r m   i y t i e         t a t t
                     e e e r e e e i u e e e s s s t y e c t i   a a s e   b r r p     p i i
                     r r r y r r r t s r r r e e e     n t   a a n r a e   u y e a     h t t
                         e e         e         s       t u g l c   e t     t   c y   s i o o
                     g o p o i i m     a d o i i t     r r r   c   a i     i s i m     e c r r
                     r r o r n n       g e r n n r     e i o t o     o     o h e e     c   s
                     o d i d v v       r l d v v u     n u r u     n     n i p n       t
                     u e n e o o       e i e o o c     g p a n         p t t       o r     p
                     p r t r i i       e v r i i t       n t     u     c m         r e     r
                         c c           m e c c u       p   s     n     h e           g   o
                         l e e         e r e e r       r   a     i     a n           i   d
                         i             n y       e     o   c     t     n t           o   u
                         n   l         t       l     c   t       n             n   c
                         e   i                 i     e   i       e             e       t
                             n                 n     s   o       l
                             e                 e     s   n
|-------------------------------------------------------------------------------
analyse market         | u c u     u       u                       m u u     u     u u   u u       u u u u
select niche           | u u u       u u                             u         u     u u         u u u u
target products        | u u u   u   u u                             u         u     u u         u u u u
plan promotion         | u u u   u   u u                             u     u u u u u u           u u u u
execute promotion      | m u           u u                           u     u u u u u u           u u u u
analyse sales          | u u u   u     u                           u u u u u u u u u   u u       u u u u
develop sales force    |                                           u     m u u m u u         u u
manage sales force     |   u   u     u                             u     m u u m u         u u
motivate sales force   |   u u   u                                 u u u m u u m u u     u u u u
qualify credit customer| c   u c                                   u u u u     u u u   u u
accept order           | m   c m c     u u                           m u u     u u u     m m
check credit           | u   m   m                                   u u       u u     u u
check stock            |     m   m     u u       u u
create back order      | u   m   m     m u u u u u     u u                           u
plan distribution routing| u   m u u       u       u         u           u   u u
schedule trucks        |   u u u         u             u                     u u
load trucks            |   u u u       u u
issue goods            |   u u u       u u
ship goods             | u   u u u m m u u                 m u               m m
invoice customer       | m   u   u c c u                   c u         u u     c c
chase cash             | m       u u                       u u         u u     u u
add product to catalogue|         c   u m         c       m       u     u u
plan demand            |   u   u     u u u u u u     u u       u       u     u u u       u u u u
develop make/buy schedule|   u       m   m m u u     m u u u u         u         u
control stocks         |   u   u     u m     u u       u                       u
plan delivery schedule |   u u u     m u u m u u     u u               u     u u u
qualify supplier       |       u u u     c c u u u u         u u u           u u u
negotiate supply agreement|     m u m c u c       u         m u     u     u u     m m
place supply orders    |       u u u m c         u         m u     u     u u u m m
accept goods receipt   |     u m u u u u m m     u             u         u u c
pay supplier           |     u   m u u u m u             c u           u c c
plan manuf'g capacity  |     u u u u   u       u u m m u       u u     u u         u u u u
make goods             |     u u       u u       u u u u             u
plan raw mat'ls needs  |     u u u u u m       u u u u u         u     u u u
plan human resource    |           u           u u u       u u u u           u u u u u u
recruit                |                                   c u   c             u u
develop/train staff    |                                     u u u u         m m
reward staff           |     u               u u u   c u u u u u       c c u u
plan cash flow         |       u         u u u     u       u u     u     u u     u u     u u
assess capital requm'ts|       u         u u u     u u u     u u     u u     u u     u u     u u
manage cash            |     u   u       u u u     u         u u     u     u u     u u     u u
produce operating stm't|         u                   u       u u u     u u     u u     u u     u u
```

Figure 8-17:   *(continued) Output from cluster program 2 - input matrix II - Data Create/Use/Modify*

```
                          s j e s c c s c g m o c c c p f c c o d l w m c c f p s p d w p p s s d s
                          k o m a u o a o e a r u u u r i a a u i e o a u u a u t u e a u r u u e u
                          i b p l s m l m o r g s s s o n s s t s d r n s s c r o r l r r o p p l p
                          l   l e t p e p g k a t t t d a h h l t g k u t t t c c c i e c d p p i p
                          l   o s o e s e r e n o o o u n     e r e     f o o o h k h v h h u l l v l
                          y m m t   t a t i m m c c     t i r c a m m r a   a e o a c i i e i
                          e a e i a i p   s e e e t i p r   b   e c e e y s i s r u s t e e r e
                          e n r t r t h   a r r r   a a e   u a n t r r   e t e y s e   r r y r
                            o e o i s t       g l y c   t c t u         e   e   s
                          g r a r c e i i i   r   m i   i c r r o   i m i p   o t a   s d
                          r   s   c o n n   o t e e   o o e i r r   n   n o   r r g   h e
                          u       t n v v   u r n p   n u n d d   v   v i   d u r   i l
                          p   p r o   o o   p a t t   n   g e e   o   o n   e c e   p i
                              r e r u i i   n     c t     r r   i   i t   r t e   m v
                              o g   n c c   s     h     p     c   c       u m   e e
                              d i   i e e   a     a     r   l e   e       r e   n r
                              u o   t     c     n     o   i       e n   t y
                              c n     l     t     n     c   n     l         t
                              t       i     i     e     e   e     i
                                      n     o     l     s         n
                                      e     n     s               e

recruit                   | u u c c       u
develop/train staff       | m m u u       u           u
develop sales force       | u u m m       u           u           u         u u
manage sales force        | u u m m       u           u           u u             u u         u
reward staff              | u u u u       u           u     u       c c c       u u u       u
plan human resource       | u u u u   u u u u u u                           u u       u             u
qualify credit customer   |   u u                         c u u u u u u u       u                 c
motivate sales force      | u u m m u   u           u         u u u u u u u     u u
chase cash                |                         u u m   u u u u u u
execute promotion         | u u u u u u u u u       m u       u u                     u       u
select niche              |     u u u u u u     u   u u       u u             u       u
plan promotion            | u u u u u u u u u u   u u       u u             u u       u
target products           |     u u u u u u     u   u u       u u             u u       u
analyse sales             | u u u u u u u u     u u u u u u u u     u u       u
analyse market            |     c u u u u u     u m u u u u u u     u u       u
produce operating stm't   |     u     u u u     u u u u u u u             u   u
invoice customer          |             c c m     c c c u u u       u u       u
manage cash               |         u u u   u       u u u u u u       u u u u       u
plan cash flow            |         u u u           u u u u u u       u u u u       u
assess capital requm'ts   |     u     u u u         u u u u u u u u       u u u u         u
check credit              |                       u   u u u u u u     m m
accept order              | u u                   m     m m m u u u     c c       u     m u
ship goods                |             m m u     m m m       u       u u       u     u u
schedule trucks           |                               u u       u u u       u u
plan manuf'g capacity     |     u u u u u u           u       u u     m m       u     u     u u u u u
qualify supplier          |               u u     u u u u       u             u u u       u     c c u u
plan distribution routing |                 u     u         u u       m u u       u u           u
plan demand               |     u u u u u           u         u u       u u u     u       u u u u u u
place supply orders       |           u           m m m u u u             u       u c u m u u u
negotiate supply agreement|           u           m m m u u u             m       u c u c m   u
plan delivery schedule    |           u                   u u       u u u       u u u u u u u u
plan raw mat'ls needs     |               u     u         u u   u u       u   u       u m u u u u u
develop make/buy schedule |               u     u             u u u   u   m       u m m m u u
accept goods receipt      |                         u u u           u m u m     m u       u u c u
pay supplier              |                   c c c     u           m u u         u     u m u u
create back order         |                   u             m m u   m         u u u u u u u u
make goods                |             u                 u u       u   u         u u u       u
check stock               |                               m m       u       u u
add product to catalogue  |     u                   m       u u           c         c m u
control stocks            |                               u u u       u           m u         u u
load trucks               |                               u u         u     u u
issue goods               |                               u u         u     u u
```

In the above example, where the cluster program appears to be suggesting the existence of natural system groupings, the clusters have been highlighted. You, the reader, must judge whether or not it is telling you anything new!

Interaction with system and data architects

It is just as vital to get the IS/IT personnel on your side as it is the business management.

The systems and data architects in your IT organization will become the custodians and implementors of the architecture products described in this chapter. If they feel that they have been disregarded or steamrollered, their resentment may be reflected in reluctance to take the products on board in a whole hearted manner, and a failure to reflect the high level architectural insights gained in the detailed systems and data designs resulting.

The solution in the case of the information architects is to have them work on the architecture products alongside other strategy team members, so that they are committed to their work automatically. They will bring benefits of thoroughness and rigor to the team, and the products will conform the relevant standards from the outset. However, tact and diplomacy may be required in helping such design staff to avoid inappropriate detail – they didn't get where they are by 'skimming over the surface'.

Needs

- Smooth hand over of concepts and materials
- Mutual regard, understanding of needs and levels of detail
- Distinguish between strategic/directional and tactical/migration

Method

- Involve the architecture group who will receive the results
- Include in training and planning
- Participation in interviews and analysis
- Presence at group consolidation meetings
- Secondment for business and systems modelling
- Negotiate use of compatible techniques, tools and conventions
- Assist in evaluating current systems
- Assist in defining/estimating new projects
- Provide for architectures maintenance in the implementation plan

Summary of process issues

Start Up

- core team
- co-operation with other groups
- techniques as compatible as possible

Business Requirements Analysis

- involve architects
- control over levels of detail
- 'traceability'

Information Architecture Definition

- use tools as servants not masters
- control over levels of detail – just sufficient
- use automated means to record main objects

Follow-through

- involve the architecture group who will receive the results
- compatible techniques and convention
- incorporate maintenance in the implementation plan

Appendix 1 to Chapter 8

Discussion of application categories

This paper embodies a number of approaches to the classification of application systems. It is made up of three parts, each offering a slightly different view. The shortest is first, the longest last. The sections are:

1.   Broad operational categories.

2.   Categories based on application layer type.

3.   An outline of a fuller approach, which includes data categories.

1. BROAD OPERATIONAL CATEGORIES

i.	Information distribution (feeds, broadcast, back-channel).
ii.	Fully protected transaction processing (measured, e.g. in TPC A/B/Cs per second).
iii.	'Batch' processing
iv.	Text editing and management;
v.	Text analysis;
vi.	Support for heavy numerical computation;
vii.	Support for general workstation functionality – mix and match, task management, presentation, MMI, etc.;
viii.	MIS type ad hoc enquiry/analysis
ix.	Network message and transaction switching;
x.	Application development activity – resource consumption per active terminal;
xi.	End user activity – clerical/managerial/specialist;

NB: Decision support type processing is seen as a combination of *v, vi, vii* and *viii.*

2. CATEGORIES BASED ON APPLICATION LAYERING

This is the set of information system types needed to support all of the needs of a typical commercial organization. The systems are defined as they are perceived by the users – therefore there is no intrusion of technology solutions here – although there may be performance, throughput or service requirement which have technology implications.

2.1   Information distribution and support - *internal*

  ■ *structured data*   ■ *document/text*   ■ *picture*   ■ *numeric*

2.2   Information distribution and support - *external*

  ■ *structured data*   ■ *document/text*   ■ *picture*   ■ *numeric*

2.3   Office Automation

- *news/intelligence propagation*
- *electronic mail*
- *document management*
- *diary/calendar*

2.4   'Batch' transaction processing

Data collection separated from asynchronous batch processing during which transactions are applied to the database.

- High volume – shared database
- Low volume – shared database
- Low volume, closed user group

NB: There is wide variation in the business scope and duration of a transaction – e.g. a settlement bargain is only fully processed and completed after several stages, over a period of days or weeks.

2.5   On-line transaction processing – Interactive processing of transactions, with immediate full database updating.

- High volume – shared database
- Low volume – shared database
- Low volume, closed user group

NB: Same comments re transaction scope.

2.5   Consolidation, monitoring and control

- *Financial*
- *Surveillance*
- *Performance measurement*
- *Service levels, networks and access*

2.6   MIS-Type Analysis and Planning

- *budgeting/planning support*
- *ad-hoc enquiry*
- *routine analysis of performance*
- *presentation-oriented*

2.7   Decision support

- *numeric*
- *text analysis*
- *knowledge-based*

2.8   Communications and delivery

- *local*
- *within UK*
- *world-wide*

3. OUTLINE OF A FULLER APPROACH, INCLUDING DATA CATEGORIES

3.1   *Nature and Purpose of the Information Pyramid*

The 'Information Pyramid' is based on the classic Anthony Triangle [Anthony, Robert N: *Planning and Control Systems*, Harvard Business School Press, Boston 1965]. It is intended to set out a generic set of information systems for any organization in a given business sector.

Thus, if starting with a clean slate, and an unlimited budget, this is the ideal target set of information systems.

It is intended as a starting point for the development of a more detailed and specific 'map' of the ideal set of application systems. Such a map may then be used as a frame of reference, against which any given state may be checked very simply. It must, of course, be developed in step with the evolution of business plans and strategies.

At any specific time, there will be a significant degree of coverage offered by existing systems, some good, some less so. The coverage offered by existing systems should be assessed on three criteria:

- The extent to which business needs and priorities are met by the applications;
- The operational stability, reliability and other aspects of service quality are met by them;
- The extent to which the applications form a suitable basis for further evolution to meet future business needs – which is a function of their design quality and enhanceability.

There will also be identifiable gaps in coverage, where high priority business needs exist and there is a good case for the construction of systems to meet the needs. These coverage gaps will vary in the degree of business priority which may be accorded to rectifying them. Thus the pyramid may be used in assigning priorities for moving the applications portfolio closer to meeting current business priorities.

As the detail of the systems map is improved, the interfaces between the applications will be highlighted and clarified. When it is in this form, the systems map may be used to evaluate the impact of alternative ways of meeting a particular information need, or of feeding data to a subsystem. Thus it becomes of value in planning of migration.

3.2   *Information System Types and Levels*

The information pyramid is divided into a number of horizontal bands, which correspond approximately to identifiable levels of information or of management responsibility. These may be varied to taste, but the levels used here have been proven in a fairly wide range of cases, and may be used in the absence of obviously better alternatives.

The basis for these bands is that there are certain distinct classes of information and support required for running any business. These may be regarded as corresponding to different 'layers' of information systems. In the attached diagram, the layers correspond to the following classes:

3.2.1 *Operational Support Systems* provide routine support to the day-to-day business activities. Examples include:

- provision of dealing support information (e.g. market prices and trading volumes) from external sources;
- electronic mail/messaging;
- provision of up to date internal reference data, e.g. party/credit, tariffs/rates, positions, etc.

3.2.2 *Transaction Processing Systems* process business transactions corresponding to bargains and other relatively high volume routine business events of the organization. They tend to be predefined, and access structured files or databases.

3.2.3 *Monitoring and Control Systems* tend to carry out predefined monitoring and exception processes resulting from the transaction processing systems. Examples include position and limit minding, and monitoring of trading volumes.

3.2.4 *Planning and Analysis*

- *Management Information Systems (MIS)* concern reporting, enquiry and analysis for management planning and control purposes – e.g. product profitability, routine compliance monitoring. The broad terms of such reporting are relatively stable. However, the level of summarization tends to be high, and there may be a high degree of flexibility needed in selection and formatting. There may also be wide variation in the degree of timeliness required of the underlying data – from up to the minute for certain types of Trading, to monthly or less for monitoring the profitability of long term client relationships or big ticket lending.
- *Decision Support Systems* generally represent a higher degree of volatility. The facilities are specifically oriented to:
- planning and budgeting;
- analysis of performance against those plans;
- forward projection of likely performance according to a variety of options.

These applications tend to have lower processing volumes, and less frequent work requests, but to have with greater volatility of requirements. They also tend to be far more heavily dependent upon good presentational interfaces, and require heavier computing power per request to support them.

3.2.5 *Business Strategy Support* facilities support the senior management strategy formulation process, as well as certain classes of operational decision – e.g. risk assessment. They may be of almost any type, with any combination of characteristics. Their inherent characteristics include:

- Heavy use of external information;
- A wide event-horizon;
- Highly interactive, even though they may be used through intermediaries, hence the user interface and presentational aspects are highly critical.

These applications may be split broadly into:

- Numerically based modelling processes;
- Text based 'intelligence' processes;
- Rule-based 'expert system' processes.

Although as time goes on we will see increasing convergence of these classes. Layers 3.2.4 and 3.2.5 together are commonly termed 'Decision Support' systems, and tend to be particularly suited to PC-based environments backed up by closely controlled downloading from mainframe databases.

3.3   *Functional Divisions*

In a similar manner, the pyramid can be divided into vertical columns. This is usually done on the basis of a functional split (where function is carefully distinguished from any consideration of the ways in which those functions may be placed in an organizational structure).

This vertical functional is not always rigid – several classes of information, e.g. Party Profile, run across many functional areas – and in any case should become clearer in the more detailed versions of the systems map into which the pyramid should evolve.

Typically, the pyramid is partitioned on the basis of a generic functional split which would apply to a wide range of business types. This is:

- Marketing ■ Product Development ■ Selling – day-to-day:

                                              Front Office
                                              Customer support

- Bargain Processing – Back Office
- Distribution
- Warehousing/Inventory holding
- Business Control
- Business – Planning and Direction
- Risk Management – Credit/Exposure
- Risk Management – Compliance

- Resource Management:
  - *people*   - *money*   - *other assets*   - *information*

These functional partitions should be customized for each particular business.

3.4   *Data Types*

The most important categories are:

- *Organizational level*   - *Management level*   - *Type of data source*
- *Data type*   - *Time dependence*

These are expanded upon below:

- *The Organizational level* at which data is most relevant helps to determine the level of sharing, and indicates the most appropriate location for holding it. Some of the most important levels are:
  - Corporate HQ;
  - Country/Region;
  - Area of business, e.g. product or service;
  - Legal entity or Trading division;
  - Departmental;
  - Individual, or small team.
- *The Management level* refers to the level of management responsibility to which the data is most relevant. This gives an indication of the level of summarization required, and the likely stability of the analyses and presentation formats likely to be needed. Some of the significant levels are, (from high to low):
  - High level decision support;
  - MIS type planning and analysis;
  - Operational control – e.g. tracking against departmental profitability objectives;
  - Processing/recording of individual transactions/deals;
  - Administrative support.
- *The Data source type* determines the degree of control which may be exercised over its quality and availability, as well as the likelihood of its being confidential. Some of the relevant data sources are:
  - Internal – from within the organization unit using it;
  - Internal, from another part of the organization;
  - Client/counterparty;
  - Market sources;
  - Other external.

The source of an item of data will have a bearing on the way in which it is regarded, and certain other decisions, e.g.:

- its 'hardness' – from rumor, through reliable projection, to proven fact, and hence its value;
- the necessary collection and maintenance process for it;
- the merit of considering alternative sources, e.g. to improve reliability;
- distribution policy within the organization;
- whether to keep internal copies, or to pay an external agent for each access.

- *Data type.* Hitherto, 'traditional' data processing systems have been almost exclusively concerned with 'files' of records, of mostly fixed format. However, increasingly, with the penetration of IT into broader areas of business support, other types of data are becomingly increasingly significant. Some of the most important are:
  - Documents, and other forms of free text;
  - Numerical models;
  - Pictures, graphs and other images;
  - Expert rules;
  - Voice recordings.

- *Time dependence.* The time dependence of an item of data may be a vital aspect of its definition in business terms. Some aspects are:
  - *historic* – how long a span must be covered;
  - *future* – horizon, and level of precision of the projection needed;
  - *level of timeliness* – how up to date must the current version be, e.g. last accounting period for financial returns, close of business on the last working day for performance reporting, or up-to-the-second for position keeping.

Appendix 2 to Chapter 8 – Trendy Products Plc Business Function Hierarchy

Introduction

The functional hierarchy identifies Trendy Products' business functions and processes independently of:

- their grouping into organizational units;
- their present IS/IT support.

In the form presented, it represents the business prior to the move into Retail.

It provides a basis for:

- identification of similar functions performed separately at present for different products or market sectors;
- identifying opportunities to consolidate common functions;
- reassessment of the most appropriate groupings of functions into organizational units;
- assessment of the potential for common IS/IT support;
- assessment and control of the functional scope of the Trendy Products' application portfolio.

As part of the follow-on architecture development work, the following tasks need to be undertaken:

- update to reflect recent changes in business scope;
- preparation of the 'Business Process Schematic', embodying analysis and documentation of 'horizontal' inter-function business inputs and outputs as 'value chains' flows;
- derivation of the corresponding idealized 'Application Systems Map';
- assessment of coverage offered by current and proposed systems;

The products from this work will confer the following benefits:

- *senior business management* will be able to identify more clearly the business impact and dependencies of any proposed development or activity;
- *the cross-functional flows* of business cost and value will become much clearer, and options for their improvement, control and simplification may be highlighted;
- *project managers* will be able to use the identified current and future systems dependencies to help manage design and change, and to thereby enable more effective future systems support of the identified business dependencies.

The function hierarchy

1.   Market products and services

    1.1   Monitor competition

        1.1.1   Collect data

        1.1.2   Analyze data

        1.1.3   Make tactical decisions

    1.2   Develop brand strategies

        1.2.1   Analyze market need

        1.2.2   Propose brand concept

        1.2.3   Test market

        1.2.4   Propose strategy

    1.3   Manage brands

        1.3.1   Determine image

        1.3.2   Determine target market

        1.3.3   Plan brand strategy

        1.3.4   Execute brand strategy

            1.3.4.1   Price brand

            1.3.4.2   Advertise brand

        1.3.5   Monitor volume and profit

    1.4   Conduct market research

        1.4.1   Produce regular reports

            1.4.1.1   Monitor consumer trends

            1.4.1.2   Monitor trade activity

            1.4.1.3   Monitor volumes

            1.4.1.4   Monitor market share

        1.4.2   Produce special reports

            1.4.2.1   Check consumer acceptance

            1.4.2.2   Exceptions and spotlights

            1.4.2.3   Price/volume sensitivity

            1.4.2.4   Ad hoc as needed

    1.5   Provide marketing training

    1.6   Provide input to motivate sales force

1.7   Monitor and report marketing performance

2   Develop products and services

    2.1   Establish requirements

        2.1.1   Assess market requirements

        2.1.2   Analyze market and consumer research data

        2.1.3   Analyze competitor activity and intelligence

        2.1.4   Assess economic, fiscal and opinion trends

        2.1.5   Formulate target product areas

    2.2   Establish constraints and targets

        2.2.1   Assess legal and consumer implications

        2.2.2   Check availability of materials and expertise

        2.2.3   Check input costs

        2.2.4   Assess quality/image of relevant present offerings

    2.3   Select product/service options to test

        2.3.1   Check manufacturing and distribution costs

        2.3.2   Check support costs

        2.3.3   Run profitability models/scenarios

        2.3.4   Select option and plan development

    2.4   Test market

    2.5   Launch/roll-out product

    2.6   Product support

    2.7   Monitor and report product development performance

3   Sell products and services

    3.1   Run wholesale sales force

        3.1.1   Promote accounts

        3.1.2   Take orders

        3.1.3   Progress shipments

        3.1.4   Monitor and control wholesale sales performance

        3.1.5   Manage and motivate sales force

        3.1.6   Progress billing and collection

    3.2   Monitor and report sales performance

4   Distribute products and services

    4.1   Determine wholesale distribution requirements

    4.2   Plan and control distribution

    4.3   Run warehousing

    4.4   Control stocks

    4.5   Run distribution fleet

    4.6   Schedule shipments

    4.7   Monitor and report distribution performance

        4.7.1   Monitor warehousing performance

        4.7.2   Monitor stocking performance

        4.7.3   Monitor trucking performance

5   Buy products, services and raw materials

    5.1   Determine purchasing requirements

        5.1.1   Aggregate demand

        5.1.2   Make or buy decision

    5.2   Identify and qualify suppliers

    5.3   Negotiate supply contracts

    5.4   Manage supply contracts

    5.5   Calculate and place orders

        5.5.1   Receive and aggregate demand plans

        5.5.2   Convert into order schedule

        5.5.3   Select source/terms

        5.5.4   Place order

    5.6   Pay suppliers

        5.6.1   Authorize invoices

        5.6.2   Issue payment

        5.6.3   Account for payables

    5.7   Monitor supplier performance

        5.7.1   Track purchase orders

        5.7.2   Track deliveries

        5.7.3   Monitor quality

        5.7.4   Monitor prices and service

6   Produce products and services

6.1   Plan manufacturing capacity

6.2   Order plant and raw materials

6.3   Receive orders

6.4   Manage demand plan

6.5   Develop production schedules

6.6   Produce goods

6.6.1   Configure lines

6.6.2   MRP

6.6.3   Shop floor scheduling

6.6.4   Tracking and control

6.7   Manage inventory

6.7.1   Raw materials

6.7.2   Intermediates

6.7.3   Finished goods stocks

6.8   Manage manpower

6.9   Manage production capacity

6.10   Monitor and report manufacturing performance

6.10.1   Service

6.10.2   Costs

6.10.3   Quality

7   Plan and control the business

7.1   Set and maintain business policy and strategy

7.2   Develop and implement business plans

7.3   Monitor performance versus plans

8   Manage finance

8.1   Manage treasury

8.2   Manage tax

8.3   Establish and monitor financial standards and policies

8.4   Control finances

8.4.1   Set financial targets

Exercises for the reader

Review the following items of information architecture and recommend amendments or improvements to reflect the recent developments in the management team and in Trendy's business scope, as reflected in the preceding chapters.

- Business function model (Appendix 2 above).
- Data entity model (Figure 8-13).
- Application Systems Map – Figure 8-8.

CHAPTER 9

Use (and abuse) of case tools and other software aids

Chapter objectives

Use of automated aids in IS/IT strategic planning is not a solved problem. This chapter is an interim status report on an unsatisfactory and rapidly changing field. In it we will:

1. Explore the use of such automated aids as are available so as to achieve the maximum effective level of automated support for the strategic IS/IT planning process.

2. Establish a set of requirements for automated aids for strategic IS/IT planning.

3. Explore the benefits and disadvantages of use of relevant CASE tools as well as other aids available.

The need for automated support in IS Strategic Planning

The most important factors which dictate the need for automated support for IS Strategic Planning include:

- the high volumes of information involved
- completeness of cover needed within truncated time scales
- complexity and variety of the documentation and its cross-linkages
- the need for rapid re-iteration and re-work:
  - scenarios within a single cycle;
  - subsequent planning cycles.
- the need for complete, accurate traceability from early business views through to projects and plan entries, which in turn implies continuity

of access to the full range of documentation

■ the need to limit the need for continuing high levels of expensive expertise

Requirements

Overview

In summary, an effective automated aid must provide effective support for:

1. Recording and analysis of management interviews – awareness of business structures and planning elements

2. Recording and analysis of business, market, industry and product structures:

   ■ *function models*   ■ *information flows*   ■ *matrix management*

3. Recording and analysis of data and systems architectures

   ■ data models

   ■ information, data and systems flows

   ■ matrix management

4. Management of inventories, e.g. of current systems and resource status

5. Comprehensive document index and retrieval and text management functions.

6. Comprehensive project definition and management

7. Resource capacity planning

8. Financial modelling

9. Management presentations

The vehicle should as far as possible be 'aware' of the nature of the objects recorded, so that it can offer intelligent validation.

Object support requirements

The toolset should ideally be aware of the following object types, and be able to track their occurrences in all elements of documentation:

■ Business function (recursive)   ■ Organization unit (recursive)

■ *Product/service* (recursive) –   ■ Objective
  needs life cycle treatment

■ Business   ■ Business strategy

- Critical success factor (C.S.F.)
- Performance measure
- *Key performance indicator* (KPI)
- Requirement item:
  - Information need
  - Support function: *{sponsor, priority}..., joint approved priority, business benefit area/basis*
- Person: *Employee, Key external party, job/role – past/current/future*
- Data entity
- Database: *Current, Logical, Future physical*
- Application system/subsystem – (full B-O-M structure) – needs life cycle treatment
  - status assessment: *current, logical, future physical*
  - business case
- *Project* (recursive) – needs life cycle treatment
  - Organizational
  - Application
  - Database
- Technical: start/end dates, {resource type, quantity}..., business case, sponsor
- Technical environment
  - Current
  - Future
- Technical component
- Human resource skill type:
  - Internal
  - External: *resource available, resource needed*

KEY:

Entity class, subtype:

  - attribute
  - {repeating group}...

Object associations

Table 9-1 indicates the inter-object associations which need to be supported.

Figure 9-1:   *Repository architecture*

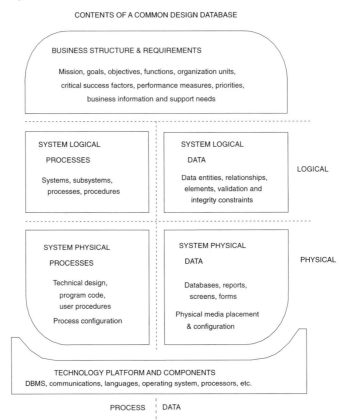

Figure 9-1 illustrates the scope of the information which will need to be held to control all aspects of systems documentation. Although our interest in IS/IT planning is limited to the upper layers of this diagram, we must remain aware that we are initiating or adding to a much larger body of documentation, which increasingly will be used by automated application generation tools and active applications.

The search for suitable tools

No present day tool-set meets even a major sub-set of these requirements on its own. We need instead to mix and match, combining the best of several types of software.

Typically such a composite tool kit will likely be based around a set of office automation software and a CASE tool.

It is important that these items should be a GUI integrated environment with data integration facilities such as such as DDE and OLE, so as to facilitate:

■   version control, e.g. by means of 'hot' OLE links from a master set;

	Business function	Org unit	Product	C.S.F	K.P.I.	Requirement item — Information	Requirement item — Support	Person/job /role	Data entity	Database — Existing	Database — Logical	Database — Future physical	Application system/subsystem — Current	Application system/subsystem — Logical	Application system/subsystem — Future physical	Project	Technical env't	Technical component
Business function	Business function hierarchy	organization mapping of functions	Product support functions	subject to	tracked by	DERIVATION	DERIVATION	unit	usage	usage	usage	usage	usage	usage	usage	sponsor		
Org.unit		organization chart	Org / product resp.	subject to	tracked by	DERIVATION	DERIVATION	holds post	usage	usage	usage	usage	usage	usage	usage	sponsor		
Product					tracked by	DERIVATION				usage	usage	usage	usage	usage	usage	needs		
C.S.F.					may lead to	DERIVATION												
K.P.I.						DERIVATION				DERIVED-NEEDED TO SUPPORT			REQUIRED TO DELIVER			DELIVERS		
Requirement item – information								Sponsor via org'n unit			DERIVED-NEEDED TO SUPPORT		REQUIRED TO DELIVER			DELIVERS		
Requirement item – support								Sponsor via org'n unit				DERIVED-NEEDED TO SUPPORT	REQUIRED TO DELIVER			DELIVERS		
Person/job/role										OWNERSHIP OR RESPONSIBILITY			OWNER/SPONSOR					
Data entity										SPECIFICATION OF MAPPINGS			DATA ENTITY USAGE			Delivery of support		
Database-existing													CREATES/USES /MAINTAINS			Migration delivery	Placement in environment	
Database-logical										MIGRATION			CREATES/USES /MAINTAINS			Migration delivery	Placement in environment	
Database-future physical											MIGRATION		CREATES/USES /MAINTAINS			Migration delivery	Placement in environment	
Application system/sub system — current																Migration delivery	Placement in environment	
Application system/sub system — logical													MIGRATION			Migration delivery	Placement in environment	
Application system/sub system — future physical														MIGRATION		Application mapping into projects	Placement in environment	
Project																	Implements or utilises	
Technical environment – current																		Make-up of environment
Technical environment – future																		Make-up of environment
Technical component																		

Table 9-1: *Key associations between SP4IS objects*

- or at least, easy cut and paste to avoid re-keying.

CASE tools (including data dictionaries)

These are mostly still immature, and are still mainly oriented towards detailed systems analysis and design. They can be of significant value if they:

- fit the method in use;
- can cope with phase deliverables.

None qualify fully today for exclusive use in SP4IS, but several can make a useful contribution.

A strong argument in favor of using even a modest CASE tool is that it is important to deliver architectural products and other design basis in form compatible with the CASE tools already in use in your organization.

Figure 9-2: *Case and application builder tools match to SP4IS requirements (based on information available at the time of publication including unverified vendor claims re functionality)*

Product	Interview analysis	Business plan structure	Business structure	Matrix management	Structured analysis	Text management	True GUI mode	Client/server builder	Comment
DESIGN/1	NO	NO	PART	NO	YES	NO		YES	
JMA IEF	NO	PART	PART	YES	YES	NO			Now marketed by Texas Instruments
Ernst & Young IEW/ADW	NO	PART	PART	YES	YES	NO			Alliance with Knowledgeware
Knowledgeware ObjectView								YES	Little information available
INTERSOLV EXCELLERATOR (Plus PRISM)	NO	PART	PART	YES	YES	NO			PRISM is add-on for planning
LBMS SYSTEM ENGINEER	NO	PART	PART	PART	YES	NO	YES	YES	Post Rel 4
PRISM (Hoskyns)	NO	NO	NO	NO	YES	NO			DesignAid from USA
CASE*DESIGNER (ORACLE)	NO	PART	PART	PART	YES	PART	YES	YES	
SOFTLAB MAESTRO 2									
SYSTEM ARCHITECT								YES	
Application development tools with strong CASE connotations (sample only)									
SAP								YES	
GUPTA SQL WINDOWS								YES	
MICROSOFT VISUAL BASIC								YES	
POWER BUILDER								YES	

Figure 9-2 and Figure 9-3 illustrate comparative analyses of a sample of relevant CASE products available. The product lists are not complete, and such an analysis will inevitably become dated extremely rapidly; and the judgements presented here should not be taken as currently valid. You should consult the vendors for up to date information (but validate it yourself!) The diagrams are presented as examples of style rather than as statements of the state of the art.

Figure 9-3:   *Methods and tools – market positioning (Based on Vendor claims for functionality and user base)*

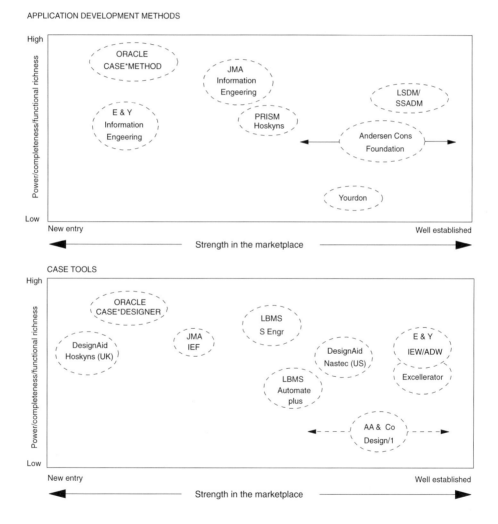

Summary and conclusions

1. IS/IT planning documentation must be accessible, controllable, complete, maintainable and must support traceability and easy re-work of conclusions. It must also support smooth flow into the later stages of the systems life cycle.

2. CASE tools are not the complete answer (yet):

    ■ conceived on too narrow a front

those which support business planning and analysis objects are very restrictive and often eccentric.

3. Close integration of a set of tools, each of which is of limited scope, within a GUI environment is often the best solution today.

4. Use whichever integrated component fits the purpose – surprisingly often, a spreadsheet! But don't ignore pencil and paper!

For specific purposes:

Type of product:	Suitable vehicle:
Interview documentation and analysis	spreadsheet, word processor, free text analyser
Business analysis	best with CASE
Data/systems analysis	best with CASE
Inventories	DBMS or spreadsheet
Document management	text manager
Text analysis	free text (NB: Free text analyzers with added intelligence have great potential)
Project definition/scheduling	spreadsheet or specialist tool
Capacity planning	spreadsheet or specialist tool
Financial modelling	spreadsheet
Presentation aids	good selection

CHAPTER 10

*Defining the IS strategic vision
and options for its implementation*

Chapter objectives

1. Derive application systems requirements and priorities.

2. Define the IS strategic vision to support the business vision, and ascertain its implications for systems implementation and IT.

3. Establish a range of options and solutions to meet the needs and deliver the vision.

Process

1. Identify and assess realistically all applications and other IS/IT assets.

2. Match with business needs identified, against the backdrop of target information architectures, and highlight gaps, weaknesses and 'soft spots' and other key needs.

3. Establish an IS strategic vision to support the business vision.

4. Derive impact of the IS vision on the application portfolio and IT support needs.

5. For strategic needs, establish a range of options and solutions for meeting them

6. Allocate and agree preliminary priorities for action.

7. Initiate direct action where appropriate.

The scope of this chapter is illustrated in Figure 10-1.

Figure 10-1:   *Establishing the strategic systems vision and options for delivery*

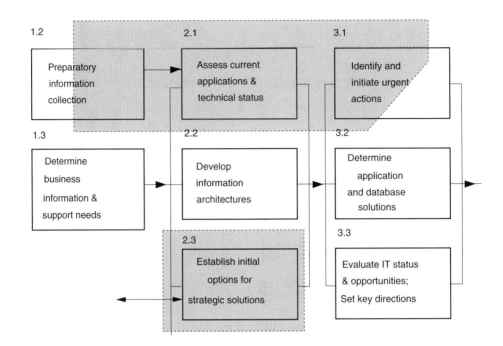

Products

1.   IS vision statement.

2.   The ideal business delivery sequence and rate – reflecting business priorities in the development sequences.

3.   Formal assessment of the current application portfolio in relation to reported business needs and with the ideal portfolio.

4.   Options for application solutions with and accompanying technology implications.

5.   Indication of opportunities for specific rapid development projects for early delivery.

6.   Refinements to the information architectures to reflect additional detail and decisions made.

Inputs

1.   Business needs and priorities, in application and data terms – from chapter 7 and chapter 8.

2.   'Ideal' data and systems architectures to support these – from chapter 8.

3. Information on fitness and coverage offered by current systems – introduced in chapter 8, and refined below.

4. Sufficient detail on current status to highlight key constraints and dependencies – form information collection initiated in chapter 4.

Figure 10-2, below, illustrates the stages in the matching process.

Figure 10-2: *Matching plans to business needs*

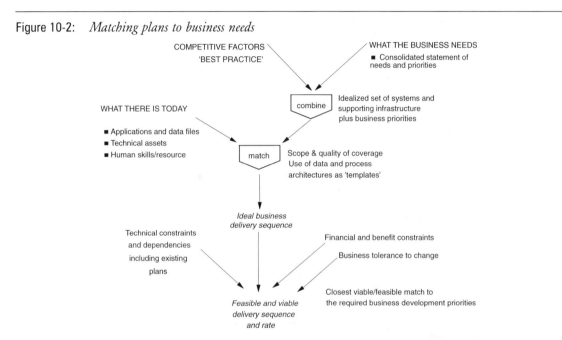

In Figure 10-3, the development of the ideal business delivery sequence and its transformation into the feasible and viable sequence are broken into more detail. This chapter addresses the activities above the dotted line; chapter 11 refers to those below it.

Evaluating IS/IT related assets

Types of asset

- Application systems
- Databases
- All hardware, software
- Communications networks
- External services
- User procedures
- Staff skills/resources – all developers, operators and users
- Plans, development projects, service agreements and other commitments

Figure 10-3:   *Application options and solutions*

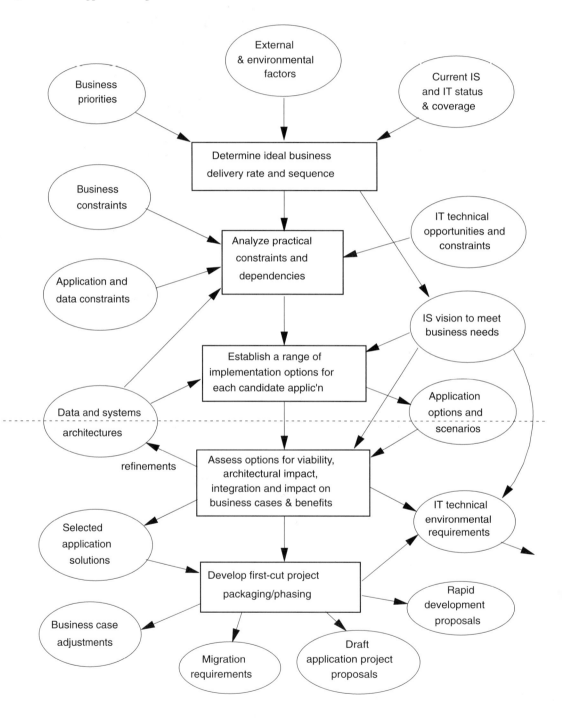

Assessment Criteria

- Meeting user needs – current and those arising from Phase 1
- Operational stability
- Workload/throughput capacity – including peaks
- Security/integrity/availability
- Effectiveness as a basis for evolution:
    - design quality/flexibility to accommodate likely business scenarios
    - code quality
    - documentation
- Nature of application in relation to its potential on the McFarlan matrix – how appropriate is the present level of investment?

Assessment Process

- Inventory – questionnaires, early start
- Assessment against criteria
- Identifying and prioritizing gaps and weaknesses in coverage
- Determine range of options for action for each
- Focus on opportunities and means for rapid development
- Redirect priorities and re-deploy resources where appropriate

The assessment of Trendy Products current systems is shown in summary form in Table 10-1.

Using application portfolio techniques

Application portfolios – uses and relevance

In assessing current systems status, in addition to the coverage assessment discussed in chapter 8, we should seek to place the present applications on such a McFarlan portfolio grid, and then examine the result and compare it to an idealized portfolio, in order to determine whether:

- the placement of current systems is appropriate in terms of the business contribution which such applications should be making;
- there are any significant gaps which need to be filled, especially in the Key Operational and Strategic categories.

In the former case, we may determine that investment is needed to upgrade or replace a system which should be playing a strategic role, but is not doing so at present. We may also identify cases where inappropriately high levels of investment are taking place in hygiene systems, and reduce it accordingly. In the

APPLICATION	Status P – plan D – dev't L –live	DATE FIRST LIVE	HARDWARE & SOFTWARE ENVIRONMENT	USER INTERFACE MODE	COMMENTS	Summary ratings - 0 (poor) to 5 (good)				
						User Satisf'n	Oper'l stability	Response and thruput	Security availability integrity	Pot base for future dev't
General Accounting	L	1984	IBM 43xx Package	Interactive	Reputable package, but failing to meet user needs at present, mostly due to inadequate coding structures and poor discipline and controls in manual systems.	2	4	3	2	4
Purchase Ledger	L	1972	ICL (Plan & COBOL)	Batch	Completely out of date; should have been entirely superseded by now, but is still in use in a few sites.	1	2	2	3	0
	L	1984	Converted to IBM COBOL	Batch	The conversion was at the code level, the revised system remains poor.					
Sales Ledger	L	1985	IBM 43xx Package	Interactive	Implemented to replace poor mostly manual transfer from Sales Order Processing, & to provide automated invoicing. User problems mostly due to inadequacies of the SOP system.	3	5	4	4	4
Payroll	L	1974	ICL (Plan & COBOL)	Batch	Does the job at present, but accounting interface is weak, and design limitations make further development difficult	4	3	3	3	2
	L	1985	Converted to IBM COBOL	Batch						
Personnel	L	1976	ICL (Plan & COBOL)	Batch	A batch-based extension to Payroll. Offers little flexibility for analysis or enquiry, due to constraints of parent system.	2	3	3	3	0
	L	1985	Converted to IBM COBOL	Batch						
Sales Order Processing	L	1975	ICL COBOL	Interactive	Limited system, lacking up to date facilities.	2	2	3	2	0
	L	1985	Converted to IBM COBOL	otherwise batch	Due to poor quality of design, potential for enhancement is now exhausted. Many requests for modifications outstanding.					

Table 10-1: *Trendy Products PLC – current systems and development plans inventory and assessment*

APPLICATION	Status P – plan D – dev't L –live	DATE FIRST LIVE	HARDWARE & SOFTWARE ENVIRONMENT	USER INTERFACE MODE	COMMENTS	Summary ratings - 0 (poor) to 5 (good)				
						User Satisf'n	Oper'l stability	Response and thruput	Security availability integrity	Pot base for future dev't
Finished Goods Inventory Control	L	1977	ICL COBOL	Interactive data entry otherwise batch	Well integrated with SOP, but lacking facilities to cope with Trendy's current multiple sites and more complex distribution arrangements.	3	4	3	3	2
	L	1985	Converted to IBM COBOL							
Sales & Marketing Analysis	L	1986	IBM 43xx COBOL, with some ad hoc enquiry	Batch limited reporting flexibility	System value is limited by quality and scope of source data. Users are disappointed by lack of online enquiry & lack of flexible formatting and analysis facilities.	2	3	4	4	3
Manufacturing Control - Luton	L	1973	ICL COBOL	Mostly Batch	Trendy's original system - now obsolescent.	2	3	1	3	0
	L	1984	Converted to IBM COBOL							
Manufacturing Control - Birmingham	L	1979	ICL ME29 - RPG, some COBOL	Mixed batch/ interactive	Custom system, moderately successful at Birmingham location. Doubts exist over its applicability to other sites due to technical env't and limited facilities.	4	4	3	3	1
Manufacturing Control - Bristol	L	1985	Hewlett Packard 3000 Package	Mixed batch/ interactive	An up to date mfg. control package, with reputable vendor and broad user base. More advanced modules (MRP & shop floor ctl.) not yet implemented in Bristol, but early plans exist to do so.	4	4	4	4	5

NB: This version does not include W.I.P projects

Table 10-1: *(continued) Trendy Products PLC – current systems and development plans inventory and assessment*

latter case, where there are gaps, then we may propose new applications, especially if these gaps are supported by high priority CBINS.

Figure 10-4 illustrates this process.

McFarlan portfolio evaluation techniques were described in chapter 8. They are of value at this stage for several reasons:

1. They provide us with an alternative approach to the modified Anthony Triangle for use as a categorization scheme assessment of coverage of business needs. This increases the confidence factor – if we arrive at similar conclusions by two alternative routes, then this reduces the risk of gross error.

2. The position of an application on the McFarlan grid can give a strong indication of the relative level of investment in it which is appropriate. The marginal rate of return in Strategic systems should remain higher than for hygiene systems above the levels of basic functionality (see the discussion of value drivers below).

3. Both the existing and the proposed 'idealized' future application portfolios may be assessed in this way. The difference between the two resulting grids highlights the key shortcomings of the existing portfolio and the proposed changes to it. The distance by which a current application is displaced from its ideal position can be taken as a measure of the strategic change which is needed in that area.

4. The position of an proposed new application on the McFarlan grid may offer some indication of appropriate options for its provision. In particular, hygiene systems are generally more suited to use of utility packages than are Strategic or High Potential systems.

Figure 10-4:   *Use of portfolios in coverage assessment*

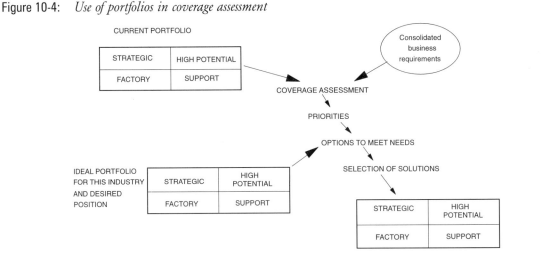

Assessing the current application portfolio using value drivers

Whilst it is easy to illustrate this process in qualitative terms, and the benefits are obvious, this technique really needs effective quantitative criteria for placement of applications on the McFarlan axes. There is no agreed approach to this, and readers are free to experiment. Systematic criteria are needed for assignment of applications into categories, along with a quantified assessment scale for placing them on the axes.

Although still under development, there is reason to believe that an adaptation of Porter's cost driver concept can be useful. This is termed 'value drivers', and is based on analysis of the likely incremental rate of return of further investment in extending the functional scope or the services delivered by an application.

Value drivers can be defined as those attributes of an application and its mode of use which govern the nature and magnitude of business benefits attained or value delivered, and may be varied by the implementors. They are quantities which, when they vary, may be related in an identifiable manner with the variation in benefit potentially or actually attainable from an application.

Many drivers will be found to affect both costs and benefits, and may prove to be a manageable and quantifiable link between the two. For example, mean response time for a business transaction system is a clear driver of the configuration cost to run the application, and may be a significant driver of user productivity benefits. In neither case is the relationship linear, and for this particular example, there is probably a region between response times of 0.5 secs and 2 secs where the benefits may exceed the costs by the widest margin – see the Figure 10-5.

Figure 10-5:   *Costs and benefits of improving response times in a transaction processing system*

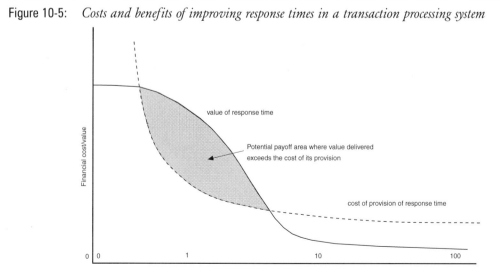

By considering their impact on current business benefits and potential future business benefits, value drivers may be used to quantify the positioning of individual applications on each axis of the McFarlan portfolio matrix. They also offer a basis for allocation of application categories; when the benefits cease to rise sharply with further increase in the value of the driver, this indicates that we are in the Support/Key Operational category region. Where the benefits continue to increase with change in the value of the driver, this places us in the Strategic or Turnaround category region.

Value drivers will vary in nature and significance:

- for different applications;
- for similar applications in different industries;
- for similar applications in different organizations at different stages of maturity in the same industry.

MODE OF USE OF VALUE DRIVERS

1. For each application, identify in discussion with users and designers the relevant factors which will influence the perception by the users of benefit arising from the application. Select the most significant; these are the value drivers.

2. For each selected value driver, for current and likely future business scenarios, identify which benefits are influenced, and in what manner.

3. For each driver/benefit/current/future combination, plot a sensitivity graph in a manner analogous to Porter's cost drivers, as illustrated in Figure 10-6.

4. Assess the shape and impact of the benefits curve.

5. Develop a cumulative score for the application on each of the two Mcfarlan axes, current and future significance.

Figure 10-6:   *Assessing the behavior of IS/IT value drivers*

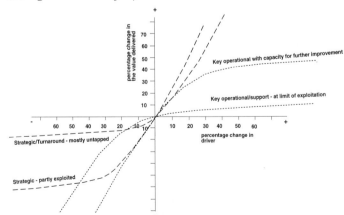

SAMPLE CANDIDATES FOR VALUE DRIVERS (A NON-EXCLUSIVE LIST)

- Richness of range functionality offered.
- Ease of use:
    - training needed;
    - error rates;
    - range of functionality which users actually utilize.

Degree of data and application integration and connectivity achieved.

- Degree of accessibility to users.
- Availability and reliability.
- Response time to a query or work request.
- Contribution of application to the productivity of the users:
    - effort to process a transaction;
    - levels of accuracy attained;
    - confidence level in decisions made.
- Scope of data access offered (applies to MIS or EIS type applications).
- Quality of stored data:
    - currency;
    - consistency;
    - integrity;
    - completeness.
- Technical platforms on which the application will run, or with which it will interoperate.
- Service levels to users.
- Service levels attained by users to their customers.
- Unit cost of service, (affecting user's willingness to use it).

Assembling the 'ideal' future application portfolio

Our aim should be to move this stage away from being seen as still one of the black arts. Inevitably, there remains a high degree of expertise and skill involved. We will draw upon our knowledge of best practice in the relevant industries, and overlay on this creative flair, inspiration or whatever to give our organization its competitive edge. Value drivers applied to the future application portfolio offer one way of tightening this process. As suggested in chapter 8, a key starting point is the business process schematic. Once the set of prioritized CBINS is overlaid on this, the bones of the future application portfolio often emerge clearly.

Each materially different business scenario (chapter 6) may require different features in the application portfolio. The position of an application in the future portfolio map must depends on where it should be under a particular business scenario, based on the net sum of the effects of the relevant IS/IT value drivers.

Flexibility and ability to adapt the application portfolio to meet rapid business change are a special case of requirement. In the past, they were often seen as excuses for not planning, whereas they are perfectly respectable (and often critical) requirements, albeit of a special and demanding nature.

Defining the IS vision

The IS vision for our target organization should express the manner in which IS will support the business over about a five year time scale. There is inevitably a significant creative element in defining the IS vision for our target organization. This makes some people uneasy – perhaps the very people who themselves, on occasion, may stake a great deal on a business 'hunch'. When accused of subjectivity, remember that one man's subjectivity is another's judgement.

We have now undertaken a great deal of systematic analysis of what the business needs, how well it is met by the current portfolio and the like, and we really ought now to have a good idea of the answer. Even so, it is a good idea to have some formal basis, and I set out below some of the categories and topics which I believe that a sound IS vision should address. This very much a guide, and you should be looking to improve on it.

Elements of an IS vision

1. An overall application portfolio framework – probably framed in terms on an overall Application Systems Map, with color coded coverage assessment, and supported by brief explanatory notes..

2. Proposed means for support of business product and service development.

3. Capability to cope with business change:

    - product or geographic scope;
    - volume;
    - competitive stance.

4. Integration with the business planning process.

5. Style of data collection:

    - once only close to source;

- validation at the point of collection;
- direct update of core databases.

6. Style of operation of core transaction systems and databases:

    - common customer view;
    - on-line processing of all core business transactions;
    - re-usable infrastructure, e.g. to support common products and functions across the organization;
    - effective reporting and analysis of key business measures such as customer and product profitability.

7. Approach to provision of timely, relevant and accessible MIS and EIS in a manner which will adapt to evolving management style.

8. Business basis for the vision.

9. Risk assessment.

10. Assumptions on which the vision is based.

11. Implications for IT strategy.

Developing options for future solutions

Considerations

- Business pressures may force consideration of short term, limited life solutions – the inevitable clash between expediency and architectural aesthetics.
- Open options carried forward will help us to keep open minds (for a while).
- Portfolio category may strongly indicate preferable types of solution.
- Data and other dependencies impose limits.
- Physical placement options start to become significant.
- Application development routes and options may impact delivery speed/cost.
- Continuing negotiation with sponsors.

The Options Development Process

I recommend a fairly systematic process for this stage, along the following lines:

1. Derive data dependencies and databases needed, in terms of:

    - quality;

- availability;
- synchronization/timeliness.

leads to Mark I trial design – broad applications and data flows

2. Look at ways to meet it from where we are – development route and options. Consider side effects/dependencies, e.g.:

    - rapid/tactical versus built for long life;
    - availability/quality of data flows especially for interim tactical options.

leads to a series of Mk II design options:

3. Negotiation with sponsors re rate, phasing and cost/flexibility options.

4. Use of matrices/clusters to analyze dependencies.

5. Consider options for mapping of functions on to locations – options for distribution of data and process.

leads to a narrowed down series of Mk III applications and database options, to be assessed and verified through later processes. Figure 10-7 illustrates the purely business-driven priorities for having application needs met.

Figure 10-7:   *Business priorities for applications*

	Priority
Corporate Control	
■ Profitability by product, outlet and region	1
Finance	
■ Cashflow planning/management	2=
Manufacturing	
■ Materials requirements planning	4
■ Shop floor control	2=
Sales	
■ Order processing	3
Warehouse/Distribution	
■ Finished goods inventory control	6
■ Distribution scheduling	5=
Retail Outlets	
■ In-store data capture	2=
■ Store-level control	5=

These are translated into a rudimentary bar chart (Figure 10-9), in which the vertical bands are really as yet only implementation groups, rather than time frames. Figure 10-8 shows business and application dependencies added to the rudimentary priority list, and in Figure 10-10 these are superimposed on the basic bar chart from Figure 10-9. Figure 10-10 also retains 'ghost' bars to remind us when the business wanted the applications.

Figure 10-8:   *Application dependencies*

	priority	requires	is prerequisite for
Corporate Control			
■ Profitability by product, outlet and region	1	Coding structures Accounting data interfaces	Cashflow
Finance			
■ Cashflow planning/mgmt	2=	Coding structures Accounting data interfaces Profitability	
Manufacturing			
■ Materials requ'mts planning	4	Item data Bill-of-materials Demand planning Mat'ls inventory ctl.	Shop floor
■ Shop floor control	2=	Mat'ls requm'ts planning	
Sales			
■ Order processing	3	Customer database Order entry Fin. goods	Profitability
Warehouse/Distribution			
■ Finished goods inventory ctl	5=	Item data	Profitability
■ Distribution scheduling	6	Outlets/routing database	
Retail Outlets			
■ In-store data capture	2=	EPOS Stores comms network	Profitability
■ Store-level control	5=	Stores comms network In-store computers	Profitability

In Figure 10-10, a number of sure are illustrated which have been taken to adapt the application plan to take account of the dependencies. In each case where we are forced to depart in this manner from the ideal sequence, a negotiation with business sponsors will be required. Often, we may be able to present sponsors with options at this stage.

It may be, as illustrated in the case of Profitability Reporting, that the sponsor favors a 'quick and dirty' interim implementation to meet a pressing business need. We must then ensure that provision is made later for this to be brought into the main stream. Such interim fixes for dependency problems are not always feasible. The Cashflow Planning and Management and Shop Floor Control applications illustrated have their delivery dates been severely impacted by intransigent dependencies. The sooner we get the sponsors involved in negotiation over such issues, the more likely we are to attain god business solutions which the sponsors will support. Sometimes we may even bring forward an application, because analysis of the dependencies indicates that is a key enabler for others. In Figure 10-10, Finished Goods Inventory is a case in point.

Although introduced here, this process of analysis of dependencies and refinement of the application delivery schedule, with concurrent negotiation with sponsors, continues during the remaining phases of the process. Real life equivalents of Figure 10-10 quickly become quite complex. It is best if they are placed on a spreadsheet or project management tool early, so that 'what if' iterations become fairly painless.

Figure 10-9:   *Business priorities for application delivery*

Figure 10-10:   *Practical sequences for application delivery*

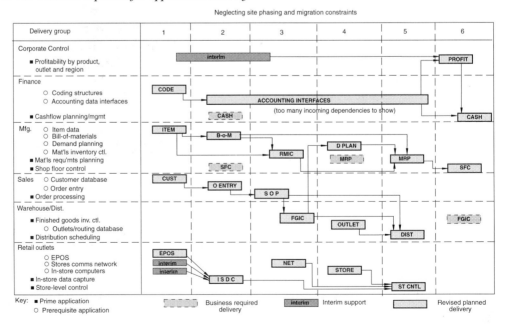

An outcome-based approach to selection of options

We can adapt further the multi-dimensional approach to business strategy selection which was set out in Chapter 6, and apply it to:

- *Selection of the overall IS support* style for business strategy implementation – this is addressed below.
- *Selection of IS implementation* options to meet business application needs – see Chapter 11.
- *Selection of IT technical options* – see Chapter 12.

Table 10-2 illustrates the approach to overall IS support style, which may be applied at any of several levels.

Table 10-2: *Selecting overall IS support style for business strategy implementation (a simplified example)*

Description	Domain/option	Decision matrix - rule definitions																	
Business criteria																			
Service/product 'family' compatibility	High / Med / Low	L	L	L	L	L	L	H	H			Y							
Venture horizon	Quick buck / long haul			Q	Q		L		L	L	Q								
Priority of business need	Critical/High / Med / Low	L	L	H	H	H	H		H	H	H	H	M	M	M	M	H		C
Expected business volumes	High growth / flat / declining			H	F	H	H		H	H	H	H	F	H	F				
Level of regulation prevailing	High / Med / Low																		
Manual process complexity	High / Med / Low	L			H											H	H	H	H
Pressure on cost per transaction	High / low			H	H				H	H	H	H	H	H	H	H			
Systems and technical criteria																			
Existence of a current system	Absent/Present	A	P						A	P	P								
System meets current business need	Well / so-so / poor		P						W	S	P								
Availability of application packages	Some / none						H					Y			Y	Y			
Level of application/data integration required	High/Med/Low						L		H	H	H	H	M						
Decisions																			
No system needed - stay manual		Y	Y																
Quick and dirty - 'throwaway' style				Y	Y														
Standalone product support - 'vertical' structure						Y	Y												
Cross-functional systems - common support								Y											
Build on present architectures								Y											
Re-engineer current systems portfolio									Y	Y									
Investigate package based family								Y				Y			Y	Y			
Least cost 'hygiene' system													Y	Y	Y	Y			
Invest in leading edge custom systems				Y	Y	Y			Y	Y	Y								Y

As before, we start with the bottom left quadrant, where we identify those decisions which need to be taken, with their alternative outcomes or options. At the top left, we identify the business criteria which may influence the decisions. In addition, we now identify relevant systems and technical criteria. The right hand half of the matrix represents some combinations of criteria which may lead to particular decisions – i.e. our view of the rules.

Once again, I must stress that the matrix presented is only a simplified example, and any experienced designer could quickly pick holes in the specific rules presented, or identify some missing criteria. The systems and technology marketplace is also in such turmoil that criteria and options will change quite quickly over time. But the approach is such that we aim to capture the knowledge of experts, and their awareness of market trends, and enlist their aid in systematizing and documenting what has hitherto been largely a black art.

Use and relevance of application packages

Considerations

Application packages are often attractive in business terms as systems solutions:

- implementation is potentially very rapid – early realization of benefits;
- users can evaluate a working system

However, package assessment is often carried out hastily and/or very poorly, before business requirements have been defined properly, and based largely on the vendor's marketing material rather than on thorough evaluation. As a result, the chosen package may:

- not meet a reasonable set of business needs;
- be in conflict with existing data, systems or technical architectures;
- be hard to amend;
- be expensive to operate.

This has led to a spate of wry jokes, along the lines of:

Question: *On which platform does the XYZ package run best?*

Answer: *A 35mm slide projector.*

Another common pitfall is to select a package on the basis that it will be modified after purchase to fit the business needs. Much time, effort and expenditure later, people who take such decisions often come to regret them.

Even so, business users who have a rapid solution to a pressing problem in sight may be hard to deflect, and they may be right. We may have let them down badly in not identifying the requirement early and accurately, and in not supporting the early stages of package evaluation. We may have to live with the consequences of this – a tactical business solution which is a poor fit with other systems. But let's get it right next time. Packages evaluated and selected in a proper manner can be effective, strategic business solutions.

Issues

Key questions asked at an early stage can help to avoid many of the pitfalls, without getting in the way of business solutions. Some of these are:

- Is the package intended as a pragmatic stop-gap or a new strategic direction? Many criteria will need to be applied much more stringently if the latter.

- What is the architectural quality of the package itself? This matters much more if we will have to live with it and modify it over a long period.

- Will it be isolated, or is it expected to co-exist with or integrate with other systems? Much more care is needed in selection of an application which will be at the core of our systems.

- Will you implement it 'vanilla' or customized? Above all, beware customization. There may be valid reasons for taking the customization route, but they are very rare.

- If the business changes – and whose doesn't these days, then how can we meet the mandatory level of enhanceability required of the package systems?

- Is there a viable migration route into and out of it – especially out? Stop-gap solutions have a habit of turning into long lived solutions. There needs to be an evolutionary plan, even where short term business needs are being met.

Package assessment procedure

There needs to established as part of the systems development standards, procedures for package assessment and implementation which cover:

- Work needed prior to commencing selection;
- Assessment of business functional fit;
- Assessment business a package's data fit;
- Assessing the applications and data architecture of a package
- Criteria for deciding when customization is necessary or valid;
- Assessing the capacity to cope with business change;
- Management of the application and technical architectural conflicts.

Application delivery options

It is useful to summarize on the Application Systems map the results of this first cut at potential solutions. Figure 10-11 illustrates a way of doing this.

Figure 10-11: *Trendy Products PLC application implementation options*

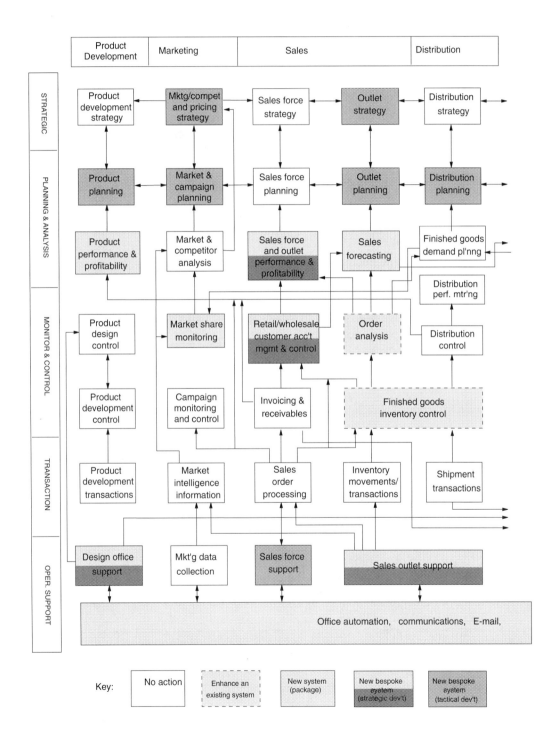

Figure 10-11: *(continued) Trendy Products PLC application implementation options*

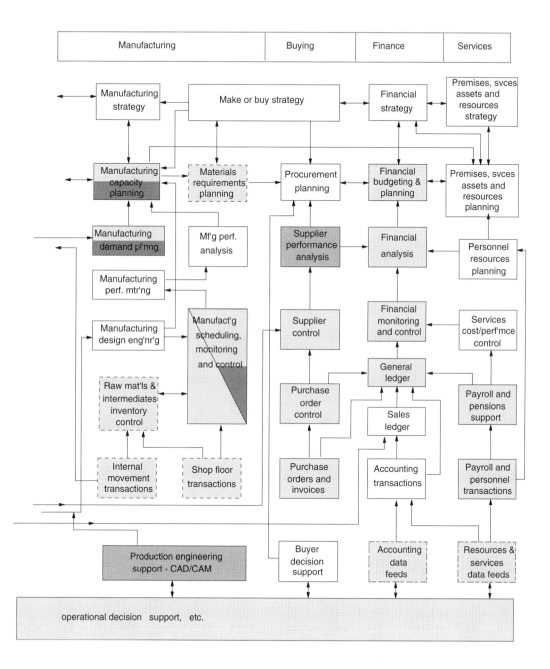

Establish the IS strategic vision and the implementation options – summary

We have now:

1. Derived application systems requirements and priorities.

2. Defined the IS strategic vision to support the business vision, and begun to ascertain its implications for systems implementation and technology requirements.

3. Assessed the extent to which current applications and other IS/IT related assets meet the business requirements and contribute to the IS vision.

4. Derived the ideal business delivery sequence and rate to rectify the gaps – reflecting business priorities in the development sequences.

5. Made a preliminary identification of key dependencies and constraints, and explored options for coping with them.

6. Established a realistic range of options and solutions to meet the needs and deliver the vision.

7. Laid the basis for continuing sponsor commitment.

8. Fed back refinements to the information architectures to reflect additional detail and decisions made.

9. Derived the preliminary implications for IT strategy.

10. Identified opportunities for specific rapid development projects for early delivery, and initiated them is suitable cases.

We now have to:

1. Select application and database solutions – in chapter 11.

2. Derive the IT strategy to support the IS vision – in chapter 12.

3. Develop a recommended portfolio of development projects and transform this into a complete plan – in chapters 13 through 15.

Figure 5-11 in Chapter 5 illustrates a useful way of presenting the manner in which the key transaction systems (the pillars of the classical temple) rest on the foundation of the core databases, the communications and operational support systems, and support the MIS and EIS systems of the organization. This view acknowledges the manner in which it may be necessary to add 'vertically' structured product support systems with at best partial integration to meet short term needs. It also makes it clear where the interfaces must lie to ensure interoperability across the organization.

Figure 5-12 in Chapter 5 takes a Mcfarlan portfolio for Trendy Products and seeks to illustrate the way in which key systems need to migrate across the sectors.

Exercises for the reader

Based on the information which you have gained concerning the present status of IS at Trendy Products Plc, consider and report on the merits of alternative application solutions options in the following cases of high priority business need:

1. Establishing improved profitability reporting by product and sales outlet.

2. Moving to a uniform approach to automation of retail store-level ordering and inventory control.

3. Completing the move to fully integrated requirements planning and shop floor control at all manufacturing sites.

Consider short term and/or interim solutions as well as longer term, and assess the merits of package based approaches where appropriate.

Compare the relative strengths, weaknesses and risks of the alternatives.

Indicate how you intend to approach selecting between options, and identify the technical and implementation issues involved.

Bear your intended approaches in mind as you read chapters 11 and 12.

CHAPTER 11

Selecting application and database solutions

Phase 3 – Determine strategic solutions

Phase objective

We have now identified business needs and the strategic IS options for meeting them. Our task now is to:

1. Assess the options and select database and application solutions to:

    - Meet business needs and priorities
    - Implement the IS strategic vision

2. Derive the requirements for the Technology Strategy needed to support the business systems solutions.

3. Lay a basis for successful implementation and migration.

4. Work with business sponsors throughout the process to translate the business cases from business needs to support for specific project initiatives

Chapter objective – determining database and application solutions

Knowing:

- Future business needs and priorities;
- Current applications and projects strengths and weaknesses;
- The strategic IS vision;
- Options for meeting them.

We will now consider application and database options and alternatives, selecting the most favorable so as to:

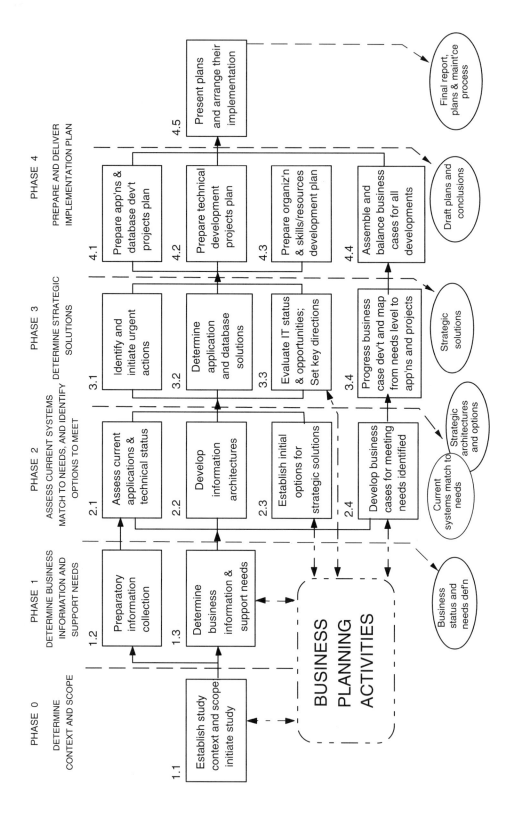

Figure 11-1: *Framework for strategic planning for information systems*

■   keep as near as possible to the ideal business delivery sequence and rate

■   provide the best chance of meeting future business needs easily

■   provide an attractive costs and benefits profile.

Figure 11-2 shows the relative placement of these tasks within the overall process.

Figure 11-2:   *Determine application and database solutions*

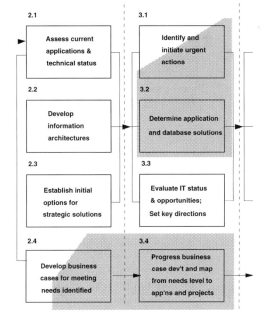

Products

1.   Review and practical confirmation of the ideal business delivery sequence and rate – reflecting business priorities in the development sequences.

2.   Selection from the candidate options for application solutions previously developed – translated into a real set of applications and databases which comes as close as possible to meeting the ideal, taking account of realities.

3.   Log of options considered and reasons for selection or rejection.

4.   'First cut' views on implementation phasing, including a draft set of development projects to deliver the above.

5.   Scope definitions for specific rapid development projects for early delivery.

Figure 11-3:   *Application options and solutions*

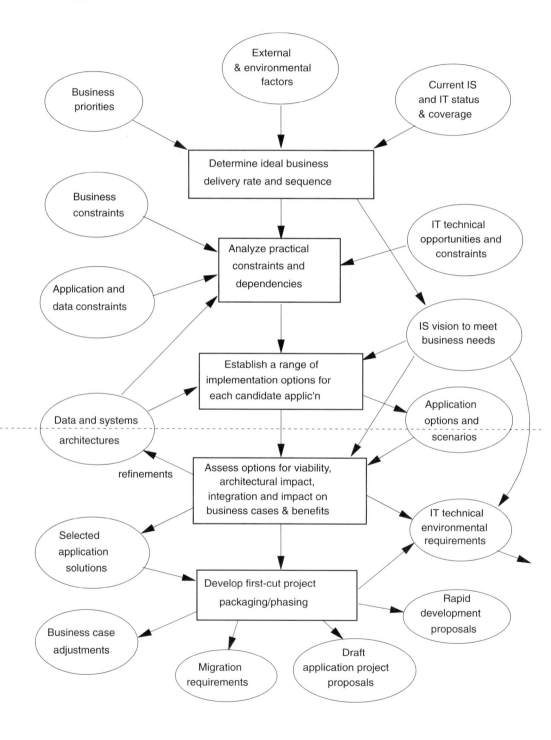

6. Refinements to the information architectures to reflect additional detail and decisions made

7. Technical environment requirements

    ■ allocation of business systems into application type categories – aggregated to workloads by type, time phase and business location of origin

    ■ technology requirements to support the above.

8. Statement of migration requirements and constraints

Inputs

1. Business needs and priorities, in application and data terms

2. The IS vision and 'ideal' data and systems architectures to support these

3. A range of candidate options for application solutions, along with preliminary views on their technology implications

4. A view of fitness and coverage offered by current systems

5. Sufficient detail on current status to highlight key constraints and dependencies

We have now shifted focus from the IS vision and options to the specific 'how tos' which we will recommend for implementation. This is reflected in the lower half of Figure 10-3 from Chapter 10 – see Figure 11-3.

Managing the application portfolios

We are seeking to fine tune the existing application portfolio and to augment it in key areas to meet new needs, or those whose priority has shifted significantly. Some of the ways in which an application's placement on the McFarlan matrix can influence our decision to implement are suggested in Figure 11-4.

Typical portfolio categories

The applicability of portfolio management concepts is not limited to application systems. The approach can be of immense value in managing a wide range of portfolios. The concepts and approaches are closely similar. Relevant categories include:

■ Businesses

■ Investments

- Products/services
- Functional units
- Organization units
- Applications
- Development tools and methods
- Technology item
- People skills and experience
- Any other asset whose selection or utilization needs management

Figure 11-4:   *Using portfolio analysis to help select between options*

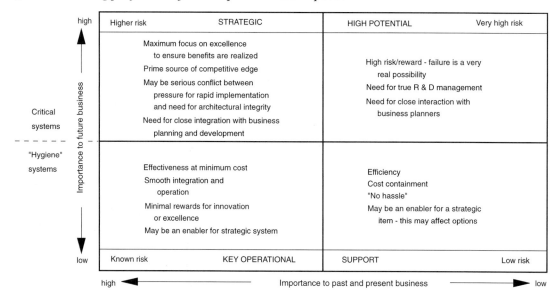

Assessment of options

For each case in which we wish to propose an application solution, we have to determine:

1.   The nature and scope of the functionality to be supported;

2.   Its relation to existing systems and databases;

3.   The options to be recommended for its provision:

   - new system or modify an existing;
   - 'cheap and cheerful' or a strategic implementation;
   - custom or package;

4.   Technical vehicle(s) and implications for IT strategy;

5.   Development medium and vehicles;

6.   Phasing and timing.

Whilst all the time keeping closely aware of the impact on business benefits delivery and thence on the stability of the business case.

Many of these options will be inter-linked, and certain key decisions will have a 'cascade' effect. We may need to set out such decisions in a decision tree in order to understand the implications of such issues. For key options, perhaps such as where and how to place implementation of a strategic database in the development program, the technique of Strengths and Weaknesses, Opportunities and Threats (SWOT) assessment is especially beneficial.

The SWOT analysis technique is very simple, and is largely illustrated by the form presented in Figure 11-5. Once key factors have been identified, they should be quantified where appropriate, and may be used as a basis for risk assessment and for evaluation of potential benefits. Recommended refinements to the basic technique are:

1.   The recognition of interactions between key decisions.

2.   The explicit links into risk analysis.

3.   Use of SWOT as a source of identification and quantification of benefits.

Figure 11-5:   *SWOT assessment*

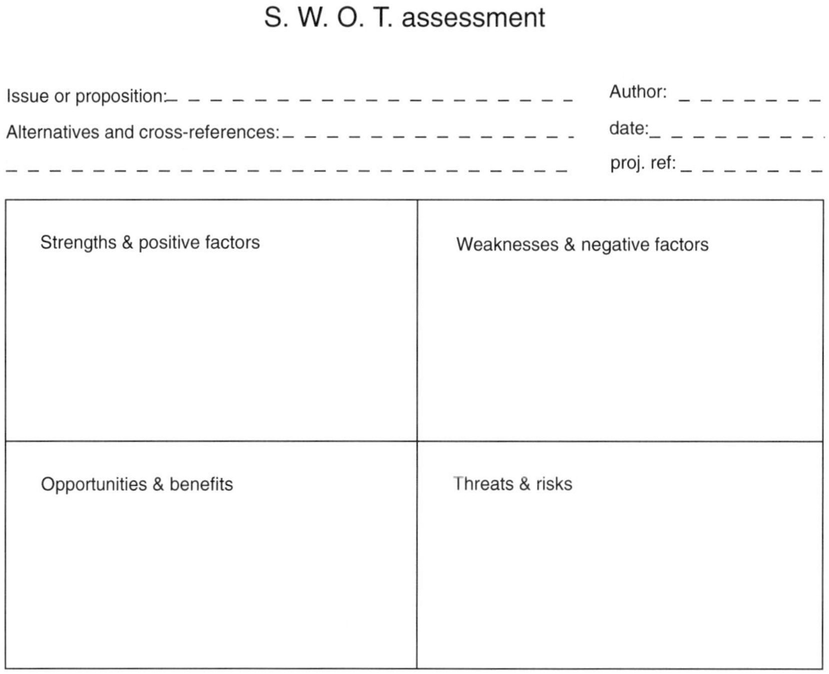

S. W. O. T. assessment

Issue or proposition:_ _ _ _ _ _ _ _ _ _ _ _ _ _ _ _ _ _ _   Author: _ _ _ _ _ _ _

Alternatives and cross-references: _ _ _ _ _ _ _ _ _ _ _ _ _ _   date:_ _ _ _ _ _ _ _ _ .

_   proj. ref: _ _ _ _ _ _ _

Strengths & positive factors	Weaknesses & negative factors
Opportunities & benefits	Threats & risks

Examples of constraints on selection of IS solutions

Selection of options is never an entirely free choice. Sometimes it may seem as if there is no freedom at all, when all of the 'givens' are taken into account. Some of the constraints which may apply are set out below; they are not all necessarily valid, but you may still be stuck with them for all sorts of reasons. Don't take on too many battles at once – play the system if you have to, and get the business sponsors to take on the 'career-limiting exposures' if you can. If they won't, maybe they know something you don't!

- Timing and integration with broader initiatives
- Business cases, priorities
- Cost and benefits profiles
- Business benefits – impact of early delivery
- Application and database dependencies
- What is a realistically achievable rate of change – 'culture shock', egos
- Balancing early delivery against building for long term flexibility
- Momentum, commitments and the need to exploit current investment.

Selecting between implementation options

- It is important to distinguish tactical decisions, taken on the basis of short term expediency and strategic decisions. Tactical is not always wrong, but may carry hidden penalties.
- Reconsider options rejected in previous cycles on T feasibility/cost grounds – reducing technology costs and expanding functionality are continually pushing the boundary of what is worth automating.
- To be considered for life extension, an existing system must be capable of withstanding the enhancements needed.
- Great care is needed over package selection (see Chapter 10).
- There may be several types of development vehicle to choose from. The application may be partitionable into:
  - peripheral subsystems which are more volatile, but are amenable to ultra-rapid development;
  - a core (e.g. of database maintenance), which is less so.

There is a hierarchy of options to consider, the very last of which is to write a new system in a low level implementation language. This is illustrated in a simple minded way in Figure 11-6.

Figure 11-6:   *Selecting options for implementation*

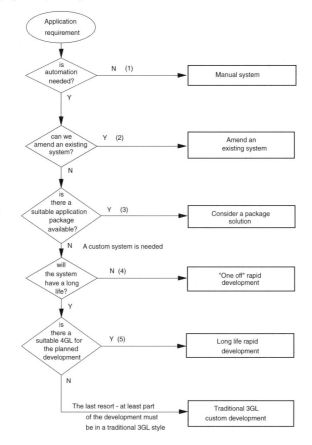

Implementation options – an outcome-based approach

A multi-dimensional approach to business strategy selection was set out in Chapter 6. It was hijacked in Chapter 10 to help with selecting of IS support style for business initiatives. We can adapt it further, and apply it to:

1.   Selection of IS implementation options to meet specific business application needs – see below.

2.   Selection of IT technical options – see Chapter 12.

Table 11-1 illustrates the approach. As before, we start with the bottom left quadrant, where we identify those decisions which need to be taken, with their alternative outcomes or options. At the top left, we identify the business criteria which may influence the decisions. In addition, we now identify relevant systems and technical criteria. The right-hand half of the matrix represents some combinations of criteria which may lead to particular decisions – i.e. the columns document our view of the rules.

Table 11-1: *Selecting specific application implementation options (a simplified example)*

Description	Domain/option	Decision matrix – rule definitions																							
Business criteria																										
Business need priority - importance	High/Med/Low	L	L			L	L	L	H	H	H	H	H	H	H	H	H	H	H	H					
Business need priority - speed of response	Immed/Soon/No rush																			I	I	I	I	I	I
Business need stability	High/Med/Low			H					M	M									M						
Competitive edge need	Critical/Med/Low					M	L	L	L			L	L	C	C	C	L	C	C						
Rate of growth/shrinkage	High growth/Flat/Declining						D	D	D								H	H	H						
Business functional integration needs	High/low																L	H	H			L	L	H	L	L	H
Systems and technical criteria																										
Existence of a current system	Absent/Present	A	P	P	P	P	P	P	P	P	P	P	P	P	P	A	A	A	A	A	A	A	P	P	P
System meets current business need	High/Med/Low	H	H	M	L	M	M	H	H	H	M	M	L	L	L	L	L						L	L	L
System operational stability	Good/Moderate/Poor		G	P		P			G	G															
System operational costs	High/Med/Low		L	H	H				H	M	L														
System maintenance costs	High/Med/Low		M					H			L	L													
System technically capable of enhancement	Good base/Limited/No way		G	N	N	N	G		G	G	L	L											N	N	N
Application/data integration	High/Med/Low																								
Performance critical need	Yes / No												N	Y		N	Y								
Availability of packages	Yes / No										Y	Y		Y			Y			Y					
System technical fit with architectures	Good/Tolerable/Poor																								
Decisions																										
Take no action		Y		Y																					
Minimise future investment – 'strangle'			Y																						
Review and tune current system – 'refresh'				Y																					
Stop running the system now – 'chop'					Y	Y	Y																		
Migrate current system to a lower cost platform								Y	Y																
Enhance the current system										Y	Y														
Replace current system with a package												Y	Y										Y		
Replace current system with a bespoke dev't	throwaway – one-off													Y											Y
–ditto–	rapid dev't for long life														Y										Y
–ditto–	traditional development															Y									
Implement a new system using a package																	Y		Y						
Implement a new bespoke system	throwaway – one-off																	Y		Y					
–ditto–	rapid dev't for long life																		Y		Y				
–ditto–	traditional development																	Y							
Further decisions, e.g. outsourcing to be added																									

Once again, I must stress that the matrix presented is only a *simplified example*; any experienced designer could quickly pick holes in the specific rules presented, or identify some missing criteria. The systems and technology marketplace is also in such turmoil that criteria and options will change quite quickly over time. But the approach is such that we aim to capture the knowledge of experts, and their awareness of market trends, and enlist their aid in systematizing and documenting what has hitherto been largely a black art.

A re-think of application development methods

The problem

Conventional 'waterfall' life cycle approaches to application definition and development have become discredited as being excessively bureaucratic and largely irrelevant to the development needs of the '90s:

- requirements are rarely stable, so why spend so much of the budget trying to lock them into a straitjacket?

- accelerated development tools such as GUI based 'point and shoot' enable small to medium applications to be developed and overhauled several times for less cost and within less time than a conventional feasibility study would take.

However, the lack of controls and unstructured patterns of working inherent in the ad hoc development methods typically used with recent generation development tools mean that most of the painful lessons of the past concerning the need for orderly methods for building large systems are being re-learned even more painfully by people who really should know better.

There is in consequence a need for a complete re-engineering and overhaul of the life cycle view of approaches to application definition, development and maintenance. There appears to be very little on offer from the theoreticians and academics, but this is the norm in an industry where practice outstrips theory with monotonous regularity.

The Coad/Yourdon books appear to be a notable exception, as does the work of Taylor and Wirfs-Brock with Smalltalk, but these approaches are techniques based, and do not really address the needs of builders of large, complex systems.

The potential of object oriented methods

Object oriented methods and techniques are seen by many as the panacea which will sort all this out. However, the benefits of these approaches are only arriving very slowly, if at all; some of the areas in which object oriented techniques need to be converged with the best features of previous conventional wisdom are:

- there is potential for formalization of data entity sub-typing and its integration with the process of object class hierarchy definition;

- the correspondence between and methods (in the formal sense of processes associated with object classes needs to be explored. There is need for rigorous definition and validation of the 'method hierarchy' associated with a class hierarchy. In particular, the potential power of association of methods name (assuming identical method names perform polymorphically similar operations) needs to be investigated – the extent to which similar processes may be invoked by recognizably similar names, even across classes.

- balance – data driven versus process driven:
  - *proposition* – does a full class hierarchy plus method set fully define an application, or do we still need function/process/driven analysis;
  - is there potential here for self-checking via two parallel routes?

- there is potential for extensive automated syntactic analysis of business documents and system specs, based on English nouns as candidate classes, verbs as candidate methods;

- there is needed class hierarchy/class/method administration/control as a key architect function.

Enhanced development methods – principles and requirements

Principles

A development method for the late '90s should:

1. Support early and informal interactive exploration of user interfaces and requirements

2. Encourage prototyping at appropriate stages, and make it easy to assemble, classify and exploit the products

3. Recognize that any or all development products may be working code (differing only in degree of testing, integration and approval for release)

4. Impose no limit on the number of permitted levels of integration and testing, save that it should discourage unnecessary levels

5. Recognize that requirements may evolve continuously, both in precision and in nature

6. Support the concept of successive system releases

7. Support validation, verification and amendment of user requirements at any stage

8. Make it easy to develop small simple systems, but provide within the same framework effective means (e.g. layering, abstraction, multiple levels of integration) to manage design and integration of large, complex systems

9. Encourage maximum re-use of pre-existing design elements and code

10. Be platform independent – vehicles, DBMS, Client/Server

11.   Support all development stages, from earliest investigations of feasibility through to maintenance/enhancement

12.   Support all classes/types of design/implementation decision

13.   Support iteration between any stages of development

These considerations lead us to the view illustrated in Figure 11-7.

Figure 11-7:   *A rethink of the systems development cycle*

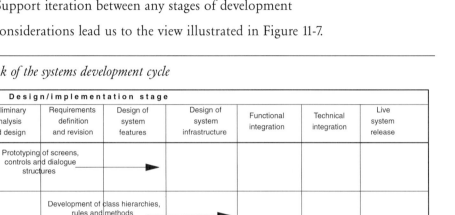

Design or implementation decision	Design/implementation stage						
	Preliminary analysis and design	Requirements definition and revision	Design of system features	Design of system infrastructure	Functional integration	Technical integration	Live system release
User interfaces	Prototyping of screens, controls and dialogue structures						
Business rules and algorithms		Development of class hierarchies, rules and methods					
System logical structure		Integration of class hierarchies; investigation of commonality in rules and methods					
System integration - intra system							
System integration - inter system				Influenced by interfacing requirements			
System internals	Use of appropriate defaults for early, rapid prototyping		Progressive refinement of the selection of vehicles and options, based on fit to task and interfacing constraints			Transfer if necessary to appropriate vehicles for live use	

Requirements

These principles lead to the following partial list of requirements for a development method for the '90s.

1.   Support preliminary prototyping

Permit and even encourage informal cycles of interactive prototyping of screens, controls, dialogues and algorithms during any or all stages and iterations for the purposes of:

-   preliminary discussions with users;
-   identification and validation of requirements;
-   design and trial of system features.

This to be able to be done using a variety of GUI tools of choice.

2.   Capture prototyping products painlessly as and where required

Capture the emerging screens, dialogues, subsystem fragments, classes and rules in such a manner that they can be refined by successive cycles and eventually integrated into releases.

3.   Operate in terms of system releases

All or most of the design/development products are 'working' subsystems. The only difference is the status of a subsystem, in terms of:

- *testing*   ■ *integration*   ■ *release approval*

4.   Support appropriate levels of functional and technical integration and testing, along with appropriate configuration management.

5.   Support iteration at various levels, including evolution of requirements

6.   Support fuzzy requirements

Support scenario based planning and design

7.   Support design and integration of class hierarchies

- Easy local class definition.
- Cross sub-system and cross-application integration of class hierarchies and methods.
- Import of standard templates – see later section

8.   Support the full range of design/implementation decision types

- User interface/dialogue behavior
- Business rules and algorithms
- System logical structure
- System/subsystem integration
- Cross application integration
- System physical structure/technical internals

Equivalences and analogues between traditional structured analysis/design objects and OOD concepts

Class hierarchy	Application or knowledge area
Class	Entity type.
Object type	Sub-type. What about domains, relationships and referential integrity? Methods seem a bit weak for these.
Object instance(?)	Occurrence – level at which key is unique
Method	logical function/process. Physical stored procedure.

Transfer of procedurality

There is a 'fried egg' syndrome, where an increasing proportion of what was hitherto regarded as discretionary procedurality is now perceived as inherently data-related, and should be pulled under co-ordinated control. Incidentally, getting better supported by RDBMS – stored procedures, business rules, triggers, validation rules, domains etc., referential integrity, etc.

Layers (from data-centered outwards):

- core 'pure' data definition;
- referential integrity, validation and other inherently declarative properties;
- business rules;
- storable procedures, remote procedure calls (RPCs), triggers etc.;

These should be implemented on the server if possible, but in the interests of an effective user interface, it must be possible to enforce the consistent mirroring of functionality on the client workstations, e.g. for interactive field validation, some screen generators can download the validation rules, so as to make controlled validation possible field-by-field.

Generally, the following functionality is best implemented at the client end.

- other procedurality which is 'methodizable' – becomes the consistent 'heavy duty' or 'service' functions as Microsoft call them;
- the residue – user interface, and other application instance-dependent procedurality and local formatting.

NB: This has a major impact on development/maintenance Organization and roles. The erstwhile DA/DBA function thus takes on a lot more common process maintenance, becoming more like a systems architecture function, needing more muscle and stature. The application programmer becomes little more than a user interface implementor.

The role and promise of OOD methods

A *method* is defined as any process which is relevant to a class. The power of the concept comes from:

- methods are *declarative* – they are properties of the class, therefore should be removed from discretionary procedural application programming;
  - point for methods and controls;
  - excellent basis for referential integrity only more so;
- typically, access to and manipulation of objects may be constrained to be done only through their associated methods – providing a strong

basis for controls, potential for more rigorous proof of correctness;

- physically, methods offer a potential extension of the stored procedure implementation approach, thus actual discretionary application code can reduce to very little;
- methods may be functions or procedures (Turbo Pascal);
- there is potential for rules requiring all classes to have certain methods defined, e.g. create, retrieve, display, modify, delete, audit/validate;
- it is possible to define extensive preventive validation, e.g.:
  - application code attempts to override methods;
  - the existence of required methods;
  - querying of possible replication of functionality, e.g. if two methods both create new instances of the same object;
  - thesaurus-based searches for clashes or gaps.

Suitable choice of method names gives great self-extending power to language; and ability for expression of algorithms in something closely akin to natural business language.

Design/expression of complex applications

Complexity management is a problem with novel GUI development environments. Most of the current generation of GUI environments appear great for building small, simple interactive processes. However, no effective proven approaches appear yet to have emerged to support structured, layered definition, design and development.

GUI applications may be best described as finite state machines (FSMs). Screens and (possibly) user state and database positions are states, events and operation of GUI controls invoke transitions. Application spec can then embody (layered) state transition diagrams and transition matrices.

Application Manager shows some signs of this. I liked the ability to take different views of the emerging application: FSM, PHD and 'dictionary' – indented list, and to maintain from all or any.

Generic templates

There is serious potential for generic object class and method templates which incorporate industry/sector requirements, features and expertise. See below re Banking.

Issues

Inheritance seems to mean that the selection of a method for a class must proceed from bottom up in the class hierarchy.

Can an object type be a member of multiple class hierarchies i.e. network type class hierarchies? Generally no - but there are some products which permit it, e.g. Choreographer (like Smalltalk only more house trained). Term is multiple inheritance. Careful qualification is needed to overcome ambiguity. Methods can probably be used to overcome limitations.

- if not, this limits ability to describe reality, e.g. owned vehicle wants to be a member both of vehicle and asset classes;

- if this is permitted, how is inheritance controlled, e.g. where both super classes have methods of the same name - potential ambiguity, e.g. via polymorphism - maybe a route qualifier?.

Can a method invoke methods of other classes, e.g. creating a customer account needs to check existence of a customer instance, and set one up if not? If not, how is referential integrity to be managed?

Version control is claimed to be a problem. Why can't the class hierarchy itself be used for this?

Banking examples of OOD

The aim is to have a natural 'grammar' in which all statements or instructions concerning the business could be expressed.

For example:

'Validate all deals involving XYZ PLC in which Party A has been an intermediary.'

'Report profitability actual versus plan, this year versus last, by legal entity, business unit, product group and customer type'

THE DEFAULT METHOD SET SHOULD INCLUDE:

C *create* **R** *read* **U** *update* **D** *delete* **P** *present* **V** *validate*; plus specials

A STARTER CLASS HIERARCHY FOR BANKING:

- *Legal entity*: private individual, Ltd, PLC, partnership, LBG, charity
- *Contract*: service, loan, bargain in financial instrument, bargain in commodity, supply of asset
- *Role in contract: principal* - buyer, seller, borrower, lender; *intermediary* - agent, broker; *observer* - advisor, regulator
- *Limit*
- *Instrument*:
  - *Simple*: domestic equity, foreign equity, foreign exchange, CD, commodity
  - *Compound*: arbitrage,
  - *Derivative*: future, option, index

- *Account*:
    - *customer*: retail, loan, trading
    - *ledger*: general, sub-ledger
    - *supplier*

A framework for rapid and iterative development

To support the above concepts, it is necessary to be able to control fragmented, rapid and iterative development. The process illustrated in Figure 11-8 can be used as a guide for this purpose. The diagram is explained by the notes which follow.

Figure 11-8:   *Rapid development cycle*

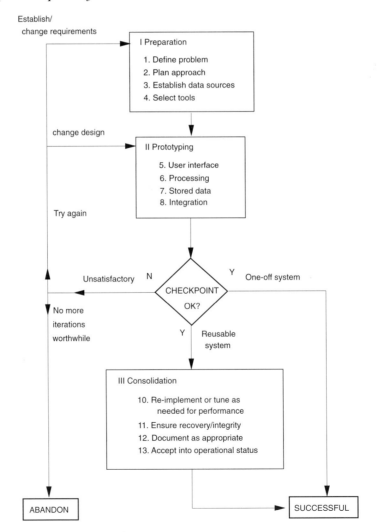

Stages of iterative development

1. PREPARATION

1. Business goals, Prototype goals, Prototype scope, Business volumes.

2. Prototyping approach, user participation, user expectations.

3. Minimum essential data and functional analysis to understand requirement, and decompose into prototypable units;

    ■ Investigate data sources and quality.

4. Vehicle selection (possibly by step).

2. PROTOTYPING

5. 'Emulation' of Man/Machine interface screens, means of user communication, etc.

6. Addition of functionality

    ■ Algorithms, etc., within single function.

7. Support for data storage

    ■ Data storage/memory

8. Integration:

    8.1   *Intra-sub-system: linking of dialogue steps*

    8.2   *Intra-system: assembly of prototype components*

    8.3   *Inter-system: testing of data sources, population of prototype with plausible data to provide realistic trial.*

9. Decision point: Abandon *or*

    Use once and discard *or* Keep for repeated use

3. CONSOLIDATION

10. Addition of performance/recovery/Integrity

11. May require re-implementation

12. Documentation

13. Package and handover for operational use.

Classes of application and their suitability for iterative or rapid development

1. 'Analytics' – numeric and graphics for DSS purposes

    ■ centralized (declining)

    ■ workstation (growing, backed by server databases)

Figure 11-9:   *Trendy Products PLC implementation options*

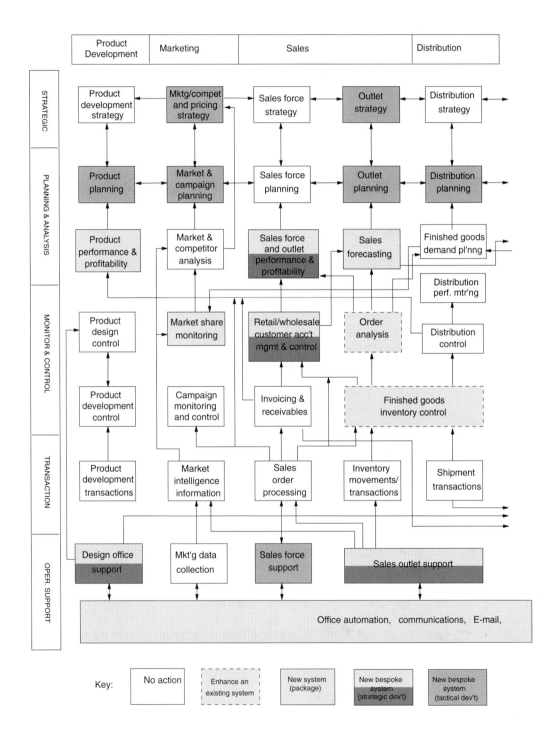

Figure 11-9:   *(continued) Trendy Products PLC implementation options*

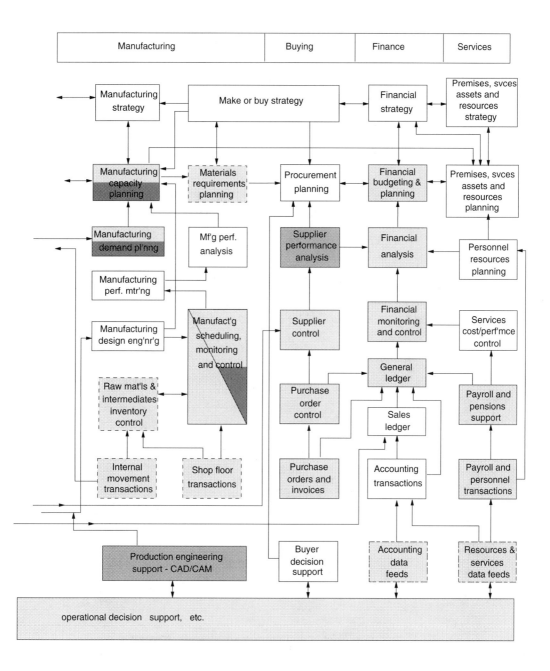

2.   MIS – enquiry and analysis of operational and/or extract databases.

  ▪ increasingly client workstation based, with interactive usage

3.   Document management and textual analysis.

4.   Transaction processing – pre-defined transactions against shared operational database:

  ▪ user interface processing to client
  ▪ database to shared server

5.   Information distribution and delivery

The results of the above deliberations will lead to updates to, and further detail in:

1.   The Application Systems Map version which is annotated to reflect implementation decisions (see Figure 11-9).

2.   The implementation bar chart which reflects phasing and dependencies (see Figure 11-10).

3.   The business cases which are being assembled jointly with the sponsors.

Figure 11-10: *Practical sequences for application delivery – neglecting site phasing and migration constraints*

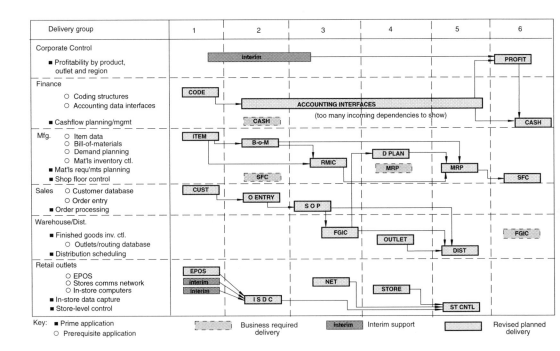

Logical distribution analysis

In general, there will be a number of business locations involved in our IS/IT strategy. At each location there may be:

1.   A variety of users, who can be divided into populations who make differing levels of use of a number of different application functions.

2.   A variety of workstations on which client type application functionality can run.

3.   One or more larger computers, which may host one or more applications, and one or more databases.

The user populations, and their patterns of function systems usage may be stable, or they may be highly variable. User locations may even be mobile.

Despite the growing capability of information technology to handle distributed processing and client/server computing, it is still much more expensive and time consuming if a high proportion of database access is remote, i.e. needs to access data at a remote site. This is despite the fact that most operators of wide area communication networks charge by connection, not by usage volume; the problem is mostly a matter of response time. There are techniques for placing composite procedures involving clusters of database access calls at the database servers, but this has its limits, and there is as yet no stable standard for this 'remote procedure call' mechanism.

We therefore need to design our overall set of systems and databases so that they are both efficient to use and run today, and can cope with likely future changes in the physical placement of users. A key issue is – do we fine-tune to optimize for today's technology, costs and business user profiles, or do we implement a simpler configuration which may not be as cheap and effective, but which will not be wrong-footed by future developments?

This is not a trivial problem, and I do not have a ready-made recipe for its solution. However, in Figure 11-11 below there is shown a form of documentation which has proved useful as an aid to thinking about the problem.

The left hand side of the chart is a matrix showing types of business location and the population of each (horizontal axis, l1..ln), versus application processes (vertical axis, p1..pn). The cells contain the total number of users at each location type who make use of each application process.

The right hand side of the chart is a matrix showing the patterns of usage of logical databases (horizontal axis, d1..dn), versus application processes (vertical axis). The cells in this example show the level of usage from low (L) to very high (VHF).

It is intuitively obvious that placement where possible of the databases accessed by a set of applications close to the user populations who make most use of those applications could be advantageous, in terms of response time and communications network usage.

As an example, it is relatively easy to derive the following conclusions from the chart:

1. Location l4 is Corporate HQ – candidate as the location for any centralized processing or database placement

2. Process p6 is used widely, uses mainly partitioned local data – candidate for dispersal to locations

3. Processes p7, p8 are used especially heavily at location 6 – candidate for processing at that location, and to hold d5 and d7 data there

4. Processes p2, p4, p5 are used heavily at HQ, and tend to pull d3, d4, d6 with them – candidate for a centralized system

5. Processes p3 and p9 are used widely, and access d1, d2, d8 heavily – candidate for centralized system, located possibly at HQ

Figure 11-11: *Sample logical distribution requirement*

Application processes

Process	I8	I7	I6	I5	I4	I3	I2	I1	d1	d2	d3	d4	d5	d6	d7	d8	...
p9		7	8		2	5	35		H	H						M	
p8			255									L	H		H		
p7			386									L	VH		H		
p6	127		13	5	175	212			L		L		L				
p5				148						L	VH	H		VH		L	
p4				75							H	VH		H			
p3	24	35	7	36	12		35		H	M				L		H	
p2				139						L	H	L		H			
p1																	
loc'n type	I8	I7	I6	I5	I4	I3	I2	I1	d1	d2	d3	d4	d5	d6	d7	d8	...
loc'n pop'n	10	3	32	1	1	5	12	1									

Aggregate user population by location type using each process | Shared access by process type to data groups

It is stressed that this approach to analysis of distribution requirements is only partially formulated, but readers may find it useful, even so.

Application definitions

We are now at the stage where it is increasingly clear to us and to the sponsors which are the key recommended applications. These need to be defined in a

succinct form for approval and agreement. Figure 11-12 illustrates a useful
format, although in practice, especially for larger applications, this may run to
2 or more pages. Note particularly the provision for backward traceability, via
CBINS references, and for forward referencing to implementation projects.

Figure 11-12: *Candidate application synopsis*

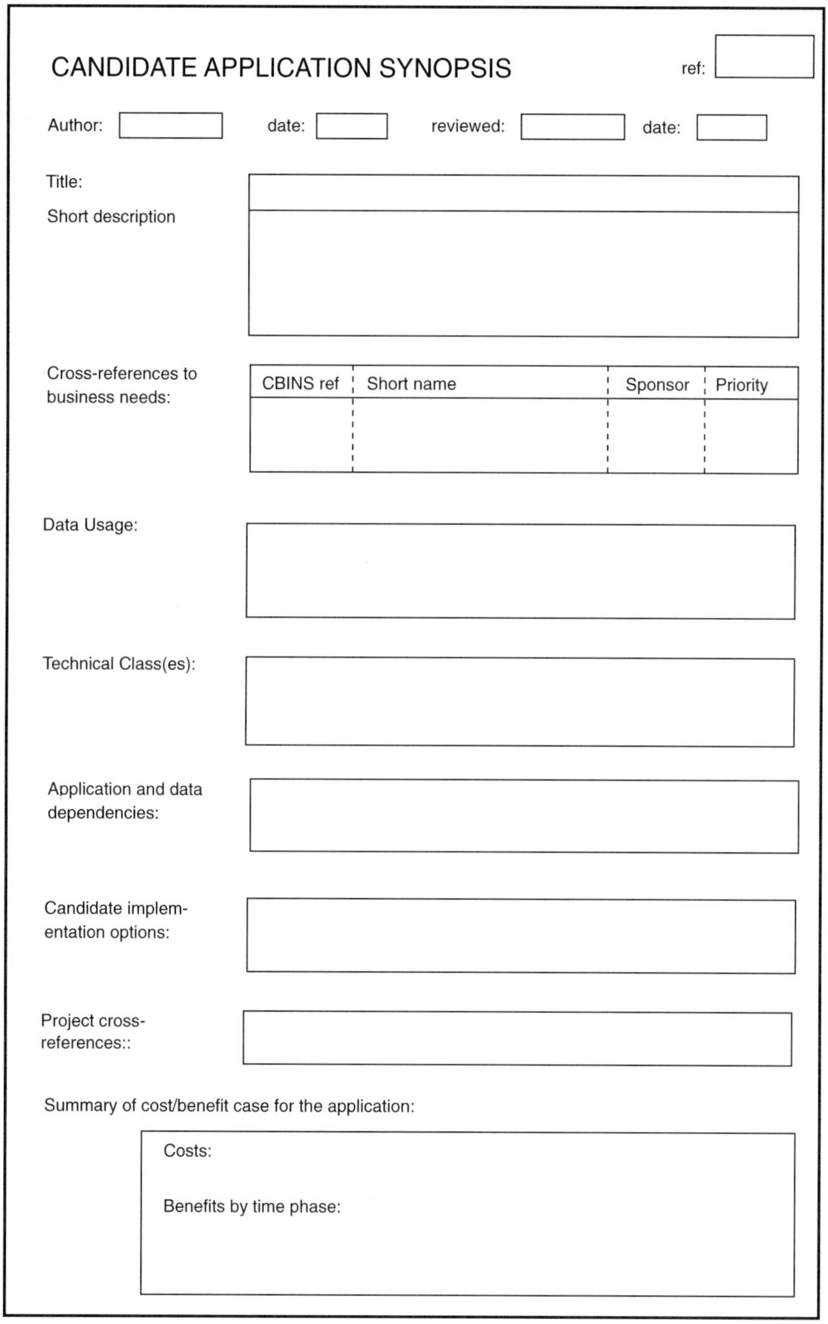

Project definitions

Of course applications, be they new or modifications of existing, only get implemented by means of projects. We now have to give thought to the nature of these projects.

Figure 11-13:   *Recommended IS/IT project synopsis*

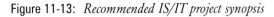

RECOMMENDED IS/IT PROJECT SYNOPSIS   ref.:

| Author: | date: | reviewed: | date: |

Title:

Type: review   feasibility study   requm'ts def'n   Design: new dev't   enhancement   custom dev't package implem'n   technical   other (specify)

Short description:

Cross-references to business needs:

CBINS ref.	Short name	Sponsor	Priority

Data Usage:

Business volumes and workload profile

Application and data dependencies/cross references:

Performance, security and control requirements:

Implementation options:

Technical requirements/ options:

Project/phase cross references and dependencies

Resource estimates:

Analysis:	Build:
Design	Test:
User:	Implement:

Implementation schedule:

Summary of cost/benefit case

Costs by time phase:

Benefits by time phase: (consider cost reduction, loss/risk avoidance and revenue/profit increases)

Risk/impact of not proceeding:

Although there is much work to do to finalize all aspects of the projects, it is valuable to start to pull together an draft view of them even this early. Figure 11-13 illustrates the nature of the Application Project Synopsis, although much of this information will not yet be finalized.

Business case development

Whilst all of this is going on, we must remain in constant touch with the business sponsors. They will need reassurance that the benefits which they expected to be delivered from having the their business needs (as defined in their CBINS) met are being preserved in the transition from needs to applications, and then to projects.

We will need their help to ensure that we do not lose sight of the overriding business priorities. They will need our help in identifying and quantifying business benefits.

It is a useful approach to develop jointly with the sponsors a document for each application or project along the following lines:

Key questions:

- What is recommended?
- Why should we do it – what will it do for the business?
- What happens if we don't do it – what are the alternatives?
- How much will it cost?
- When will you deliver it?
- How will it be achieved?

What? – TITLE AND ONE PARAGRAPH DESCRIPTION OF WHAT IS PROPOSED.

Cross-references to acknowledged business needs, e.g. CBINs or other specific user sponsored initiatives.

Why? – BUSINESS RATIONALE FOR THE DEVELOPMENT – QUALITATIVE

Business benefits – costs/headcount saved:

- Risks controlled or losses avoided
- Revenue or profit improvement

Impact/risk of not doing it

How much? – TOTAL COSTS, SPLIT BY:

- Internal staff
- External contractors
- Software licenses or services
- Equipment

When? – BY DATE:

- Deliverable
- £ spend, by:
- £ amount of benefit delivered

How? – WHO WILL DO IT

- With what training or other purchased assistance
- With what technology
- Key risks and control measures
- What are the dependencies, impacts and side effects, and how are they to be controlled.

Selecting application solutions – summary

We have now achieved:

1. A clear vision of application and database strategy – where we want to get to.

2. Specific selections from the database and application implementation options.

3. Implementation and phasing options identified – basis for migration planning.

4. Impact on business delivery sequence and business cases cleared with the sponsors – basis for business cases.

5. Sponsors fully involved in the process of formulating business cases based on applications and projects.

6. Impact on information architectures actioned.

7. Technical environment requirements drafted.

8. Rapid implementation projects launched.

CHAPTER 12

Establishing technology strategy

Introduction

This chapter both puts forward a process for establishing and maintaining a technology strategy, and also addresses a number of the most relevant issues involved.

Figure 12-1: *Establish technology strategy*

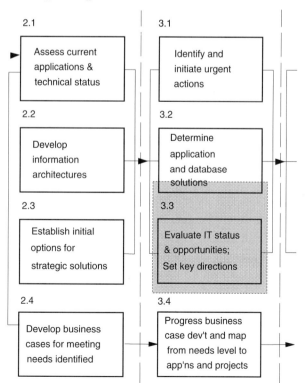

Whilst the process set out in the first half of the chapter should remain valid, by and large, for a considerable period, the relevance of the specific issues raised is likely to vary quite rapidly, and to be supplanted by other, as yet unforeseen issues. To an even greater extent, the particular technical options and solutions discussed, whilst valid as of mid-1995, may quickly become of little more than historic interest.

This phenomenon does not invalidate the process, which is designed to provide a high degree of insulation against just such rapid obsolescence.

Chapter structure

- Products from the stage
- Recommended process for setting IT strategy
  - Objectives of setting IT directions
  - Approach to setting IT directions
  - Determining requirements
  - Useful categories
  - Formulating the strategy – technical options and direction statements
- Review of key IT issues and options
- Approaches to sizing and costing

Products from this stage

Where we want to get to in technical terms

- Technology (IT) vision to meet the emerging IS vision, or even to drive it where appropriate
- Identified opportunities for IT to make a proactive contribution to the business
- Recommended overall technical strategy
- Specification of technical environments to support applications
- Refresh of industry and vendor status, promises and intelligence
- For technical components, options, preferences and basis for selecting solutions, short and longer term, to build the environments

Basis for technical implementation and migration

- Realistic assessment of current IT assets and status
- Analysis of dependencies and constraints
- A firm basis for planning, sizing and costing

- quantified workload patterns for business and application scenarios
- performance characteristics of candidate components
- Position statements on key issues, uncertainties and risks – any further work required

Goals of the IT vision and supporting technical strategy

- Good support for and enabling of the business and IS visions
- Stability:
  - *application code*
  - *user interfaces*
- Cost control:
  - *max. value for money*
  - *predictable*
- Flexibility to meet changing business needs/volumes
- Flexibility to exploit technology advances:
  - better cost/performance
  - business/product opportunities
- Minimize diversity

Technical Strategy – scope and process

An IT Technical Strategy needs to cover recommended solutions, guidelines, standards and approaches for all computer and communications technology within all Business Units and locations of the Organization. In the relatively high level IT strategic review, there may remain continuing uncertainty concerning the suitability of certain specific technical components. If this is so, then this should be indicated, and a program of further specific work recommended. As illustrated in this Chapter, a typical IT strategic statement should cover:

1. A sample set of target technical environments needed to host a typical application portfolio and the associated databases.

2. Sample criteria for assigning applications and databases into the technical environments. These will vary over time, according to the nature of the application workload, and to the capabilities of the environments.

3. A sample set of recommended technical components to be used to construct the technical environments.

4. The criteria for selecting and combining technical components from the recommended set to construct technical environments.

5. A recommended approach to identifying, maintaining and updating the set of preferred technical components, as a subset of the available range of vendor offerings and options. This should take account of the

variation over time of vendor and component functionality, reputation, cost/performance and potential.

6. Recommended approaches to sizing and costing the usage of technical environments and components.

7. Other agreed statements of requirements, policy and preference.

8. The criteria, definition of responsibilities and process for maintaining items 1 through 7.

The scope of such an IT strategy is illustrated in Figure 12-2.

Figure 12-2: *Formulating technical strategy*

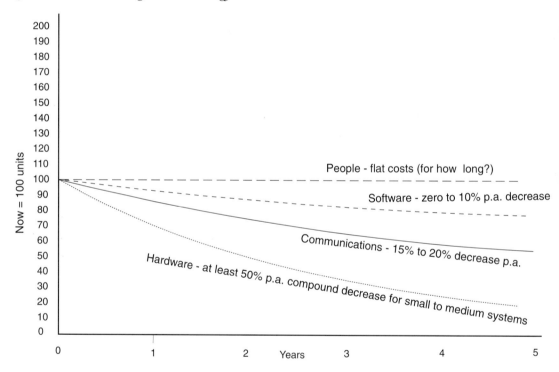

IT direction statements

Purpose

SCOPE

- All computers – largest to smallest, specialized and general purpose
- All use of external and quasi-external IT services
- All communications – voice and digital, including mobile units

- Application development methods, techniques, tools and vehicles
- People, accommodation and ancillary logistics
- Vendors
- Options, risks, capacity and costs
- Assessing current IT status
- Present installed hardware
- Software systems, languages and databases
- Personnel skills
- Commitment to the present systems
- Contentment with the present systems
- Work planned and in progress
- New start ups
- 'Givens'

Defining technology requirements

- Workloads – types of activity, aggregated by application class
- Physical locations at which service is required
- Performance, security, integrity, resilience, auditability
- Workload volumes analyzed by the above
- Profiles – variation over day, week, month, year
- Forward projections
- Contingencies
- Constraints imposed by current investment, skills limitations, etc.

A layered approach to IT strategy

Background

Traditionally, applications have been assessed on an individual basis for their technology needs. This is illustrated in Figure 12-3. According to the perceived application characteristics and requirements, and constrained by the available technical platforms and capacity, a suitable set of technical components is selected and assembled to meet the application's needs. This approach has led in the past to a variety of problems:

- a multiplicity of solutions to closely similar problems, each dependent to some degree on the background and views of the individuals taking the decisions. This spurious diversity has led to excessive support costs;
- the absence of clear criteria for good practice;
- limited opportunities to learn from experience gained elsewhere;

- great difficulty in establishing commitment to any form of coherent technology architecture;
- limited ability to gain the benefits of economies of scale.

Figure 12-3:   *Technology planning - application level solutions*

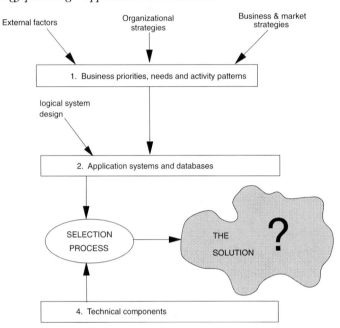

Recommended approach

Our recommended approach to technology strategy is based on the idea that business requirements should be filtered through a number of layers, in which they are transformed firstly into a set of loadings on an application systems portfolio, and then into a set of workloads which are supported by a set of technology environments.

The behavioral characteristics of the environments and the criteria for assignment of application into them are kept independent of the manner in which the environments are made up from technology components. Applications need no longer be matched directly to technology components on a piecemeal basis. Figure 12-4 illustrates the effect of interposing this technical environment layer.

Independently, alternative candidate technical components for the technology platforms may be assessed, sized and costed, based on the aggregate application workload imposed by the assigned applications.

In more detail, a given set of business requirements, comprising a quantified set of activity patterns and support priorities is taken as a sample scenario (layer 1 in Figure 12-4). This set will vary over time, in a manner which may depend on a variety of factors, each subject to a degree of uncertainty. Additional scenarios for evaluation may be developed by varying any or all of:

- the set of business activities;
- the initial workload volumes;
- the variation in activity mix and volume parameters over time.

Figure 12-4:   *Technology planning using an environmental layer*

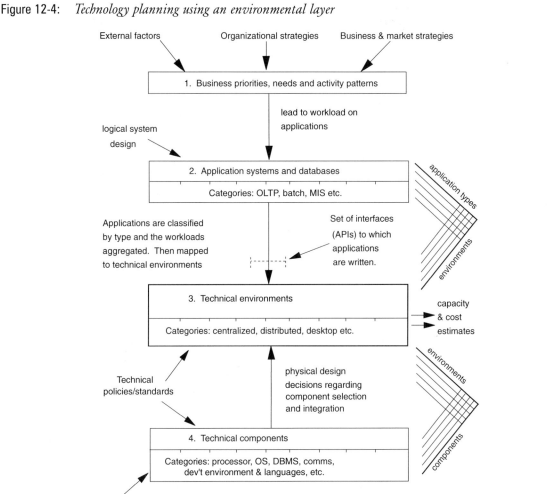

Each scenario to be considered is transformed into a set of workloads placed on an assumed application portfolio (layer 2 in Figure 12-4, in which each type of application is assumed to exhibit certain characteristics which will lead to its requiring to be supported by a suitable technical environment or platform (layer 3 in Figure 12-4).

Each type of technical environment can be made up in a number of ways from technical components (layer 4 in Figure 12-4). Alternative formulations may be assembled and evaluated on paper. It is intended that applications should be constructed in such a manner that their use of technology is expressed in terms of what they expect the platform to do for them, and not how it is made up from components. In this way, it should be possible to vary the physical formulation of the platform, e.g. for reasons of integration compatibility, risk management or cost/performance, with little or no impact on the application code itself.

It is the intention that, by this means, application implementation decisions should become limited to selection of the appropriate type of technical environment. It becomes a separate issue how such an environment is to be supported from time to time, and is no longer a concern of the application designer or user.

The relevance of Open Systems

Much was expected of Open Systems Interconnection (OSI) and related standards, such as OSI, XPG, POSIX and the UK Government's GOSIP variant (now subsumed in EPHOS - the European Procurement Handbook for Open Systems). Although they proved of critical importance in breaking the proprietary stranglehold of powerful vendors in the 1980s, they never really delivered on the promises of their strongest adherents. Such formalized panaceas have now most likely reached their peak of popularity, although, under pressure from large public sector customers, most major vendors now offer compliance with them.

It is becoming increasingly clear as this is written in 1995 that true 'openness', in the sense of interconnectivity of separately developed systems has less and less to do with OSI, and more and more to do with market forces, driven especially by such co-operative efforts as the Internet protocol stack TCP/IP, and by powerful players such as Microsoft, with their OLE and ODBC quasi-open standards.

Such *de facto* standards increasingly make it possible for applications to be written to a set of standard application programming interfaces (APIs) in such a way that they are protected from change to the underlying components, so long as they adhere to the conventions embodied in the APIs.

Benefits of the recommended approach

By following this approach, the following benefits can be obtained:

1.   Provision of ready-made, proven solutions to standard business requirements and problems.

2.   More effective sharing of core databases across the business where relevant and appropriate.

3. Improved ability to provide IT technical support to new business or Organization units, so that they are free to focus on their business development.

4. Easier provision by Organization units of timely, accurate, information flows in standard format

5. Standardization of information flows between Organization units where relevant and appropriate.

6. The ability to sustain efficient information flows and support to units of the business through most likely business evolution scenarios.

7. More effective integration of application systems and technical solutions. The need to assess technical component compatibility and to provide for effective integration of technical components is provided for explicitly in the stage of assembling components into environments.

8. More effective technical solutions may be attained through requirements being clearly identified and common elements highlighted.

9. Through computer modelling of the sizing and costing of technical environments, it will be made easier and more efficient to assess the effect of alternative activity patterns and to explore alternative technical options and configurations. In this way, the impact of alternative business scenarios on a selected technical strategy may be explored. Similarly, several alternative technical configurations for a particular environment may be evaluated with ease.

10. The range of recommended technical components may be treated as a single pool of candidate solutions. This helps in recognition of spurious diversity and redundancy, and in managing economically the provision of expertise and support.

11. The questions of vendor and component qualification, range capacity and inter-component compatibility may be addressed once, rather than separately for each environment or solution.

Assumptions underlying the approach

Our approach is predicated on the following assumptions, which are the result of experience and best practice observed across a wide range of organizations and situations.

1. It is possible to divide the application portfolio, both current and likely future versions, into a set of application categories which, if carefully chosen, will:

   ■ each exhibit a clear-cut set of characteristics, in terms of function, distribution and performance, which will have clear implications for the IT technical environments on which they need to reside;

- act as a focus for development of a time-phased, quantified statement of requirements for technology support, based on predicted patterns and volumes of business activity;

- act as a basis for the specification of a stable set of requirements for each type of technical environment

- remain stable despite continuing evolution in the underlying technology.

Examples of technical environments are:

- a centralized computing environment which supports high volume transaction processing against a shared database and concurrent MIS;

- a distributed multi-user computing environment which supports transaction processing against distributed shared databases and concurrent Office Automation and other general purpose work-group processing;

- a single user desktop general purpose environment which also hosts MIS and EIS delivery and presentation facilities.

2. There can be identified a set of categories of technical components, for example computing processor, operating system, DBMS, LAN protocol, VDU screen, which:

- can be combined to make up technical environments;

- act as a focus for drawing up short-lists of preferred candidate components.

These environmental requirements will be capable of being met by a variety of alternative combinations of specific hardware and software components. The cost/performance and the additional capabilities of the technical components may be expected to continue to evolve, but should not impact the applications' view of the environments.

3. There can identified for each class of technical component an identified list of candidates, selection of which is recommended in preference to other options. These recommendations will vary over time.

4. For each technical environment, there can be drawn up a set of recommendations regarding preferred make-up, which may vary according to details of the requirement. These recommendations will vary over time.

Defining application requirements

General goals and requirements

BASIS FOR EVOLUTION

Any future computing platform must offer a good basis for long term evolution in an environment where there will remain the likelihood of further change in markets, products and business Organization and control style.

FLEXIBILITY

There will be a continuing need to support further evolution of business strategy and Organization. This implies the need for great flexibility as to:

- the types of business support which the platform can sustain;
- the locations of users, processing nodes and database locations;
- the range of workload required to be handled at any location;
- the scale computing power required at any one location;
- the range of types of network connectivity required, and volatility in the physical topology itself;
  - the environmental tolerance of the equipment;
  - network topology/capacity.

RISK MANAGEMENT

There are a number of areas of potential business risk associated with IT strategy options. The requirements include assessment of these and provision of effective means of control in each case. The risk areas include:

- Getting 'wrong footed' by radical business/market scenarios:
  - *functionality*   ▪ *flexibility*   ▪ *network topology/capacity*
- Higher than expected rates of change of external factors, e.g.:
  - political/economic climate;
  - business patterns/volumes;
  - technology capabilities and options.
- The organization's ability to cope with rate of change becoming a constraint.
- Limitations of management calibre and capability.
- Limitations of technical support capability.
  - Excessive diversity of components may over-stress the technical skills base.
- Equipment and software failing to meet vendor's promises:
  - *delivery date*   ▪ *functionality*   ▪ *capacity*   ▪ *cost*

This may lead to failure of solutions to deliver the sought for cost/ performance or functionality.

- Difficulty of migration – may fall victim to vendor 'lock-in' strategies.

- It may be hard to initiate radical change, due to inability to overcome the momentum of previous investment and 'imposed' Corporate standards.

- The true complexity and difficulty of the business ambitions or application requirements, or of the technical solutions considered may be seriously underestimated.

SPECIFIC REQUIREMENTS

Any Technical Strategy which is to offer a long term basis for evolution for an Organization should address the following requirements:

1. The equipment and software should be able to do the required job efficiently.

2. Solutions should be cost effective.

3. Application development and maintenance should be easy, fast, certain and cheap.

4. Effective control is required over integrity, availability and resilience.

5. Effective control is required over security.

6. A good platform for packages is necessary.

7. The facilities should enable easy compliance with mandatory standards and also provide the opportunity to exploit other attractive standards and common practices.

8. The set of services should appear integrated to the user, available through a uniform set of menus; their availability should depend only on his/her access rights, not on the location from which access is attempted.

9. Access to services should appear uniform, regardless of the physical location of the user, the database(s) and of the computer undertaking the processing.

10. Effective control is required over physical distribution.

11. A wide range of useable 'scaleability' will be necessary.

12. Support is needed for key networking roles, especially client/server.

13. The ability is needed to move applications easily between:

   - large and small implementations of the same platform;
   - different platforms offering a common environment.

14. The ability is needed easily to migrate into the environment, and to be able to follow a satisfactory evolutionary path once within it.

15. Effective data management is needed covering:

    - standards compliance;
    - local/central/distributed;
    - range of functions;
    - range of data types;
    - integration with application development vehicles.

16. Good support is required for business devolution.

17. A high level of environmental tolerance is required for the smaller more populous computers.

18. The computing environment should require minimal human intervention, and place low demands on user expertise.

APPLICATION PORTFOLIO

The application portfolio is assumed to be developed and maintained through an Information Systems Planning process in the manner outlined in the introduction. This process performs the derivation of the application and database portfolio (layer 2) from business requirements (layer 1) in Figure 12-4 above.

As with business activities, this needs to be by means of a 'hot link', in a prescribed format, from the business unit planning groups into the models used for technical strategy formulation.

There must be provision made for continuing refresh of the quantitative aspects of this section as business and IS plans evolve.

Types of application

The application types introduced here are intended to be:

- easy to assign, based on examination of the application in question;
- useful as a basis for selection of technical environment;
- between them, to cover all of the application portfolio.

The correspondence of each with the technical environments is defined below. In addition to the type, at this stage, other application attributes need to be identified, as they will also influence the selection of technical environment:

- workload and database volumes;
- performance requirements;
- availability requirements;
- security requirements;

- special requirements, such as real time data collection, mobility, etc.

Applications are classified under the following categories:

- Transaction processing (OLTP) systems.
- Management information, enquiry and reporting (MIS) systems.
- High level management planning and analysis aids and decision support (known as Executive Information Systems (EIS) or Decision Support Systems (DSS).
- Office automation (OA) and other associated clerical and administrative support systems and productivity aids.
- General desktop utilities.

Future applications will tend to place more focus on high volume OLTP, and may in addition require a composite category of specialized systems such as those for:

- operational decision support;
- source data collection in a variety of hostile or open air environments;
- providing capability to maintain operational control over fast changing situations (frequently termed 'command and control').

This classification of applications is intended to lead painlessly to the corresponding technical environment categories.

Technical environment types

Transaction Systems

- High volume
  - Worst case is high integrity, high availability and geographically dispersed user base
- Low volume
  - shared data, geographically dispersed user base
  - personal, disjoint

Monitoring and Control Systems

- High volume – Regular analysis of large databases
- Low volume: *shared, up-to-date data*; *disjoint*
- Specialized, e.g. process control
- Key issue – timeliness of data

Management Decision Support

- Highly consolidated MIS type data
- Planning and modelling – 'analytics'
- 'Intelligence'
    - Management and analysis of text and other data formats search, much external, high uncertainty

Operational Support

- Office Automation
- Operational Decision Support
- Communications
- Text Management
- Command and control

Client/Server

Client/Server computing is undoubtedly a key issue in the mid-nineties, and is addressed in the second half of this chapter as such. It is not treated here strictly as either an environment, nor as a set of components. I see the concept rather a means for using a set of components, which will vary over time, to meet environmental needs in the most economical and effective way. I do not consider Client/Server to be a truly strategic issue – it is rather a migration aid, and a means for avoiding or deferring inappropriate strategic decisions, and substituting for them reversible tactical decisions instead.

Strategic decisions and tactical decisions

People often seem to feel bound to rush into strategic decisions under entirely inappropriate circumstances, e.g. when they should be looking for means to leave options open. The approach to procurement which the EC and GATT rules are tending to impose, at least on public sector organizations can be especially damaging.

I have, on more than one, occasion watched powerless as an Organization very carefully, thoroughly and fairly – and in full compliance with all relevant rules and legislation – selects on the one hand a strategic supplier for software, such as a relational DBMS, whose use is to be mandated at Corporate level, and simultaneously on the on hand, selects an application package which will be rolled out into many sites, which requires a different RDBMS!

Usually, what is needed is the insight to realize that a strategic product decision is not needed at that time. In the example above, the strategic decision should be to use a certain level of distributed ANSI SQL, and there needs to be flexibility to explore one or more products on a tactical basis.

Where strategic procurements are taking place, then interdependencies need to be acknowledged. Otherwise, just as sailors can have radar assisted collisions at sea, so, I believe, can IT strategists have procurement rules assisted collisions on land.

Assignment of applications into technical environments

- Application are assigned technical environments, and particular components selected for the environment according to:
- the application type, and behavioral characteristics;
- the application workload and data volumes;
- the availability and performance requirements of the application sub-systems;
- the characteristics and constraints of any candidate application packages which are under consideration as solutions;
- the types of users, and the geographic distribution and mobility of users and data sources;
- the derived consequences for physical placement of data storage and processing capacity, and hence for local and wide area communications;
- the manner in which any of the above are likely to change over time.

All of this is tempered by consideration of cost constraints and other 'givens', and of any special purpose requirements. Selection and sizing of technical components for technical environments is covered later in this Chapter.

An overall process for making these mapping decisions is set out in Figure 12-5.

Technology components

Technology components can be regarded as the raw material for assembling the technical environments discussed above.

The very strength of the IT industry, its constant re-invention and renewal of itself; the profusion of solutions, each genuinely cheaper and faster than the last, but each subtly or not so subtly incompatible with the previous, is its greatest weakness. The one certainty is that today's 'best buy' will be tomorrow's expensive dinosaur; that the more finely we tune our favorite technology solution for optimal cost/performance, many other vendors will claim to have rendered it obsolete tomorrow. And some of them may be telling the truth! This is the reason for the stress in this approach on the technical environment layer, which we hope will offer stability and the ability to swap technology components almost at will, whilst keeping applications and user interfaces stable. It is not always that simple, but that's the general idea. These concepts are also central the Open Systems movement, and the Client/Server approach, which will be discussed in more detail later.

Technical component categories

Technical components are best considered under the following categories (or your preferred refinement or decomposition of them).

- Processor
- Storage
- Operating system
- Data management – data types and DBMS types
- Communications – LAN and WAN
- Development methods tools and techniques
- Development vehicles

It may appear grossly insensitive to consider human skills and resources under this head as yet another technology component category, but it often proves the most effective approach. Certainly capacity planning for staff skill types, and meeting the re-skilling needs can often be a key limiting factor in planning technical change.

Rather than provide details of particular technical components which will both offend their vendors and almost certainly be way out of date by the time you read this, I have confined the remainder of this chapter to the discussion of issues which I believe will remain relevant for some time.

Figure 12-5: *Technical strategy implementation – selecting an environment for an application*

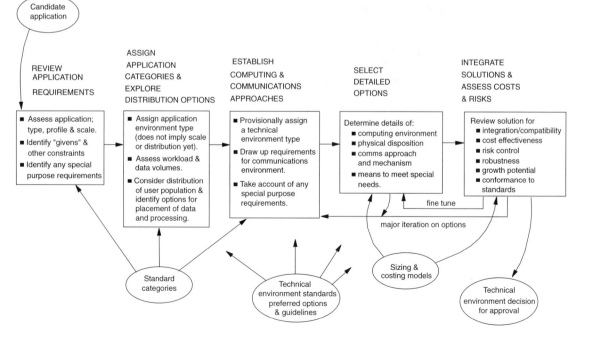

Technical options selection – a multi-dimensional approach

INTRODUCTION

The multi-dimensional analysis approach to the taking of decisions based on complex criteria, first introduced in chapter 6 in a business context, and then extended to selection of IS support options in chapters 10 and 11 may also be applied to technology decisions. One such application is outlined below in Table 12-1. One difference is that at the technical level, there are many more relevant but distinct times at which decisions are to be made. A list of these is suggested, but the matrix presented in Table 12-1 considers only one of these.

As before, we start with the bottom left quadrant, where we identify those decisions which need to be taken, with their alternative outcomes or options. At the top left, we identify the criteria which may influence the decisions. There is now greater emphasis on the domains of the criteria and the options. The right-hand half of the matrix represents some combinations of criteria which may lead to particular decisions – i.e. our view of the rules.

Once again, I must stress that the matrix presented is only a simplified example, and any experienced designer could quickly pick holes in the specific rules presented, or identify some missing criteria. The systems and technology marketplace is also in such turmoil that criteria and options will change quite quickly over time. But the approach is such that we aim to capture the knowledge of experts, and their awareness of market trends, and enlist their aid in systematizing and documenting what has hitherto been largely a black art.

Decision times to consider

- Strategic IT Architectures – system/network/platform configuration (see Table 12-1).
- Business requirements mapping to application services
- Selection of technical options
- Detailed physical design – including placement of databases and application processes
- System build/integration
- System roll-out
- Service start-up – shift / day
- Taking backups
- Time of fault occurrence
- During recovery
- During reversion from standby to normal

Key points

- Earlier decisions can close off or enable later options
- Leaving options open is often cheap – even where it may be quite expensive subsequently to activate them
- Therefore the leverage of early decisions, and the cost of getting them wrong, is very high

An example of decision-time analysis – for decision time

System /network/platform configuration

Here, we are establishing capabilities of the environment, and guide-lines for implementors of systems on it.

Table 12-1:   *A simplified example of a decision table reflecting the above approach for decision time:system/ network/platform configuration*

Decision criteria/drivers	Domains	Sample rules							
Max level of recoverability	24 X 365 no break	Y	Y						
	24 X 365, short breaks			Y	Y				
	long shift					Y	Y		
	9 to 5							Y	Y
Level of degraded service	none	Y		Y				Y	
	local notepad				Y				
	simulated					Y			
	live		Y		Y				Y
… and so on									
Resulting decisions	Decision options								
Database protection	local logging only							Y	Y
	remote logging			Y	Y	Y	Y		
	on-the-fly backup	Y	Y	Y	Y				
	remote mirroring	Y	Y						
Client application placement	always co-locate with DB							Y	
	always on user's wkst'n		Y		Y				Y
	moveable as needed								
Local replica database	indicative only						Y		
	overnight update					Y			
	real time updated		Y		Y				Y

The lists below represent a reasonably full set of decision types and options, and the first few of each are placed on the matrix in Table 12-1 (above), with some simple illustrative rules. The reader is encouraged to extend this analysis if they find it fruitful do so

DECISION TYPES AND OPTIONS

Database configuration:

- single centralized;
- physically distributed
- database physical partitioning – none / row / column / value based
- database redundancy – none / cached / replicated slave copies / replicated synchronized

Server CPUs:

- vendor
- O/S
- single / SMP / AMP
- standalone or clustered
- how fault tolerant

Client application placement:

- always co-located with database on server;
- always on user's workstation;
- moveable between server(s) and clients
- option for separate application server

Treatment of data-related procedurality – e.g. validation rules, referential integrity, RPCs, derived data algorithms etc.:

- always on database server;
- always on client – uncontrolled;
- always on client – controlled – how?

Database protection:

- RAID;
- mirroring;
- remote mirroring;
- remote logging.

Database access protocols:

- DCE / SAG SQL;
- OLEn;
- ODBC;

- OMG, etc.

WAN:

- bandwidth
- service type
- protocols for file/bulk mode transfer;
- protocols for interactive fast response.

DECISION CRITERIA

Maximum level of recoverability which will be required:

- 24 hour 365 days p.a., no break, ever;
- 24 hour 365 days p.a., short tolerable breaks;
- long working days;
- normal working days

Level of degraded local service when WAN or servers are out:

- none;
- local notepad only;
- simulated service for critical functions;
- full real time service.

Level of data access across WAN links in normal mode:

- *none* ▪ *low* ▪ *high*

Level of data access across WAN links in fallback mode:

- *none* ▪ *low* ▪ *high*

Level of data access across WAN links in minimum critical service mode:

- *none* ▪ *low* ▪ *high*

This analysis is not presented in its entirety for the simple reason that it has not been completed. It covers only a single decision time, and neither the list of decision types and options nor the decision table is fully populated.

There follows a skeleton list (which the reader is invited to explore) of:

- Other relevant decision times
- Decision types and options
- Decision criteria

1.   IT Strategic architecture – system and network configuration

See above.

2.   Business requirements mapping to application services

Decision types and options

- Placement of workstations
- Delivery of services to locations
- Decision criteria
- User location
- User mobility
- Workload mix
- Business volatility
- Required service levels by function
- Data integrity

3.   Selection of technical options

Decision types and options

- Selection of DBMS
- Database server configuration
- Methods and tool-sets for: *data management*; *application development*; *configuration management* and *system management*
- Server placement
- Utilization of WAN and LAN links: *normal mode* and *fallback mode*

Decision criteria

- Design goals and targets:
- value for money;
- future flexibility;
- application availability;
- service levels

From here on, only categories are listed.

4.   Detailed physical design – including placement of databases and application processes

5.   System build/integration

6.   System roll-out

7.   Service start-up – shift/day, whatever.

8.   Time of backup

9.   Time of fault occurrence

10.   During recovery

11.   During reversion from standby to normal

Technical issues

Specific topics and categories

Specific topics and categories addressed in the remainder of this chapter include:

- Application development environments
- WAN and LAN communications
- Environments or brand names; proprietary or open/standard architectures
- Data management
- Transaction processing
- MIS, DSS, EIS
- Distributed computing and client/server
- Cost / performance:
  - bench-marking
  - capacity estimation and costing

Application development issues

(See also relevant elements of Chapters 10 and 11)

- Alternative development methods and techniques – fixed life cycle versus iterative versus parallel. Discussed in Chapter 11.
- Project management and control are radically different using rapid or iterative development methods.
- Problems and approaches vary according to:
  - application size
  - complexity;
  - expected lifetime;
  - who is to develop it;
  - required levels of integration with other systems and databases.
- *Types of vehicle.* It used to be valid and useful to distinguish between 'fixed function' pre-defined transactions, and the most suitable means for their development, versus what were, in effect, user customizable functional packages, such as spreadsheets. This is now less valid, as the macro languages marketed by such as Microsoft, Borland and Lotus in their functional packages such as the Office set are converging strongly with languages such as Visual Basic, a strong candidate for Client based application development.

- *Portability.* Retention of the option to switch platforms, either for the DBMS or for the client application engine pushes us towards use of an application development vehicle which can 'port' to several alternative platforms, and can talk effectively to several DBMS, preferably simultaneously. This extremely tall order appears to be arriving in the form of database drivers allied with the application development macro languages discussed above.

- Exploitation of cheap desktop mips versus maintenance of central control. Criteria for placement of:
  - development activities
  - application processes
  - core data integrity management processes
- Selection of support tools – CASE/IPSEs
- Choice of development environments and languages

Evolution of development vehicles

The evolution of application development techniques and vehicles appears to be accelerating. This is illustrated in Figure 12-6, where the higher layers represent the more recent developments.

A few years ago, it was considered bold to use a procedural fourth generation language (4GL) to develop applications, instead of a 3GL, on the grounds that although the amount of code to be written would be less, the resulting application may run slowly. Now 4GLs are regarded as well nigh obsolete for many purposes, being supplanted by the newer generation of GUI based 'point and shoot' development tools, even though their demands on computing power are very high; there are several reasons for this:

1. These new tools are vastly more productive and responsive for most types of application development.

2. All hardware is becoming cheaper and faster. Especially on the desktop, this effect is running at between 40% and 60% compound p.a. This means that an almost unlimited amount of cheap computing power can be used to save development manpower.

3. Client/server computing, which depends on effective distributed database management is becoming feasible and economical. This makes it possible to place a substantial proportion of the application computing on the cheap desktop vehicle, even for critical systems.

4. The resource utilization differential between 3GLS, 4GLs and GUI tools is not as great as it used to be because the technology of interpreters and run time dynamic linking and loading has improved by leaps and bounds.

Figure 12-6: *Alternative development environment levels and paths*

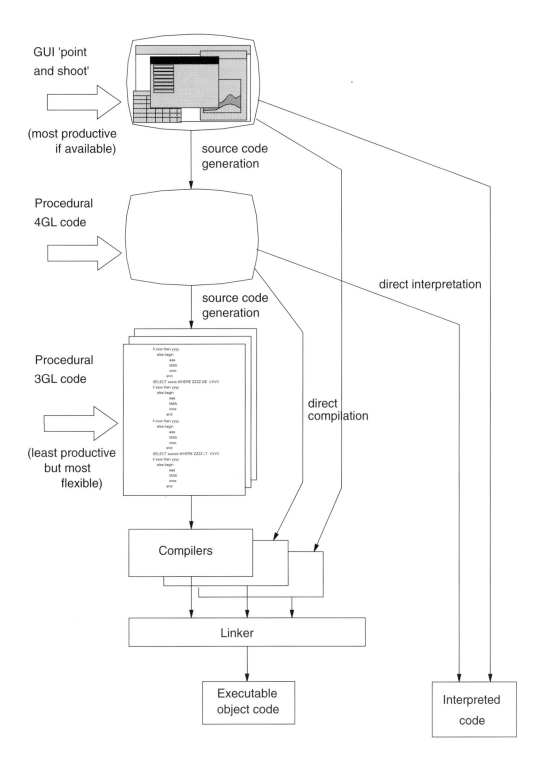

Traditional distinctions between application packages such as word processors and spreadsheets and custom development tools are becoming diluted by such developments as Microsoft's making a dialect of VisualBasic, one of the leading GUI custom development tools into the standard macro language for their package product range.

This rate of change means that it is neither necessary nor advisable to make long term binding strategic commitments in this area. We must also remember that the potential of these tools does not ease the problem of maintenance of very large legacy systems, built in 3GLs and running often on mainframes which are still expensive to operate and upgrade.

Data management

Distributed database management

Much of the potential of modern development methods and tools rests in the ability to place both applications and databases on the most suitable vehicles, even where these are neither the same architecture, nor co-located. The viability of this depends directly on the ability of database management to cope efficiently and with total reliability with high volume concurrent database access under these circumstances. Therefore 'bomb-proof' but efficient database management is the single most critical factor underpinning the technical strategy and the architecture which implement it. For this reason, we will undertake some brief revision of fundamental principles.

GOALS AND CONSTRAINTS

Benefits Sought

- Ability to optimize operational costs
- Improved physical control
- Responsiveness to local users
- Resilience: *partial network failure; ability to reassign work of a failed node*
- Ability to represent business responsibility structure

Design Goals and Constraints

- Easy and safe to re-locate data and processing
- User to be unaffected by physical location(s) of data or process
- Application code to be independent of physical location(s) of data or process
- All data and processing recovery and integrity to be 'bomb-proof' regardless of physical location(s) of data or process

Potential Benefits

- Improved control
- Able to match configuration to organization's responsibility structure
- Easier resilience
- More flexibility
- Full integrity of distributed data
- Economy of communications costs

PRINCIPLES OF DATABASE INTEGRITY

Maintenance of effective database integrity is based on a number of principles, which should be regarded as inviolate. Any system or DBMS, whether distributed or not, which fails to meet them is unacceptable. The principles are:

- No irretrievable data loss, ever.
- No release of invalid partial results to users or other processes, ever.
- High integrity transaction processing.
- No failure should ever lead to perception by a user or another uninvolved application of inconsistent data – the 'commitment unit' principle. This is addressed by the distributed two phase commit protocol, which is safe, but extremely bureaucratic and resource intensive, especially in communications overheads. The term ACID (atomicity, consistency, isolation and durability) has been coined as a mnemonic.
- The commitment unit concept should not be diluted, ever, even across a network with multiple database servers.
- Database safe update and integrity protection are so important that application designers and programmers should not be allowed to alter or improvise recovery mechanisms, or to override system features – although they may need to select from available options, or even press the vendor to improve them.
- No software which violates these principles is safe for on-line access to important data.

Other issues

- *Large reports.* Reports and analyses involving scans of large amounts of data are a especially demanding in terms of database integrity if they have to run concurrently with protected transaction processing problem, as their database views may need to be held consistent.
- *Granularity.* The finer the locking unit, the more concurrency can take place, and hence the better the potential transaction response in heavy traffic, but the harder the database integrity control mechanisms have to work. Conversely, if we lack large units, such as files or database tables, then the admin. is simpler, but processing is heavily constrained. A good

RDBMS will offer a range of such 'granularities'.

Derived requirements

- The following requirements can be derived directly from the above principles.

- Full support for commitment unit management – local and distributed, i.e. recognition of transactions and their integrity.

- Transaction back-out as well as full database restoration capabilities.

- Full recovery from all classes of contingency.

- Effective management of consistent database views for reporting and analysis.

- 'Transparency', i.e. an application should neither know or care about the location(s) of any of the databases which it is accessing, nor about its own location; it should be unaffected if any of the components are moved.

- Ability to support 24 hour availability, e.g.:

  - concurrent long and short commitment units

  - 'on the fly' backup and recovery

  - Remote logging – to protect against complete destruction of the location at which the database is held currently.

  - Realistic compromise options to help manage performance: *a range of granularities for locking and contention management; duplication and logging options; caching and replication options.*

Distribution of data – state of play

- The problem is on us already – the issue is how to control it.

- Where is the data now?

- Authenticity.

- Vendor credibility.

- Synchronization of data states.

- Access control.

- Heavy communications traffic for 'red tape'.

- Downloading and uploading.

- Theoretical solutions are increasingly being implemented respectably – generally based on distributed two phase commit.

- Vendors have in the past delivered slogans, not effective solutions:

  - *'interoperability'*   ▪ *LU 6.2*   ▪ *APPC*   ▪ *'co-operative processing'*

There are *real* benefits lurking out there once solutions are delivered.

Database integrity – options and compromises

Achieving the above can be cumbersome and costly. The impact on response times can be severe. Therefore, we do break the rules, but hopefully in a risk-controlled manner. Some of the most important and useful rule violations are:

- Database partitioning by table, row or column.
- Selective replication, with customizable 'lag' on synchronization. This is termed 'Replication server technology'.
- Ability to turn off 'belt and braces' options and continuous operation features if performance or integrity requirements do not demand them.
- Performance monitoring and tuning facilities.

Data distribution issues

- Location of: user, processor, data.
- Processing style: centralized, distributed, dispersed.
- Data bases: single master, partitioned and/or replicated.

Data distribution options

- Single image
- Replicated
- Partitioned
  - by table
  - vertical, i.e. by row key
  - horizontal, i.e. by column
- Cached, i.e. copies are held locally to points of heavy usage. This raises issues such as:
  - frequency of refresh
  - who is entitled to update which copy
  - synchronization of multiple copies

Standards efforts

One of the most significant efforts is been made by the Open Software Foundation (OSF), who, since the merger of the contending UNIX camps have re-focused on making their Distributed Computing Environment (DCE) open and general. This is now supported by all of the key vendors – IBM shipped a SDK for it in September 1993. Their commitment was reinforced by decisions made in March 1994. DCE release 1.1 shipped around the end of 1994.

However, this still lags the requirements badly – DCE remains file-oriented, and therefore unsuited to high volume transaction processing. It therefore needs to be supplemented by a transaction monitor such as Transarc, Tuxedo or CICS, which IBM are moving into the UNIX and OS/2 domains.

Distributed processing architecture

Figure 12-7 illustrates the major components which need to be considered. Later, under Client/Server, Table 12-2 illustrates the key options.

Other database issues

Increased variety in data types

- 'Structured' i.e. traditional record formats
- Document
- Picture
- Binary object
- Numerical model
- Voice
- Assertion/rule

DBMS and development vehicles – key distinctions

- 'Pure' DBMS – server functionality
    - orientation – transaction processing or high throughput, e.g. for scans
    - proprietary versus SQL versus object based
- Application development – often bundled with a DBMS, but logically distinct
    - orientation – transaction processing or MIS/EIS
    - best if separable: *client process remote from database; client process can access several DBMS types*
- Multipurpose tool – viable stand-alone, but also connectable to a variety of DBMS
    - e.g. Spreadsheet such as Excel, Quattro or Lotus for Windows, or front end DBMS such as MS Access or Paradox

MIS, EIS and information database issues

- Shared access to operational data, or rigorous separation

Figure 12-7: *Distributed data access architecture*

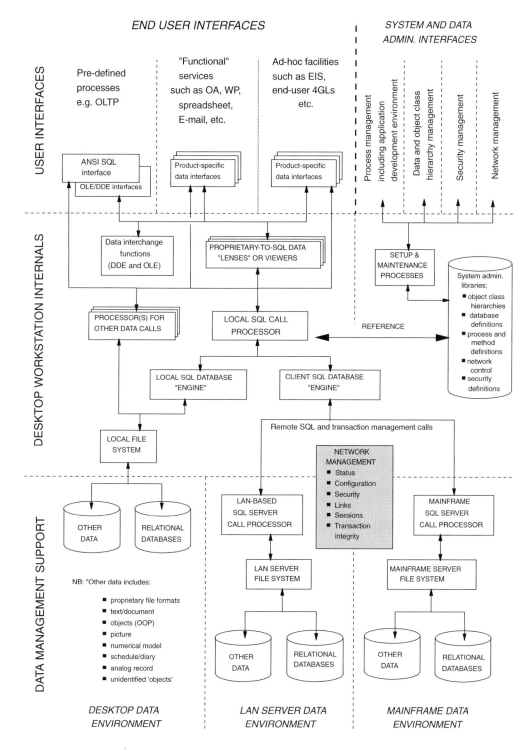

- Data refresh mode and lag if separate
- Delivery and presentation architecture and costs
- MIS/EIS user enquiry and reporting facilities:
  - fixed function or user customizable
  - integrity of reported data
- Status of user derived results
- Controls over user originated changes to operational data

Figure 12-8 Illustrates these issues

Figure 12-8:   *Information database architecture*

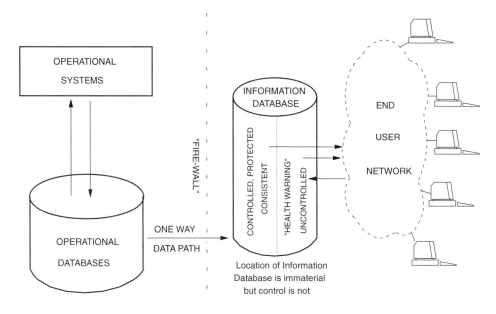

MIS/EIS technical environments

There is a very rapid rate of change in the technology for providing regular and ad hoc MIS and EIS type analysis. The days when expensive, specialized software required hours of mainframe time for these purpose are numbered. Nowadays, it is much more effective, and more flexible, to assemble a set of familiar components, such as spreadsheets, graphic presentation aids and SQL access drivers, and grant access from the interactive front end to the relevant databases through mapping its tabular interface onto view of the distributed databases.

Modern spreadsheet software has presentational and analytic capability far beyond that of traditional vehicles. Issues which now remain are more to do with:

- authentication of spreadsheet prints purporting to be official financial reports;
- security and control;
- effective management of multiple data dimensions;
- the performance implications of allowing casual users to browse operational databases.

But these are soluble without recourse to the EIS megaliths of a few years ago.

These considerations should not be allowed to impede effective, flexible business access. Figure 12-9 illustrates a typical MIS/EIS configuration.

Figure 12-9:   *MIS and decision support typical technical environment*

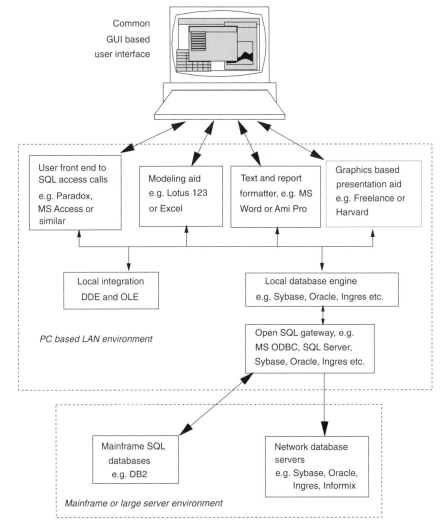

The 'father' of relational databases, Ted Codd, has apparently recently coined 'The 12 rules of OLAP' (on-line analytical processing systems), but on first reading they are repetitive and non-orthogonal, at least six of them concerning multi-dimensional access capability, and the remainder dwelling on user interface and concurrency issues.

Client/Server

I do not consider Client/Server to be a truly strategic issue. It offers certain benefits, but has a certain entry cost – and I am sure that it will prove to have exit costs too, we just haven't looked for them yet!

It is treated here as:

- a means for using a set of technical components, which will vary over time, to meet environmental needs in the most economical and effective way;

- an approach whereby applications can be developed and run on the most appropriate platform, which is often desktop based, without sacrificing either effective development controls or system integration;

- a migration aid, whereby existing databases especially, can be left on their existing platforms, but opened up to a wider range of types of access, subject to the capacity of the platforms to cope with the traffic. Market forces can be allowed to dictate when and to what platform the databases are eventually moved;

- a means for avoiding or deferring inappropriate strategic decisions, and substituting for them reversible tactical decisions instead.

Figure 12-10: *Client/Server – idealized view*

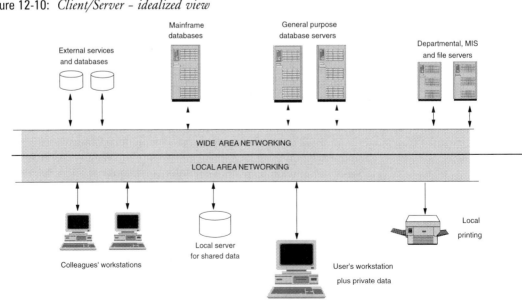

Using Client/Server in this way makes certain demands on the technology, the most important of which is that the database management software should be able to cope with concurrent access and update to distributed databases, possibly on heterogeneous platforms, with complete 'bomb-proof' data and transaction integrity. This is by no means a trivial proposition, and it places heavy demands on the communications infrastructure. We will come to this later. Figure 12-10 illustrates a typical present day scenario in which existing legacy systems are co-existing with an evolution towards a fuller implementation of Client/Server.

Client/Server – the vision

- Better, longer life, applications, built faster, cheaper to operate
- Cheap desktop mips
- More responsive user interface
- Effective rapid development tools
- Longer application code lifetime:
  - portability of application
  - tolerance of change to DBMS and server type

Client/Server – architecture

SERVER

- Manages database(s) shared across network(s)
- Responds to data access calls
- For integrity, needs to know about: *logical transactions*; *data copies*
- Controls database integrity, recoverability

CLIENT

- May request services from one or more database servers, regardless of their location
- Needs to register transaction start/end
- Controls progress of logical transaction

ACCESS PROTOCOLS

- There is need for a common set of extensions to SQL to enable fully controlled access to a heterogeneous population of shared database servers.
- The competitive nature of the RDBMS market is impeding this development.

ARCHITECTURE

Table 12-2 represents the original Gartner Group model for Client/Server (Gartner 1993). The original Gartner view fails to take account of the following considerations:

1. The amount of data-related processing which can be done on the database server may vary.

2. Recognition of the option to separate data and process physically (or not to do so – or to migrate between co-hosting and separate).

3. The critical effect of the distinction between dumb or smart terminals. Client/Server may be run with dumb terminals, full smart GUI terminals, or smart but non-GUI terminals. In the first and third cases, presentational processing may of necessity be separated from the terminal itself, but should still be done close by, so as not to involve excessive WAN traffic.

4. Some or all of: the database server, the application server and presentation processor may be physically separated; therefore there may be several network links, some of which run over WAN.

5. The required ability to have an arbitrary number of database servers, of the same or different platform type.

6. The frequent need for incorporation of legacy databases as database servers – and requirements for doing so, e.g. basis for non-dramatic migration.

Table 12-2:   *Gartner Client/Server model (Based on Gartner 1993)*

Traditional centralised	Remote presentation	Distributed logic	Remote data management	Distributed database
Data management	Data management	Data management	Data management	Data management
Application logic	Application logic	Application logic	Network	Network
Presentation	Network	Network	Network	Data management
Network	Network	Application logic	Application logic	Application logic
Presentation (limited)	Presentation	Presentation	Presentation	Presentation

Table 12-3 is an adaptation and extension of the Gartner work, in which Client/Server systems are classified according to the placement of the network link.

	Traditional centralised Dumb terminals	Traditional centralised GUI front ends 'Remote presentation'	Single database server Dumb terminals Separate application server(s) 'Distributed logic'	Multiple database servers Dumb terminals Separate application server(s) 'Distributed logic' and distributed database	Multiple database servers Smart terminals 'Distributed logic' and 'Distributed database'	Multiple database servers Full GUI front ends 'Distributed logic' and 'Distributed database'	Multiple separate DB and App servers Full GUI front ends 'Distributed logic' and 'Distributed database'
Database	Single, centralised	Single, centralised	Single server	Multiple	Multiple	Multiple	Multiple
Data related common procedurality	none	none	on server	on server(s)	on server(s)	on server(s)	on server(s)
network link			yes	yes	optional	yes	yes
Application - specific algorithms			application server(s)	application server(s)	optional application server(s)		application server(s)
network link		yes					yes
Presentational formatting							
network link					yes		
User interface driving logic							
network link	yes		yes	yes			
Physical screen/ keyboard							

Table 12-3: *An adaptation of the Gartner Client/Server model layers and extensions*

This extension takes account of the shortcomings listed above, and recognizes that:

1. Databases may be replicated wholly or in part.

2. Applications may run on client workstations or 'application servers' or both.

3. It may be required to incorporate legacy databases, at some or all of the following levels:

   ■ interactive access;
   ■ file extract/transfer;
   ■ via filter process.

4. Applications and databases may be co-hosted

Table 12-3 attempts, in perhaps an over-simplified way, to establish some rules for placement of components in a Client/Server system.

Table 12-3:   *Guidelines for placement of data and system features in a Client/Server environment*

Attributes of data and process	Recommended placement/treatment		
	Database server Developed once, maintained as a common resource. Enforced automatically at the Client.	**Optional application server** May be co-located with groups of users or centralized, according to performance needs.	**Client environment** Faster response. Cheap mips. Best place for features which may vary at the discretion of the user or the client application developer.
Screen, panels and controls			✓
Local processing algorithms			✓
Dialogue and sub-system structure			✓
Sub-system specific data manipulation		✓ if available 'thin client'	✓ 'thick client'
Common business rules and core functionality, not especially database-related, but meriting of centralized control		✓ if available 'thin client'	✓ 'thin client'
Common data access and manipulation processes: eg Create, Read, Modify, Delete, Browse, integrity control, RPCs etc.	✓		Selected processes may be 'shadowed' into the Client environment to improve response or useability, but even so should remain centrally controlled
Basic data-related processes, eg validation rules, common algorithms etc.	✓		
Data structure, type and properties.	✓		

Common protocols and standards for Client/Server

The goal

A common set of extensions to SQL to enable any client to pretend that it is accessing a single, integrated database, when in fact it is accessing a heterogeneous population of shared database servers.

Fully distributed on-line transaction processing is required, with real time update, across multiple heterogeneous servers, with complete integrity/recoverability regardless of the data server types.

Offerings

Mostly originating from proprietary developments, but now based on the SQL Access Group (SAG) protocols – also influenced by OSF DCE.

Mostly still incomplete, especially in distributed update and in heterogeneity.

- **DRDA** – IBM – still incomplete
- **ODBC** – Microsoft – narrow SQL product focus; supported in products, SDK available. Growing pragmatic acceptance from 1993 on.
- **IDAPI** (was ODAPI) – Borland, Novell, IBM
  - DOS, OS/2, Windows, Netware
  - WordPerfect, Ingres, Informix, Sybase, USL
  - Apple, UNIX 'expected soon'
  - No SDK yet; to be supported in 'next versions'
- **ODBC/IDAPI interoperability** – half-hearted promises only

Communications – special performance considerations

Even with modern high bandwidth communications, there remains a problem with high volumes of SQL calls taking place across WAN links. Not only does each such call involve several messages to be safe under distributed 2 phase commit, but each WAN transfer may involve half a second or more if using X.25 or similar. Transaction response times can thus involve several seconds solely due to comms delays.

Solutions to this involve:

1. Optimizing database server placement so as to minimize WAN traffic. This must be done, but may involve frequent re-tuning, and may still not be satisfactory – consider the distribution scenario represented by Figure 11-11 in chapter 11.

2.   Grouping SQL calls together into packages – termed stored procedures or remote procedure calls (RPCs). These are handled differently by different RDBMS at present, but standardization is tightening.

3.   Transferring larger, object-based data aggregates less frequently.

Options 2 and 3 place more core, data-related procedurality at the database server, where application programmers cannot code it wrongly.

Due to such performance considerations, capacity planning and modelling of distributed or Client/Server systems is a complex proposition. It is especially important that the whole integrated system be modelled 'end-to-end'.

Bob Jones, President of the Socrates Corporation, based in Redmond, WA, has produced a project profile worksheet, which is aimed at risk assessment of Client/Server projects – but it actually has far wider applicability. Following a dialogue with him, we jointly produced an extended form of this worksheet, which is produced, with his permission, at the end of this chapter. This thorough assessment approach is applicable to any development project which contains significant elements of:

- rapid development;
- Client/Server operation;
- distributed data and/or processing

and its use is highly recommended, both at project inception, and at regular checkpoints through development.

Risk assessment

Typical technical risks

- Business functions and needs may alter so radically as to invalidate the technical architecture
- Business volumes may be much higher or lower than foreseen
- The selected approach and its implementation may fail to deliver the cost/performance goals
- The viable life cycles of key technical components may prove too short to enable benefits to be realized
- Technical support and expertise may prove excessively costly
- Components may prove difficult to integrate effectively
- The vendor may fail:
  - to deliver commitments, e.g. function, performance, service levels, range continuity or reliability
  - to remain in business

- The strategy selected may be attacked or circumvented by powerful vendors
- Strategy may be superseded early by technology breakthrough
- The strategy may become invalidated early by an acceleration of evolutionary developments

Technical risk assessment process

- Identify full range of specific threats and risks to be considered
- Identify impact of each, and cost of failure to avoid/control
- Assess probability of each, and develop a score as a function of impact and probability
- Explore options to avoid or pre-empt
- Explore measures to control or mitigate their impact
- Undertake sensitivity analysis
- Integrate and review overall plan

Specific upgrade related risks

- Ease/cost of upgrade
- Lead times versus capacity forecast accuracy
- Cost of asset under-use, versus penalty of under-capacity
- Vendor range capacity limits
- Difficulty in matching capacity plan with:
  - application portfolio evolution
  - future business processes
  - future business volumes

These considerations are illustrated in Figure 12-11. As a simple example of good risk assessment practice, Table 12-5 sets out a sample contingency analysis in simplified form. For each mini-pie chart, there would be expected to be some form of quantified analysis to back it up. For each avoidance measure and recovery measure proposed, there should be a statement of options considered and reasons for the selection of the recommended approach.

Figure 12-11:   *Capacity estimation risks*

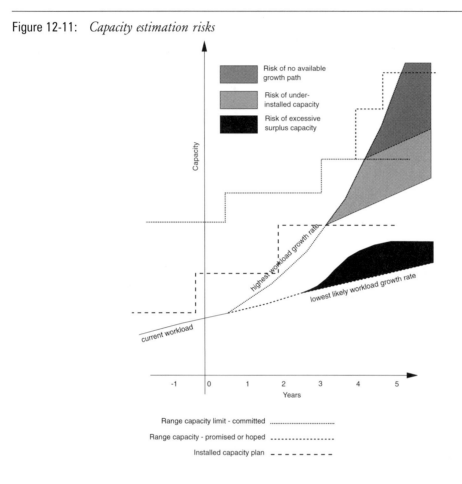

Capacity and costs assessment and planning

Making the strategy quantitative

- Map business activities to applications
- Aggregate by type
- Map application workloads to technical environments
- Develop broad capacity estimates and derive likely costings
- Repeat for relevant alternative business scenarios and technical solutions
- Repeat for alternative business and application scenarios
- Test for sensitivity
- Assess risks

Threat/contingency	Probability of occurrence	Potential impact	Avoidance measures	Recovery mechanisms
1. Application logic error, causing logical database corruption which is not detected immediately	(pie)	(pie)	Thorough testing	External mechanisms, involving users and/or customers – the worst case
2. Application program failure: a) abnormal termination b) deadlock/back-out	(pie) (pie)	(pie)	a) as above b) unavoidable – see recovery mechanisms	Rapid recovery – requires full transaction isolation and back-out
3. Physical disk failure	(pie)	(pie)	Reputable supplier, effective SLA For continuous operation – replicated physical storage – mirroring or RAID	Database re-build from backups plus update logs – serious impact on service. Mirroring/RAID may be accompanied by background re-build of copy.
4. Logical database corruption	(pie)	(pie)	Thorough testing; good operating procedures. Detection may be problematic.	Database re-build as above. NB mirroring/RAID are no help whatsoever.
5. CPU/memory failure	(pie)	(pie)	Reputable supplier, effective SLA. Duplication of components or hot standby.	If this causes complete system failure, treat as appropriate combination of contingencies 2, 3 and 4.
6. Complete destruction of computer site	(pie)	(pie)	Good physical security. Remote standby site, eg hot mirroring or logging. Network switch-over may be most difficult.	Dependent on mechanisms in place. Recovery can never be faster than that provided for by mechanisms, though it may be slower if mechanisms or procedures are faulty.
7. Network failure a) partial b) complete	(pie) (pie)	(pie) (pie)	a) unavoidable – duplication of links, effective protocols. b) good supplier; effective SLA. For LANs, good diagnostics and training.	Good supplier; good diagnostics, good SLA.
8. Demise of supplier	(pie)	(pie)	Open systems – no dependence on single-sourced component.	Hire the staff; buy up spares; third party maintenance.
9. Serious software faults	(pie)	(pie)	Exhaustive testing whenever software configuration is altered. Provide fall-back plan.	Revert to stable software base. Recovery from system and database damage may be major.
10. Deliberate sabotage	(pie)	(pie)	Good physical and network security. Keep staff happy.	Damage may be any of the above contingencies; recovery is dependent on the nature of the damage.
11. Fraud	(pie)	(pie)	As 10, plus appropriate controls.	Damage may be more to financial position and to service/image rather than to systems or data. Recovery is a business issue.

Table 12-5: *A typical contingency analysis (threats and assessments are indicative only)*

Stages at which sizing and costing are relevant

BROAD ESTIMATES, RELATIVE COSTS

- Costing business strategy, product and process options and scenarios
- Establishing IS strategic options
- Evaluation of viability of technical solutions under different business/application scenarios

SPECIFIC, BUT STILL RELATIVE COSTS

- Quantifying requirements
- Assessing vendor claims
- Assessing alternative implementation options

Assessing the impact of alternative different business/product scenarios

SPECIFIC, AND ABSOLUTE COSTS

- Assessing vendor tenders
- Capacity/cost risk assessment
- Committing to a specific business case
- Setting specific performance budgets or committing to service levels
- Specific configuration for major application projects
- Preparing costs and capacity plans

IT cost drivers

Identifying, predicting and managing the key components if IS/IT costs. See Figures 12-12 and 12-13.

- Hardware
  - cost per useable mip
  - cost per Gb of disk
- Networking costs: *basis – volume related or not; management/control costs*
- Systems software
- Application (variation by source type)
- Staff
- Premises

Figure 12-12: *Basic IS costs trends (cost per unit of capacity)*

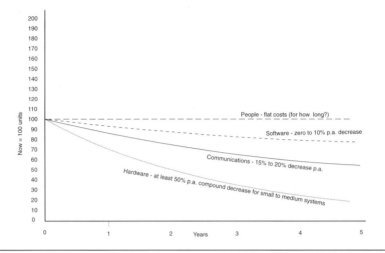

Figure 12-13: *The infrastructure iceberg*

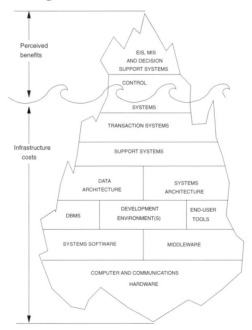

IT costs – useful composite measures

FIVE YEAR COST OF OWNERSHIP PER BUSINESS TRANSACTION PER SECOND – COVERS:

- Capital, development and ongoing costs
- Hardware, software, premises and people
- Engineering/maintenance/licence fees

- Vendors don't like it, so it must be valuable!

Transaction processing cost/performance – 'standard' benchmarks

TRANSACTION-BASED

- DEBIT/CREDIT, TP-1
- RAMP/C
- ET/1 (no connection)
- Protected or unprotected – the con
- The 'Vendor-Neutral Council on the Debit/Credit Benchmark'
  - TPC-A, TPC-B, TPC-C

OTHER MEASURES

- Mips, RISC mips, VUPS etc.
- Specmark
- Neal Nelson

The Transaction Processing Council (TPC)

The TPC are a widely respected body, backed by a consortium of hardware manufacturers, who have produced a series of public domain benchmarks for on-line computer performance. The benchmarks are tightly specified, are run under controlled conditions, and are stringently audited. The TPC publish regular summaries of benchmark 'league table' results posted, and 'full disclosure' statements of detail backing up results are available.

All significant hardware vendors have become obliged to conduct and make public TPC benchmark tests for their current mid-range equipment, despite the considerable cost of doing so. I have even heard un-verified recent (late 1993) reports of IBM re-entering the fray with their mainframes, reporting over 3000 TPC-A transactions per second under TPF software, and over 1000 transactions per second with IMS Fastpath. These reports should be treated with caution, as the TPC specifications require SQL compliant processing, and the IBM claims may prove not to be fully compliant.

The TPC benchmarks have real teeth; it is a common requirement in public sector procurement that bidders are required to quote TPC results for the equipment and software range quoted. It is not uncommon for claimed TPC results to be withdrawn or revised by the vendors following audit. However, it is important to remember that, despite the TPC's efforts at creating a 'level playing field' and controlling the grosser circumventions such as turning off logging, all standardized public domain benchmarks only tell you about the performance of a particular configuration running a particular workload. However, they are good for:

- broad relative cost/performance comparisons;
- drawing up a short list of serious candidates;
- forcing vendors to provide directly comparable cost/performance data.

Any significant procurement should only proceed on the basis of verification of vendor and TPC claims by means of custom benchmarks or other quantitative evaluation based on your own data, applications and workload.

In brief, the TPC benchmarks are as follows:

TPC-A

Based on a distributed banking system, with fairly simple enquiry and update transactions, with a specified percentage of transactions hitting accounts held at remote sites. Covers all aspects of networking, as well as the core transaction processing aspects.

TPC-B

Focuses on the core database maintenance aspects of the TPC-A application only.

TPC-C

The most recent released benchmark, TPC-C, is of most relevance to mixed commercial workloads; as of late 1993, the first TPC-C results were beginning to be reported. It resembles an updated, vendor-neutral and more tightly specified version of the well known IBM Ramp-C benchmark. There is also a late draft under review of a TPC-D benchmark covering Decision Support/EIS type processing.

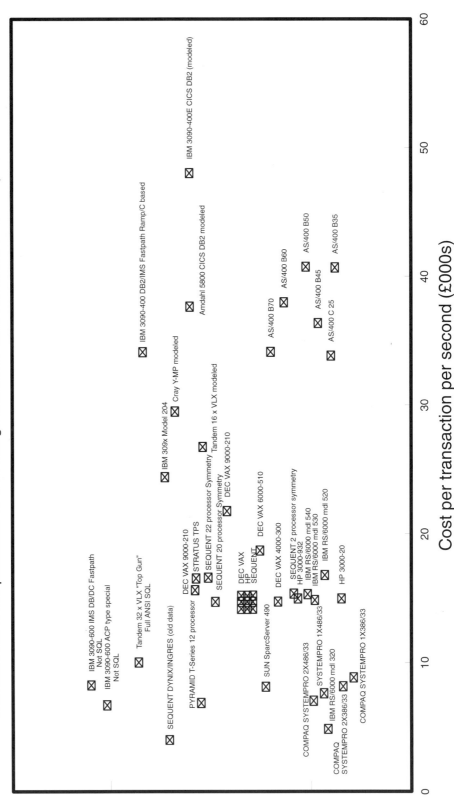

Figure 12-14: *Summary of OLTP results*

Figure 12-15: *Summary of OLTP results*

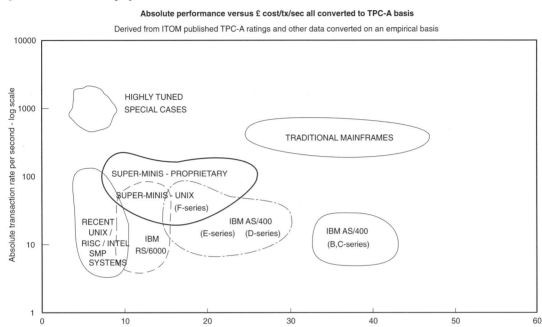

Absolute performance versus £ cost/tx/sec all converted to TPC-A basis

Derived from ITOM published TPC-A ratings and other data converted on an empirical basis

The analyses presented in Figures 12-14 and 12-15 of TPC and similar results are of necessity out of date. Anyone seeking to use TPC results as a basis for procurement is strongly advised to contact the TPC direct in order to obtain up-to-date information – which is available for a modest fee. They are at:

> The Transaction Processing Council
> c/o Jayne Russell Gilbert, Shanley PR
> 777 North Street, Suite 6000
> SAN JOSE, CA 95112-6311
> USA
>
> Tel: 1-408-295-8894   Fax: 1-408-295-9768

Inputs to the sizing process

- Requirements (see above)
- IT options and configurations
- Component capabilities
- Previous experience, external benchmarks
- Vendor's claims and sizing aids

Sizing metrics

- Processor power
- Disk capacity
- Disk throughput
- Communications throughput – and, increasingly, response
- End-to-end transaction response – importance of end-to-end modelling

Categories of workload

- User type
- Application class
- Priority or service level band
- Penalties for departure from service targets
- Location of origin and recipient
- Profile over time period – hour of day, month, year

Developing load profiles

- Pick major transactions
- Gross up for the rest
- Produce typical profiles
- Estimate resources:
  - CPU
  - Disk capacity
  - Disk traffic
  - Communications, especially the impact of remote SQL calls

Capacity modelling – levels of detail

- Pick level of detail to suit needs
- Coarse modelling to identify good options and highlight problem areas
- More detailed modelling of each key option/feature
  - capacity/cost
  - balance system
  - system sensitivity to load changes
  - look for bottle-necks
- Use appropriate modelling package for each level

Figure 12-16 illustrates the components of 'end-to-end' modelling. Figure 12-17 illustrates why it is dangerous to extrapolate from a few sample points on a modelled scale. Based on a real life example, at low transaction rates, configuration B offered a significant cost/performance edge over configuration A. However, once transaction rates became higher, configuration A was found to 'scale' in a more linear fashion than configuration B, due to a different design of inter-system bus. The message in this case was – if you're sure the transaction rates will stay down, buy B and bank the savings; if transaction rates may shoot up, bite the bullet and buy A.

Figure 12-16: *Approach to modelling IT costs and capacity*

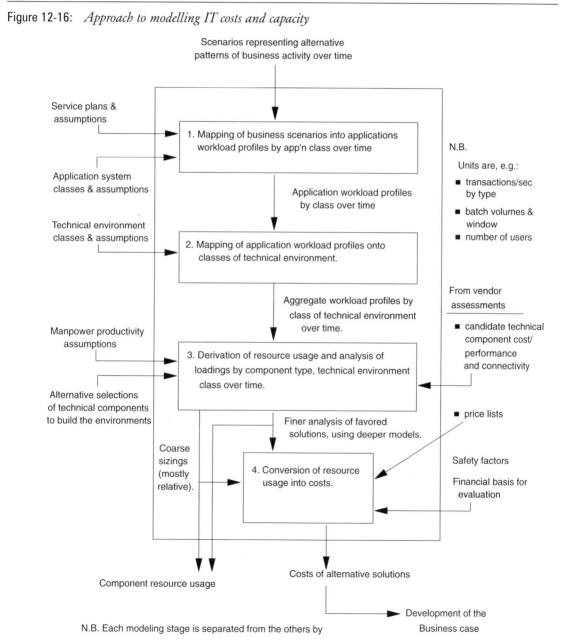

N.B. Each modeling stage is separated from the others by manual assessment. Each also has coarse and fine variants.

Figure 12-17: *Volume/cost sensitivity*

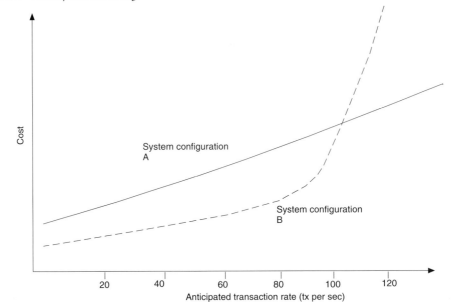

Products from the stage

1. Statement of IT vision and supporting technical strategy, which embodies:

    ■ Good support for and enabling of the business and IS visions

    ■ Stability: *application code; user interfaces*

    ■ Cost control: *max. value for money; predictable*

    ■ Flexibility to meet changing business needs/volumes

    ■ Flexibility to exploit technology advances: *better cost/performance; business/product opportunities*

    ■ Minimized diversity

    ■ Identified opportunities for IT to make a proactive contribution to the business

2. Specification of technical environments to support applications

3. Practical implementation guide lines

    ■ For technical components, options, preferences and basis for selecting solutions, short and longer term, to build the environments

4. *Basis for the recommended strategy, and for its maintenance and evolution*

    ■ Realistic assessment of current IT assets and status

    ■ Analysis of dependencies and constraints

- Position statements on key issues, uncertainties and risks – any further work required

5. A firm basis for planning, sizing and costing

- Quantified workload patterns for business and application scenarios
- Performance characteristics of candidate components

6. Technical options statements for each key requirement area

- Definitive where possible, else a few clear alternatives
- Clear criteria for selecting between options – including contingencies and assumptions
- Supported by rationale and risk assessment
- Scope and terms of reference for in-depth work needed.

Project profile

Worksheet

This worksheet is designed to help you evaluate any proposed Client/Server project to assess its overall risk and complexity. The worksheet will expose two important characteristics of the project: (1) any specific items that need attention, and (2) the overall risk level of the project.

To use this worksheet, answer each relevant question by circling the appropriate number on the 1–5 scale, where 1 indicates low risk, 5 indicates high risk, and 2–4 indicate increasing degrees of risk.

If you don't know the answer, or if you don't understand the question, circle 5.

Project Identification

Client:_____

Project name:_____

Project manager:_____

Assessment performed by:_____ Date:_____

Infrastructure Characteristics

Vision and Architecture	Low				High
Business technology vision defined	1	2	3	4	5

Have the business principles which define how information technology will be applied to business opportunities been decided and written down?

Business technology vision communicated to all developers   1   2   3   4   5

Has the business technology vision been communicated to all people affected by that vision, including, (but not limited to) all information technology developers?

Architecture project team in place   1   2   3   4   5

Has your environment identified and chartered a team of people to establish your application (logical) and technical (physical) architectures?

Application architecture defined   1   2   3   4   5

Has your architecture team defined the application architectures that will be used to develop client/server applications in your environment?

Data architecture issues defined   1   2   3   4   5

Is there an up to date Corporate data model which covers the project area? Has the architecture team identified the key issues relating to whether and how you will distribute data?

Distributed data access strategy defined   1   2   3   4   5

If you have decided to distribute data, have you determined the partitioning and/or replication criteria, and is it clear how replicated data will be kept synchronized?

Technology architecture process defined   1   2   3   4   5

Has the process by which technology choices are made been defined in a manner which will assure that the process is applied effectively for the selection of all distributed computing technology throughout the organization?

Technology architecture process in use   1   2   3   4   5

Has the technology architecture process been applied successfully to the choice of distributing computing?

Architecture total score:___divided by number of questions answered:___equals risk factor:___

Staff	Low				High

Experienced client/server developers   1   2   3   4   5

Does your development team include a reasonable proportion of people who have developed successful client/server applications in the past using similar environments?

Training planned and budgeted   1   2   3   4   5

Do you have an adequate training budget established and have you included 'just-in-time' training for every member of the team?

Help desk budgeted and staffed   1   2   3   4   5

Does your organization have a trained help desk that will provide support for this application when it is deployed?

Experienced consultants identified   1   2   3   4   5

Have you identified, qualified and retained experienced consultants to help with both planning and development throughout the entire project?

Staff total score:___divided by number of questions answered:___equals risk factor:___

Technology – networks and servers	Low				High
LAN in place	1	2	3	4	5
Is a LAN in place at all sites where this application will be deployed?					
LAN compatible between all locations	1	2	3	4	5
Are all locations using the same LAN protocols and network operating systems?					
LAN has adequate bandwidth	1	2	3	4	5
Does the LAN support adequate bandwidth to support the anticipated load of this application?					
WAN in place	1	2	3	4	5
Are the wide area networking links which will be required in place?					
WAN has adequate bandwidth	1	2	3	4	5
Has the WAN been configured based on a capacity plan which takes account of the characteristics of the proposed application?					
WAN capacity overload contingency plan established	1	2	3	4	5
Are there contingency plans to cope with bottlenecks and/or unexpected changes in business location or activity volumes?					
Wide area network systems management	1	2	3	4	5
Is there an effective wide area network management process in place?					
Centralised network management	1	2	3	4	5
Is there centralised administration of the wide area network?					
Automated WAN support tools	1	2	3	4	5
Are WAN support procedures supported by up-to-date automation?					
Wide area network support team on board and trained	1	2	3	4	5
Does your organization have a team of people who are trained and dedicated to supporting the enterprise network?					
WAN support team accessible to developers	1	2	3	4	5
Are these people accessible to your development team to help with any problems that may arise?					

Network technology:
total score:____divided by number of questions answered:____equals risk factor:____

Technology – servers	Low				High
Server platform(s)	1	2	3	4	5
Have you selected the hardware and operating combination for all servers?					
standardized server environments	1	2	3	4	5

Are all servers that will participate in this application running on the same hardware, under the same operating system, i.e. you don't have multiple operating systems to support and program? Is this covered by your configuration management procedures?

Provenness of components	1 2 3 4 5

Are all of the hardware and software components of your networks and servers current shipping versions, i.e. you are not dependent on beta products or promises of future functionality?

Server database engines selected	1 2 3 4 5

Have you selected a server database engine for use by this application?

Single database technology selected	1 2 3 4 5

Have you selected a single database technology vendor or are you integrating multiple different database technologies?

Server database engines experience	1 2 3 4 5

Does your team already have experience using the selected database engine(s) together with the server operating systems?

Servers in place	1 2 3 4 5

Are all servers that will be used by this application already in place, configured, programmed, and tested?

Network and server platform sharing	1 2 3 4 5

Will the networks and servers be dedicated to the application under assessment?

Server technology:
total score:____divided by number of questions answered:____equals risk factor:____

Technology – desktop environments	Low	High
Desktop platform(s)		1 2 3 4 5

Have you already selected the hardware, operating systems and other software which will run on all desktops?

standardized desktop environments	1 2 3 4 5

Are all desktops that will participate in this application using the same hardware configuration, operating system/graphical environment?

Configuration management procedures	1 2 3 4 5

Are all participating desktops managed by your configuration management procedures?

Proven components	1 2 3 4 5

Are all of the hardware and software components of your networks and servers current shipping versions, i.e. you are not dependent on beta products or promises of future functionality?

Desktops in place	1 2 3 4 5

Does each end user of the system already have a desktop in place that can support the proposed system?

Trained end users	1 2 3 4 5

Are users trained in the use of the desktop environment?

Trained support staff	1 2 3 4 5

Is your internal support staff in place and trained to support these desktops?

Compatible desktops & servers	1 2 3 4 5

Are the desktops and servers that will participate in this application proven to be compatible with each other?

Desktop to server connectivity experience	1 2 3 4 5

Do you have people on staff who have experience in connecting the desktop and server environments?

Desktop data access interface(s) selected	1 2 3 4 5

Have you selected a desktop database interfaces for use by this application?

Single or multiple data access interface(s) selected	1 2 3 4 5

Have you selected a single database API (LOW risk) or will you be using multiple database access interfaces?

Data access interface provided by DBMS vendor	1 2 3 4 5

Is the data access interface provided by the same vendor as the server database engine?

Database engines experience	1 2 3 4 5

Does your team already have experience using the selected database engine(s) together with the desktop and server operating systems?

Desktop workstation sharing	1 2 3 4 5

Will the desktop workstations be dedicated to the application under assessment? LOW score 1; if this is dominant score 3; else score 5.

Desktop environment:
total score:____ divided by number of questions answered:____ equals risk factor:____

Development tools and environment	Low	High
	1 2 3	4 5

Development methods selection	1 2 3 4 5

Have you selected a development method for the proposed application (LOW) or will you use an ad-hoc approach (HIGH)?

Rapid application development method	1 2 3 4 5

Does the selected development method support iterative requirements definition, design and development and user interface prototyping?

Maturity of development method	1 2 3 4 5

Is your selected development mature, with a proven track record for developing distributed client/server GUI applications?

Development methods – experience	1 2 3 4 5

Does your team already have experience using the selected development method?

User involvement with development	1 2 3 4 5

Does your development method provide for full time end-user involvement at all stages of the development process?

Development tools selected   1 2 3 4 5

Have you selected the desktop GUI development tool(s) to be used for this project?

Development tools support for database engine   1 2 3 4 5

Does the development tool you selected have close integration with the database engine(s)
you have selected?

Development tools – experience   1 2 3 4 5

Does your team already have experience using the selected development tools, together with
the selected RDBMS and the development method?

Number of different development environments proposed   1 2 3 4 5

How many different development environments is it proposed to use? For one score 1; for 2
score 3; for over 2 score 5.

Business rules development tools   1 2 3 4 5

For any high level largely non-procedural environment – score 1; for C or C++ – score 5. For
any other procedural environment score 3.

Business rules tools experience   1 2 3 4 5

Does your team already have experience using the selected business rules tools together with
the selected database engines, desktop and server operating systems?

User interface tools selection   1 2 3 4 5

Have you already selected the tools that will be used to implement the desktop elements of the
applications?

User interface development tools style   1 2 3 4 5

Will the end-user interface run under a mainstream GUI?

Desktop tools support GUI   1 2 3 4 5

Does the selected development tool-set support the desktop GUI effectively? For a mature version of any market leader GUI based tool-set score 1; for C or C++ – score 5; for anything
else score 3.

User interface development tools experience   1 2 3 4 5

Does your team already have experience using the selected user interface development tools
together with the selected business rules tools, database engines and desktop and server
operating systems?

Application development support tool-set selected   1 2 3 4 5

Have you already selected the supporting tool-set(s), including test harness, version control
and configuration management that will be used to build, test and control the applications?

Support tool-set is compatible with configuration management tools   1 2 3 4 5

Are all of the supporting tools compatible with your configuration management and system
management regimes?

Application development support tool-set experience   1 2 3 4 5

Does your team already have experience of using the selected support tool-sets in conjunction
with the other selected software?

Approach to performance engineering   1 2 3 4 5

Is there a mature process in place for capacity planning and performance engineering that
addresses all stages of the design and construction cycle?

Performance engineering process supports LAN/WAN	1	2	3	4	5

Does it cover LAN, WAN and server environments?

Performance engineering process uses automated tools	1	2	3	4	5

Is your capacity planning and performance engineering process supported by automated tools? Are the results of operational performance monitoring fed back into the models?

Performance engineering process covers aggregate work load	1	2	3	4	5

Does your capacity planning and performance engineering approach take account of the aggregate workload arising from other applications sharing the platforms?

Performance engineering process measures end-to-end response	1	2	3	4	5

Does your capacity planning and performance engineering process take account of end-to-end response time requirements?

Development methods, tools and environment:
total score:____divided by number of questions answered:____equals risk factor:____

Application Characteristics

Application	Low				High
Availability requirement	1	2	3	4	5

Is this application critical to your ability to do business? If the application fails totally, will your business still be able to operate successfully? For normal working day availability, with reasonable tolerance for limited down-time, score 1. For 24 hour cover, 365 days/year, score 5.

Delivery time-scale	1	2	3	4	5

Must this application be completed and operational by a specific date? If the date is not met, will your business be materially affected? Score 5 if a specific date must be met.

Analytical vs OLTP	1	2	3	4	5

Is this application strictly analytical (read-only) or both analytical and operational (OLTP)? Score 1-2 for analytical, or 3-5 for OLTP.

Analytical components can be separated	1	2	3	4	5

If the application contains both analytical and OLTP components, can the analytical components be fully implemented as a separate project that will complete before the OLTP project begins? Score 1-2 if analytical application can be implemented and deployed before more complex OLTP components, or 3-5 if all components must be implemented in the same time frame.

Application and business scope	1	2	3	4	5

Is this application limited in its scope or does it touch many areas of the business and many other systems? If it is large and/or complex, can it readily be broken down into a series of delivery phases, each with clear business scope? (A system with very limited scope could be implemented on entirely separate hardware without any need to access other systems.)

Business process definition and understanding	1	2	3	4	5

Are the business processes that are being implemented in this system well understood, well defined and formally documented?

	Low				High
Users agree with process definition	1	2	3	4	5

Are the users of the system in agreement that these processes are well understood?

Perceived value added	1	2	3	4	5

Does implementation of this system provide substantial value to the ongoing operation of the organization? If the system succeeds, will it have a significant positive impact on the organization?

Transaction volumes	1	2	3	4	5

A transaction is a set of changes to the database that must occur as a single entity. For example, a customer order with 10 line items would be a single transaction. This metric should measure the total number of transactions of all types that the system must support. A transaction volume of 1 per second is very low. Any volume over 20 TPS would be considered high.

Average transaction complexity	1	2	3	4	5

Is the average complexity of the transactions low? A transaction that makes only a single change to a single table is very simple; however, a sales order entry transaction is very complex. This measure should reflect the 'average' transaction complexity.

Application total score:___divided by number of questions answered:___equals risk factor:___

Data characteristics	**Low**				**High**
Data models – definition	1	2	3	4	5

Is the data being used by this application well documented and understood? Are the rules for default values, mandatory vs. optional, valid values and ranges defined for each data element? Are the relationships between data entities and elements well understood and documented?

Data models – complexity	1	2	3	4	5

Is the data model on which the databases are based of low complexity. For 10 or less entity types, score 1; for 100 or more entity types or subtypes score 5.

Data access volumes	1	2	3	4	5

Does this application require access to less than 1Gb of data? For over 10Gb score 5.

Data volatility	1	2	3	4	5

Does the data change slowly, i.e. less than 5% per day? (50% per day = very fast)

Database sharing	1	2	3	4	5

Are databases dedicated to this application – i.e. not shared with other applications?

Data timeliness requirement	1	2	3	4	5

Does the application require access to extremely timely data, i.e. must the data be up to the minute (score 5) or can the data be current as of a period end such as last night, last week or last month (score 1–2)?

Data total score:___divided by number of questions answered:___equals risk factor:___

Distribution	Low				High
Users at single site	1	2	3	4	5

Will this application serve users at only a single geographic site, i.e. not involve users at multiple distributed sites? If all users are at a single site, score 1. If users are at multiple sites, but all sites are physically nearby, score 3. If users are distributed at multiple distant sites, score 5.

Number of users	1	2	3	4	5

For under 10 users, score 1; for over 200 users score 5.

Level of remote database access	1	2	3	4	5

Will all high volume database access involve only high bandwidth LAN links? If not, is provision made for sufficient WAN bandwidth to cope with access peaks? Does this picture change if the system needs to be re-configured, e.g. after server failure? Does the capacity plan take account of this?

Data at single site	1	2	3	4	5

Will all data accessed by this application be kept at a single site on a single database server? If single site, score 1; for multiple servers at a single site, score 3–4; for multiple sites, score 5. If you scored a 1 on this question (i.e. all data will be kept in a single database on a single server), then skip the remaining questions in this section.

Physical partitioning of data	1	2	3	4	5

Is the data involved readily 'partitionable'? Can it be sliced like a pie with each piece stored in separate databases, possibly on separate servers? If it can be partitioned, then only a single copy of the data will exist, but the overall collection of data may be distributed to many servers. If data is easily partitionable, score 1; otherwise score 5.

Number of servers	1	2	3	4	5

How many database servers are envisaged? For a single server, score 1; for a small number of servers co-located on a single LAN score 3, for over 10 physically dispersed servers score 5.

Data update sources	1	2	3	4	5

Will all updates to each database table occur from a single location (score 1) or can a table be updated by users at multiple locations (score 5)?

Data replication	1	2	3	4	5

Will there be a single copy (score 1) or multiple copies (score 5) of each database table? If you score a 1 on this question (i.e. data is NOT replicated) then skip the remaining questions in this section.

Single or multiple database vendors	1	2	3	4	5

Does replicated data exist in database engines provided by a single vendor (score 1–3) or are multiple database vendors involved (score 5)?

Data synchronization	1	2	3	4	5

Must updates of replicated data be synchronized in real time (i.e. all databases must be updated simultaneously (score 5) or can updated be made as soon as possible (score 3).

Experience with replicated data	1	2	3	4	5

Does your development staff have experience developing with systems involving distributed replicated data?

Distribution total score:____divided by number of questions answered:____equals risk factor:____

Business Support	Low				High
Senior level sponsors	1	2	3	4	5
Does this application have the support of very senior level sponsors within the organization or is it a 'grass roots' application with little or no high level support?					
Support commitment	1	2	3	4	5
Does the support that exists translate to commitments to spend money and commit resources?					
End users want the application	1	2	3	4	5
Do the users of this application really want it (score 1) or is this application being forced on the user organization (score 5)?					
End users commitment to the application	1	2	3	4	5
Is the end user organization ready to commit people full time to the project to assure its success?					
End user commitment to the development process and their role in it	1	2	3	4	5
Do the users of this application appreciate their roles in the development process? Are they committed to meeting their obligations as to participation?					
Monitoring of end user involvement	1	2	3	4	5
Is end user involvement monitored as part of the project planning and control process?					

Support total score:____divided by number of questions answered:____equals risk factor:____

Project Planning and Control	Low				High
Project planning and estimating	1	2	3	4	5
Is there a complete and realistic project plan.					
Risk identification process	1	2	3	4	5
Does the project plan include a regular and repeating process to identify risks which should be managed and integrate risk containment strategies into the project plan?					
Proven estimation model	1	2	3	4	5
Are project estimates based on a proven estimating model which has been calibrated for this environment and tool-set? Is there sufficient contingency?					
Frequent deliverables	1	2	3	4	5
Does delivery of system components take place at frequent intervals of not more than three months?					
Funds included for tools, training, equipment and research	1	2	3	4	5
Are there funds included for tools, training, equipment and research?					

Project planning/control:
total score:____divided by number of questions answered:____equals risk factor:____

Financial	Low				High
Project business case	1	2	3	4	5
Does the project have a clearly identified cost justification with a measurable return on investment that will be realised quickly?					
Validated ROI	1	2	3	4	5
Has the ROI analysis been signed off by appropriate financial analyst or management?					
Benefits delivery	1	2	3	4	5
Are clear responsibilities agreed for delivery of business benefits? Is there commitment to tracking this delivery post implementation?					
Project approval status	1	2	3	4	5
Is the budget for project capital, labour and expenses approved?					

Financial total score:____divided by number of questions answered:____equals risk factor:____

Overall Project Risk

Sum of risk factors from all ten sections: divided by 11 equals project risk factor:

A factor of 2 or below indicates a relatively low risk project. High potential business returns may justify higher risk levels, but only if there are no lower risk alternatives, and if the risks are well managed. You should not attempt a high-risk project without substantial prior experience and strong support. Architecture, staff, support, project planning and control and financial sections must have low risk factors for a project to succeed.

Exercises for the reader

For your preferred IS solutions for Trendy Products Plc, consider and report on alternative technical and implementation approaches to support:

1.   Integrated support for the retail outlets, covering:

   - data collection;
   - communications;
   - local computing power;
   - local functionality;
   - performance monitoring and reporting.

Issues include:

   - 'quick and dirty' solutions for the bulk of the stores, versus longer term solutions, and migration from one to the other;
   - the data collection approach to be used;
   - the right level of computing power in stores, and whether it should be integrated with other functions;
   - communications facilities.

2.   Consolidated Group level profitability reporting and associated MIS.

Issues include:

   - means for data collection and assembly
   - choice of technical environment for routine and ad-hoc reporting and analysis
   - security and integrity controls.

3.   Wholesale level sales order processing and finished goods inventory control.

Issues include:

   - what stays on the mainframe, versus what moves out
   - co-ordination of shared databases, e.g. product and customer
   - provision for on-line transaction processing and database integrity
   - integration of packages if used.

4.   Warehouse and distribution depot automation and networking.

Issues include:

   - placement of computing and database power
   - LANs and WANs
   - selection of suitable mid-range platform(s)

- 'roll-out' program and change control in a multi-site environment.

Describe at least two distinct alternatives for each, and compare their strengths, weaknesses and risks.

CHAPTER 13

Migration planning

Stage objectives

A strategic vision is useless if it is unattainable. The steps towards it must not only be feasible; they must individually be low in risk and attractive in business terms, i.e. there must be an effective and robust migration plan. Producing the migration plan is one of the most important stages in the entire IS/IT planning process; in it we must:

1. Validate the strategic targets by establishing viable evolutionary routes to them.

2. Establish an effective basis for implementation by ensuring that the IS/IT plans are integrated with relevant organizational and process changes. Figures 13-1 places this work in context.

Figure 13-1: *Migration planning*

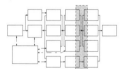
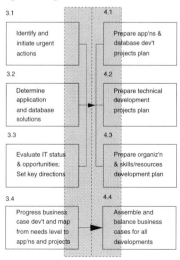

Key considerations

- The recommended target has to be a good place to be, and to move on from
- It has to be possible to get there from here
- There have to be sound and compelling business reasons for heading there, and for taking each step en route

Are you ready to start migration planning?

- In order to plan a migration, we must know accurately:
  - where we are coming from;
  - where we plan to end up.
- Targets defined
- Constraints and dependencies are clear
- Other 'givens' are identified, and whether each is mandatory or optional
- Ground rules for evaluating interim steps are defined

Products from migration planning

1. The preferred migration targets, being as close as possible to the ideal business delivery rate and sequence

2. Viable migration routes to each, supported by:
   - impact analysis
   - risk assessment
   - business cases for the interim steps

3. A proposed set of development projects to deliver the above

4. Workload profiles for development and operation, by:
   - application and activity type
   - time phase
   - business location of origin

5. Technology requirements to support the above.

Inputs to migration planning

1. Reminder – the ideal business delivery sequence and rate.

2. A translation into a real set of applications and databases which comes as close as possible to meeting the ideal, taking account of realities.

3. First cut set of development projects to deliver the above

4.   Urgent action projects already initiated

5.   Allocation of business systems into application type categories

6.   Aggregated workloads by: *type*; *time phase*; *business location of origin*

7.   Technology requirements and constraints to support the above.

Migration considerations

- Need for frequent, phased deliverables to the business
- Seek and exploit opportunities for early delivery of benefits
- Do not discount 'throwaway' solutions, e.g. to provide interim support an interface, or to deliver business benefit early
- Need to 'balance' the business case
- It should be clear that you have evaluated alternative routes/options, assessing cost/benefits of each
- The business sponsors are the ultimate arbiters

The search for a migration route which is low risk, attractive in business terms and feasible technically may require extensive iteration. Figures 13-2 and 13-3 illustrate different ways of looking at this. Our project based implementation bar chart (Figure 13-4) will now be becoming both quite complex and, hopefully, stable. It continues to form a centre-piece in all negotiations with sponsors.

Figure 13-2:   *Evaluation migration options*

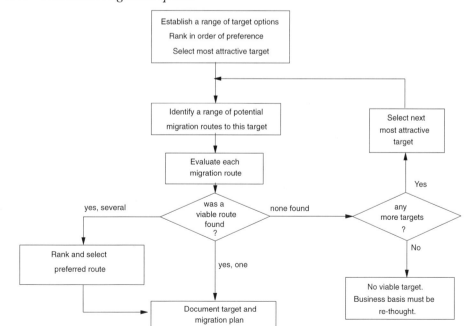

Figure 13-3:   *Process for migration options assessment*

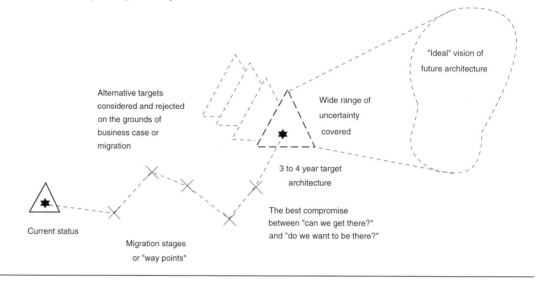

Figure 13-4:   *Practical sequences for application delivery (neglecting site phasing and migration constraints)*

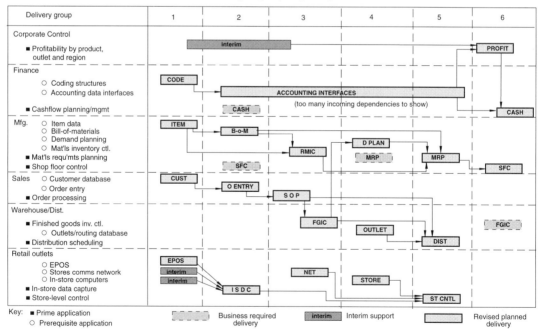

Migration decision drivers

There are many factors which influence migration decisions. These include:

■   Business priorities

- The desire for early, incremental delivery
- Risk management
- The need to maintain existing service levels
- Business dependencies
- Business case structure
- Information dependencies
- Application sequencing/interfaces
- Development options, routes and rates
- Organization culture shock
- Staff skills/resources
- IT technical constraints

Mapping charts for complex environments

Migration can often be a complex process, with many options for how best to address it. The multi-dimensional analysis approach introduced in Chapters 10, and developed in several others can easily be adapted to help analyze the options here; this exercise is left to the reader. Note that, even where the application migration sequence may be relatively straightforward, there may be a maze of technical options to be considered.

In addition, there is a particularly useful technique which I have found to be of real value – 'T' diagrams. In a complex environment, e.g. where a set of ageing vertically oriented product support systems are being replaced by a new unified 'horizontal' system, migration planning can become especially complicated. Figures 13-5 and 13-6 below illustrate how 'T' diagrams may be used to help manage this complexity.

Figure 13-5:   *Migration mapping – data*

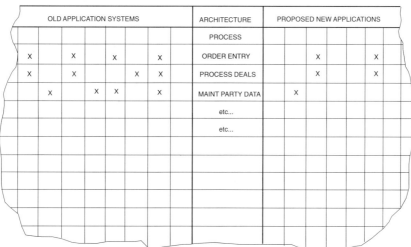

In each case, the components of the old systems are on the left, and the new on the right. The architecture components are used as the 'pivot' in the mapping. The aim should be to implement a subset of the element of the data or process architecture cleanly in the new systems or databases. By looking along the relevant rows, you can check – or decide – which components of the old systems or databases are to be included in a particular phase. This way of looking at the problem also helps consideration of precedence.

Figure 13-6:   *Migration mapping – application*

OLD FILES/DATABASES								ARCHITECTURE	NEW DATABASES					
								DATA ENTITIES						
	X		X			X		PRODUCT	X					
								LOCATION						
X			X		X			TRANSACTION					X	
X			X					LEGAL ENTITY		X		X		
	X		X					Customer		X				
				X				Agent		X				
	X							Counterparty		X				
					X			Competitor				X		
	X							Advisor		X				

Supporting business process and organizational change

IS/IT strategy implementation is inseparable from business evolution. Business process, IS/IT and organizational developments must be treated as mutually interdependent. This requires:

■   a clear view of dependencies – IT developments will often be a key enabler for the proposed business change;

■   effective overall coordination.

There may be potential uncertainty or over:

■   the rate of change achievable;

■   the best responsibility groupings for the new Organization;

■   physical location of functions;

■   relative priority of needs in future.

Organizational change is also amenable to analysis by means of T diagrams. The example in Table 13-1 represents a transition from a rather muddled old Organization – perhaps due to a series of mergers, to a streamlined new Organization. As always, the architecture is key – the central column of logical business processes. In a similar vein, I have found it useful to construct columns representing product support for particular lines, with the idealized support functions comprising the vertical axis. With this technique, organizational anomalies just 'jump out and grab you'.

Table 13-1:

Old organization units								Business process	Proposed new organization					
u1	u2	u3	u4	u5	u6	u7	...		U1	U2	U3	U4	U5	etc
	X			X	X			p1	X					
		X	X			X		p2		X				
X			X	X				p3			X			
	X			X			X	p4				X		
		X		X				p5					X	
X			X			X		p6						X
	X			X				p7			X			
								p8						
								p9						
								p10						
								etc						

CHAPTER 14

Plan assembly and integration

We have now done most of the work. The results and key recommendations are clear, at least to the project team. It now remains to ensure that what we deliver is a viable plan, to which management can commit, with clear costs and deliverables, and which can be followed in a controllable manner.

Figure 14-1: *Plan assembly and integration*

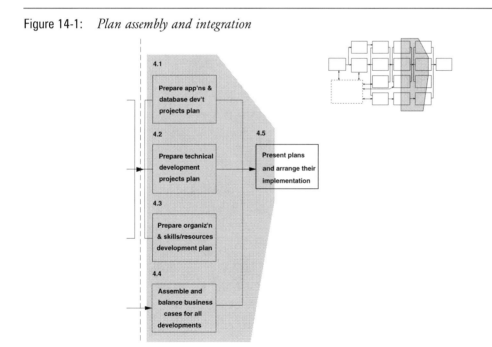

Chapter scope

The plan must now be assembled and integrated fully with existing work programs and tactical plans. This is addressed under the following headings:

1.   Applications and databases development.

2.   Technology development.

3.   IT Organization, human resources and skills.

4.   Balanced business case.

5.   Means for continuing review and maintenance.

Phase 4 – prepare and deliver the implementation plan

Finalize and deliver all elements of the strategic IS and IT plans

The elements if the IS and IT plans which we will deliver comprise:

- The overall IS/IT vision.
- Applications development plan.
- Information architectures development plan.
- Provision to establish and maintain technology environments.
- Organization, skills and resources.
- Financial and business cases.
- The process and management control structure for implementation and maintenance of the plans.

Part I: The applications and database plan

Purpose: *to transform the results of the previous stages into a viable and coherent plan acceptable to Business and IT Management*

The applications and database plan

- Provides the main results of the project
- Confirms interpretation of Information Needs to business management
- Provides basis for cost/benefit management
- Provides starting point for detailed development projects
- Provides basis for detailed (tactical) planning
- Shows outline schedule for developments in each quarter (Table 14-1)
- Includes synopsis of each project (Figure 14-2)
- Shows technical and resource requirements
- Shows costs and benefits

Figure 14-2:   *Recommended IS/IT project synopsis*

RECOMMENDED IS/IT PROJECT SYNOPSIS

ref.: [   ]

Author: [   ]   date: [   ]   reviewed: [   ]   date: [   ]

Title: [   ]

Type: review [ ]   feasibility study [ ]   requm'ts def'n [ ]   Design: [ ]   new dev't [ ]   enhancement [ ]   custom dev't package implem'n [ ]   technical [ ]   other (specify) [ ]

Short description: [   ]

CBINS ref.	Short name	Sponsor	Priority
Cross-references to business needs:

Data Usage: [   ]

Business volumes and workload profile [   ]

Application and data dependencies/cross references: [   ]

Performance, security and control requirements: [   ]

Implementation options: [   ]

Technical requirements/ options: [   ]

Project/phase cross references and dependencies [   ]

Resource estimates:

Analysis:	Build:
Design	Test:
User:	Implement:

Implementation schedule: [   ]

Summary of cost/benefit case

Costs by time phase:

Benefits by time phase: (consider cost reduction, loss/risk avoidance and revenue/profit increases)

Risk/impact of not proceeding:

Package applications into projects

- Review and complete the application synopses
- Classify by business area and technical category
- Analyze all dependencies – produce precedence network
- Carry out trial packaging to projects – seek best compromise fit between:
  - *business target dates*   - *skills/resource*   - *spend rate*   - *risk*
- Document project packaging – re-group application synopses to projects
- Audit traceability so as to facilitate subsequent review and maintenance
- Summarize effort by type
- Smooth resource loadings
- Agree date revisions with sponsors
- Agree schedule with IT management

NB: Several iterations may be needed for each technical group. In practice this is done in parallel with technical and staff planning.

Figure 14-2 illustrates the full form of the project specification document which we will now be completing. Note that for significant projects, it may run to several pages. Figure 14-3 is a reminder that we are also working with the now fully developed form of the dependency chart, which will now include existing tactical plans and work in progress, as well as new conclusions from this study.

Accuracy considerations

- Avoid spurious accuracy
  - tactical plans will vary in detail due to short term priorities and resource availability
  - strategic plan is intended as a good guide not exact schedule
  - quarterly time frame
- Validate estimates
  - involve IT staff who will be responsible for carrying out the projects in assessing effort and duration
  - agree with IT Management

Types of project

We will not be recommending only large, new development projects from an IS/IT strategy study. There are many other relevant outputs.

- Application development
  - *new, large scale*   - *new, small or rapid development*
  - *enhancements of existing applications*

- Amendment of the implementation or roll-out programs for applications already developed.

- Review, e.g. of a current initiative which may need to be redirected. Some initiatives may be stopped or curtailed.

- Feasibility studies:

  - *new developments*   - *enhancements*
  - *joint with the business, e.g. product or service formulation*

- Infrastructure development

- Skills development

- In depth study e.g. of a set of technical options or application packages

  - *paper evaluation*   - *hands on trial or benchmark*

Figure 14-3:   *Practical sequences for application delivery – neglecting site phasing and migration constraints*

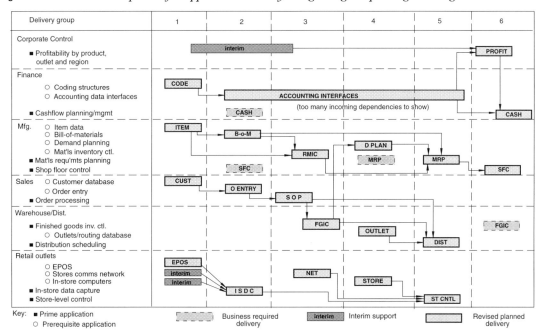

Remember that one certain way to lose friends among senior management is to run a study which only recommends further studies!

- Procurement activity

- Installation, e.g. of a package or network already selected

Data planning

Data availability and dependencies remain one of the most critical considerations.

- Database priorities must be related to application priorities.
- Derive the database creation/migration plan from the application schedule.
- Database conversion may be a major dependency:
  - *finding the data* ▪ *data control* ▪ *quality* ▪ *distribution/dispersal*
- Interim gateways and/or data extracts or feeds may be necessary.

Plan integration

- Check feasibility:
  - *technical* ▪ *data availability* ▪ *user involvement*
  - *business tolerance of phasing and delivery of benefits*
- Adjust the application plan if necessary

Delivery format of application plans

- Application Project Schedule by Business Area
- Application Project Schedule by Technical Category
- Urgent Action Program
- Resource summary by skill type
- Cost/Benefit Summary by Business Area

Part II – Technology planning

Section structure

- Making decisions – meeting requirements, narrowing options
- Quantifying solutions – see also Chapter 12
- Assembling the plan

Technology planning objectives

- Deliver a viable, coherent IT strategy which supports the business goals and application plans
- Make decisions re solutions for all IT areas
- Highlight and quantify risks and issues
- Define and scope detailed work needed to finalize the strategy
- Deliver outline capacity plan and costs
- Produce a phased plan for IT development projects and supporting logistics

Table 14-2 illustrates how IS/IT objectives can be linked to business objectives. Table 14-3 takes this a stage further and links IS/IT objectives to IS/IT strategies and tactics.

Table 14-1:   *Trendy Products PLC - information systems strategy application development projects overall schedule*

BUSINESS AREA / PROJECT NAME	Development man yrs	style	1995/6 Q1	Q2	Q3	Q4	1996/7 Q1	Q2	Q3	Q4	1997/8 Q1	Q2	Q3	Q4	98 on man yrs
SALES															
Sales order processing and finished goods inventory	8.75 / 0	Pack	3	4	8	8	6	4	2						
Sales analysis phase I	1.5	Rapid		2	2		2								
Sales analysis phase II	1	Rapid						2	2						
Customer perf./profitability	1	Rapid					2	2							
Wholesale outlet support	2.25	Trad									1	3	3	2	
Retail outlet support	2	Trad											2	2	1
Sub-total	16.5		3	4	10	10	10	8	4	0	1	3	5	4	1
FINANCE															
Revised coding structures	1.25	Manual	2	3											
G/L interfaces	1.75	Mods	3	2	1	1									
Improved financial ctl reports	2.25	Rapid			1	2	2				2	2			
Budget planning support	1.13	EUC		1.5	1.5	1.5									
Cashflow planning model	1.63	EUC		1.5	1.5	1.5			1	1					
Cash management	2.5	EUC							2	2	2	2	2		
Sub-total	10.5		5	8	5	6	2	0	3	3	4	4	2	0	0
MANUFACTURING															
Bristol	0														
Mat Req. Planning	3.75	Pack	2	3	2										2
Shop floor control	2.5	Pack						2	2	2					1
	0														
Luton	0														
Basic HP systems	2.25	Pack				1	3	3	2						
Mat Req. Planning	3.25	Pack							2	2	1				2
Shop floor control	3	Pack									2	2			2
	0														
Birmingham	0														
Basic HP systems	2.25	Pack							1	3	3	2			
Mat Req. Planning	3.25	Pack										2	2	1	2
Shop floor control	4	Pack											2	2	3
Sub-total	24.3		2	3	2	1	3	5	7	7	6	6	4	3	12
MARKETING															
Marketing analysis phase I	1.5	Trad		2	2	1	1								
Marketing analysis phase II	3.25	EUC				1	2	2	2						1.5
Campaign analysis	1.25	EUC										1	1	1	0.5
Sub-total	6		0	2	2	2	3	2	2	0	0	1	1	1	2
DISTRIBUTION															
Distribution control pilot	1.75	Pack						2	2	2	1				
Distribution – all sites	7.5	Pack										2	4	4	5
Sub-total	9.25		0	0	0	0	0	2	2	2	1	2	4	4	5

Table 14-1:   *(continued) Trendy Products PLC – information systems strategy application development projects overall schedule*

BUSINESS AREA / PROJECT NAME	Development man yrs	style	1995/6 Q1	Q2	Q3	Q4	1996/7 Q1	Q2	Q3	Q4	1997/8 Q1	Q2	Q3	Q4	98 on man yrs
(Shows no. of development staff by quarter)															
PRODUCT DEVELOPMENT															
Product dev't support	1	EUC		2	2										
CAD/CAM facilities	2.5	Pack					1	2	2	3	2				
Sub-total	3.5		0	0	2	2	1	2	2	3	2	0	0	0	0
PURCHASING															
Purchasing system replacement	1	Pack	1	1	1	1									
Sub-total	1		1	1	1	1	0	0	0	0	0	0	0	0	0
PERSONNEL & SERVICES															
Payroll/personnel system replacement	4.5	Pack							2	4	2	2			2
Office automation pilot	1.5	Pack					1	2	2	1					
Office automation (fuller)	3.25	Pack										1	2	2	2
Sub-total	4.5		0	0	0	0	0	0	2	4	2	2	0	0	2
GRAND TOTALS – MAN YEARS	75.5														22
GRAND TOTALS – MANPOWER			11	18	22	22	19	19	22	19	16	18	16	12	

Table 14-2:   *Relation between business objectives and IS/IT objectives*

Typical IS/IT Objective	Type of business objective					
	Improve customer satisfaction	Gain market share	Reduce costs	Improve profitability	Develop new/ improved products	Develop new markets
Support business processes and priorities	✓	✓		✓	✓	✓
Detect changes in business need and respond quickly	✓	✓	✓	✓	✓	✓
Develop and enhance applications faster and cheaper	✓	✓	✓	✓	✓	✓
Systems to be adaptive and flexible to changes in business need or volumes	✓	✓			✓	✓
Meet service level targets at minimum costs	✓		✓	✓		
Provide effective business perf. measurement and analysis	✓	✓	✓	✓	✓	✓
Gain maximum return on investment in IT R&D	✓		✓	✓	✓	
Provide and operate cost effective, flexible technology infrastructure	✓		✓	✓	✓	✓

Preparing the IT plan

- Establish the demands
- Select/confirm options to meet the demand
- Evaluate risks and external factors

- Size and cost IT preferred options
- Build the plan

Elements of the IT plan

- Policies, guide-lines and strategies
- Computing and communications hardware and software
- Application development and maintenance methods, tools and techniques
- People/skills
- Accommodation
- IS/IT Organization
- Provision for maintenance of the plan
- Synchronization with application development and business schedule

Technology planning products

- Statement of IT strategy which supports the business goals and application plans
- Decisions and recommendations re solutions for all IT areas
- Assessments of risks and issues
- Definitions of detailed work needed to finalize the strategy
- Outline capacity plan and costs
- Phased plan for IT development projects and supporting logistics

Table 14-4 illustrates a typical IT development plan.

Part III – IT organization, human resources and skills

Purpose

To define staff and organizational requirements arising from application and technical Plans

- Refine schedules allowing for staff constraints
- Initiate personnel related projects
- Refine cost benefit analyses
- Provide manpower planning information
- Develop planned and business oriented culture in IT
- Facilitate IT exploitation in User Departments

IS/IT OBJECTIVE

IS/IT Strategies	IS/IT Tactical measures	Support business processes and priorities	Detect changes in business need and respond quickly	Provide effective systems for business perf. measurement & analysis	Develop and enhance applications faster and cheaper	Meet service level targets at minimum costs	Gain maximum return on investment in IT R&D	Systems to be adaptive and flexible to changes in business need or volumes	Provide and operate cost effective, flexible technology infrastructure
ISSP process closely linked with business planning to identify and track business needs and changes		✓	✓						
Effective integration of strategic, tactical and operational plans		✓	✓	✓					
Improved application development process, tools, techniques			✓		✓	✓		✓	
Maximum effective devolution of responsibility to users		✓	✓						
Common service level strategy				✓		✓			
Appropriate levels of investment in data and IS architectures				✓				✓	
Follow best practice in project management			✓		✓	✓	✓	✓	
Exploit innovative technologies for cost/performance and flexibility	Exploit Client/server				✓	✓	✓	✓	✓
Implement 80/20 business solutions		✓	✓		✓	✓		✓	
Implement applications in via frequent, phased deliveries		✓	✓		✓	✓		✓	
Implement a common MIS/EIS architecture and delivery system				✓	✓			✓	✓
Manage and control IT R&D		✓				✓	✓		✓

Table 14-3: *Relation between IS/IT objectives and IS/IT strategies/tactics*

Subject areas

- Application planning, design, development, maintenance
- IT planning, implementation, support
- Computers, networks, services
- Sponsorship, requirements definition, development, training, customer role

Development skills

- Cost/benefit management ▪ Organization to meet business objectives
- Business analysis and account management
- User involvement ▪ Quality management ▪ Requirements definition
- System design ▪ System building ▪ Analyst/programmer roles
- Data administration ▪ Development techniques ▪ End user support

Technical skills

- Specialist management   ▪ Database management
- Equipment and software evaluation ▪ Productivity aids
- Development tools   ▪ Network planning and design
- Performance/capacity planning and measurement

Operations skills

- Network management   ▪ Procurement
- Development support   ▪ Automated tools
- Performance monitoring and tuning ▪ Data collection
                                 ▪ Distributed hardware support
- Distributed systems management (this is at least 50% about management)

User departments skills

- Project sponsorship
- Benefit management
- System/data ownership
- Central development involvement
- Secondment to IT
- End user computing
- Office automation

TECHNICAL CATEGORY & POTENTIAL PROJECTS	Tech man years	how critical 1=max	95 Q1	95 Q2	95 Q3	95 Q4	96 Q1	96 Q2	96 Q3	96 Q4	97 Q1	97 Q2	97 Q3	97 Q4	97+ (man years)
Central Mainframe Hardware	0.00														
Capacity planning for main hardware	2.25	1	1	1	0.5	0.5			0.5	0.5			0.5	0.5	1
Complete move from ICL to IBM	2.25	1				1	2	4	2						
HP installation in Luton	1.00						2	2							
HP installation in Birmingham	1.00										2	2			
Wide Area Networks	0.00														
Network replacement	2.00	1			1	1					2	2	2		
Local area networks	0.00														
Head office PC/OA integration & associated LANs	1.25	4									0.5	0.5			1
Terminals, local MCs & PCs	0.00														
Re-equipment of terminals	0.63	4					0.5	1	1						
Retail/Wholesale outlet on-site equ'pt selection	0.75	2		1			1	1							
Systems Software	0.00														
IBM - DOS/VSE to MVS upgrade	2.50	5			1	1			4	4					1
Data Management	0.00														
Main operational systems – DB2 & afterwards	1.25	2		0.5	0.5										
Central information database DBMS and language for MIS	1.25	1						1	1	2					
Local & PC data management & connectivity to centre	0.31	3			0.25		0.5	0.5	0.5						
Development environment	0.00														
Analyst/designer workbench	0.50	3			0.5			0.5	0.5	0.5			0.5	0.5	
3GL programmer workbench	0.25	3			0.5			0.5	0.5	0.5					

Table 14-4: *Trendy Products PLC – information systems strategy, technical development projects overall schedule*

Table 14-4: *(continued)* Trendy Products PLC – information systems strategy, technical development projects overall schedule

TECHNICAL CATEGORY & POTENTIAL PROJECTS	Tech man years	how critical 1=max	95	95	95	95	96	96	96	96	97	97	97	97	97+ (man years)
Development languages															
End-user app'n dev't language	0.25	3					0.5	0.5							
DP rapid dev't shop use	0.25	2					0.5	0.5							
Standards & Methods	0.00														
Implement up to date application development standards for all types of applications	1.25	1	2	2			0.5	0.5							
Special methods/options to suit small/med projects	0.13	1	0.25				0.25								
Prototyping adjuncts to major project dev't standards	0.13	2	0.25				0.25								
End user dev't methods & support approaches	0.88	2	0.5	0.25			0.25	0.25							
ISD Skills & org'nl dev't															
Architecture group	0.25	1	0.25	0.25			0.25								
End-user support group	0.25	1	0.25	0.25			0.25								
Skills conversion/update for ISD staff	0.63	1	0.25	0.5			0.5	0.5			0.5				
Architecture/Strategy Dev't	0.00														
In depth data & functional analysis of business needs areas, as needed to precede key app'n dev'ts scheduled	1.19	2	1	1			0.5	0.5			0.25	0.25			0.25
Integration & control of architectures by architecture group	0.38	2	0.25	0.25			0.25				0.25	0.25			
Specials															
Business, market & product modelling tools & techniques	1.38	2	0.5	0.5			0.25	0.25			0.25	0.5			1
Techniques for collection & analysis of external intelligence	1.50	4	0.25	0.25			0.25	0.25			0.25	0.5			1
TOTALS – MAN YEARS	23.38														
TOTALS – MANPOWER LEVELS			2.00	3.50	9.50	9.00	7.75	12.00	12.75	10.00	5.00	5.50	3.00	1.50	4.25

Inputs to user departments' personnel planning

MANAGEMENT ASPECTS

- responsibility for sponsorship
- delivery of benefits
- involvement in development

DEPARTMENTAL COMPUTING

- development – central or user staff
- operation – IT or user staff
- end user computing – support, standards, control

DEVELOPMENT METHODS

- structured methods
- joint application design
- end user developments

Part IV – Business case integration

Components of the business case

- Costs
- Tangible benefits
- Intangible benefits
- Timing of costs and benefits

Business case development cost items

- Side effects on other systems
- Users
- DP human resource
- Computer resource
- Software licenses – packages and 4GLs
- Training
- Premises/facilities/materials

Business case conversion cost items

- Users
- Equipment/services
- Special activities

- DP human resource
- Computer resource

Business case operational cost items

- Users
- IS/IT staff costs
- Computer resource
- Software licenses
- Premises/facilities/materials
- Growth rates
- Supplies
- Missed business opportunities from delays

Business case benefit items

COST REDUCTION

- Headcount displacement
- Cost management
- Reduction in inventory
- Reduction in overhead costs, e.g. transport, due to better scheduling/utilization

IMPROVED BUSINESS RESPONSE AND CONTROL

- Improved management effectiveness and/or productivity
- Inherent benefits from more accurate, accessible information up to date e.g. as an enabler to key personnel effectiveness.
- Tighter margins, 'just in time'
- 'Knowing what's going on'

INCREASED REVENUE

- More repeat business from better service
- Better recognition of business/market opportunities
- Ability to recognize and avoid pitfalls before competition

VALUE ACCELERATION

- Bringing forward benefits as a result of earlier implementation
- Risk avoidance or control
- Risks avoided
- Improved control over unavoidable risks – finer tuning.

RISKS OF EXCESSIVE OR BLINKERED COST CUTTING

- Short term gains, long term damage

- Unforeseen side effects
- Inappropriate or limited KPIs – e.g. improved margin on declining market share

WHY DOES COST CONTAINMENT DO SO MUCH DAMAGE?

The second law of thermodynamics applies to business systems – see Figure 14-4

- When adding value – focus closely on pay-back, to keep curve relatively shallow
- When pruning costs – assess realistically the loss in quality or function, and whether this is worthwhile and/or reversible

Figure 14-4:   *Cost/performance/quality tradeoffs*

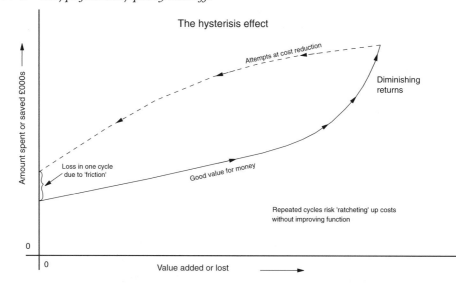

Business cases

Every budget manager, and every finance director has his own preferred way of presenting business cases for major projects. The only rule is to follow the rules laid down in your Organization. But if there's an option, full life cycle cost benefit analysis offers one of the more balanced ways of looking at a proposal. The spreadsheet in Table 14-5 is a simplified example, illustrating sample cost and benefit lines. It is based on current costs, but the reader is welcome to superimpose their own preferred cashflow discounting process on it.

Overall financial summaries

Table 14-6 presents the whole plan integrated and summarized on a single page. Figures 14-5 and 14-6 illustrate useful alternative ways for presenting the overall summary at senior management level.

Figure 14-5:   *Trendy Products PLC information systems budgets by year at current costs*

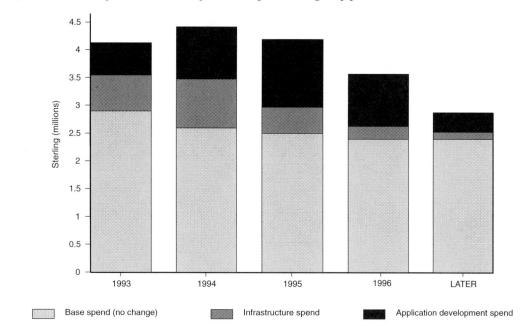

Base spend (no change)   Infrastructure spend   Application development spend

Figure 14-6:   *Trendy Products PLC - information systems plan (Summary of costs and benefits)*

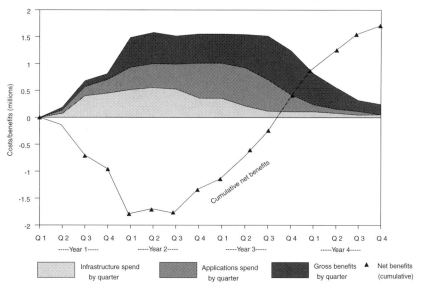

Infrastructure spend   Applications spend   Gross benefits   ▲ Net benefits
by quarter   by quarter   by quarter   (cumulative)

	Year 1				Year 2				Year 3				Year 4				Year 5			
	Q1	Q2	Q3	Q4	Q1	Q2	Q3	Q4	Q1	Q2	Q3	Q4	Q1	Q2	Q3	Q4	Q1	Q2	Q3	Q4
Costs - non-recurring																				
Analysis/design - human	20	40	50	30	20															
Programming/testing:																				
■ human		10	50	80	80	50	30													
■ computer time			100																	
Package purchase						200														
Development – premises									300											
Installation – premises									50											
Communications – installation																				
Computer hardware – capital	300			500		200														
Software – capital	120			220		50														
Roll-out - installation staff				25	25	10	10													
Roll-out - training				15	5	5	5	5												
QTLY TOTALS - non-recurring	440	50	200	870	130	515	45	5	350	0	0	0	0	0	0	0	0	0	0	0
CUMULATIVE - non-recurring	440	490	690	1,560	1,690	2,205	2,250	2,255	2,605	2,605	2,605	2,605	2,605	2,605	2,605	2,605	2,605	2,605	2,605	2,605
Costs - recurring																				
Communications – circuit rental			1	2	4	4	7	10	13	13	14	14	15	16	17	18	19	20	21	22
Hardware maintenance					80				130				130				130			
Software licenses					66				104				111				111			
Application maintenance					36				90				90				90			
Premises - rental/maintenance	30				1	2	2	2	2	2	2	2	2	2	2	2	2	2	2	2
Staff - operational						2	2	2	2	2	2	2	2	2	2	2	2	2	2	2
Energy/utilities					0	0	0	0	0	0	0	0	0	0	0	0	0	0	0	0
QTLY TOTALS - recurring	30	0	1	2	187	8	11	14	341	17	18	18	350	20	21	22	354	24	25	26
CUMULATIVE - recurring	30	30	31	33	219	227	238	252	592	609	627	645	995	1,015	1,036	1,058	1,412	1,436	1,461	1,487
QTLY COST TOTALS	470	50	201	872	317	523	56	19	691	17	18	18	350	20	21	22	354	24	25	26
CUMULATIVE COSTS TOTALS	470	520	721	1,593	1,909	2,432	2,488	2,507	3,197	3,214	3,232	3,250	3,600	3,620	3,641	3,663	4,017	4,041	4,066	4,092
Benefits																				
Cost avoidance - staff						110	225	330	380	440	440	440	440	440	440	440	440	440	440	440
Cost avoidance - other							110	118	250	25	75		100		75		90		90	
Risk avoidance						50	50	75	75	75	100	100	75	100	100	100	100	100	100	100
Revenue/profit improvement								5	25	75	110	11	120	120	120	130	131	132	133	134
QTLY BENEFIT TOTALS	0	0	0	0	0	160	385	528	730	615	725	551	735	660	735	670	761	672	763	674
CUMULATIVE BENEFITS	0	0	0	0	0	160	545	1,073	1,803	2,418	3,143	3,694	4,429	5,089	5,824	6,494	7,255	7,927	8,690	9,364
NET CUM (COST)/BENEFIT	(470)	(520)	(721)	(1,593)	(1,909)	(2,272)	(1,943)	(1,434)	(1,394)	(796)	(89)	444	829	1,469	2,183	2,831	3,238	3,886	4,624	5,272

Table 14-5: *IT systems – full life cycle cost/benefit model (Costs in $000s, with no discounting)*

Table 14-6 is a wide financial summary spanning four years by quarter. All monetary values are in thousands of pounds sterling at current costs.

PROJECT AREA	Total man years	Total Costs	Total Benefits	Y1 Q1	Y1 Q2	Y1 Q3	Y1 Q4	Y2 Q1	Y2 Q2	Y2 Q3	Y2 Q4	Y3 Q1	Y3 Q2	Y3 Q3	Y3 Q4	Y4 Q1	Y4 Q2	Y4 Q3	Y4 Q4
BUSINESS APPLICATIONS AREAS																			
Sales	17	£850	£2,300		£120	£185	£160	£160	£146	£65	£14								
Finance	11	£480	£1,200			£60	£80	£75	£80	£86	£75	£24							
Manufacturing	25	£1,500	£3,500			£75	£65	£135	£150	£135	£145	£215	£160	£120	£85	£75	£75	£65	
Marketing	5	£160	£1,750			£20	£30	£25	£25		£20	£40							
Distribution	9	£300	£840							£40	£50		£60	£65	£30	£55			
Product Development	4	£170	£700					£30					£35	£45	£60				
Purchasing	1	£55	£350						£10					£30	£15				
Personnel & Services	5	£185	£130				£15				£25	£55	£75		£15				
APPLICATIONS TOTAL	75	£3,700	£10,770	£0	£120	£340	£350	£425	£411	£326	£329	£334	£330	£260	£205	£130	£75	£65	£0
TECHNICAL INFRASTRUCTURE																			
Mainframe Computers	7	£1,700			£300			£650			£350				£400				
Networking	3	£350				£200	£150												
Workstations	1	£1,010							£220	£85	£225		£50	£300		£65	£65		
Systems Software	3	£148										£45	£20	£28	£55				
Data Management	3	£375					£45	£45	£65	£85		£135							
Application Dev't Tools & Env'ts	1	£135						£25	£20	£45		£20			£25				
Standards & Methods	2	£85				£25	£15	£5	£5	£5	£5	£5	£20						
ISD Staff/skills Development	1	£75				£25			£5	£5		£5	£35						
IS/IT Architectures	2	£110			£15	£15	£10	£10	£10	£10	£10	£25	£5						
Specials	3	£275									£50			£25	£30	£45	£15	£50	£55
INFRASTRUCTURE TOTAL	26	£4,263	£0	£0	£315	£265	£220	£735	£325	£235	£638	£240	£130	£355	£510	£110	£80	£50	£55
OVERALL TOTAL	100	£7,963	£10,770	£0	£435	£605	£570	£1,160	£736	£561	£967	£574	£460	£615	£715	£240	£155	£115	£55
COSTS BREAKDOWN																			
Hardware		£2,095				£450		£680				£550							
Building		£480											£65						
Software		£818			£150	£30	£45	£45	£130	£110	£150			£28	£50			£50	
Manpower — tech support		£240		£10	£15	£15	£15	£15	£15	£15	£15	£15	£15	£15	£15	£15	£15	£15	£15
analysts		£592		£35	£45	£40	£50	£45	£42	£40	£35	£30	£30	£35	£40	£35	£30	£30	£30
programming		£1,175		£45	£45	£60	£75	£80	£80	£95	£85	£80	£85	£105	£90	£80	£70	£50	£50
users		£1,450		£50	£110	£120	£110	£130	£130	£130	£110	£110	£85	£85	£60	£60	£60	£50	£50
External services		£1,113		£50	£88	£150	£225	£175	£130	£95	£110	£55	£35						
Distribution of Benefits		£0	£10,770	£0	£111	£360	£540	£650	£965	£975	£870	£970	£884	£855	£954	£836	£760	£460	£580
Cumulative Costs				£0	£435	£1,040	£1,610	£2,770	£3,506	£4,067	£5,034	£5,608	£6,068	£6,683	£7,398	£7,638	£7,793	£7,908	£7,963
Cumulative Benefits				£0	£111	£471	£1,011	£1,661	£2,626	£3,601	£4,471	£5,441	£6,325	£7,180	£8,134	£8,970	£9,730	£10,190	£10,770
Running DR/CR Balance				£0	-£324	-£569	-£599	-£1,109	-£880	-£466	-£563	-£167	£257	£497	£736	£1,332	£1,937	£2,282	£2,807

Table 14-6: *Trendy Products PLC – overall financial summary (thousands of pounds sterling at current costs by quarter)*

Part V – Means for continuing review and maintenance

Key prerequisites

- Plans to become and remain visible.
- Management to be committed to following and maintaining them.
- Performance/adherence properly tracked and controlled.
- Effective integration of planning cycles and process:
  - tactical and strategic;
  - corporate, business unit, IS and IT.
- Effective responsibility structure for review and maintenance:
  - enabling efficient integration across the planning cycles and layers;
  - supported by appropriate management disciplines and cultural awareness.
- Accessible, largely automated documentation, supported by maintainable computer models which support 'what if' usage.
- Accurate 'traceability' in the working papers/files from early business intent through CBINS and applications to projects and verification of benefits delivery.
- Core human expertise to support rapid, responsive iteration both on regular and 'event-driven' criteria.
- Clear criteria for identifying the need for change.

Key planning baselines

- Business plans
- Business process models:
  - function hierarchy;
  - business process schematic.
- Consolidated statement of business needs (CBINS).
- Inventory/assessment of IS/IT status and quality.
- Current IS/IT strategic and tactical plans.
- The planning process itself.

For the maintenance process itself – see chapter 16.

CHAPTER 15

Plan delivery and implementation

We have now apparently finished. But have we?

Quality – are you ready to deliver the plan?

- Have you got a clear recommendation?
- Does the recommendation embody a clear vision for business support, IS and IT?
- Are you still in touch with the mood of the business and market? Are you solving the *right* problems?
- Is it clear what management need to do to approve the plan?
- Have sponsors agreed with you and among themselves as to how to allocate costs and benefits?
- Is presentation material clear; presentations rehearsed?
- Have you prepared the ground with potential sceptics/opponents?
- Is back-up material available if needed - e.g. alternatives considered/ rejected?
- Does the plan provide for regular review and maintenance?

Objectives of this stage

1. Finalize the plan for presentation
2. Present the plan and ensure that it is understood
3. Gain acceptance, and agreement as to how to proceed
4. Ensure proper integration with business planning cycles and with IS/IT tactical plans
5. Initiate the implementation of the plan

6.   Ensure effective provision for future tracking and maintenance – the biggest pitfall of all!

First, in Figure 15-1, a reminder of the process which we have followed.

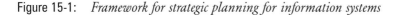

Figure 15-1:   *Framework for strategic planning for information systems*

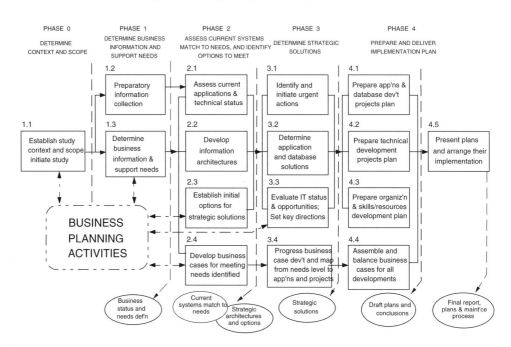

Presenting the plan

You can do: the *right study* at, the *right time* and deliver the *right answer*
– and still fail to gain acceptance on presentation.

Finalizing the plan for presentation

- Good report and presentation is critical
- Manage expectations and avoid surprises
- Get the sponsors to lead – they must carry the can for the business cases
- Provide in the plan for:
  - monitoring of implementation;
  - linkage into subsequent business planning cycles;
  - means to reflect sudden changes – contingency, scenarios;
  - review and update cycles.

Presenting the plan and ensuring that it is understood

- Be ready with answers, and to proceed.
- Act like you expect to succeed.

Critical factors for success

- There must be overwhelmingly attractive business benefits of doing it.
- Make it clear what dire consequences will happen if this action is not taken.
- Ensure the presentation is clear, aimed at recipients, and offers something they can commit to.
- Follow rules, e.g. for business cases, capital expenditure, etc.
- Make it clear why alternatives were rejected.
- Ensure the plan is implementable - tangible, no howlers.
- Make sure the timing is right - when decision makers can listen and concentrate, and when they can commit if they're convinced.
- Gain and keep sponsors' commitment - give them what they want - they'll then do the rest for you.
- Ensure that suppliers of funds keep their nerve - don't scare them.
- Ensure that those who can sink it don't - psychological warfare held at bay:
  - know the key players at Board level.
- forestall middle management snipers - get them committed as sponsors.

Gaining acceptance and agreement as to how to proceed: *The project is not successful until the results are acted upon - the report is not the end product.*

As Figure 15-2 reminds us, planning and control is a closed-loop process.

Figure 15-2:   *The closed loop planning and control cycle*

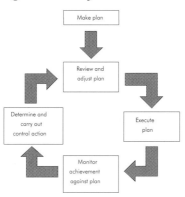

Following the plan, tracking performance and amending both the activities and the plan are essential elements of the process. Figures 15-3, 15-4 and 15-5 illustrate the maintenance cycle in progressively more detail.

Figure 15-3: *IS/IT plan creation and revision process*

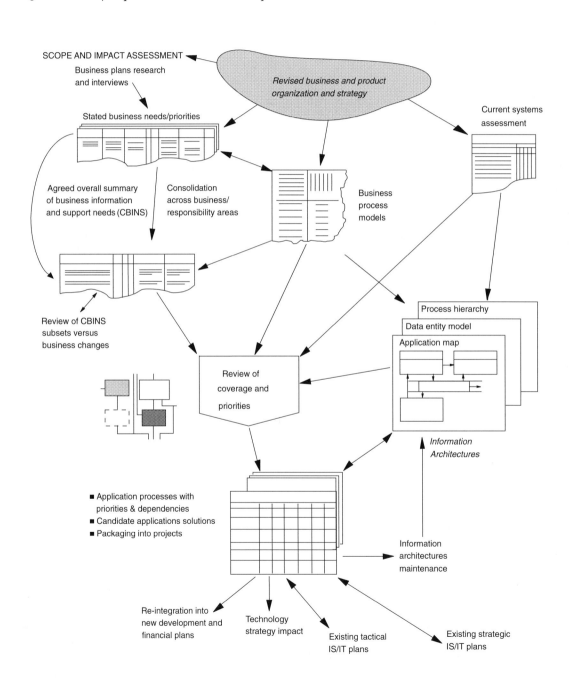

Initiating plan implementation

- The plan must maintainable
- The plan must be maintained – provide for subsequent cycles of plan review and adjustment

Follow-up – you can:

- do the right study at the right time;
- deliver the right answer and present it well;
- gain acceptance,

and still fail on follow up. There must be an effective mechanism and commitment to follow and maintain the plans.

Figure 15-4: *The IS/IT strategic planning cycle*

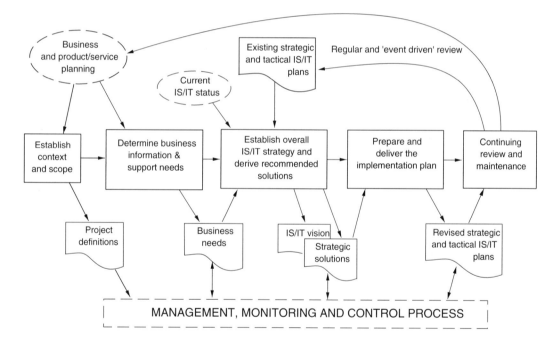

Figure 15-5:   *IS planning cycle key decision points*

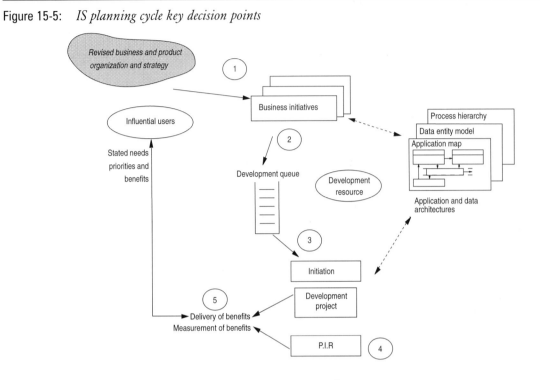

Strategic planning for information systems – products

Remember to focus your products on the appropriate audience. Senior business sponsors will not appreciate the elegance of your entity modelling technique, and will become quite irritable if you insist on trying to enlighten them.

Key end products

- Statements of strategic solutions for information systems and technology
- Phased development plans for:
  - application systems and databases
  - IT development projects
  - staff skills upgrade
- Basis for implementation and migration
- Business case with financial plan
- Criteria and process for plan review, tuning and maintenance

Business-oriented intermediate products

- Consolidated and agreed statement of business information and support needs and priorities.
  - the 'charter'
  - basis for managing change
  - may be used to generate scenarios
- Indication of key areas of risk and uncertainty on which the viability of the recommended solutions depends
- Assessment of current information systems in terms of the extent and quality of coverage achieved of business needs
- Urgent actions plan for interim 'quick fixes'
- Complete audit trail and basis for traceability from requirement to solutions

IS and IT oriented products

- Assessment of current IS and IT status:
  - objective – what there is
  - judgemental – its quality and current and future relevance
- Log of options and solutions which were considered and rejected, with reasons
- Target applications and database architecture
- Target IT architecture
- Target Organization and skills/resource strategy

Strategic planning for information systems delivers a set of plans which are:

- Manifestly necessary – linked to business priorities
- Achievable
- Affordable
- Manageable
- Understood by IT and the business
- Maintainable

And which will be implemented, maintained and continue to be followed. There follows a sample set of documents typical of those required to set up and manage the maintenance cycle.

IS/IT strategy steering group

Draft terms of reference

The IS/IT Steering Group for Trendy Products Plc should consist of a sub-set of the main board plus the General Manager, IT. During an IS/IT strategic review, the project manager for that review should attend as an invitee. The Steering Group should meet on a regular basis bi-monthly, and, exceptionally, on an as-required basis. Their duties will comprise:

1. Approve the project scope and t.o.r., and direct and steer the IT strategy review in accordance with it.

2. Receive progress and quality assurance reports. Action or monitor high level issues and exceptions arising.

3. Facilitate the project by ensuring where necessary that resources are available, and dependencies e.g. on parallel initiatives, are managed.

4. Provide guidance on high level issues of business intention or direction.

5. Address and resolve high level business priorities and other issues; manage and resolve any out of scope issues raised by the project.

6. Approve guidelines for establishing and evaluating business cases.

7. Receive, review and approve the project interim deliverables, final report and findings.

8. Oversee the implementation of the IS/IT strategy and the maintenance process, and act as the top level change control authority for the Trendy Products IS/IT strategic plans.

9. Ensure the proper coordination of business, IS and IT strategic and tactical plans for Trendy Products in the future.

IS/IT strategy working group(s)

Draft terms of reference

The work of the IS/IT Steering Group should be supplemented by one or more working groups. Each such group will report to the IS/IT Steering Group, and will comprise the relevant business general managers, including the IT GM as well as the IS/IT planning co-ordinator in all cases. The working group(s) should meet on a regular basis, approximately monthly, and, exceptionally, as-required. Each such working group should have as a member at least one member of the IS/IT Steering Group. They may invite other IT or business line managers to meetings, or may commission work from them.

For their area of authority, each working group will:

1. Own and direct the implementation of their sections of the IS/IT strategic and tactical plans.

2. Act as change control agents for the relevant sections of the CBINS and the IS/IT strategic and tactical plans.

3. Review changes in business or product support need or priority and direct the work of modifying the strategic or tactical plans accordingly.

4. Review proposals and requests for significant addition or change to the existing application portfolio and direct the work of modifying the strategic or tactical plans accordingly.

5. Monitor status and achievement against the IS/IT strategic and tactical plans, and consider and recommend remedial action as appropriate.

6. Recommend to the overall IS/IT Steering Group changes in priority or funding where relevant.

7. Respond to requests for the business for assessment of business or product scenarios, in terms of IS/IT lead times, costs or feasibility.

IT strategy project – steering group

Draft agenda for the first meeting

1. Presentation of project scope, rationale and t.o.r.

2. Overview of project approach to be followed.

3. Project management process, including milestones and steering group meetings.

4. Process for providing high level Trendy Products business vision and directional input.

5. Management interview groupings and schedule.

6. Review of actions c/f.

7. A.o.b. and date of next meeting.

IT strategy project – steering group

Sample agenda – later meetings

1. Review of actions c/f

2. Project status report

3. Review of scope or other relevant steering issues, e.g. dependencies or priority conflicts

4. Review of actions c/f

5. Next meeting and a.o.b.

Draft role definition

Manager of IS/IT strategic planning services

1. **Overall objective**

    Establish and manage within Management Services an IS/IT strategic planning group which will:

    - act as the prime focus for provision of effective IS and IT strategic planning services for all Association Business units;
    - help to ensure that all provision of IS/IT services to the business units is accurately aligned to business goals and priorities;
    - help to ensure that all business unit demands upon Management Services are framed in a common format which promotes identification of common architectures and potential economies of scale, as well as facilitating internal planning and resource loading.

2. **Functional responsibilities**

    Methods, skills and techniques

    2.1 Establish, maintain and make available appropriate methods and techniques, including software support, for strategic planning for IS and IT for the business units.

    2.2 Ensure on a continuing basis that these methods remain:

    - effective;
    - up to date;
    - in line with perceived external best practice;
    - consistent and well integrated with the business planning ethos, conventions and cycles of the Association;

- compatible with systems design, development and maintenance procedures.

NB: This includes identification of the need for and management of the provision of outside support and services where appropriate.

2.3   Monitor the continued effectiveness of the methods and their results as delivered in practice; take appropriate measures to revise and upgrade the methods, techniques and skill sets where necessary.

2.4   Develop or recruit and maintain a sufficient level of skilled and experienced staff resources to support the demand for the IS/IT planning services. This involves:

- maintaining a demand plan for the service;
- planning and conduct of recruitment, training and development to meet the needs;
- arranging rotation of staff so as to propagate the skills within Management Services and keep the body of practitioners "fresh".

Launch and conduct of IS/IT strategy studies and reviews

2.5   Maintain contact with Association business units at Board and General manager level so as to most effectively:

- identify demand for the IS/IT planning services;
- market and sell them;
- deliver the services;
- track the success of the outcome;
- ensure an appropriate level; of business unit participation in the process;
- provide appropriate review and maintenance support.

2.6   Position and oversee the conduct of specific IS/IT planning studies and reviews for Business units, covering all aspects of quality, timeliness, customer satisfaction and business relevance. Specific aspects include but are not limited to:

- advising on project management and steering groups;
- provision of skilled resources and methods;
- balancing the mix of project team skills and background;
- liaison with sources of specific technical expertise

Maintenance and review of existing plans

2.7   Provide appropriate resources and approaches to help ensure effective maintenance and support of existing IS/IT plans. This includes but is not limited to:

- meeting both routine/cyclic and meeting ad hoc needs;
- ensuring that planning and reporting cycles are integrated effectively across:
    - business and product planning, IS and IT;
    - both short and longer term time scales.

2.8   Fulfil where requested the role of custodian of Business-owned planning documentation and materials.

Meeting Management services internal needs

2.9   Help to ensure that all demands for systems and for Management Services resources are framed in accordance with a common 'template', i.e. in a standardized, common format which facilitates identification of opportunities for delivery of common functionality and for other economies of scale.

2.10   Liaise closely with the Corporate groups responsible for more detailed data, systems and technology architectures over matters of potential or actual commonality.

2.11   Assemble, maintain and provide a consolidated demand plan covering the stated load by resource type on Management Services from Customers, so as to give maximum assistance with skills and resource planning and control

2.12   Help to ensure that both in terms of methods and techniques, and also in the specific IS/IT planning deliverables, there is near "seamless" integration into the later stages of the systems life cycle. This scope should include, but is not limited to:

- business plans, models and requirements;
- systems development phase deliverables and formats;
- data, information systems and technical architectures;
- project schedules and scope definitions.

2.13   Liaise effectively with the account management function as appropriate.

3.   Scope and span of control

3.1   For all Association business units, act as the Management Services link with the business units and business general management concerning matters of:

- IS/IT strategy development and maintenance;
- effective alignment of provision of IS/IT with business plans and priorities;
- reaction to changes in business need or market conditions, in terms of impact on IS/IT strategy;
- effective integration of IS/IT plans with business and product plans, and of strategic plans with tactical.

3.2   Be responsible for planning, developing and delivering Management Services methods, techniques and staff skills/resources to achieve 3.1.

3.3   Ensure that the methods, and the plans delivered are compatible with the systems development methods, techniques and tools used in subsequent life cycle stages.

4.   Impact and contacts

4.1   Within Management Services

- *Training*   ▪ *Skills planning*   ▪ *Staff scheduling*   ▪ *Methods liaison*

4.2   With other Association Business Units – *see 2.1*

4.3   With external bodies/third parties

Keeping abreast of best practice

Jointly with business units, selection of contractors, and management of provision of external IS/IT strategic planning services where required.

5.   Experience and qualifications

5.1   General IS/IT background

At least 5 years systems analysis and design experience – mandatory.

5.2   Project management

Solid grounding – mandatory.

5.3   Staff and line management

Mandatory to a level appropriate to the management of:

- up to 5 concurrent IS/IT planning projects;
- up to 10 internal staff;
- multiple client relationships;
- external services procurement and project management on an exception basis only.

5.4   IS/IT planning experience

Several completed IS/IT Planning in a variety of business types is highly desirable. If this cannot be met, then:

- business and management experience requirements are more stringent;
- post holder should participate "hands-on" in several IS/IT Planning at an early stage;
- limited continuing external consulting support should be planned for.

5.5   Business experience

Several years non-IT experience in relevant business areas is highly desirable. If this is not met, then the requirements for IS/IT planning and line management experience are more stringent.

5.6   Knowledge of the Association

Several years experience is highly desirable as a basis for Customer confidence and credibility, some at a management level involving significant visibility. If not met, then the requirements for IS/IT planning and business experience are more stringent.

6.   Training and development requirements

Any needed in the short term to rectify shortfalls in immediate needs.

Continuing measures to keep in touch with developments in IS/IT planning methods

The post holder should participate hands on (i.e. 50% or more of their time in all phases) in an IS/IT strategy plan development or revision every so often. The requirement for this is more stringent if previous business or IS/IT planning experience is light.

It may prove effective if this role were to be held for a period by each Business Account manager, or by persons who are candidates for such posts.

CHAPTER 16

Maintenance, evolution and enhancement

Prerequisites for successful handover and maintenance of the IS/IT strategic plan

Successful implementation of any IS/IT strategic plan depends on a number of factors:

1. The IS/IT combined strategic and tactical plans should be visible, maintained, followed and controlled.

2. There must be effective integration of tactical and longer term plans for:

    - business;
    - products;
    - information systems (IS);
    - information technology (IT).

3. The IS and IT plans need to be integrated with the relevant IS Department internal procedures and plans.

4. The plans need to be embodied in maintainable models with 'what if' support.

5. Agreed business requests for change or development must be notified promptly and clearly to a single co-ordination point, which will be responsible for:

    - assessing and balancing priorities and resource requirements;
    - making recommendations to and seeking approval from the appropriate level of systems review committee;
    - assessing side effects and arranging, where appropriate, to produce common solutions to common problems;
    - maintaining the IS/IT plan;

- initiating and monitoring approved developments.

6.   Plan iterations should be able to be carried out quickly and efficiently; the smaller the underlying change, the smaller the revision task should be. Also, rapid, approximate assessments should be possible;

7.   There should be clear, agreed criteria for recognizing the need for change, and for determining the means to respond;

8.   Requests should be considered jointly, and in a sufficiently broad context, for priority, call on resource and side effects. Decisions regarding scope and implementation must be approved by sponsoring business users.

9.   The joint priorities must be formally reviewed, both on a cyclic basis, and, where necessary, on an event-driven basis

10. Resulting changes should change the documented tactical plan, not lead to its circumvention or abandonment.

11. Both business unit line and IS management must be committed to:

- maintaining and following the plan;
- delivering the benefits from it;
- funding an appropriate portion of IS Department' support for the planning process and the associated data, systems and technical architectures.

12. Implementation progress and delivery of business results must be monitored properly.

13. The IS Department must be committed to:

- supporting the planning process;
- managing and controlling the data, application and technical architectures;
- maintaining an appropriate level of resourcing to fulfil these roles.

14. There must be agreement as to the maintenance responsibilities and process.

This section sets out how these requirements are to be met.

Relation to business and IS planning and budgeting cycles

The potential modes of use of the IS/IT plans include the following:

Regular review cycles

These must be linked to the quarterly and annual business planning cycle.

Event driven

There must be a for plan review on an exceptional basis, e.g.:

- significant change in business direction, (for internal or external reasons);
- development/launch of a major new product;
- senior management reorganization;
- material change in Government policy;
- significant new technology.

'What if' planning support

Use in evaluation of business and product proposals, options and scenarios.

Timing

Typically, IS planning should be phased to complete slightly after the relevant business planning exercise. Likewise, IT planning should lag slightly from IS planning. In both cases, this displacement should not be too great, as it is important to be able to run IS/IT cost and feasibility checks on particular business and product options or scenarios during the business planning cycle.

Key baseline documents – purpose and use

The primary baseline documents required to support plan review and iteration are as follows:

Business needs and/or priorities

Consolidated summary of needs – CBINs. This is the key baseline for business requirements, consolidated and agreed. It forms the preferred base for plan and priority reviews. If invalidated by lapse of time, reorganization or significant change in business direction, then it must be partially or completely reconstructed by consolidation from interview analyses.

Detailed interview analyses reflect individual manager views and requirements; approved by him/her, but not subject to consensus. Not maintained formally as a baseline document. Re-created as necessary, e.g. due to change of job or job scope. Often (but not always), it may be productive to use the previous interview analysis as a starting point.

IS/IT status and capability

Current systems assessments are held in detailed and summary form. Both of these documents need to be maintained, as there is a significant rate of change, both in systems functionality, as plans are implemented, and in perception of quality and relevance to business needs. They provide the main source of reference concerning the degree to which current systems and committed plans meet the business needs identified in the CBINs above.

Business process model

The business process model (chapter 8), also known as the function hierarchy, identifies the inherent business functions and processes needed to run the business, independently of their grouping into organizational units or their present IS/IT support. It provides a basis for assessment of the appropriateness of current Organization and of organizational proposals to meet new needs, and will provide a valuable launch point for Business Process engineering activities. Product support matrices (see chapters 7 and 8), which reflect the current organizational and systems approaches to product support are relevant.

Incoming requests for change or service

These are the raw material of plan maintenance. Frequently, the need for review arises as a result of an accumulation of individual needs or pressures, and is not necessarily articulated at senior management level. It is important that changes resulting from such circumstances result in the plan being maintained, and not by-passed.

The current business and IS/IT plans

These will form the baseline for the plan review in each case.

The continuing IS/IT planning process

Whereas the results of the IS/IT planning process are owned by the business sponsors, responsibility for plan review and maintenance, and for execution of the future IS/IT planning cycles will be joint between the business and the IS Department. Provision needs to be made for the skills and resources to perform this role.

The process as defined in this manual provides an effective means of developing consensus on requirements, priorities and solutions across the business. The decision processes are based as far as reasonable on quantitative criteria, but these must in all cases be tempered with business judgement.

The rationale which underlies the recommendations in the plan should be made as clear as possible. It is especially important that business focus and issues remain clear to all staff working on the plan, regardless of their role. In a corresponding manner, the impact of IS and IT opportunities, constraints and options should be clear to senior business management, as should be the basis for recommendations.

Plan maintenance

The plan should be maintained on the basis of both regular and exceptional or event-driven reviews. These reviews are usually coupled with business-related events or cycles, and the association is as set out above in *Relation to business and IS planning and budgeting cycles*.

Maintenance activity may be classified as follows:

a.   Regular, cyclic

Small to medium changes should normally be carried out by review and adjustment at the CBINs level, with, exceptionally, re-interview where necessary. Note that even where needs do not change, priorities may shift quite dramatically, and the impact on the plan can be significant.

b.   Event-driven

A review of business and/or IS/IT plans may be needed at short notice. It is difficult to define a significant business change unambiguously; it is recommended that the IT Steering Committee should be the final arbiter of this. It is clear that the definition will include any of the classes of event set out above. The scope of a plan change can usually be limited according to the nature of the event. The severity of the impact can be of any level; re-interview or new interviews for new responsibility areas may be appropriate, followed by re-integration into the CBINs.

c.   Review due to change of senior management job or job scope

This type of review should be quite limited, according to the seniority of the position(s) involved. Re-interview or new interviews for new responsibility areas will be appropriate, followed by re-integration into the CBINs.'

d.   'What if' evaluation of business or product options

Feasibility reviews of this nature should be able to be done quickly, at short notice. Often it may be appropriate to extrapolate from an existing similar example of the option whose evaluation is required. Usually, incorporation of hypothetical entries or priorities in the CBINs is the key starting point.

e.   Major revision

Every 4 years or so, possibly much less if there has been a period of high volatility, the level of change of business climate and senior management personnel will dictate that a complete overhaul of the strategic IS and IT plans is needed. This should, of course, take place in the context of a similar revision of business strategies, and be phased accordingly. Even during this type of revision, the existing CBINs and information systems and data architectures should form a valuable basis for the next cycle.

The goal of efficient, rapid iterations of the planning process means that maximum viable use is made of the results of previous planning activities (see above re use of baseline documents). To support this, key baseline documents and other materials must be:

- maintained;
- accessible and processable on magnetic media.

The plan working papers should be embodied in PC-based software media, which have generally been selected on a pragmatic basis. At the present state of CASE and workstation software, the most suitable software set is one which permits a variety of document, tabular, diagram and financial modelling formats to be:

- maintained as an inter-linked set;
- transferred where appropriate to the diagram and file formats required for later stages in the systems life cycle,

and which supports change management through object linking mechanisms - i.e. so that changes to a master are automatically propagated across secondary documentation

Any of the current generation market-leading 'Office suites' meet this requirement, if used with care. Their use should be supplemented by a CASE tool of choice.

As CASE tools mature further, it is a key objective that as much of the documentation as possible should be either delivered in the CASE tool of choice, or should be readily and automatically transferable into it. However, this goal must not be allowed to obstruct clarity or efficiency of the planning process or its products.

Responsibilities and ownership

The recommended responsibilities for provision of service, control and ownership are as follows:

- Responsibility for control of the process - *IS Department*
- Provision and support of the process - *IS Department*
- Provision of planning resources - *joint business and IS Department*
- Maintenance of baseline documents - *joint business and IS Department*

Development and maintenance of architectures. This includes data, application and technical architectures, as well as other infrastructure, such as software used in common by several business units. Primarily IS Department, but should be jointly funded and resourced with the business.

- Ownership of the resulting application plan - *sponsoring business units*
- Ownership of the technical plan - *IS Department*

It is noted that funding of IT infrastructure activities, i.e. those which are not wholly related to a single application development for a single customer, such as architecture definition, infrastructure development or maintaining the capability to undertake ISSP projects, is an issue which is outside of the scope of this report. However, a case can be made for a general overhead charge to cover such activities on the grounds that the critical mass achieved means that IS Department can offer economies of scale, compared to Business units carrying out such work individually. For this case to be valid, the following have to apply:

- the activity or investment has to be of sufficient intrinsic value - i.e. there must be clear tangible business benefits;
- IS Department need to be competitive on price, service and quality;
- there needs to be a 'critical mass' of business units pursuing broadly the same path.

The case for the first of these is addressed below. The second and third will require time and investment by IS Department investment to achieve. A case can be made for investment by IS Department in the mean time, both in the necessary capability and in the marketing.

Information architectures utilization and maintenance

There are four classes of architecture which are delivered from this project. In each case, the level of detail delivered is appropriate to a strategic level view, and continuing evolution, refinement of detail and maintenance is critical to the effectiveness of the Information Systems function, and to the ability of IS Department to deliver service.

The architecture products are:

- The functional, or 'business process' model
- The data entity model;
- The application systems architectures;

- The IT technical architecture.

The relevance and benefits of each is discussed briefly below, along with recommendations for control and resourcing of the necessary work.

Business process model

The business process model (see Chapter 8), also known as the function hierarchy, identifies business functions and processes independently of their grouping into organizational units or their present IS/IT support. It provides a basis for:

- identification of similar functions performed separately at present for different products or market sectors;
- identifying opportunities to consolidate common functions;
- reassessment of the most appropriate groupings of business functions into organizational units (together with items a and b, this process which has become known as 'business process re-engineering');
- assessment of the potential for common IS/IT support;
- continuing assessment and control of the functional scope and coverage of the application portfolio.

The product support matrices (chapters 7 and 8) represent an analysis of present approaches to organizational and systems implementation of the product support functions.

Data models

Logical data models (also known as entity models, see chapter 8) express the inherent, logical structure of business data, independently of the implementation form. They provide a basis for:

- the ability to integrate data views across business areas in ways which were not necessarily foreseen originally;
- delivery of business benefits which cannot be delivered effectively by any other means, such as the ability easily collate data from diverse sources to support key important performance indicators (KPIs);
- provision of systems which can be extended or changes much more easily, giving reduced marginal cost/time of enhancements
- more effective impact analysis and change control;
- more rapid and effective assessment of application packages.

Application architectures

The recommended application (or information systems) architectures are embodied in the Application Systems Maps (ASMs). They indicate at the logical or ideal level the main application systems and subsystems, and the information flows between them. In the IT planning process, they provide a basis for indicating business needs priorities in relation to potential IS support; and assessing the coverage offered by the present application portfolio. They were discussed in detail in chapter 8, and their usage further explored in chapters 10 and 11.

In later stages of the system development cycle, they can be valuable in:

- facilitating rapid, controlled change;
- assessing the business impact and dependencies of any proposed development or activity;
- control and management of design and change;
- more rapid and effective assessment of application packages.

Initial implementation steps

The following activities are involved:

a. Approval/acceptance of the final draft report;

b. Hand-over and implementation - responsibilities;

c. Dissemination, communication and selling - "hearts and minds";

d. Follow the plan;

e. Track progress;

f. Maintain the plan;

g. Extend, maintain and utilize the architectures.

IS department responsibilities

Process support and coordination

Considerable awareness and knowledge now exist as a result of the participation of IS Department personnel in the planning project. The main additional need is for a IS Department middle manager to be designated the co-ordinator for the strategic planning process and relationships with the Businesses. He or she should have sufficient resource available from September onwards to ensure continuity into:

a. consolidation of the strategic planning process and accompanying techniques and materials into IS Department procedures

b. follow-through into the first stages of implementation (see below)

c. support for the scoping and launch of further planning studies as required by the other businesses;

d. integration of the IS/IT strategic planning process with the relevant business and systems tactical planning cycles;

e. establishing a mechanism for tracking business events and planning activity so as to identify the need for review of existing IS plans.

Architecture standards and policies

Definition and ratification of standards and policies covering:

a. data architectures;

b. application architectures;

c. technical architectures.

Costs and resources estimation and refinement

This should further refine the results from the planning project, being aimed at developing realistic detailed estimates for application development as well as computer and network capacity projections. These estimates will need to reflect:

a. the limited amount of detail available in any strategic plan, and the consequent tolerances necessary for contingency;

b. previous experience both within the Group and from elsewhere;

c. the need for the resulting estimates to be owned and committed to by the personnel who will be implementing the plans

Plan handover and acceptance

Acceptance by IS Department of delivery of:

a. the information systems and technical architecture products;

b. computer and networking capacity requirements;

c. recommended technical development plans produced by the project;

Integration of the above with other relevant materials and with IS Department internal plans and procedures.

1. Adoption as appropriate of the strategic planning process itself, associated standards, use of software and absorption of experience in customization gained during the project.

2.   Full awareness of:

  ▪ the project results
  ▪ the rationale and basis for the conclusions
  ▪ the application development plans delivered

3.   Transfer of custodianship of all working files and papers.

Plan implementation and follow up

This provision covers:

a.   planning for use and support of the process in other business areas;

b.   consolidation and extension of the information systems and technical architectures, and their use as tools for quality management and change control (see the architecture projects identified in Section 5);

c.   support for maintenance of the information systems plans owned by each of the business units;

d.   conduct of the application developments recommended by the project;

e.   maintenance of the technical plans owned by IS Department.

This represents a continuing commitment which is best resourced by a full time architectural specialist. During slack periods, this specialist can become available to give specialist advice to key design projects. When the ISSP process is in operation for several business units, then there will be workload peaks during which additional resource will need to be co-opted. This will provide valuable familiarization and skills transfer.

Conduct of specific architecture development projects

These include:

a.   Business process model refinement;

b.   Application systems architectures refinement / integration;

c.   Integration of the business and information architecture products across the Group;

d.   Confirmation and refinement of architectural details through use of affinity analysis techniques;

e.   Development and use of Migration Architecture support materials.

Resource requirements for this will be driven by the state of play and complexity of the migration issues being addressed at any time. Specific resources should be funded from the budgets of the relevant implementation projects.

Activities a through d should run in parallel after handover. After initially peaking at approximately 2 persons full time, the workload should drop to a maintenance level of between half and one architecture analyst. This role would best be combined with the task of reviewing project and design proposals for compliance with the architectures.

Identification and evaluation of new technology opportunities

Most of the plan development and maintenance process described above is strongly business needs driven. However, every so often, significant innovations or marked changes in cost/performance of information technology may occur which, if exploited effectively, can offer significant business opportunities. It is likely that only a small proportion of such opportunities, even where detected, may prove worth pursuing. These opportunities are relatively unlikely to be detected by the business sufficiently early for them to be exploited for competitive advantage. The plan maintenance process should provide for this form of input.

IS Department should continue to play a key role for each business unit in detecting, evaluating and supporting the exploitation of such opportunities. There should be a formally identified Research and Development fund for this purpose, to which Business units contribute. This activity should include tracking the use of advanced IT by competitors.

APPENDIX I

References and bibliography

Allen, B. (1987). *Make Information Services Pay its Way.* Harvard Business Review Jan/Feb '87.

Alloway, R. M. and Quillard, J. A. (1981). *Top Priorities for the Information Systems Function.* Sloan School of Management, MIT. CSIR no 79, Sept '81.

Anthony, R. N. (1965). *Planning and Control Systems.* Harvard Business School Press, Boston.

Boar, B. H. (1993). *The Art of Strategic Planning for IT.* Wiley & Sons NY.

Bullen, C. V. and Rockart, J. F. (1981). *A Primer on Critical Success Factors*, Sloan School of Management, MIT. CSIR no 69, June '81.

Bunn, G., Bartlett, C., McLean, D. (1989). *United Kingdom Government CCTA Information Systems Guide A2: Strategic Planning for Information Systems.* John Wiley & Sons Chichester.

CCTA (1993). *Applying Soft Systems Methodology to an SSADM Feasibility Study.* HMSO.

Checkland, P. B. (1981). *Systems Thinking, Systems Practice*, Wiley, Chichester, Sussex.

Cottrell, N. and Rapley, K. (1991). *Factors critical to the success of executive information systems in British Airways.* Eur. J. Inf. Systs Vol 1 no 1 '91.

Coveney, P. and Highfield, R. (1991). *The Arrow of Time*, Flamingo.

Datamation Magazine. (1987). *Industry by Industry IS Survey.* Datamation Sept. '87.

Davenport, T. H. and Short, J. E. (1990). *The New Industrial Engineering: Information Technology and Business Process Redesign.* Sloan Management Review, Summer '90.

Drucker, P. F. (1993). *Post Capitalist Society.* Butterworth-Heinemann, Oxford.

Ernst and Young USA (1990). *The Navigator Systems Series - Overview Monograph.* Ernst and Young USA.

Feeny, D. F., Edwards, B. R. and Earl, M.J. (1987). *Complex Organisations and the Information Systems Function - A Research Study.* Available from the Oxford Institute of Information Management, The Oxford Centre for Management Studies, Templeton College, Oxford.

Fredericks, P. and Venkatraman, N. (1988). *The Rise of Strategy Support Systems.* Sloan Management Review Spring '88 Vol 29 no 3.

Galliers, R. D. (1987). *Information Systems Planning in the United Kingdom and Australia - a Comparison of Current Practice.* Oxford Surveys in Information technology, Vol 4, '87.

Galliers, R. D. (1987). *Information Analysis - Selected Readings.* Addison Wesley.

Galliers, R. D. (1991). *Strategic information systems planning: myths, reality and guidelines for successful implementation.* Eur. J. Inf. Systs Vol 1 no 1 '91.

Gartner Group (1993). *Client/Server Computing Strategies for the 1990s: Part 1.* InSide Gartner Group This Week. July 28, 1993.

Gerrity, T. P., and Rockart, J. F. (1986). *End-User Computing: Are You a Leader or a Laggard?.* Sloan Management Review Summer '86.

Goold, M. and Campbell, A. (1987). *Many Best Ways to Make Strategy.* Harvard Business Review Nov/Dec '87.

Hammer, M. (1990). *Reengineering Work: Don't Automate, Obliterate.* Harvard Business Review July/August '90.

Hammer, M. and Champy, J. (1993). *Re-engineering the Corporation - a Manifesto for Business Revolution.* Nicholas Brealy.

Hardaker, M. and Ward, B. K. (1987). *How to make a Team Work.* Harvard Business Review Nov/Dec '87.

Hussey, D. E. (3rd ed 1983). *Introducing Corporate Planning.* Pergamon Press.

Kearney, A. T. & Co. (1985). *The Barriers and Opportunities of Information Technology - A Management Overview.* Sponsored by the IAM and the UK Government Dept. of Trade & Industry.

Kearney, A. T. & Co. (1990). *Barriers II (to the effective use if Information Technology).* Sponsored by the IAM and the UK Government Dept. of Trade & Industry.

Keene, P. G. W. (1978). *Decision Support Systems - An Organisational Perspective.* Addison Wesley.

la Belle, A. and Noyce, H.E. (1988). *Whither the IT Organisation?* Sloan Management Review Spring '88 Vol 29 no3.

Lovett, P. D. (1988). *Meetings that Work - Plans Bosses can Aprove.* Harvard Business Review Nov/Dec '88

Martin, J. (1982). *Strategic Data Planning Methodologies.* Prentice Hall.

McFarlan, F. W. (1981). *Portfolio Approach to Information Systems.* Harvard Business ReviewSept/Oct '81.

McFarlan, F. W. (1984). *IT Changes to way you Compete.* Harvard Business Review May/June '84.

Meyer, N. D. and Boone, M. E. (1987). *The Information Edge.* McGraw Hill.

Nolan Norton & Co (1985-87). *Stage by Stage - The Economics of Computing in the Advanced Stages.* Series of Client Newsletters.

Oliva, T. A., Day, D. L. and DeSarbo, W. S. (1987). *Selecting Competitive Tactics - Try a Strategy Map.* Sloan Management Review Spring '87.

Parker, M. M. and Benson, R. J. (1989). *Information Economics.* Prentice Hall.

Penrose, R. (1989). *The Emperor's New Mind.* Vintage Press, London.

Peters, T. J. and Waterman R. H. Jr. (1982). *In Search of Excellence.* Harper & Row.

Porter, M. E. (1980). *Competitive Strategy.* Free Press.

Porter, M. E. (1985). *Competitive Advantage.* Free Press

Porter, M. E. (1987). *From Competitive Advantage to Corporate Strategy.* Harvard Business Review May/June '87.

Price Waterhouse & Co. (1991, '92, '93). *Information Technology Review.* Price Waterhouse & Co.

Remenyi, D. S. J., Money, A. and Twite, A. (1993). *A Guide to Measuring and Managing IT Benefits.* 2nd ed NCC Blackwell, Oxford.

Rouse, W. B. (1993). *Catalysts for Change.* Wiley & Sons NY.

Somogyi, E. K. and Galliers, R. D. (1987). *Towards Strategic Information Systems - Volume 1.* Abacus Press.

Tozer, E. E. (1988). *Planning for Effective Business Information Systems.* Pergamon Press.

Ward, J., Griffiths, P. and Whitemore, P. (1990). *Strategic Planning for Information Systems.* Wiley.

APPENDIX II

Sample work programs

Approach

This Appendix comprises two separate example sets. No apology is made for this – it comes out different every time.

Key principles are:

- Start with a clear vision of what you have to produce
- Identify key intermediate deliverables and process stages
- Consult standard templates, task lists and deliverables sets, and select the subset which is most appropriate
- Customize and prune
- Prune again
- Complete estimates and resource loadings
- Review availability of skilled staff
- Prune again until you can show that you can deliver what is needed within realistic resource and time scale constraints
- Make absolutely clear what management have to do to contribute their share of effort to the process – it will be far more than they thought!
- Review and adjust the plans again

Sample set 1

Phase 0 Determine context and scope

1.1.a   Establish study scope and context

Work step	Product
1. Initiate the scoping review	■ Agreed team, management framework, plan and schedule for the scoping review. ■ Agreed specification of the process to be followed and the timing, format and review process for all deliverables.

2. Information collection and analysis:
  ■ review of business plans & status
  ■ selected senior management interviews
  ■ analysis of all other relevant documents
	■ Complete set of materials and scoping level interview results on which to base conclusions.
	■ Results of investigations and analysis ready for synthesis stage.
	■ Clear identification of all material issues, and a plan for the resolution of each.

3. Synthesis:
  ■ what studies are needed (if any)
  ■ what are the key issues, risks, CSFs and dependencies for them
  ■ what risk control measures are needed
  ■ what overall coordination mechanisms are needed
	■ Identification of each area where IS or business strategy needs to be formulated or overhauled.
	■ For each:
	  ■ outline project brief for strategy review where needed
	  ■ risk assessment
	  ■ dependencies
	  ■ definition of external key issues needing senior management resolution

4. Integrate and document conclusions	■ Scope, terms of reference and plans for each strategic review ■ Specification of the steering and control mechanisms ■ Brief for project management and risk control processes

1.1.b   Project initiation

Work step	Product
1. Establish team, brief participants fully	
2. Arrange project environment	
3. Set up Project Log	■ Project Diary ■ Personnel Profiles ■ Scheduled Absence List ■ Milestones Log ■ Change Control Log ■ Performance Index ■ Progress Log ■ Assumptions ■ External Constraints
4. Set up Steering Group, brief Group on roles and responsibilities	Steering Group composition, scope and terms of reference
5. Set up QA/review procedures	Agreed review procedures
6. Set up cross-project liaison with other relevant concurrent business and IS/IT projects.	Agreed liaison procedures

7.	Develop, review and confirm statement of scope and terms of reference and expected deliverables from the assignment	Agreed definition of scope objectives, terms of reference and deliverables
8.	Specify and agree all relevant planning assumptions and other 'givens'	Specification of assumptions and 'givens'
9.	Draw up detailed work plan and load project resources	Detailed work plan and resource schedule, with commitment to meet it.
10.	Complete team building and training	Committed team, with requisite skills
11.	Prepare format of key deliverables for agreement	Key deliverables format
12.	Agree procedure for transfer of knowledge and processes to the staff of the organisation to support planning cycles	Agreed plan and participants for knowledge transfer

Phase 1 Determine business information and support needs

1.2   **Preparatory information collection**

1.2.a.   **Assess business plans, directions and vision**

	Work step	**Product**
1.	Determine approach to be followed and obtain senior management agreement.	Agreed plan and approach Outline specification of process to be followed. Senior management commitment to participate.
2.	Prepare generic templates and business models.	First draft templates and models
3.	Prepare planning assumptions statements and draft topic lists for workshop sessions	Planning assumptions. Draft topic lists and other starter materials.
4.	Identify workshop participants and facilitators; allocate other roles for workshops	
5.	Schedule workshop sessions	Agreed schedule
6.	Conduct first stage business directions workshop session	Agreed division of business topics, responsibilities, process and time scale to address them
7.	Run parallel business task groups between workshops	Deliverables to second workshop as agreed at first workshop.
8.	Conduct second stage business directions session	Statements of business vision, direction and areas of likely priority or volatility as needed to direct to IS/IT strategy.
9.	Analyse conclusions and update assumptions and business models	High level business direction statements supported by assessment of options, impact and contingency. Clearly identified assumptions and identification of critical business issues and factors. Revisions to business models

1.2.b	Determine current IS/IT systems status	
Work step		**Product**
1.	Assemble inventory of all current systems, hardware and software, including:	IS/IT Inventory
	■ applications ■ databases	
	■ package software ■ systems software	
	■ communications ■ DBMS	
	■ external services ■ user procedures	
	■ committed plans and development projects	
	using existing documentation and expertise wherever possible	
2.	Obtain systems upgrade/development plans already proposed/being actioned.	Systems development/upgrade plans and their approval/implementation status.

1.3	Determine business information and support needs	
Work step		**Product**
1.	Arrange interview schedule in each selected Business Unit, and Group Function.	Senior management interview schedule.
2.	Analyse Business strategies and objectives for each Business Unit and Group Function	Documented queries and clarifications of Business strategy and objectives
3.	Analyse product plans for each Business Unit and Group Function	Documented queries and clarifications of product strategy.
4	Analyse IT strategies and objectives for each Business Unit and Group Function	Documented queries and clarifications of clarifications of IT strategy.
5	Tailor interview questionnaire and organisational unit pro-formas	Interview questionnaires. Organisational Unit pro-formas.
6	Review background information on interviewee including job description, performance objectives, previous interviews, etc.	Pre-interview analyses
7	Conduct structured interviews with key Senior Management to update/confirm understanding of Business goals and strategies, and to determine the most effective approach to confirm/update Business needs	Documentation of: ■ Business objectives and strategies ■ Key features of business functional structure ■ Key features of Business information structure ■ CSFs and performance measures ■ Key issues and priorities
8	Prepare post-interview analysis and verify with each interviewee	Post Interview Analyses with confirmed needs, Statement of key issues & Priorities. (To be progressively refined) Business Function Hierarchy Decision summaries.
9	Confirm key Business processes, objectives and priorities	Business functions, objectives and priorities statement. Business function hierarchy.
10.	Confirm information needed by management to perform functions	Information needs analyses Information needs statement for each Business Unit and Group Function selected. Statement of priorities.

11.	Prepare draft consolidated statement of Business information and support needs	Consolidated statement of Business Information and support needs (CBINS)
12	Conduct follow up group sessions attended by key managers/staff to reach consensus on top needs, key issues, priorities, unresolved matters, etc., across each area.	Top needs and issues for for each business.
13.	Integrate the CBINS across Business Units and at Group level	CBINS further consolidated across business units and operating companies.
14.	Prepare a statement of key concerns identified and prioritized by management.	Statement of Consolidated Issues.
15.	Conduct workshop with key Business Management to confirm Top Needs and Issues and to recruit and confirm sponsors.	Signed off CBINS with agreed priorities and sponsors Action plan for each sponsor or area
16.	Commence sponsor support – preliminary identification of business benefits	Agreed basis for definition of business benefits. Initial basis for key benefit areas

Phase 2 – establish information architectures, identify strategic targets and options

2.1 Assess current IS/IT status

	Work step	Product
1.	Analyse systems key strengths and weaknesses, making use of any recent work already done.	Strengths and weaknesses statement for each system against five criteria: ■ meeting user's business needs ■ operational stability ■ response and throughput ■ security, availability and integrity ■ potential as a basis for future development
2.	Evaluate status against emerging requirements, and assign preliminary priorities for attention.	Preliminary priorities for IS/IT attention
3.	Arrange for urgent, easy to implement enhancements to be actioned.	Urgent, easy to implement enhancements to current systems.
4.	Identify/assess current current IT skills by: ■ systems ■ business area ■ technical skill ■ management skill to evaluate the suitability of current resources for future requirements and to formulate resultant training plans	IT personnel assessments including skills matrix.
5.	Analyse current and planned work in progress in relation to agreed business priorities.	Analysis of IT Work in progress

2.2 Develop and refine business process model, is and data architecture

	Work step	Product
1.	Using available architecture products, set up frameworks for the data model and application systems map.	Early draft of business process schematic. First draft data model. Outline application systems map.
2.	Infer the main application delivery & feeder subsystems and associated data needed to deliver the stated information and automation needs (working from CBINS)	Information needs analysis statements. Application systems processes. Preliminary identification of data subject area databases.

3.	Progressively map the application processing identified into the application systems map.	Growing detail on the application systems map.
4.	Progressively map the data entities identified into overall data models.	Draft subject databases Draft data models.
5.	Refine business function definitions	Business process model Refined and extended definitions of business functions.
6.	Refine data analysis to yield conceptual data models	Firm corporate data model and data subject area definitions.
7.	Perform usage/sensitivity analysis of data entities by: ■ Data Entity/Function ■ Data Entity/Application Process ■ Function/Application Process ■ Function/Organisation Unit	Data usage priorities and maintenance responsibilities. Usage matrices and cluster analysis results. Data redundancy. Redundant systems/processes Basis for interaction with Business process reengineering activities
8.	Analyse product support functions, responsibilities and use of systems	Identification of replicated functionality and/or duplication of systems. Basis for rationalisation and /or design of multiple use systems.
9.	Analyse user department and business function use of data and systems	Definition of data creation and usage responsibilities.
10.	Preliminary grouping of functions into applications areas.	Draft Application System Schematic.
11.	Preliminary identification of conceptual databases	Relation of subject data areas to conceptual databases.

2.3   Establish initial options for strategic solutions

	Work step	Product
1.	Map current and planned systems/projects to the application systems map.	Statement of current and planned coverage.
2.	Rate current systems, development projects and committed tactical plans on a McFarlan Portfolio matrix to assess the level and type of investment made or planned in relation to that which is which is appropriate.	Populated McFarlan matrices showing for each system: ■ its actual position in relation to its optimal position ■ the nature of its expected contribution and hence investment merited
3.	Map current data structures to target data architecture	Current and planned data coverage.
4.	Indicate coverage ratings/identify gaps	Target systems and data shortfall analysis.
5.	Identify mismatches with consolidated business requirements and add commentary to CBINS to support sponsor negotiation	Identified application areas with high associated business priority but weak or absent current application cover
6.	For each mis-match, identify a range of options for addressing it	Preliminary application options for each key need: ■ new system/enhance old ■ package or custom ■ quick and dirty vs. long life system

2.4	Initiate development of business cases	
	Work step	**Product**
1.	Agree business case approach	Agreed guidelines for quantifying business benefits and for formulating business cases.
2.	For each CBINS entry, reconfirm identification of sponsors and supporters and progress the identification of business benefits and development of business cases for each requirement.	Extended CBINS with benefits and systems coverage commentary. Results of sponsor negotiations re priority and benefits. Outline business cases.

Phase 3 Determine strategic solutions

3.1	Identify, agree and initiate urgent actions	
	Work step	**Product**
1.	Identify high priority business needs which can be met by projects which: ▪ Are not dependent upon long term outcomes. ▪ Can be implemented using rapid development methods.	Recommendations for urgent action and revision to project plans and resource schedules.
2.	Produce short project definition for each recommended urgent action.	Urgent action project definitions.
3.	Identify any areas which are at present using significantly higher resources than priorities merit.	Recommendations of revision to plans and schedules.

Note: urgent actions relate to small resource, short time scale requirement projects which address high priority/high payback needs.

3.2	Select and integrate strategic solutions	
3.2.a	**Application priorities/solutions**	
	Work step	**Product**
1.	Refine definition of application systems areas & priorities	Refined overall application systems schematic showing data flows and agreed coverage assessments. Reflection of CBINS priorities onto application systems. Synopsis for each candidate application subsystem, with statement of options for meeting it.
2.	Refine Definition of Refined Conceptual Databases	Corporate Data Model. Refined Definition of Subject Databases. Refined Application Systems/Data Usage Matrix.
3.	Assess strengths, weaknesses opportunities & risks of each candidate option for each key area of application need	Options assessment worksheets for each key application need
4.	Draft first cut synopses of application solutions	Definition of each 'real' application system and database.
5.	Perform logical distribution analysis (data and process), based on location(s) where service is required	Access requirements for data and process by type, location, user population and workload volume.
6.	Logical distribution analysis for data & process by business	Access Requirements for Data & Process by location location & user classification.

3.2.b	Derive technical classes and platform requirements	
7.	Determine classes of application to be supported (e.g. Transaction, MIS, EIS, DSS, OA, etc. and split by size)	Class Definitions Allocation of Application Processes to Class
8.	Determine technical characteristics needed to support each class of application	Technical architecture requirements for each Application Class.

3.2.c	Establish migration priorities/dependencies & systems groupings	
9.	Determine physical distribution policies	Computer sites/facilities Communications network policy.
10.	Identify key implementation priorities, constraints and options	Statement of priorities, dependencies and constraints.
11.	Assemble business volumes & relate to functions needed	Business workload volumes projected by application & scenario over time.

3.3	Evaluate IT status/set key directions	
	Work step	**Product**
1.	Collect, review and analyse current technical plans and strategy	Statement of current and technical plans and strategy.
2.	Define technical classes to meet the needs of application classes	Definition of technical characteristics needed to support each class of application. Identity of Technical class.
3.	Assess nature and broad volume needs by class of technical architecture	Basis for developing capacity needs by application class and time phase.
4.	Assess current support for each class of technical architecture	Verified statement of current status for all IT items. Assessment of Strengths & Weaknesses.
5.	Define list of technical areas, principles & options	List of areas. Statement of principles and options for each area.
6.	Consult vendors & industry sources for each key IT component	Assessment of Vendors & Key Directions.
7.	Assemble & assess expertise on status & direction for each key technology component	Statement of opportunity, direction & risk for each technology area, showing preferred options.
8.	Develop a direction statement for each technical architecture class, showing: ■ component type ■ broad capacity needs ■ recommended policies and directions for 3 to 5 years out.	IT strategic direction statements.

3.4	Progress preparation of business cases	
	Work step	**Product**
1.	Maintain dialogue with sponsors as candidate applications emerge. Ensure that business criteria are reflected in the options selection process. Ensure that sponsors understand the implication of dependencies, and exercise appropriate judgement over timing of benefits, interim solutions, etc.	Committed sponsors who understand and support the way in which their business needs are reflected in the emerging solutions, and who will follow through into supporting the projects. Business cases which support the emerging solutions.

Phase 4 Prepare and deliver implementation plans

4.1   Develop applications and database development plans

	Work step	Product
1.	Agree ideal target state	Agreed version of target application and database strategic targets and solutions from Phase 3.
2.	Verify achievability of target states	Potential interim migration milestones, with associated business case issues. Results of assessment of business and technical viability of end-point.
3.	Confirm key milestones to be achieved in moving to the strategic target	Definition of milestones Definition of transition route and options.
4.	Undertake dependency analysis and identify other planning issues	Statement of all factors relevant to a practical, workable plan.
5.	Analyse options, priorities, interfaces, dependencies and compare with ranking criteria	Impact on ideal business development sequence of application & technical dependencies.
6.	Iterate with business sponsors until most satisfactory project phasing/packaging solutions are attained	Alternative targets and migration assessments of each. Recommended compromise on delivery order & rate for key systems.
7.	Package migration steps into appropriate phased development projects.	Agreed project synopses and phasing solutions.
8.	Assess technical and financial feasibility and iterate	Result of evaluation. Agreed cost/benefit outlines for systems. Agreed application development schedule.
9.	Write synopsis for each priority project/action	Synopsis for each systems project /action.
10.	Integrate with technical & organisational plans showing complete set of application systems and technical projects to be undertaken to achieve milestones	Project definitions • application processes • database usage • resources • time scales • business cases.

4.2   Develop technical development plan

	Work step	Product
1.	Confirm allocation of applications and databases to technical environments/platforms	Agreed placement of applications and databases to technical platforms
2.	Confirm physical placement of applications and data	Recommended mapping of applications and databases to physical locations.
3.	Derive placement of IT components to implement platforms for preferred target & interim states.	Recommended physical for all components
4.	Iterate with technical constraints	Impact analysis of alternative physical distribution options. Confirmed recommendations for physical distribution

5.	Map business volumes into project & technical units & develop capacity needs by application, technical environment & time phase	Human & computer workload & capacity needs by application, technical environment, development & time phase. Assessment of quantity & type of computing capacity at each site. Communications network capacity estimates.
6.	Review and confirm technical strategy, take technical selection decisions where appropriate, else define follow-on projects to confirm	Updated technical position statements for each topic. Technical development plans covering all work needed to establish: ■ Mainframe H/W & S/W ■ Network & Terminals ■ OA Facilities ■ DBMS & TP S/W ■ Application Development Environment ■ MIS/EIS delivery system
7.	Define all technical development projects	Technical development project synopses
8.	Develop Technical Cost/Benefit	Tech/Infrastructure Cost/Benefit Statement Linked to Business Benefit.
9.	Integrate & Confirm Broad Capacity Plan for Each resource Type	Broad Capacity Plan. Project Definition & Scope For More Detailed Capacity Plan If Needed.
10.	Document Technical Plan	Summary List Of Technical Development Projects & Costs. Resulting resources schedule.

4.3   Develop staff skills/resources/organisation plans

	Work step	Product
1.	Identify Business, Corporate Function organisational impact.	Recommendations & Observations Statement.
2.	Define IS Division Organisational Impact	Roles & Responsibilities By Function & Location. Skills/ Resource Requirements By Time Phase.
3.	Define Complete set of functions for IS organisation	Definition Of Role & Skill Requirements. Job Description For New/Revised Roles.
4.	Integrate Skills/Resources Required from other plans	Consolidated Skills/Resources Profile.
5.	Compare skill requirement with Current skills	Statement of Training Needs/Upgrades for Skills/ Resource Levels.
6.	Define Organisation Groupings	Revised ISD Organisation Plan and Job Descriptions.
7.	Assess how to meet recruitment, development & training plans	Recruitment & Skills Development Plan.

4.4   Assemble and balance business cases for all developments

	Work step	Product
1.	Integrate plans and cost/benefit schedules	Integrated costs and benefit schedules. Phased resource plan
2.	Obtain/reaffirm business sponsor support	Sponsor commitment to all recommendations

4.5	**Present plans and arrange their implementation**	
4.5a	**Prepare draft report**	

	Work step	**Product**
1.	Summarise findings and present verbally in draft	Board/Steering Group presentation. Findings accepted in principle
2.	Agree main report structure and contents; review/ approval process	Agreed report structure Agreed report review and approval process
3.	Draft main report sections.	Main report first draft.
4.	Issue main report draft for review and approval.	

4.5.b	**Finalise main report**	
5.	Manage QA review cycle	
6.	Include modifications.	
7.	Present final report	Final report

4.5.c	**Carry out handover**	
8.	Arrange and give seminar for handover of planning process.	Seminar. Planning Process.
9.	Finalise transfer of planning process and deliverables	Information Planning process and deliverables.
10.	Agree and implement change control and maintenance procedures for IS/IT strategic and tactical plans.	Working, documented mechanism & procedure for plan maintenance
11.	Ensure integration of IS, IT and business strategic and tactical planning cycles	Effective, integrated business and IS/IT planning cycles

Ongoing tasks

	Work step	**Product**
1.	Project management	Project Log.
2.	Administration	
3.	Sessions with key management/staff as required in order to: ■ keep informed on progress ■ ensure active participation, commitment to project and benefits ■ ascertain changes in business directions and priorities	Reconfirmation of business plans, levels of support, priorities and outline benefits.
4.	Quality Assurance process	Reviewed process and key deliverables.
5.	Project Steering	Minutes and decisions.

Sample set 2

	TASKS	PRODUCTS	Original estimates			
Ref	Description		Estimating basis	Man days	start date	end date

Phase 0 – Establish Study Context and Scope

1.1   Establish study context and scope; initiate the study

Ref	Description	Products	Estimating basis	Man days		
1.1.1	Assess business status, environment, existing plans and strategies	▪ summary of key business directions and options ▪ high level assessment of current plans and their relevance ▪ summary of key business, is and it issues	Dependent on the business size and complexity, and on the volatility of the environment	5.0		
1.1.2	Determine the need for development or revision of business, is or it plans	Inventory of planning needs and rationale for each		2.0		
1.1.3	Develop business case & scope definition for each study	Business case and scope definition for each study		5.0		
1.1.4	Identify and recruit senior management sponsor(s).	Committed sponsor		2.0		
1.1.5	Specify arrangements for overall coordination of planning activities	Definition of overall coordination and control process		1.0		
1.1.6	Specify steering and control arrangements for the is strategy study	Definition of steering & control arrangements		1.0		
1.1.7	Develop work plans for the study	Work program, with resource & timescale estimates.	Customize this version	2.0		
1.1.8	Select and assemble team	Initial team in place & trained as necessary.	Interviews, training	5.0		
			Phase 0 sub-total	**23.0**		

Phase 1 - Determine Business Information & Support needs

1.2   Preparatory Information Collection

Ref	Description	Products	Estimating basis	Man days		
1.2.1	Identify information sources and allocate responsibility for assembling each class of information.	▪ list of sources. ▪ agreed responsibilities & schedules for information collection ▪ resource estimates for information collection.		2.0		
1.2.2	Draw up and modify/customize questionnaires and forms for information collection.	Forms, procedures and questionaires for information collection.	Modify material supplied	2.0		
1.2.3	Assemble and review all relevant materials on business plans, organization, position competition and marketplace.	Inventory of all relevant business materials.		10.0		
1.2.4	Draw up priority list of topics needing to be resolved prior to commencing the interview cycle.	Commentary/questions to be resolved, with plan for resolution of each.	Covered in 1.2.3	1.0		

	TASKS	PRODUCTS	Original estimates			
Ref	Description		Estimating basis	Man days	start date	end date
1.2.5	Assemble inventory of current applications and databases, including ongoing development projects and tactical plans.	Complete inventory of applications, with preliminary assessments of each.	highly variable	10.0		
1.2.6	Collect and assess inventory of current it assets/equipment, including computers of all kinds and sizes, external services used, staff skills resources, and systems software, including plans.	Complete inventory of it assets, both current and planned.	highly variable	10.0		
			sub-total 35.0			
1.3	Determine Business Information and Support Needs					
1.3.1	Review business plans and strategies as documented prior to interviews.	Documented clarifications of business planning documents.	Follow on from 1.2.2/ 3	6.0		
1.3.2	Arrange first cycle of interviews	Senior management interview schedule	secretarial	2.0		
1.3.3	Conduct interviews with board and senior management team, plus selected other key personnel. **NB:** In a small to medium sized organization, there may be only a single cycle of interviews needed – omit steps 1.3.8 to 1.3.11 in this case.	1. key issues summary 2. interview analyzes 3. preliminary statement of business inf. needs	2 persons/interview For 1.3.3 thru 1.3.5, allow 20 to 25 man hrs per interviewee. 5 interviews assumed	15.0		
1.3.4	Analyze first cycle of management interviews	4. preliminary statements of: ▪ business goals & strategies ▪ key features of business functional structure. ▪ key features of business inf. structure.	included in above			
1.3.5	Review and feedback to agree results of interviews and analysis.	Agreed statements of need and priority at individual level.	consensus meeting 3 team members @ 1/2 day plus analysis/amendment	3.0		
1.3.6	First management checkpoint	Agreement on key business directions, finalised, scope, objectives & time scale for the study. finalised scope, objectives & time- scale for the study.	Steering group meeting	1.0		
1.3.7	Review detailed plans and estimates for the main body of the project	▪ agreed schedule for second cycle of interviews interviews ▪ documentation formats ▪ resource estimates and timescale ▪ schedule of deliverables		2.0		
1.3.8	Arrange remaining management interviews.	▪ extended and revised management interview schedule		2.0		

	TASKS	PRODUCTS	Original estimates			
Ref	Description		Estimating basis	Man days	start date	end date
1.3.9	Carry out second cycle of management interviews		2 persons/interview For 1.3.9 thru 1.3.10, allow 20 to 25 man hrs per interviewee. Assumed 10 single interviews @ 3 m.d. + 5 groups @ 5 m.d.	55.0		
1.3.10	analyze second cycle of management interviews	▪ interview analyzes ▪ key issues summary ▪ progressively refined stmnt of buss. inf. needs ▪ integrated business fn hierarchy ▪ analysis of product/service support approach and needs	included in above			
1.3.11	Review and feedback to agree results of interviews and analysis.	Agreed statements of need and priority at each individual level.	included in above			
1.3.12	Consolidate & prioritize business information needs, based on results of all interviews	▪ consolidated & prioritized business info. & support needs statement for each business area and information level. 'cbins'	2 man hrs/interview	7.0		
1.3.13	Review and confirm with line managers, then across functional boundaries. finally, obtain consensus with senior management.	▪ approved version of statement of business information and support needs, with committed sponsors.	3 group sessions plus one at Board-level, each ' 2 m.d.	8.0		
			sub-total	101.0		
			Phase 1 sub-total	136.0		

Phase 2 – Establish Information Architectures and Options

2.1   Assess Current Applications & IT Technical Status

2.1.1	Assess all current application systems and projects, incl. end user & external. assess & document the key strengths & weaknesses of each.	Strengths & weaknesses statement for each system, covering: ▪ user opinion ▪ reliability ▪ maintainability ▪ design quality ▪ basis for evolution	1/2 man day per application area; 20 areas	10.0		
2.1.2	Assess current inventory of it technical items, and staff skills/resource base, along with future plans.	▪ verified inventory of all hardware, communications and related equipment. ▪ assessment of status, strengths & weaknesses of each		5.0		

	TASKS	PRODUCTS	Original estimates			
Ref	Description		Estimating basis	Man days	start date	end date
2.1.3	Assess degree of match of the current application systems with the new statements of business information needs	■ assessment of the degree of cover offered by current systems, project and plans for the new/revised statements of business information and support needs (CBINS)	Dependent on complexity	5.0		
2.1.4	Assign priorities for urgent attention.	Urgent priorities, ranked		1.0		
2.1.5	Agree criteria for cost/benefit	■ cost/benefit criteria ■ agreed sponsorship roles		1.0		
			sub-total	**22.0**		
2.2	**Develop Information Architectures**					
2.2.1	Set up initial frameworks for the data entity models and application system flows.	■ outline data model ■ outline application framework	depends on complexity	4.0		
2.2.2	Infer the main application delivery and feeder sub- systems and associated data needed to deliver the stated information and support needs.	■ information needs analysis statements ■ application system processes ■ preliminary informal identification of data subject areas.	depends on complexity	5.0		
2.2.3	Progressively map the application processes identified into the application framework.	■ draft application process map – overall & by functional area.	Growth in detail in application systems process	3.0		
2.2.4	Progressively map the data entities identified into overall data models.	■ first draft subject databases ■ first draft data models		2.0		
2.2.5	Progressively develop and refine the application systems process flows and definitions.	■ application system process map ■ refined & extended definitions of applications system processes	20 application areas @ 1/2 day each	5.0		
2.2.6	Refine data analysis prior to identifying subject databases	■ firm (but not detailed) corporate data subject database definitions. ■ data entity definitionsmodel & data		2.0		
2.2.7	Perform usage/ sensitivity analysis ■ data entity/function ■ data entity/ application process ■ function/ application process ■ function/organization unit ■ product support processes and responsibilities	■ usage matrices & cluster analysis ■ basis for defining data usage priorities & maintenance responsibilities ■ raw material for potential re-engineering and/or rationalization of of business processes.	relatively informal allowance for greater depth, e.g. in re-engineering is not included	5.0		

	TASKS	PRODUCTS	Original estimates			
Ref	Description		Estimating basis	Man days	start date	end date
2.2.8	analyze user departments' and business functional use of data and application systems elements.	■ definition of data creation & usage responsibilities ■ raw material for potential re-engineering and/or rationali-zation of of business proc-esses.	relatively informal allowance for greater depth, e.g. in re-engi-neering is not included	3.0		
2.2.9	Preliminary grouping of application proc-esses into natural units – systems and sub-systems.	■ application process map grouped into preliminary subsystems – the ideal appli-cation portfolio		2.0		
2.2.10	Preliminary identification of conceptual databases.	■ initial grouping of data enti-ties into conceptual data-bases		2.0		
			sub-total	**33.0**		
2.3	**Establish initial options for strategic solutions**					
2.3.1	Review coverage assessment from 2.1.3. Identify preliminary options for meeting key gaps and weaknesses in current cov-erage.	■ specific needs framed in terms of application function with draft relative priorities associated ■ current application portfolio matched to the ideal	50 priority CBINS entries @ 5/day	10		
2.3.2	Review and agree relative priorities with sponsors	■ agreed 'ideal' business delivery rate and sequence	More meetings!	3.0		
2.3.3	Develop a range of alternative outline application solutions for each related group of needs	■ sets of alternative candidate enhancements to the appli-cation portfolio	10 key areas, 1 m.d.	10		
2.3.4	Feed back interim results to information architectures	■ modifications to information architectures		2		
			sub-total	**25.0**		
2.4	**Develop business cases for meeting business needs**					
2.4.1	Assign sponsorship role for each needs area	Committed sponsors		1.0		
2.4.2	Agree business case approach	Agreed headings & criteria for business case		2.0		
2.4.3	Develop business cases	■ business cases for all high priority needs ■ understanding of the way in which business benefits must phase in	20 areas @ 1/2 day	10.0		
			sub-total	**13.0**		
			Phase 2 – sub-total	**93.0**		

	TASKS	PRODUCTS	Original estimates			
Ref	Description		Estimating basis	Man days	start date	end date

Phase 3 – Determine Strategic Solutions

3.1   Identify and initiate urgent actions

Ref	Description	Products	Estimating basis	Man days
3.1.1	Identify high priority business needs which can be met by projects which: -are relatively independent -can be implemented safely using rapid development techniques	■ rapid development project definitions ■ urgent skills upgrade plans. ■ purchase proposals for 4GL e.t.c.	Mostly clearly apparent	3.0
3.1.2	Identify any areas which are at present using significantly higher or lower levels of resource than merited by priorities	■ revised project plans ■ revised resource allocation		2.0
3.1.3	Develop & agree definitions of rapid dev't projects	■ rapid dev't project proposals ■ short term plans	10 projects @ 1/2 day	5.0
3.1.4	Carry out redeployment of resources, retraining, etc	■ revised resource/skills schedule	highly variable	1.0
			sub-total	**11.0**

3.2   Determine application and database strategic solutions

Ref	Description	Products	Estimating basis	Man days
3.2.1	Assemble complete information on: ■ candidate options and solutions ■ dependencies and constraints	■ complete basis for selection of strategic solutions		1.0
3.2.2	Undertake logical distribution analysis analysis for data and process by business site	■ access requ'mts for data & process by location and user classification.		2.0

3.2.3	For each key needs area evaluate options established in stage 2.3 and select the preferred candidate; log the reasons and rationale for the conclusions	■ definition of preferred application and database solution for:
		  ■ each application need
		  ■ each real database.
				5.0

NB: this step to include consideration of issues such as new versus modify, custom versus package etc.		■ reasons for selections made ■ preliminary costs & benefits by subsystem		
3.2.4	Consider integration aspects of the application solutions; tune and modify decisions accordingly	Updated outputs from 3.2.2/ 3.2.3	included in above	
3.2.5	Determine classes of application to be supported (eg transaction,mis,dss,etc, and split by size).	■ application class definitions ■ allocation of application processes to classes.		1.0
3.2.6	Determine technical characteristics needed to support each type of application	■ tech. architecture requirements for each app'n class	6 technical classes @ 1/4 day each	1.5

	TASKS	PRODUCTS	Original estimates			
Ref	Description		Estimating basis	Man days	start date	end date
3.2.7	Refine definition of applications and database architectures	■ refined overall app'n process map, showing data flows ■ synopsis for each application subsystem ■ reflection of cbins priorities onto application systems ■ refined corporate data model. ■ refined def'n of subject databases. ■ refined application system/ data usage analysis.	30 applications @ 1/ 4 day each	7.5		

3.2.8	Identify and take account of all key technical and implementation priorities, constraints and options.	■ statement of priorities dependencies and constraints:
		  ■ business
		  ■ application
		  ■ technical
		■ assessment of impact on emerging solutions.
				2.0		

3.2.9	Assemble business volumes and relate to functions needed.	■ business workload volumes projected by application and scenario over time.	May need research	5.0		
			sub-total	25.0		
3.3	**Evaluate IT status and opportunities, and set key technical directions**					
3.3.1	Define technical classes to meet needs of app'n classes	■ definition of technical characteristics needed to support each class of application. ■ identity of tech. classes		1.0		
3.3.2	Assess nature & broad volume of need by class of technical architecture.	■ basis for developing capacity needs by application class and time phase		2.0		
3.3.3	Assess current support for each class of technical architecture.	■ verified statement of current status for all it items. ■ assessment of strengths & weaknesses		5.0		
3.3.4	Determine physical distribution policies.	■ computer sites & roles ■ approach to inter-site communications		1.0		
3.3.5	Define list of technical areas, principles and options	■ list of areas ■ for each, a statement of principles and options	May vary according to the range of technical environments. Say 5 areas @ 2 m.d.	5.0		
3.3.6	Consult vendors & industry sources for each key it component	■ assessment of vendors & key directions	Highly variable	5.0		

	TASKS	PRODUCTS	Original estimates		
Ref	Description		Estimating basis	Man days	start date / end date
3.3.7	Assemble & assess expertise on status and direction for each key technology component	■ statement of opportunity, direction & risk for each technology area, showing preferred options	incl in below		

3.3.8	Develop a direction statement for each class of architecture showing:
	- component types
	- broad capacity needs
		■ for each class of tech. architecture, a statement of:
		  ■ target coverage in 2 & 5 years
		  ■ capacity needs.
			8 areas @ 1 day	8.0	

			sub-total	**27.0**	

3.4 Progress business case development; map from needs to projects

3.4.1	Draw up clear presentation materials showing how the CBINS have been translated into applications and thence to projects.	■ presentation materials ■ traceability recodes to support conclusions		3.0	
3.4.2	Negotiate with sponsors as to how project based costs impact business cases, the allocation of infrastructure costs, and how benefits may best be quantified and allocated to projects	Iterative development and refinement of: ■ sponsors' commitment ■ project packaging ■ implementation phasing ■ allocation of costs and benefits ■ business case formulation		5.0	
3.4.3	Revise and tune as appropriate: ■ project formulations; ■ implementation phasing; ■ allocation of costs and benefits; ■ formulation of business cases	■ business case cost and benefit statements now oriented towards likely application delivery phases, and committed by sponsors	40 project cases @ 1/4 day each	5.0	
			sub-total	**13.0**	
			Phase 3 sub-total	**76.0**	

Phase 4 Prepare & Deliver the Implementation Plan

4.1 Prepare Application & Database Projects Plan

4.1.1	Identify key landmarks to be achieved in short & long term	■ definition of landmarks ■ definition of transition route & options ■ traceability records	4 key streams @ 1 days	4.0	
4.1.2	Review all priorities and dependencies	■ statement of all factors relevant to development of a practical, workable plan		1.0	
4.1.3	Review results of phase 3 selection and solution decisions and effects of constraints & dependencies. iterate with business sponsors so as to tune the business cases.	■ impact on ideal business development sequence of application & technical dependencies. ■ preferred implementation groupings and phasing by business area.		4.0	

	TASKS	PRODUCTS	Original estimates			
Ref	Description		Estimating basis	Man days	start date	end date
4.1.4	Confirm 'ideal target' state.	▪ preferred business & systems architecture.				
4.1.5	Verify achievability of target state.	▪ potential interim migration points, with associated business case analyzes.	included in above			
4.1.6	Vary target until it is achievable in business terms.	▪ alternative targets and migration assessments of each. ▪ recommended compromise delivery order & rate for key systems. ▪ associated adjustments to the business cases.	Depends on the extent of operation needed with sponsors	3.0		
4.1.7	Determine optimal physical placement of it components for preferred target and interim states. (closely with 4.2.x tasks)	▪ preliminary mapping of processes & databases to sites ▪ preliminary assessment of quantity & type of computing capacity at each site ▪ preliminary comms network capacity estimates.		5.0		
4.1.8	Package migration steps into appropriate phased dev't projects.	▪ draft project synopses & phasing options.	40 projects @ 1/4 day	10.0		
4.1.9	Recheck with business rationales & priorities.	▪ results of alternative business case	4 group meetings with sponsors	5.0		
4.1.10	Check with technical constraints	▪ impact analysis of alternative implementation sequences.		1.0		
4.1.11	Map business volumes into project & technical units, & develop workload & capacity needs by app'n, tech. env't & time phase. (closely with 4.2.x tasks)	▪ human & computer workload & capacity needs by app'n, tech. env't & time phase, for dev't & operation.		5.0		
4.1.12	Assess feasibility & iterate.	▪ result of evaluation ▪ agreed cost/benefit outlines for systems ▪ agreed app'n dev't schedule		2.0		
4.1.13	Refine project synopses.	▪ synopsis for each application systems project.		5.0		

4.1.14	Integrate with tech & organization plans, showing complete set of application systems & technical projects to be undertaken to achieve landmarks.	▪ project definitions :
		  ▪ application dev't
		  ▪ database dev't
		  ▪ resources
		  ▪ timescales.
		▪ project costs/benefits statements
			Iterative integration of all concurrent threads	3.0		

4.1.15	Develop resource, skill-level profile. & balance with business benefit statements	▪ resource, cost & skill-level profiles. ▪ phased resource plan		2.0		

	TASKS	PRODUCTS	Original estimates			
Ref	**Description**		**Estimating basis**	**Man days**	**start date**	**end date**
4.1.16	Document application dev't plan	▪ application dev't plan		3.0		
			sub-total	**53.0**		
4.2	**Prepare IT technical development projects plan**					
4.2.1	Confirm direction of tech. strategy; take tech selection decisions where appropriate, else define in-depth follow-on projects to confirm.	▪ technical position statements for each topic	10 topics @ 1/2 day each (could be very much greater)	5.0		
4.2.2	Consider sequencing options in rel. to app'n plan			1.0		

4.2.3	Define all technical development projects.	▪ technical development plans covering all work needed to establish:
		  ▪ all kinds of computing facility;
		  ▪ all types of networking and systems management
		  ▪ database servers;
		  ▪ EIS/MIS delivery and presentation services;
		  ▪ application development methods, techniques tools and environments
			5 key project areas @ 1/2 day each	2.5		

4.2.4	Develop technical project cost/benefit cases	▪ tech infrastructure cost/benefit statement linked to business benefits		2.0		
4.2.5	Integrate & confirm broad capacity plan for each resource type	▪ broad capacity plan ▪ project def'n and scope for more detailed capacity plan if needed		2.0		
4.2.6	Document technical plan	▪ summary list of tech. dev't projects & costs resource schedule		2.0		
			sub-total	**14.5**		
4.3	**Prepare organizational and skills/resources development plan**					
4.3.1	Define business organizational impact	Summary of recommendations & observations statement to senior management. should have become clear earlier in the study - this is only to formalize the delivery.		1.0		
4.3.2	Define information systems division organizational impact.	▪ roles & responsibilities by function and location ▪ skill/resource requirements by time phase		1.0		

	TASKS	PRODUCTS	Original estimates			
Ref	Description		Estimating basis	Man days	start date	end date
4.3.3	Define complete set of functions for is organization.	■ definition of role & skill requirements for, eg: ■ end-user support ■ architecture admin. ■ job descriptions for new/ revised roles		2.0		
4.3.4	Assess current skill/ resource personnel profiles.	Statement of upgrade needs for skills/resource levels		1.0		
4.3.5	Integrate skills/resource requirements resulting from other plans	Consolidated skills/ resources profile.		1.0		
4.3.6	Determine how the altered profile is to be achieved	Recruitment/training needs		1.0		
4.3.7	Define organization groupings.	■ revised isd organization plan & job definitions		1.0		
4.3.8	Assess how to meet recruitment development & training needs.	■ recruitment & skills dev't plans		1.0		
4.3.9	Document the IS/IT organization plan	■ documented plan		1.0		
			sub-total	**10.0**		
4.4	**Integrate costs and business cases**					
4.4.1	Confirm cost/benefit approach	Statement of 'the rules' including criteria for exceptions, eg rapid dev't		1.0		
4.4.2	Assemble costs & benefits from all planning areas	Assembled, consistent set of cost/benefit papers		1.0		
4.4.3	Evaluate, adjust & iterate as necessary - altering phasing, spend rate, etc where appropriate. includes integration with current tactical plans.	■ finely tuned benefits delivery plan, linked into development projects and their business cases. ■ fine tuning to short term plans where needed	Mostly negotiation – could be greater	5.0		
4.4.4	Document overall cost/ benefit summaries & conclusions	Overall cost/benefit summaries		2.0		
			sub-total	**9.0**		
4.5	**Prepare and present plans and negotiate implementation**					
4.5.1	Summarise conclusions.	■ Draft management presentations.		2.0		
4.5.2	Re-confirm the business priorities & benefits on which the plan is based	■ Financial summaries approved		5.0		
4.5.3	Write reports	■ Summary & main final reports final draft delivered	Should not take longer	10.0		
4.5.4	Present as necessary	■ Presentations delivered	Highly variable	1.0		
4.5.5	Cycle of review & approval of recommendations	■ Fully approved recommendations	Highly variable	3.0		

	TASKS	PRODUCTS	Original estimates			
Ref	Description		Estimating basis	Man days	start date	end date
4.5.6	Agree status of baseline documents for change control	■ Baseline documents under control ■ Agreed process for change management	All handover, very approx	3.0		
4.5.7	Define and agree responsibilities and process maintenance of the IS/IT plan in response to changes in business needs or priorities	■ Agreed responsibilities and resourcing resourcing for maintenance of business/systems plans				
4.5.8	Define and agree responsibilities and process for maintenance of the information and technical architectures in response to changes to the plans or other IS/IT status.	■ Agreed responsibilities and resourcing resourcing for maintenance of information and technical architectures and plans		1.0		
4.5.9	Complete handover of the IS plans, including integration of strategic and tactical plans and schedules.	■ Handover completed ■ Process and responsibilities for maintenance in place and working		1.0		
4.5.10	Complete handover of the IS and technology architectures	■ Handover completed ■ Process and responsibilities for maintenance in place and working		1.0		
4.5.11	Complete documentation and handover of the planning procedures	■ Handover completed ■ Process and responsibilities for maintenance in place and working		1.0		
			sub-total	**29.0**		
			Phase 4 sub-total	**115.5**		
			Overall total	**653.8**		

APPENDIX III

Checklists and reference materials

Many examples and reference materials are provided in-line in the main chapters. This Appendix includes additional material which is of more general relevance, especially in the initiation and early phases of an IS/IT planning project.

Contents

A-III-A   Strategic planning for information systems – quality assurance guidelines

1. Objectives

- Support and help maintain project focus. Ensure that the scope and terms of reference remain valid, and are being complied with.

- Monitor relevance of the project activities and products so as to ensure that project objectives are being achieved and that maximum business benefit will accrue.

- Monitor the level of detail of the work done from the viewpoint of strategic materiality.

- Undertake reviews at the end of each project phase, in order to determine whether the phase may be declared complete, and to ensure that all prerequisites for commencing the next phase have been met.

- Undertake review of drafts of nominated deliverable documents prior to their formal issue for consistency, accuracy and completeness.

- Review any proposed departures from or modifications to the methods and approaches used to ensure that the most appropriate approach is used.

- Identify in good time, and recommend control measures for, material risks to schedule, budget and quality of delivery.

2.   Approach

2.1   *General style*

The primary focus in this QA plan is on review of a nominated set of deliverables. In addition, phase start/end checkpoint reviews are be used in support of risk management activity.

The phase start/end checks , which are set out in Appendix A, add value in terms of supporting identification and assessment of risks of failure to meet time scales, and of failure to produce results which are appropriate. However, formal adherence to them, to the extent of stopping work at each point may disrupt momentum. Therefore, under controlled circumstances, such checkpoints may be observed less formally, and (slightly) retrospectively. They should be carried out as soon as possible after each major phase end when relevant materials become available.

The remainder of this section sets out the manner in which the approach adopted meets the stated objectives.

2.2   *Overall business focus and relevance*

In this context, the QA activities should pay regard to:

- the means used in the treatment of uncertainty and foreseeable change in business climate, business plans and technology opportunities;

- the stability and clarity of business priorities and directions identified;

- the accuracy of alignment of plans emerging with identified business priorities;

- the balance achieved between expediency and long term flexibility.

2.3   *Strategic materiality*

The reviews should check that all issues which are material at strategic level have been covered, and that the level of detail covered is sufficient without excessive effort being consumed on non-strategic issues. There should be clear criteria established for stopping work on a task or deliverable, e.g. key issues and business information needs, when sufficient detail has been generated.

In view of the need to compromise on schedule and quality, acceptable tolerances on timeliness, levels of detail and the degree of management consensus achieved will need to be agreed. There is also a need for means for ensuring continuity between this work and the subsequent design and implementation phases. This should involve arranging the transfer of unresolved items through to architecture groups, and to the functional/technical design teams.

2.4   *Deliverables*

The following classes of deliverable are recognized:

a)   the final reports and their sections and subdivisions;

b)   other formal project end-products;

c)   key intermediate documents, which may be required for traceability of conclusions and/or the re-work of conclusions on successive cycles;

d)   other working papers which may be needed for reference.

Items of type (a) and (b) should be subject to the full review process. Items of type (c) should also receive close attention, although the type of review should be tailored to the nature of the document, and its purpose in the process. Type (d) items should be accessed for reference purposes only - review comments should be offered on an exception basis only, and review of these is not guaranteed to be exhaustive or complete.

2.5   *Risk management*

The review team should co-operate closely with Project Management and the Steering Group for this purpose. We should follow a conventional process of:

■   identify risks;

■   assess their impact and priority for attention;

■   develop/recommend control measures;

■   where necessary, report to the Steering Group concerning risks identified and control actions taken.

If necessary, the Steering Group may be asked to authorize or facilitate action needed to control risks. The scope of QA interest in this area in relation to the responsibilities of project management and the Steering Group needs to be defined.

The project team should prepare and agree with QA a start-up statement of assumptions, perceived risks, expected impacts and control measures. At the end of each phase, and also as and when necessary on an exception basis, the project team should prepare a risk management summary covering progress on control of perceived risks and any changes.

3.   Roles, responsibilities and process

3.1   *Team*

The review team should consist of the project manager and an independent QA monitor of appropriate experience, who should report directly to the project Steering Group. They should review project plans and proposed amendments to them, as well as all nominated items in draft and final form. They should also conduct the phase end reviews. Additional user management may be nominated to review certain documents.

3.2   *Responsibilities*

The *project team* should provide the following items to the review team to an agreed schedule which allows time for review and any necessary re-work prior to final delivery (generally 10 working days - see below):

- work plans and schedules, and updates to them;
- an initial schedule of deliverables, and revisions to it as appropriate;
- notification of all material changes to plans, schedules, scope definition and document issue dates, and will indicate the approval status of these items;
- drafts of key documents for review, as defined in Appendix B.

The *reviewers* should provide within five working days of receipt of the draft document, written comments, in a format which clearly indicates:

- the document identity and version;
- the reviewer;
- type of comment, e.g. omission, inconsistency, need to explain basis for conclusion, request for clarification, etc.;
- severity of the comment, ranging from 'observation only' through 'must rectify before release'
- recommended for action.

Wherever possible, subject to location and time scale, and certainly in the case of significant issues, the reviewing team should jointly agree and provide a consolidated set of such comments.

The *project manager* should schedule and manage additional reviews by user management, including the consolidation and timely delivery of their comments to the project team.

The *project team* should respond to review comments within five working days of receipt by:

1.   Providing a summary acknowledging the comments and the manner in which they should be implemented, including:

- 'accepted as-is' to be actioned;

- comment modified after discussion, to be actioned;
- action deferred to a later stage;
- comment superseded by a revised version of the document (in this case, revised document sections must be provided with the response if not before);
- comment rejected – with reason, e.g. as trivial, or erroneous, due to misunderstanding by the reviewer).

2. Issuing if necessary a revised version of the document or sections of it. This should normally be the first formal release of the document, which should be 'baselined', i.e. placed under formal change control at this stage.

3.3   *Review process & cycle*

The review process is based on the issue of draft and final versions of each document. The process, which telescopes the more formal process which is typically used on very large projects, is outlined in Figure A-III-1. Only nominated reviewers should receive the draft versions, and the project team may, at their discretion, continue work on the materials whilst the drafts are being reviewed.

Figure A-III-1 *A typical formal QA process*

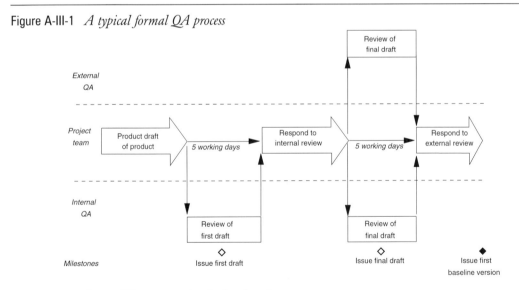

4.   Phase start/end checkpoints

4.1   *Level of formality*

Phase start/end checkpoints are acknowledged as adding value, in terms of supporting identification and assessment of risks of failure to meet time scales, and of failure to produce results which are appropriate. However, formal phase start/end checkpoints, phased in with start/end of project tasks are felt to be inappropriate due to the need to meet stringent overall time scales.

Instead, such checkpoints should be observed less formally, and retrospectively, as soon as possible after the relevant materials become available. Thus they should not delay work; however, the checks should be carried out in due course, and it should be noted that the impact of risks identified as a result may be greater, due to the lapse of time.

There should be one QA checkpoint at start of the project, one between each major phase, and one just prior to presentation of the final report. These checks, which are primarily aimed at risk control, are discussed further below.

4.2   *General goals*

a).   Determine whether the preceding phase may be declared successfully completed:

- tasks completed;
- deliverables present to acceptable standard;
- conclusions are consistent with facts and analysis documented;
- management commitment and consensus obtained.

b).   Establish whether all prerequisites for commencing the next phase (if any) are met, so that it may commence:

- prerequisites in place;
- availability of inputs, materials, skills and resources;
- timing and dependencies are within limits;
- risk assessment satisfactory;
- authorization and budget cleared;
- management climate and environment are prepared.

The phases are:

1.   Establish context and scope

2.   Determine business information and support needs

3.   Establish information architectures and options

4.   Determine strategic solutions

5.   Prepare and deliver the implementation plan

The reviewable documents comprise:

1.   The final reports

2.   Other formal deliverables

3.   Other items for review

4.   Background items which may be needed for reference

Specific check-lists for each phase are in appendix A.

5.   Criteria for review of deliverables

5.1   *Reviewable documents*

The reviewable documents comprise:

1.   the final reports and their sections and subdivisions;

2.   other formal project end-products;

3.   key intermediate documents, which may be required e.g. for traceability and/or re-work of conclusions on successive cycles;

4.   other working papers which may be needed for reference.

5.2   *Final reports*

Final reports may comprise several volumes. These are nominated in the list of deliverables. Each should be subject to review against the following criteria:

1.   Partitioning into volumes as specified.

2.   Format, scope and contents are in accordance with specification.

3.   Conclusions are consistent with and substantiated by the facts and analysis documented. (This may require access to several layers of working papers).

4.   Conclusions and approach are sensitive to business priorities and climate.

5.   Due regard is paid to feasibility, in terms of the organization's commitment to implementing the solutions and its ability to manage change, the consensus process, technical and business risks and dependencies.

5.3   *Other formal deliverables*

These should be reviewed against the following criteria:

1.   Format, scope and contents are in accordance with specification.

2.   Conclusions are consistent with and substantiated by the facts and analysis documented.

3.   The level of detail is appropriate.

5.4   *Other items for review*

Key intermediate documents (type 3) should also receive close attention, although the type of review should be tailored to the nature of the document, and its purpose in the process. In particular, it is important that the document provides a basis of traceability for re-working conclusions in later iteration cycles, e.g. when inputs have altered. Type (4) items should be accessed for reference purposes only – review comments should be offered on an exception basis only, and review is not guaranteed to be exhaustive or complete.

Annexes to QA guidelines

A. phase start/end check-lists

Comprising only those items specific to particular phases, over and above checks implied by the general goals.

0. ESTABLISH CONTEXT AND SCOPE

- Have the study scope and terms of reference been clearly specified, reviewed and approved?
- Have effective arrangements been made for proper synchronization of this study with any other relevant concurrent activities?
- Is there a clearly identified core of committed management sponsors, with the appropriate 'clout' for the exercise?
- Does the business really need this study?
- Is the timing right (or near enough)?
- Are project plans, estimates and schedule done and approved?
- Is the project steering group and associated management structure in place?
- Do you have a full team? Are there sufficient qualified members available?
- Are the Business Units/Segments clearly identified and agreed?
- Do you know the status of business plans, and have you access to the necessary business expertise?
- Has liaison been established with the Business Planning function
- Is information collection under way?
- Has an Architecture Control function been set up, including data Administration?
- Are the first cycle of interviews scheduled?
- Are key road-blocks identified – do you have a plan for each?

1. END OF DETERMINE BUSINESS INFORMATION AND SUPPORT NEEDS

- Have all planned interviews been conducted, analyzed, documented, signed off by the interviewee and the results consolidated, including late changes?
- Has consensus been achieved on needs definitions and cross-functional priorities?
- Are support requirements clear, as well as information needs?
- Are key candidates emerging as potential sponsors, are they really 'fired up', and do they have funding authority?
- Is there a realistic perception of the possible impact and costs of the likely outcomes from the study?

- Has the information collection process been successful; is the factual information available and complete for:
  - business Organization and plans;
  - current systems, projects and plans;
  - current IT technical status, assets, commitments and plans;
  - human skills/resources skills and experience.
- Are the assessments and judgements realistic, and is there consensus on key shortcomings?

2. END OF ESTABLISH INFORMATION ARCHITECTURES AND OPTIONS

- Are high level data architectures visible?
- Are high level potential application systems, with priorities visible?
- Have the architecture control groups participated in developing the data and systems architectures?
- Do relevant users understand the application maps and their implications?
- Has the usage of data by applications been mapped?
- Is the traceability of application requirements from information and support needs clear?
- Has coverage assessment been carried out, are the sponsors committed to the results and are resulting priorities clear?
- For each group of proposed applications and database, are there a set of realistic options set out for consideration?
- Are the criteria for assessment of options and selection of solutions clearly defined?

3. END OF DETERMINE STRATEGIC SOLUTIONS

- Are willing, committed sponsors now identified for all requirements?
- Are the strategic directions clear, and are the sponsors committed to their pursuit.
- Have appropriate urgent actions been identified, and is their implementation under way?
- Have resulting business delivery priorities been negotiated with sponsoring users?
- Do sponsors appreciate what is needed to assemble the necessary business cases?
- Have the ground rules for financial evaluation been defined?
- Have constraints/dependencies been analyzed, and their impact assessed?
- Have other 'givens' been identified, and whether each is mandatory or optional?
- Have the ground rules for evaluating interim migration steps been defined?

- Have IT technical implications and directions been established, and any further work needed to establish quantified requirements and to resolve issues been identified?

4. END OF PREPARE AND DELIVER THE IMPLEMENTATION PLAN

- Is there a clear set of recommendations?
  - application portfolio;
  - core databases;
  - technical environments and platforms;
  - technical components - identification, capacities and costs;
  - migration phasing
  - application development environments;
  - people skills and resources.
- Do the recommendations embody a clear vision, and are they internally consistent?
- Has the range of validity of the recommendations been spelled out; i.e. under what scenarios will they remain valid, and under what circumstances may they become invalid?
- Are you still in touch with the mood of the business and market? Are you solving the right problems?
- Do the sponsors understand their sections of the plans, do they understand clearly what they have to do next, and are they committed to driving through the implementation?
- Are financial and business cases for all the key initiatives, including technical developments and other infrastructure projects ready?
- Is it clear what management need to do to approve the plan?
- Have sponsors agreed with you and among themselves as to how to allocate costs and benefits, especially those relating to shared infrastructure?
- Is presentation material clear; presentations rehearsed?
- Have you prepared the ground with potential sceptics/opponents?
- Is back-up material available if needed – e.g. detailed working papers, alternatives considered/rejected?
- Have the architecture control groups accepted handover of the data and systems architectures?
- Has clear provision been made for continuing review and maintenance of the plans in the future.

B. Document schedule for review (based on the project plan)

B1 THE FINAL REPORTS AND THEIR SECTIONS AND SUBDIVISIONS

B2 OTHER FORMAL PROJECT END-PRODUCTS

1. Consolidated BINS statement embodying agreed priorities.

2. Recommended application development projects plan

3. Recommended infrastructure developments plan

4. Cross function and area joint/common systems developments statement.

5. Recommended Organization and skills/resources development plan.

6. Recommended technical strategy and infrastructure solutions.

7. Recommended technical development projects plan.

8. Business cases - refined.

9. Presentation materials.

10. Review and maintenance criteria and procedure for the implementation plans.

B3 KEY INTERMEDIATE DOCUMENTS, REQUIRED FOR TRACEABILITY AND/OR RE-WORK OF CONCLUSIONS ON SUCCESSIVE CYCLES

1. Decision summaries from Group Sessions.

2. Business key issues summaries.

3. CBINS priority analysis.

4. Consolidated assessment of current application status

5. Consolidated assessment of current IT technology status.

6. Technical strategy direction statement.

7. Business process model.

8. Data entity model.

9. Affinity matrices: data/business process/Organization unit/application process.

10. Application process map - overall and by business segment.

11. Systems coverage assessment.

12. Data coverage assessment.

13. Shortfall analysis assessment.

14. Definition of application priorities.

15. Application solutions - alternative scenarios.

16.   Technical infrastructure solutions - alternative scenarios.

17.   Definition of migration milestones.

18.   Selected options rationale.

B4 OTHER WORKING PAPERS NEEDED FOR REFERENCE

1.   Project proposal, scope and terms of reference, planning assumptions and project plans and work schedules.

2.   Project progress reports as and when delivered.

3.   Recommended formats and contents lists for all key deliverables (especially where these depart from the agreed standards in use).

4.   Statement of constraints and dependencies.

5.   Dependency analysis.

6.   Application and technical projects synopses and definitions

7.   Results from capacity planning models.

A-III-B   MEMORANDUM

From: **Managing Director**
To: **Board members and General managers**
CC: **IS Strategy project team**
Date:
Subject: **Information systems strategy (IS) project**

Resulting from the recent review of business and IT planning requirements, we are about to launch a short project to re-establish an integrated IS/IT strategy for Trendy Products PLC. This is to be to be carried out by a joint team of internal staff and consultants, and will be led by ∗∗∗∗∗∗. The project will report to me through the IT Director.

We intend the project to commence before the end of ∗∗∗∗∗∗, and its aims are to deliver by the end of ∗∗∗∗∗∗ an integrated set of strategic and tactical plans for the future development of the information systems and supporting technology of Trendy so as to best support the current and likely future needs of the business.

A full project initiation statement, covering the project's goals and objectives, scope and terms of reference, along with the project plan, will be presented to the Steering Group at its first meeting.

Some of the business benefits which Trendy may expect to gain from this exercise are:

1.   Enhanced flexibility:

      ■ ability to respond more quickly to product innovation or market change – getting IT off the critical path;

      ■ coping better with rapid growth in volumes or diversity without over-stressing the company infrastructure or growing a bureaucracy.

2.   Improved and more timely management information, especially on performance and profitability of business units, customers and products.

3.   Ability to access and exploit the existing base of client relationships more effectively for Marketing purposes.

4.   Cost containment – a sustainable reduction in internal administrative costs.

This study will need to keep very closely in touch with the business throughout its duration. To ensure this, we plan to establish a project Steering Group, consisting of a nominated sub-set of the Trendy Main Board, plus ∗∗∗∗∗∗ and ∗∗∗∗∗∗. This Group will meet at key project milestones to receive reports, and to review progress, and who will receive and approve the final report.

Suggested terms of reference for the Steering group are attached (A).

The key project milestones, with which Steering Group meetings will coincide, are:

1.	Project launch	w/b ******
2.	End phase 1 – Consolidated statement of business needs and priorities	w/b ******
3.	End phase 2 – Identification of cover offered by current systems, and options to meet gaps and future needs	w/b ******
4.	End phase 3 – Strategic solutions	w/b ******
5.	End phase 4 – Draft plans and conclusions	w/b ******
6.	Project close – dependent on the speed of the review cycle, early	**********

NB: These dates are approximate, although they represent our best intention; they depend on the availability of senior management for interview and review sessions, and on the actual start date. We have also yet to confirm them by detailed planning and resource loading.

Apart from the Steering Group's role, there are three other ways in which the project will need to gain business input.

1. 1.A view as to the Group's overall business vision and directions Prior to establishment of the revised formal business planning process, we plan to address this by means of a two stage workshop, involving the Main Board and selected General Managers, early in the project. This will involve two working sessions of half a day, separated by a period of not more than 3 weeks, with some work to be carried out in the intervening period. An outline of the approach which we plan to follow is attached (B).

2. 2.A cycle of interview and consensus to take place during ******* and ******, involving the Senior Management team. In this process, we will review their functional responsibilities and objectives with managers and Directors, and with their help derive their requirements for information and support. These will subsequently be consolidated, agreed across the business and prioritized. This activity will require approximately an additional 1/2 day from each Board member, Senior manager and selected other staff during this period.

3. 3.For each high priority need identified, it is expected that a Trendy manager will assume a sponsorship role. Typically, a sponsor in this context is the person who will deliver the business benefits resulting from a systems need being met. The project team will work closely with

the sponsors in formulation of business cases and recommended projects.

In view of the critical nature of this project, and its importance as a key element of our move to a more planned culture, I would be grateful if you will give the project your close attention, and make your time available so as to enable the project to meet its demanding schedule.

A-III-C   Trendy Products PLC: information systems and technology strategy study

Scope and terms of reference

1. INTRODUCTION

Resulting from the business review recently carried out, we are about to launch a short project to establish an integrated IS strategy for Trendy Products. This is to be to be carried out by a joint team of Trendy Products staff and consultants. We intend the project to commence before the end of February, and its aims are to deliver by the end of June an integrated set of strategic and tactical plans for the future development of the information systems and supporting technology of Trendy Products so as to best support the current and likely future needs of the business.

This paper defines the scope and terms of reference of this project.

2. OBJECTIVES AND BENEFITS

The overall goal of this project is to identify and establish integrated strategic and tactical plans for the development of the information systems and supporting information and communications technology of Trendy Products so as to best support the current and likely future needs of the business.

Specific objectives are as follows:

1.   Identify current and likely future business requirements, including especially those areas where there is high uncertainty or volatility of requirement.

2.   Facilitate consensus across the Trendy Products Board and Senior Management team as to these priorities, and arrange allocation of management sponsorship responsibilities for their pursuit.

3.   Identify the most appropriate strategic systems solutions to meet the needs identified, and to cope with the types of change foreseen.

4.   Assess current systems, developments and technology assets in the light of the requirements and identify the most important changes needed.

5.   Recommend a program of projects aimed at development of the applications, staff skills and technology so as to achieve efficient and responsive implementation of the strategic solutions.

6.   Establish a mechanism and basis for continuing to keep the IS/IT plans in step with developments in the business vision and direction - thereby laying the basis for evolution by Trendy Products to a more complete, integrated set of business and IS/IT planning cycles

Some of the business benefits which Trendy Products may expect to gain from this exercise are:

1.   Enhanced flexibility:

   - ability to respond more quickly to product innovation or market change - getting IT off the critical path;
   - coping better with rapid growth in volumes or diversity without over-stressing the company infrastructure or growing a bureaucracy.

2.   Improved information on product and customer profitability.

3.   Ability to access and exploit the existing base product, customer and market information more effectively for Marketing purposes.

4.   Cost containment - sustainable reduction in administration costs.

3. SCOPE

UK – all products, all locations, all systems

Overseas – identify cases where use of UK approaches is likely to prove appropriate; identify scopes of relevant local reviews.

4.   DELIVERABLES

4.1   *Business oriented end products*

- Statements of strategic solutions for information systems and technology
   - Phased development plans for:
   - -application systems and databases
   - -IT development projects
   - -staff skills upgrade
- Basis for implementation and migration of current systems into the recommended environments
- A set of supporting business cases with appropriate financial basis
- Recommended process for continuing plan review, tuning and maintenance, so as to keep it in step with developments in the business.

4.2   *Business-oriented intermediate products*

- A consolidated and agreed statement of business information and support needs and priorities. This forms the 'charter' of agreement between the business users and IT, and acts as a continuing basis for managing future change. It may, for example, be used in the assessment of alternative business/product scenarios.
- A statement of business assumptions on which the recommendations are based, including an indication of key areas of risk and uncertainty on which the viability of the recommended solutions depends.

- Assessment of current information systems in terms of the extent and quality of coverage achieved of business needs.
- An urgent actions plan for interim "quick fixes".
- A complete audit trail providing a basis for traceability from requirement to solutions.

4.3 *IS and IT oriented products*

- Assessment of current IS and IT status:
  - objective - what there is
  - judgemental - its quality and current and future relevance
- Log of options and solutions which were considered and rejected, with reasons
- Target applications and database architecture
- Target IT architecture
- Target Organization and skills/resource strategy

5. APPROACH/METHODOLOGY

The approach to be used is well proven, having been used successfully to develop IS and IT strategies for a large number of Organization, many in the finance and financial services sectors.

A key feature of the method is the attention paid to establishing a clear top-down business driven definition of business needs and priorities, (termed Consolidated Business INformation and Support needs, or CBINS), which is committed to by all relevant management sponsors. This CBINS statement acts as the basis for derivation of solutions during the planning project, and also acts as the fulcrum for all subsequent change control.

General Characteristics

- Business/priority driven – 'tuned in'
- Top/down, focused – 'rifle bullet' approach
- Open architecture – flexible, continuing to evolve; the framework is distinct from the techniques
- Estimatable, controllable
- Complete – delivers implementable plans
- May be used in a manner which is compatible with HM Government CCTA guidelines for Strategic Planning for Information Systems
- The process and results are understandable, verifiable
- The process is:
  - proven
  - efficient in elapsed and management time
  - iterative
- Key analytic tasks are amenable to automation

- The quality process is integral and explicit
- The plans as delivered are designed for maintenance & enhancement

6. STEERING AND CONTROL ARRANGEMENTS

This study will need to keep very closely in touch with the business throughout its duration. To ensure this, we plan to establish a project Steering Group, consisting of the Trendy Products Board, who will meet at key project milestones to receive reports, and to review progress, and who will receive and approve the final report. Suggested terms of reference for the Steering group are attached.

A-III-D   Trendy Products plc IS/IT strategy study: Steering Group – T.O.R. and draft agendas

T.O.R.

1. Approve the project scope and t.o.r., and direct and steer the IT strategy review in accordance with it.

2. Receive progress and quality assurance reports. Action or monitor high level issues and exceptions arising.

3. Facilitate the project by ensuring where necessary that resources are available, and dependencies e.g. on parallel initiatives, are managed.

4. Provide guidance on high level issues of business intention or direction.

5. Address and resolve high level business priorities and other issues; manage and resolve any out of scope issues raised by the project.

6. Approve guidelines for establishing and evaluating business cases.

7. Receive, review and approve the project interim deliverables, final report and findings.

8. Oversee the implementation of the IS/IT strategy and the maintenance process, and act as the change control board for the Trendy Products IS/IT strategic plans.

9. Ensure the proper coordination of business, IS and IT strategic and tactical plans for Trendy Products in the future.

IT strategy project – steering group

DRAFT AGENDA FOR THE FIRST MEETING

1. Presentation of project scope, rationale and t.o.r.

2. Overview of project approach to be followed.

3. Project management process, including milestones and steering group meetings.

4. Process for providing high level Trendy Products business vision and directional input.

5. Management interview groupings and schedule.

6. Review of actions c/f.

7. A.o.b. and date of next meeting.

SAMPLE AGENDA – LATER MEETINGS

1. Review of actions c/f

2. Project status report

3. Review of scope or other relevant steering issues, e.g. dependencies or priority conflicts

4. Review of actions c/f

5. Next meeting and a.o.b.

A-III-E   Pre-start checklist for IS/IT strategic planning

PURPOSE OF THE CHECKLIST

This checklist is intend for use during the gestation period for a potential study. Aims are to:

- highlight management pain areas and factors which may be used to justify a study;
- head off opponents who may try to stop or hijack it;
- identify areas of potential benefit;
- assess environment and climate; flush out risk areas

USES OF THE CHECKLIST

Primarily internal, and with caution – it contains enough material to scare off almost anyone who may want one! Select items from it and use them to raise issues during the selling and project initiation processes.

Status of business planning

Is there a business plan? Do people know it and support it? Do they feel they own it? Can they relate to it and do something positive to implement it? How do you know when it's working? How do you know when it needs to be changed?

1. *Is there a business plan*

    - at the top level?
    - at each operating division level?

2. Is the plan accessible to and understood by people who need to know it? Are they committed to following it?

3. Does the plan make it clear what actions need to be taken, by whom, with what goals and success criteria?

4. Does the plan take account of information technology (IT) opportunities for product/service formulation & delivery, and for support of management planning and analysis?

5. Do you know what you have to do to meet your responsibilities under the business plan?

6. Did you/your department contribute to the plan?

7. Can you tell how you are doing against it?

8. Is there provision for periodic review of progress against the plan?

9. Is there provision for maintenance of the plan and modification of it in the light of changing circumstances, both on regular cycles and on an exception basis?

BUSINESS PLANNING STYLE

Is your current business planning style right for your Organization and industry?

10.   What depth/formality of Business, IT and IS planning are needed in your Organization?

        Over-planning is probably worse than under planning. It stifles entrepreneurial flair, and gets planning a bad name.

11.   Is the plan pitched at the right level for your Organization and industry, in terms of level of detail and the prevailing degree of business uncertainty?

12.   How far ahead do you need to plan? How far ahead can you plan?

13.   Is there a high degree of uncertainty concerning the future levels of activity and types of demand in your market place?

        There are specific techniques (such as scenario planning) which are efficient, and which are suited to areas and times of high uncertainty.

14.   Is a distinction made between planning (about actions), and budgeting (about money)?

        Planning is creative, usually difficult, and concerns actions and business goals. Budgeting is easier, and is often done instead, whereas it should only be done within the context of a business plan.

15.   Is business planning candid and realistic, or is it done reluctantly, in a perfunctory manner?

CURRENT STATUS OF INFORMATION SYSTEMS (IS) AND IT PLANNING

Are you doing IS/IT planning right (or at all) today?

16.   Are there clear criteria for setting IT/IS priorities for investment in relation to other demands on business expenditure? Are these criteria understood and followed?

17.   Does the planning process ensure that IS and IT strategies are linked to the business plan in a manner which facilitates joint review?

18.   Are current IS/IT strategic priorities clearly defined?

19.   Are they visible at executive board level? Are they regularly reviewed for focus and balance as part of a more general planning and assessment process?

HOW MUCH DO YOU NEED AN IS/IT PLAN

Do you need an information systems strategy plan at all?

20.   Are there obvious shortfalls in IS support of business operations or MIS?

21. Are there priority conflicts and contention for investment resources, involving IS/IT options?

22. Are your competitors investing heavily in IS/IT, and is this apparently doing them any good?

23. What percentage of your business revenue is channelled into investing in IS/IT? How does this compare to market leaders, and other competitors in your business? Are you happy with this?

24. Are IS or IT getting into your product delivery chain, or even into the product itself?

25. Does your product/service R&D cycle take account of IS/IT opportunities?

     Technology push, rather than market pull is of increasing importance in many areas.

26. Are IS/IT development time scales & support costs considered in your product development cycle?

TIMING OF AN IS/IT PLANNING STUDY

Is this the right time to do commence an IS/IT planning study?

27. When and how often should you carry out an IS/IT plan?

28. Are there any take-overs, mergers or major reorganizations pending?

29. Is a business planning cycle about to start?

30. Have business plans or directions recently changed markedly?

31. Are you about to initiate investment in major IS/IT projects? Are you sure that this is the best way to spend the money?

32. What are the real motives and objectives of those arguing that this is not the right time?

33. What will happen if you do not do the study now?

CRITERIA FOR SUCCESS

How can we be sure it's going to work out?

34. Do senior management understand what is proposed; are they showing the necessary levels of leadership and commitment; will they implement the conclusions?

35. Do you have the necessary skills and resources to do it?

36. Are the other necessary criteria met for a successful planning study?

37. What must you do before and during the study to make sure that the results will be implemented?

A-III-F   Management interview questionnaire for business functions, objectives & information needs

I. BUSINESS PLANS & ORGANIZATION

1. What is your general area of responsibility? (please define your principal accountabilities and major activities).

2. What is the status of business plans in your area, and what are the main components of those plans?

3. What are the overall business objectives in this area?

4. What are your primary overall goals? (i.e. measurable targets).

5. For each function for which you are responsible:

    - what are the objectives?
    - what are the specific goals?
    - which strategies are you following to achieve them?
    - what factors govern success or failure in achieving them?

6. In what ways are your objectives, goals and strategies likely to change over time?

7. What measures do you use to gauge whether you and your area are performing successfully?

8. How do you detect deviations from plan?

9. What types of control action can you take when you detect deviations from plan?

10. What are the greatest problems you have met in achieving these objectives/goals within the last year?

11. What are the main strengths which the company has in your area?

II. MARKETS & PRODUCTS

1. What are the primary needs of your market sector(s)?

2. How are products or services directed to meet these needs?

3. In what way do you expect the market – and your products and services – to change with time?

4. Are current volumes of business in your area likely to increase/decrease?

5. What do you see as the company's main strengths and weaknesses in relation to the competition? (Please specify business sectors, nature of strengths or weaknesses, benchmarks and information sources).

6. What factors do you monitor to assess your business position in relation

to the competition?

7.   What information do customers/dealers/third parties need from the company to monitor the performance of the relationship?

8.   What information does the company need from customers, dealers or third parties to monitor the level of service performance?

III. INFORMATION AND SUPPORT NEEDS

1.   For each type of operational decision which you have to make, and for each key factor which you monitor, what information do you require?

2.   For each type of operational function for which you are responsible, what types of support process is carried out? Which of these:

  - is automated currently;
  - is a potential candidate for automated support.

3.   What relative priorities do you assign to these information and support needs?

4.   In the case of information, how up to date it be, e.g. up-to-the-minute, daily, weekly, etc.?

5.   In the case of support functions, what levels of availability and responsiveness are required?

6.   For each piece of information received currently, how good is it, in terms of completeness, accuracy and timeliness?

7.   What are your most important sources of current information?

8.   In which areas do you most urgently need better information at present?

9.   Which information sources lie within your direct control as opposed to outside?

IV. CURRENT COMPUTER SYSTEMS

1.   Which of the company's computer systems do you use most?

2.   How good do you rate your information support services within the Organization? Do you feel you are getting value for money? What do you see as the main strengths and weaknesses of information services?

3.   Are there any major changes anticipated in your area in the next year? If so, do you see them affecting the way information systems are operated in the company?

V. AUTOMATION OF PROCESSING AND SUPPORT

1.   In which areas do you see most potential for automation of routine processing?

2.   In which areas of supporting services do you see most potential for

improved automation?

3. Please assign priorities to these areas

VI. Close

1. What do you expect/hope will result from this study?

2. Do you have any additional thoughts or comments?

A-III-G   Strategic planning for information systems checklist for evaluation of current systems

To be completed for each currently operational application, of all types, including end-user and externally run; also, complete relevant sections for current development projects. (But see alternative for small systems)

SYSTEM:

> completed by: Date:
> reviewed by: Date:

1. SYSTEMS FUNCTIONS

1.1   What present needs does the system address?

1.2   Have the economic benefits identified been obtained?

1.3   Have the projected clerical savings been realized?

1.4   Are performance reporting procedures installed to help ensure that clerical savings continue to be achieved?

1.5   Have business conditions remained constant?

2. USER CAPABILITY AND SATISFACTION

2.1   Are users satisfied that the system is meeting objectives?

2.2   Is there evidence that users are using the system properly?

2.3   Does the accuracy of input meet expectations?

2.4   Do users understand the system logic? Is this apparent when errors occur?

3. OPERABILITY

3.1   Do the computer programs operate smoothly, reliably and on time?

3.2   Are runtime errors due to user errors at acceptable levels?

3.3   Are there controls to ensure that rejects are reprocessed?

3.4   What level of programming modifications are outstanding?

3.5   Are the databases accurate and up to date?

3.6   Are integrity controls currently being maintained?

3.7   Are they operative?

3.8   Are reports generally delivered on time?

3.9   Are operating procedures being maintained up to date?

3.10   Are user procedures being maintained up to date?

3.11   Is a disciplined scheduling approach followed?

3.12   Is the system test model being maintained?

3.13   Are the security checks on files and equipment adequate?

3.14   Is there effective control over updating of the operational programs?

3.15   Are program testing procedures enforced for changes?

4. SYSTEMS ORGANIZATION

4.1   Are there personnel who maintain all aspects of the system?

4.2   Have procedures been established for the maintenance of standards, procedures and other key aspects of the system?

4.3   Is the accuracy of reporting up to expectation?

4.4   Are the actual workloads and deadlines consistent with plan?

4.5   Is equipment usage acceptable?

4.6   Is there control over pending program modifications?

4.7   Has the user liaison activity been established?

4.8   Have they arranged a subsequent review of the system at later time?

5. CRITICALITY

5.1   How critical is this system to the business?

5.2   What is the business impact of:

- Significant output errors
- Database corruption
- Loss of the system for: one hour, one day, one week, longer.

5.2   What contingency arrangements exist for the following?

- For manual operation during fallback
- For degraded-mode computer operation
- For resumption after repair
- For operation at an alternative site.

6. DESIGN QUALITY

6.1   Is the design documentation:

- Available?
- Up to date?

6.2   Is the functional structure readily identifiable?

6.2   Are the computer programs well designed and implemented?

6.2   Are end users protected from having to know details of technical aspects of the system?

7. MAINTAINABILITY

7.1   When was the system first implemented?

7.2   In what language?

7.3   Who is responsible for maintenance?

7.4   What is the average maintenance expenditure in man-days per year?

7.5   What is the backlog of essential maintenance in man-days?

7.6   Is maintenance usually done on budget?

7.7   Can maintenance be carried out easily by staff who are not deeply familiar with the system?

8. FURTHER DEVELOPMENT PLANNED

For each planned enhancement, please provide:

- description
- release date
- development estimates
- business benefits
- side effects and impact

9. TECHNICAL DETAILS

9.1   Date first live

9.2   Batch/on-line balance.

9.3   Workload profile:

- over 24 hours
- over a month
- over a year

9.4   Technical environment (hardware, software, any special middleware).

9.5   Size of database(s) used.

9.6   Dependence on other systems, and dependence of other systems on this.

9.7   Average maintenance workload generated in a year.

9.8   Current maintenance backlog.

9.9   Type and quantity of operational fault reports in previous year.

Alternative questionnaire for PC-based applications

1. APPLICATION

1.1   Name:

1.2   Description:

1.3   Author:

1.4   Person responsible:

1.5   User department:

2. SYSTEM FUNCTIONS

2.1   What existing business needs does the system address?

2.2   By how many people is it used?

2.3   What system documentation exists?

3. EFFECTIVENESS

To what extent does the system meet the users needs for

- Accuracy
- Level of service
- Capacity
- Capability for future enhancement or increased scope of use?

4. CRITICALITY

4.1   How critical is this system to the business?

4.2   What is the maximum tolerable loss of service?

4.3   What is the impact of loss of data?

4.4   What is the impact of errors in the data?

5. IMPLEMENTATION

5.1   When was the system first implemented?

5.2   On what existing PC hardware and software is it based?

5.2   Is the system networked?

5.2   Is the system connected to a mainframe?

If so:

- which?
- By what means?
- What is the frequency and volume of access?

6. DATA

6.1   What are the main areas of data covered by the system?

6.2   Does the system deal in 'auditable' data, i.e. financial data or other information going to outside parties?

6.3   What external sources of data are used by the system?

6.4   What internal sources of data (other computer systems) are used by this system?

6.5   What data is passed from this system to other systems?

6.6   What is the total volume of data held by the system? number of records, documents, or other measure as appropriate).

7. FUTURE DEVELOPMENTS

7.1   What changes are expected in the area of business supported by the system?

7.2   What changes are planned in the way this system supports the business?

Technical and human resources status questionnaire

1. Inventory of all computing and communications hardware and system software including release and engineering levels.

2. Inventory of all service and supply contracts relating to computing and communications hardware, system software and services.

3. Current strategy and policy statements, constraints, standards and guidelines, internal and mandatory external.

4. The development plans for computing and communications hardware and systems software.

5. Systems and technical projects in progress: title, scope, function, cost, timetable and current status.

6. Current and planned application portfolio, including relevant business plans and projections on which it is based. To include a note of the assignment of applications and databases to technical platform.

7. Summary of all computing and communications equipment by location; operating statistics for the last year, number of breakdowns, length of breakdowns, number of recoveries, number of jobs run and work volumes per day.

8. Indication of current and planned special equipment and software, such as text processing, digitization/scanning equipment, CD ROMs, CAD/graphics and mobile stations.

9. Indication of the current and planned placement, including workload and database volumes of all applications and data on the computing locations and equipment.

10. Current computing and communications capacity plans and projections; supported by actual measurements where possible.

11. All external systems, including those run on external bureaux and on micros or other distributed equipment.

12. Use of all external services, e.g. Reuters, Swift etc.

13. The level of human resource, summarized by:
    - years experience;
    - years of service;
    - skills, training and qualifications;
    - actual responsibility;
    - forecast of level of responsibility in one year's time.

14. Volume of transactions for each major Transaction Processing (TP) or

data collection system classified by:

- Memo posting
- On-line data collection
- Asynchronous updating
- On-line updating.

15. For multi-user sites, machine operating schedule (TP, batch, maintenance).

16. Typical daily batch schedules (day, week, month, quarter etc.).

17. Inventory and description of the local and wide area networks and associated communications equipment. To include all terminals, personal computers and other transmission equipment, LAN operating systems, DBMS, communications protocols, cabling approach.

18. Operating plans and budgets.

19. The annual plan covering hardware, software, network, office automation, premises and human resources.

20. Information services organization chart.

Data and systems management questionnaire

The following checklist highlights key areas for attention by a quality assurance unit. The checklist is not exhaustive but serves as a guideline from which individual units can derive their own lists.

In the case of a large complex organization, this questionnaire should be completed separately by each business unit, and at the Corporate level.

1. PLANS AND INFORMATION ARCHITECTURES

1.1   Is there in existence a statement of business information needs and priorities, based upon an analysis of the business development plan?

Please supply copies of the relevant business plans and of the consolidated business requirement statements based on them.

1.2   Are these statements related to and maintained in step with statements based on the plans of associated business units?

What control measures are in place to ensure that this is so?

1.3   Is there a definition of systems and database architectures to support the provision of information needs and business support functionality?

Please supply copies of the high level versions of the data models and application flow architectures.

1.4   Are these architectural definitions related to and maintained in step with similar architectures for associated business units, if any?

What control measures are in place to ensure that this is so?

1.5   Is there in place a strategic plan for information systems development aimed at the implementation of the target application portfolio?

1.6   Are development and maintenance of systems and implementation of databases taking place within the scope of such a plan and in accordance with the architectures?

What control measures are in place to ensure that this is so?

Please supply copies of the systems development plan, the database schemes and the specifications of key feeder data flows.

1.7   Are these developments on schedule?

1.8   Is there an information technology (IT) infrastructure plan in place covering all required technical environments and their enabling technology?

1.9   Is this plan revised regularly and does it reflect current information technology in terms of:

- Facilities
- Opportunities
- Costs?

What control measures are in place to ensure that this is so?

Please supply an inventory of IT equipment and systems software.

2. ORGANIZATION

2.1   Is there an organization unit responsible for integration and maintenance of systems and database architectures?

2.2   Is there an organizational unit responsible for integration and maintenance of technical architectures and infrastructure?

2.3   Is there an organizational unit responsible for technical infrastructure and architectures for:

- Operational transaction and control systems;
- Management DSS;
- End-user information delivery systems;
- End-user facilities for personal computing;
- All aspects of communications?

2.4   What are the arrangements for direct support for end-user computing?

3. STANDARDS AND METHODS

3.1   Is there in use a recognized system development methodology? Which (name(s) and source(s))? Date first implemented?

3.2   What exceptions, if any, are permitted to its adherence?

3.3   Are review and quality management procedures in place to ensure that:

- The standards and methods are followed properly
- Benefits sought from application development are gained?

3.4   How are application development and operational productivity measured?

3.5   What arrangements are there for:

- induction training;
- staff development training;
- measurement of staff productivity gains;
- retention rates?

3.6   What procedures and techniques are there in use for:

- Business needs analysis;
- Data analysis;

- Functional analysis;
- Design and verification of business systems and user interfaces;
- Technical design and performance prediction of systems?

3.7 Are these methods consistently followed?

3.8 Are the techniques and the resulting documentation compatible with those used by associated business units?

3.9 Are data and information systems architectures reconciled on a regular basis with those of associated business units where there is a requirement for information transfer interfaces?

3.10 What computer-based support aids, including data dictionary, CASE tools and IPSEs are in use for:

- Information systems strategy planning;
- Data analysis;
- Functional analysis;
- Support of system design documentation;
- Support for database administration;
- System technical design;
- Program development and testing?

3.11 What methods are used by end users to develop their own systems? How are they supported?

3.12 What are the selection criteria for:

- End-user or specialist development;
- Which development language/vehicle to use;
- Physical placement of process and data;
- Selection of technical platform to use to run the system (e.g. micro, mid-range or mainframe, and which DBMS)?

3.13 What controls exist covering:

- The quality of end-user developed systems;
- The quality of information supplied from end-user systems?

4. INFORMATION PROCESSING

4.1 Are there standards covering:

- Character sets;
- Coding structures;
- Data validation rules;
- User authorization aids;
- File transfer formats;

- Document interchange format?

4.2   Are these supported by current systems, including:

- Mainframe;
- Microcomputer;
- Mid-range;
- Office automation;
- Other specialized equipment and interfaces?

4.3   What DBMSs are in use? For each:

- what platform(s) do they run on;
- how many licenses are held;
- how many operational databases are supported;
- how many users are supported?

4.4   What high-level languages are in use?

For each:

- what platform(s) do they run on;
- how many licenses are held;
- how many applications are implemented in them;
- how many users are supported?

4.5   What are the criteria for determining the technical platform, including hardware, DBMS and development vehicle?

4.6   What is the ratio of users to terminals for:

- Managers and administrators;
- Secretarial and PA staff;
- Clerical staff;
- Shop floor/blue-collar staff;
- Scientific/engineering staff?

4.7   What controls exist to ensure that:

- Information input is processed and updates all relevant databases - and no others;
- Information output from a process is received by all of the authorized receiving process or users and no others;
- Information input comes only from an authorized source in an authorized manner;
- Inter-system data flows operate correctly and on time?

4.8   What controls are there over acceptance of new systems or updated version into production, covering the following?

- Functional accuracy;
- User ease of operation;
- Ease of computer operation;
- Performance and integrity;
- Maintainability;
- Audit and financial controls?

5. SECURITY

5.1   Is there in existence an up to date computer security plan covering the following?

- Integrity of data sources;
- Integrity of databases;
- Integrity of information delivery;
- Access authorization and control, both from remote users and for the physical sites;
- Stored data back-up and recovery from:
    - user error
    - system error
    - physical damage;
- Disaster recovery, including:
    - fire
    - terrorist or other criminal act
    - strike.

5.2   Are formal procedures in place for its maintenance?

5.3   When was this plan last tested? What was the outcome?

Checklist for candidate rapid development projects

In each of the main questions below, a 'yes' answer implies a probability of success for rapid development. In some cases, supplementary questions are offered to clarify the position further.

1. Does the proposed development meet a clearly defined high priority business information need, and is there a committed management sponsor for it who has the clout to drive it through?

    Things only get done if they are accorded priority and resources by management. A committed sponsor is therefore essential for any systems project.

2. Are there good source data available?

    Too many attempts at MIS have failed because, although they can deliver the requested format to the right manager at the right time, the content is out of date or unreliable. Attention to data sources before implementation will ensure that only feasible solutions are attempted, and that any approximations and compromises needed are cleared with the users before you start.

3. Is an incremental approach to implementation acceptable?

    Is it feasible and acceptable to implement the required application in stages?

    How much design work should be done in advance of implementation?

4. Are you willing to scrap the system if the prototype doesn't work?

    Starting implementation early implies change. The changes may be unexpected, and a totally different solution may be applicable.

5. Is an approximate, rapid answer desirable in business terms?

    All too often, business users who want a quick, approximate answer get instead a 'Rolls Royce' system, too late to solve the business problem. If they are in charge of the priorities, they can make the trade-off.

6. Are request volumes low?

    The sort of tool which suits the user may not be acceptable for a high volume system, because of computer resource consumption.

7. Do the users have experience of the development tool?

    They better had! The moral is that it is necessary to undertake research and development into likely rapid development tools, so that experience is available when one comes to be used 'for real'.

8. Are computer resources a serious constraint?

Computer resource usage will almost certainly exceed the first estimates. However, computer resources are the cheapest resource, and the only one which is getting cheaper. It is important to determine where the cut-off point is for truly excessive consumption for this application, and to be willing and able to go to that limit.

9. Is there understanding by the sponsoring management of the nature and likely range of benefits?

Benefits for systems suitable for rapid development tend to be difficult to quantify, and when quantified, the value tends to be very sensitive to assumptions, and to possible changes in business conditions. It is important that sponsoring management go into the project with their eyes wide open to these facts.

10. Have you decided how you will document rapid development projects?

Less, but some documentation will still be needed. Ideally, it should emerge as an automatic by-product of the development environment - but this is too much to hope for with most tools at present.

11. Is there in place a rapid development cycle which can be used to manage and control this development.

APPENDIX IV

Sample deliverables

Organization

This index lists the working papers which would be used during or produced from an Information Systems Strategy Study.

The papers are arranged in the natural sequence of their production, except that, of course, some products emerge in draft form at an early stage, and become progressively refined during subsequent stages of the study.

IV.1 Inventory of sample products

PHASE 0 – LAUNCH – DETERMINE CONTEXT AND SCOPE

A. Preparatory materials

A.1   Scope and terms of reference

A.2   Work Program

A.3   Introductory Memorandum

A.4   Steering Group Structure & Terms of Reference

B. Team composition

B.1   Resources & skills needed

B.2   Staffing and reporting lines

C. Inventory of input documentation

C.1   Business plans

C.2   Previous IS/IT plans

C.3   Systems and equipment inventories

PHASE 1 – DETERMINING BUSINESS INFORMATION AND SUPPORT NEEDS

D. Determination of business information needs

D.1   Interview Schedule

D.2   Interview Questionnaire

D.3   Key Issues Summary - individuals, and integrated

D.4   Interview Analysis

D.5   Consolidated Statement of Business Information Needs

D.6   Statement of business assumptions, impact and scenarios considered

D.7   Sponsorship support and guide-lines

D.8   Business case guidelines

E. Analysis of business strategies

E.1   Interpretation of corporate mission and goals

E.2   Competitive positioning

E.3   Product portfolio analysis

E.4   Future directions and options

PHASE 2 – ESTABLISH INFORMATION ARCHITECTURES AND OPTIONS

F. Documentation from current systems & status assessment

F.1   Current Systems Questionnaire

F.2   Current Projects Inventory

F.3   IS Division skills/resources Inventory

F.4   Technical Status Questionnaire

F.5   Equipment/Software Inventory - current & on order

F.6   Data & Systems Management Questionnaire

F.7   Current Systems Quality and Coverage Assessment

G.   INFORMATION ARCHITECTURE DOCUMENTATION

G.1   Organization Chart

G.2   Business Function Hierarchy

G.3   Business Process Schematic

G.4   Business Function/Organization Unit Analysis

G.5   Business Function/Product Support Responsibility Analysis

G.6 Process re-engineering opportunities and options

G.7 Data Entity Models

G.8 Data Entity/Business Function Matrix

G.9 Data Entity/Application Process Matrix

G.10 Application Process Map - Logical

G.11 Data Entity List & Definitions

G.12 Application Process Map - physical, with current systems coverage mapped to it

H. Business systems options

H.1 Systems implications for each business need - benefits, risks, options

H.2 Outline candidate applications

H.3 Primary constraints and dependencies

PHASE 3 – DETERMINE STRATEGIC SOLUTIONS

I. Application & database definitions

I.1 Business Application Groupings/Priorities

I.2 Application synopses

I.3 Conceptual Database Groupings

I.4 Analysis of Business Dependencies (giving feasible priorities)

I.5 Analysis of Application Dependencies (giving candidate application projects)

I.6 Analysis of Technical Dependencies (giving real projects, and technical tasks)

I.7 Candidate projects synopses

J. Statements of technical strategy

J.1 Assessment of current technology policies and status

J.2 Technical Architecture categories

J.3 Technical Position Papers

J.4 Technical Architectures Statements

J.5 Assessments of Technology Components

J.6 Candidate technology development projects

PHASE 4 – PREPARE AND DELIVER THE IMPLEMENTATION PLAN

K. The application development plan

K.1   Urgent Action Program

K.2   Application Development Program.

K.3   Application Development Project definitions

L. The technical development plan

L.1   Technical Development Plan - summary

L.2   Technical Development Program - project definitions

L.3   Technical Capacity Plan - summary

L.4   Technical Capacity Plan - commentary

M. The organization plan

M.1   Business Organization Impact Statement

M.2   Information Systems Functions

M.3   Information Systems Organization Chart

M.4   Manpower Capacity Plan - Skills & Resources by time phase linked to application & technical plan

N. Overall business case

N.1   Business case approach - benefits and risk appraisal

N.2   Information Systems Cost/Benefit Summaries

O. Management report

O.1   Contents list for full report

O.2   Sample Management Summary

Final report structure and contents

Volumes

I. **MANAGEMENT SUMMARY**

II. **FULL REPORT**

III. **APPENDICES**

Management summary contents

1. Introduction

2. Business needs

3. Observations and findings

4. General recommendations

5. Application recommendations

6. Technical assessment

7. Means for plan implementation and maintenance

8. Financial summary

9. Next steps

Full report contents

1. INTRODUCTION

1.1 Background

1.2 Scope of the study

1.3 Summary of sources

1.4 Report structure

1.5 Revision process

2. BUSINESS REQUIREMENTS

2.1 Process followed

2.2 Business needs – high priority, inadequate/no cover

2.3 Business needs – satisfactory cover

2.4 Business needs – proposed as early deliverables

2.5 Business needs – requiring non-systems solutions

3. SUMMARY OF CURRENT COVERAGE

4. OVERALL IS/IT VISION

5. RECOMMENDED APPLICATIONS SOLUTIONS

strategic plan

I

N–O

P

Q-R

S

U–Z